Children's
Group Therapy

Children's Group Therapy

Methods and Case Histories

MORTIMER SCHIFFER

The Free Press
A Division of Macmillan, Inc.
NEW YORK

Collier Macmillan Publishers
LONDON

The Free Press
A Division of Macmillan, Inc.
866 Third Avenue, New York, N.Y. 10022

Collier Macmillan Canada, Inc.

Printed in the United States of America

printing number
1   2   3   4   5   6   7   8   9   10

Library of Congress Cataloging in Publication Data

Schiffer, Mortimer.
    Children's group therapy.

    Includes bibliographical references and index.
    1. Group psychotherapy. 2. Child psychotherapy.
I. Title. [DNLM: 1. Psychotherapy, Group—in infancy
& childhood. WS 350.2 S333c]
RJ505.G7S35   1984   618.92'89152   84-47659
ISBN 0-02-928090-7

The author gratefully acknowledges permission to reprint the following material:

Fanny Milstein, "Activity-Interview Group Psychotherapy of Latency-Age Girls," unpublished paper. Reprinted with permission of the author.

Leslie Rosenthal and Leo Nagelberg, "Limitations of Activity Group Therapy," *International Journal of Group Psychotherapy*, 6, 2: 166–179, 1956. Reprinted with permission of the American Group Psychotherapy Association, Inc., and of the authors.

John C. Coolidge and Margaret G. Grunebaum [Frank], "Individual and Group Therapy of a Latency-Age Child," *International Journal of Group Psychotherapy*, 14, 1: 84–96, 1964. Reprinted with permission of the American Group Psychotherapy Association, Inc., and of the authors.

S.R. Slavson, "Activity Group Therapy—Five Case Histories," unpublished paper. Excerpted and reprinted here as "Cooperative Therapy of Mother and Child—Leon," with permission of the author.

Margaret G. Frank, "Treatment of Ego-Impoverished Latency Children Through Modified Activity Group Therapy," unpublished paper. Reprinted with permission of the author.

Saul Scheidlinger, "Experiential Group Treatment of Severely Deprived Latency-Age Children," *American Journal of Orthopsychiatry*, 30, 2: 356–368, 1960. Copyright © 1960 the American Orthopsychiatric Association, Inc. Reprinted with permission of the American Orthopsychiatric Association, Inc., and of the author.

To those who help children

Contents

ix

Foreword

IT IS MY PRIVILEGE to prepare the reader for a panoramic view of the field of children's group therapy as it exists today, after a half-century of pioneering activity, increasing technical sophistication, and creative accomplishment.

This book delineates the scientific principles governing the use of the various methods of children's group therapy and richly documents the application of these principles. It impresses me as being a definitive account of children's group therapy at this advanced stage of its development, and it is undoubtedly unique in the abundance and variety of the extensive case history studies and session protocols it presents.

The emotional understanding and technical expertise needed by the beginner cannot be derived solely from a book. These are acquired through basic training and supervised practice under the guidance of preceptors such as Mortimer Schiffer and the other recognized authorities in the field who have contributed chapters to this book. However, the book constitutes an important addition to the reference library of the experienced practitioner working with children and their parents, while providing the intellectual information needed by the student entering the field.

The message that the book communicates is that children do improve in group therapy. They behave better. The group experience enhances their intellectual performance. They are found to be more socially acceptable at home, in the classroom, and in the community.

With children, as with adults, the key to realizing the healing potential of the therapeutic group setting is, in one word, specificity. Each child must be treated on the basis of his individual therapeutic needs, that is, the particular problem or problems he presents. These may dictate the use of one method or a combination of methods, applied concurrently or in succession. Judgments need to be made on the method or methods that would be most suitable at that period in the child's development when he requires psychological help. But specificity begins before a treatment plan is formulated, with the taking of a detailed history, making an accurate diagnosis, and carefully evaluating the child's personality, family background, and the social setting in which he lives.

The organization of this book also reflects the historic development of group therapy for children. The first four chapters are devoted to activity group therapy, introduced by S. R. Slavson and his co-workers in 1934, at the Madelaine Borg Child Guidance Clinic in New York City. This first, basic method of group treatment is applicable to latency-age children with behavior disorders, character problems, and other conditions. As therapists acquired experience in the group approach in treatment, they ventured to apply still other group methods to children with more serious, neurotic disturbances. Activity–interview group psychotherapy, an early and direct offshoot of the original approach, is the subject of chapter 5. A depressed, neurotic girl is focused on in this description of the use of verbal intervention in combination with activities in group treatment. The limitations of activity group therapy for certain problems are described again in the first of two chapters (chapter 6) devoted to combined therapy—individual and group; the second case (chapter 7) presents protocols that demonstrate the progress of a latency-age child with a serious personality problem and below-normal intelligence in individual play therapy and activity group therapy. The combined approach had the effect of socializing him and raising his intelligence level. Cooperative therapy, the term applied to concurrent treatment and/or counseling of children and their parents, is the next treatment approach recorded in the book (chapter 8). The last two chapters are devoted to group methods designed for children suffering from severe ego pathology, who are encountered frequently today in community agencies and are difficult to treat.

The various methods discussed thus constitute a spectrum of sorts, in terms of the relative severity of the problems that they are designed to correct, as well as in the order of their historical development.

The literature on the subject of children's group therapy is exceptionally well classified in a comprehensive bibliography. Also included is a glossary of terms and appendices containing practical information on designs of the treatment rooms and on furnishings and therapy materials.

Mortimer Schiffer, a psychologist, who began his career as a teacher of science, was associated for many years with the late S. R. Slavson in the development of children's group therapy. In the first film on the subject, he was the therapist conducting an actual group of child-patients. Since 1952, when he stopped conducting groups, he has played a leading role as a trainer, supervisor, and consultant in the promotion of group therapy in clinical settings and in public schools.

Mr. Schiffer devoted several years to bringing this book into being because he shared with Slavson the view that case history material was, in his words, "sadly needed" to demonstrate the therapeutic value of children's group therapy. The fascinatingly detailed protocols he has assembled should help children's group therapy fulfill its promise as an effective method for children with a wide range of psychologically reversible emotional and learning disabilities.

It is conceivable that these illuminating protocols might contribute to progress now being recorded in another field. In this era, when the understanding of human psychology, emotional disturbances, and psychosomatic illness is becoming accessible through the teachings of both psychology and the neurosciences, it is my impression that these minutely detailed descriptions of what goes on in the psyches of children in group situations could serve as a basis for correlating psychological changes with changes in the functioning of the central nervous system.

Hyman Spotnitz, M.D., Med. Sc.D.

Preface

THE USE OF A GROUP MODALITY to treat emotionally disturbed children originated at the Madelaine Borg Child Guidance Clinic in New York City in 1934, under the aegis of S. R. Slavson, a pioneer in group psychotherapy. In the ensuing four decades it has developed into one of the two fundamental modalities of psychotherapy; the other is individual treatment.

There is a considerable body of literature on the subject of children's group therapy. *Activity Group Therapy* was the first method devised. Much information is available in books and journal articles concerning various group methods that are employed in psychotherapy, as well as in the counseling and guidance of children (see Bibliography). It is the technical differences among the standard group treatments that are of practical interest to therapists who are presently engaged in treating children or contemplate doing so. In addition, practitioners are interested in the applicability of each method according to the nature of children's presenting problems. Such considerations can be described more definitively through case history studies *in extenso*, dealing with the start of group treatment through termination. A case history approach helps to clarify such relevant questions as: initial diagnoses and the choice of treatment, which may be one of several group methods, individual therapy, or a combination of both; the selection of clients to ensure psychological balance in a group; necessary variances in therapists' roles and functions in the different group methods; the therapeutic influence of the group as a whole on its members; settings and furnishings; crafts, play, and game equipment; safety precautions; and other subjects.

This volume is divided into six parts. In the introduction to Part I, the underlying principles and practices of activity therapy are described, followed in Chapters 1 through 4 by comprehensive descriptions of therapeutic play groups that are composed of young latency-age children. In the longitudinal study of each group, extensive protocols of group sessions are given, starting with the beginning of treatment through termination after one or more years. In each group report one or several children are focused on to show the relation between a purely activity method, the diagnosed problems, the nature of the noninterpretive activity therapy, and its corrective influence. After initial descriptions of the presenting problems, the treatment process is followed in detail through progressive stages of a therapy group's evolution: initiation of treatment, the period of acclimatization, regression and catharsis, corrective reexperience, reality testing, sublimation, and termination. Interpretations of children's behavior and group dynamics are interpolated in the records of the group sessions to illuminate the methodology and its psychological rationale. "Dos and don'ts" of therapeutic interventions are clarified within the context of significant events that take place during group sessions.

In activity group treatment, explanations and interpretations of feelings and behavior are entirely eschewed. After an initial testing period by the children, a benign, positive transference relationship is established with the therapist. Supported by this, in a setting characterized by extraordinary permissiveness and unconditional acceptance of the children as they are, individual and group behaviors undergo significant alterations. The group as a whole matures, and it exerts corrective social constraints on its members.

A wide range of children's problems is described in the case histories—problems typical of latency-age children who are referred for treatment to community agencies and in schools. In their general nature they range from shy, very withdrawn children to some with neurotic or character problems; to those who act out and are impulsive and prone to delinquency; and to still others with more serious problems. For reasons to be explained in the records, some of the children who are described in Chapters 1 through 4 would probably not have received any psychological assistance whatsoever but for the group therapy programs available in their respective schools.

Soon after activity group therapy started in 1934, it was discovered that certain kinds of problems did not yield, wholly or in part, to the influence of a purely activity group method when it was employed as the exclusive treatment. Another method of group therapy came into existence, one that depended on both activities and verbal analytical interventions by the therapist. In this procedure, children's attention was drawn to conscious and unconscious motivations for feelings and behavior. At propitious moments, a therapist offered explanations, interpretations, and suggestions to encourage children to reflect about events occurring in the therapy group and how these could relate to circumstances in their lives. This was the origin of *Activity-Interview Group Psychotherapy*, a method that is described in Part II. It is usually employed with children who have symptoms of a neurotic nature in addition to behavior problems. The case of Katie, a depressed, neurotic girl, is central in the study of a girls' activity-interview group presented in Chapter 5.

Still other kinds of children's problems may call for *combined* treatment—both individual and group therapy. There are several permutations of this approach, each dependent on diagnoses, idiosyncratic factors of children's problems, and circumstances peculiar to their families. In combined treatment, the separate approaches are usually carried out by different therapists. In some cases, group therapy may be used following a course of individual treatment as a tapering-off experience, or the reverse may take place. In still other instances, a child's treatment may alter periodically between individual, combined, and exclusive group therapy, again as determined by clinical considerations. Chapters 6 and 7 of Part III describe two children who were in combined treatment.

In child-guidance and family agencies, both children and parents are seen concurrently in what is termed *cooperative therapy*. Several therapists are used in working with various family members, separately and sometimes in conjunction with family therapy. The methods used in therapy or counseling are contingent on the diagnoses, the degree of accessibility of family members, and changes in the treatment program that are based on periodic evaluations.

In Part IV, Chapter 8, Leon and his mother are the focal patients in an extended, intricately involved course of psychotherapy during which the boy's treatment alternated between combined, individual, and exclusive activity group therapy, and his mother was seen regularly in casework treatment. The report is a comprehensive documentation of the treatment of a seriously disturbed, marginally retarded latency-age boy and his equally troubled mother. The integration of the clinical resources of an orthopsychiatric agency is also described in detail in the discussion of this case.

Part V is concerned with a special child-patient population, one that agencies increasingly have to contend with. These children have been described as "ego-deficient," "ego-weak," "ego-impoverished," and "children with severe ego pathology." They are notably resistive to individual therapy when it is attempted. Characteristics of this problem are: archaic personality; impulsive, destructive behavior; minimal or no manifestations of guilt or anxiety; absence of sublimation; and other, psychologically primitive qualities.

In Chapters 9 and 10 descriptions are given of children manifesting this severe pathology. To manage such problems in groups—with children noted for a lack of inner controls—alterations had to be devised in the standard activity group method, particularly with respect to the role of the therapist and the quality and degree of permissiveness used in the group.

The Appendix has two parts. Appendix I presents scale drawings of room designs for group therapy, to guide persons who have not had experience in fashioning them. Appendix II lists basic room furnishings and work, play, and game materials suitable for the different group methods.

A glossary of terms commonly used in children's group therapy is presented, followed by a bibliography that lists most publications on this subject from 1934 until the present. The bibliography is divided into publications on the general subject of children's group therapy; publications on group procedures used with special populations of patients, such as schizophrenic and autistic children and delinquents; and publications concerning treatment in residential, school, nursery, and other settings. It should prove to be a valuable resource for persons who are interested in special group methods in a wide range of different settings and with special clients. In addition to these references, the bibliography includes publications concerning paratherapeutic group methods used in counseling and guidance.

The author wishes to express his appreciation for the contributions of John Coolidge, M.D., Margaret G. Frank, C.S.W., Fannie Mendelson, M.S.W., the late Leo Nagelberg, Ph.D., Leslie Rosenthal, Ph.D., Saul Scheidlinger, Ph.D., and the late S. R. Slavson, each of whom has made notable contributions to children's group therapy. The author is particularly grateful to Hyman Spotnitz, M.D., Med. Sc.D., who studied the manuscript and wrote its Introduction. It is hoped that this volume will prove helpful to persons presently engaged in children's group treatment, and that it will encourage others to use the group modality as a part of clinical treatment.

I am deeply grateful to Kitty Moore and Eileen DeWald of The Free Press for their editorial expertise which contributed in large measure to this book.

Mortimer Schiffer
April 1984

Children's
Group Therapy

Part I _____

Activity Group Therapy

Group treatment of emotionally troubled children is one of the two fundamental, corrective psychological modalities, the other being individual treatment. This has been affirmed after more than four decades of clinical experience with a great number of children in many therapy groups.

Special Value of the Group

The group approach, in its several proven forms, is a particularly efficacious form of therapy because it is usually employed during a phase in children's growth and development when socialization has become a prominent feature of daily life. With the passing of the stage of nurturance and dependency, when there is a tight bond to the immediate family, children become increasingly sensitive and responsive to extrafamilial group influences.

During early latency, a child is impelled to further substantiate his identity as he moves beyond the emotional ties to the family. Passage toward the outer world provides emotional distance between the child and his primary, libidinal objects. This assists him in resolving problems associated with parents and siblings and gives rise to new feelings and attitudes toward persons outside the family. In particular, experiences with peers fos-

1

ter identity formation, broaden a child's social parameters, and provide much support during the transition.

When children require help with their emotional problems, they generally find group psychotherapy more tolerable than individual psychotherapy because it complements the growth tasks associated with normal social maturation. Participation in a peer therapy group tends to augment the developmental process while, at the same time, providing the necessary treatment. Consequently, children are notably less resistive to the introduction of group therapy than they are to individual treatment.[1]

During advanced latency, prepuberty, and into adolescence, the needs for social acceptance and for behavioral modes that reinforce personal identity become substantially more imperative. Thus, should psychotherapy become necessary, the group approach offers experiences that buttress social aspirations. It is the syncretism of group psychotherapy goals and social-growth needs that constitutes a special advantage inherent in group treatment.

The Nature of Activity Therapy

The therapeutic play group, the subject of Chapters 1 through 4, is an activity, noninterpretive method that is employed with young latency-age children whose problems are of a nature which will yield to the penetrating influence of significant interpersonal relationships with a therapist and other children in a group setting. Active probing, explanations and interpretations, and other interventions used by therapists in analytical treatment of children with problems of neurotic etiology to explore their feelings and behavior are not present in activity groups.

In a large number of cases, activity group therapy can be used as the exclusive treatment. Sometimes it is properly used as a tapering-off treatment following a course of individual therapy. In still other instances, activity groups may be helpful in preparing some children for more intensive individual analytical therapy when such is indicated, particularly with those who adamantly resist the dyadic approach to start with. Finally, some children require *combined* therapy—individual and group simultaneously.

Children's Discovery of a "New" Adult

In the benign, therapeutic climate of an activity therapy group, children discover an entirely novel adult in the person of the therapist, in addition to a

---

[1] This, however, does not negate the need for a dyadic treatment method when diagnoses and other factors indicate this approach.

unique set of conditioning circumstances (actually, deconditioning and reconditioning). Behavior which in places other than the group meeting room would be considered boisterous, undesirable, or "bad" is never subject to question, denial, rejection, censure, or punishment from the therapist, although such prohibitive responses are common on the part of parents, teachers, and other adults. Such unusual acceptance of children by a therapist is not the same as giving sanction to their acting-out behavior.[2] The children are accepted as they are, without question, but not necessarily their behavior.

The prevailing climate of an activity group is one of essential freedom, wherein children quickly learn that they may participate without directions by or interference from the therapist. However, they also discover that the therapist is always available to them when they have need, regardless of the quality of their behavior, which may be obstreperous at times. In such a *conditioned* (not controlled) environment, psychologically corrective influences are brought to bear.[3]

A child's response to the benign transference to the therapist, which develops in due time, creates in him feelings of trust, confidence, and fondness. It is these emotions which influence the psyche and ameliorate the deleterious effects of past (or, often, continuing) psychonoxious experiences with parents and siblings. Occasional negative transference expressions toward the therapist occur during the early sessions of an activity group. These are tolerated without comment or prohibitory responses. This therapeutic approach differs from what happens in analytical groups, wherein negative transference behavior is purposively dealt with by the therapist at psychologically opportune moments, in keeping with the exploratory method.[4]

With behavior disorders in particular, children who have suffered much frustration, prolonged nurturance deprivation, and rejection, the penetrating influence of *unconditional acceptance* as it is experienced in an activity group has to continue for considerable time. Only then can the children's characteristic defensiveness and hostile behavior be eased. Older latency children, from approximately nine to eleven years of age, require two years of group therapy as a minimum term before behavior disorder problems can be altered in significant degree. Because of the greater plasticity of younger children, shorter periods of therapy may be sufficient.

[2]M. Schiffer, "Permissiveness Versus Sanction in Activity Group Therapy," *International Journal of Group Psychotherapy*, 1:115, 1952.

[3]A *conditioned environment* is one that helps children express feelings in a safe atmosphere while it fosters interactions between members of a group that provide eventual relief from tensions. It also offers other gratifications through engagement in creative work and play activities. See S. R. Slavson and M. Schiffer, *Group Psychotherapies for Children: A Textbook*, International Universities Press, New York, 1975.

[4]See Chapter 5.

Corrective Reexperience

The extraordinary degree of psychological nurturance in an activity group is the basis of *corrective reexperience*. In essence, what has been produced in a child as atypical emotionality because of past psychonoxious experiences in the family, can be undone through ego-strengthening influences in an activity therapy group. The prefix "re" is used because the group is psychologically a homologue to the real family. Thus, a child is enabled to *repeat* many of the fundamental experiences of early development in the context of a "psychological family." Through the displaced transferences from actual family members to the members of the group, children have opportunities to develop reconstructive psychological relationships with substitute libidinal objects. Such transference is a penetrating influence that is capable of modifying the psychic constituents of a child's personality. A redistribution of libido occurs; the superego is relaxed and its oversevere regulatory effects become modified; and an improved self-image evolves with feelings of well-being.

Selection of Clients for Activity Groups

Two criteria determine the suitability of children for activity groups. First, they should possess *social hunger*, which is an elemental need for the company of others. Secondly, there must be sufficient ego resilience to render a child capable of altering his attitudes and conduct in response to ameliorating influences. With respect to the first criterion, a child's history should reveal the existence of a positive relationship with at least one person earlier in life, usually a parent, sibling, grandparent, or other significant libidinal object. To meet the second requirement, somewhere in a child's history there should be a demonstrated success, even marginally, in adapting to new environments, such as a school, camp, Cub Scouts, or other social group entity.

   Activity groups are efficacious as exclusive treatment for a large variety of presenting problems. As noted earlier, they are especially recommended for children with primary behavior disorders and some character problems.[5]

Primary Behavior Disorders[6]

A primary behavior disorder is so designated because the manifest behavior of a child constitutes the essential, nuclear problem. This disorder is distin-

---

[5]S. R. Slavson and M. Schiffer, *Group Psychotherapies for Children: A Textbook*, International Universities Press, New York, 1975, pp. 33, 34, 108, 298.

[6]See J.H.W. Van Ophuijsen, "Primary Conduct Disturbance: Their Diagnosis and Treatment," in *Modern Trends in Child Psychiatry*, N.D.C. Kewis and B. Pacella, eds., International Universities Press, New York, 1961.

guished from the problems of children who possess neurotic traits, symptoms, habits, and conduct patterns that reflect the influence of internalized conflicts. The primary behavior disorders are sometimes referred to as reactive disorders. During early development, such children have been subjected to marked parental inconsistency in handling; uncertainty and ambivalence caused by double-bind experiences; premature pressure for early maturation and independence beyond children's capacities to achieve this; or rejection by one or sometimes both parents, on conscious and unconscious levels.

Much of this psychomalignant experience takes place during preoedipal years, and it usually continues. Under the extraordinary strains of such parental mismanagement, during a period of development when the paramount needs are for physical and emotional nurturance, children must acquire coping defenses to protect themselves against what they perceive and react to as overwhelming threat. As a result, some children become inordinately suspicious in relationships with other persons, resentful of authority, impulsive, aggressive, and sometimes vengeful and destructive. The acting-out behavior characteristic of a primary behavior disorder, which has its genesis within the family, is typically displaced against teachers, other adults, and peers. All these individuals become unconsciously and almost automatically identified with parents and siblings—the original targets.

In addition to aggressive, hostile behavior, a child with a primary behavior disorder may acquire neurotic features from failure to resolve the oedipus complex.

Character Disorders

Children with character disorders are typified by behavioral maladaptations that are global rather than symptomatic or impulse reactions. Character problems are ego-syntonic personality defenses that are becoming habituated and persistent, even in young latency-age children. Among these problems are children with weak or defective sexual identities, viz., feminine boys and masculine girls; passive-dependent personalities; infantilized, overprotected, narcissistic children; nonpathological social isolates; children with inadequate egos; some only children. As with primary behavior disorders, character disorders are mostly preoedipal in etiology, the result of pathogenic circumstances in the family during the earliest years of child development.

A child with a primary behavior disorder will act out impulsively against persons and situations which he considers frustrating and onerous, his behavior varying considerably from one situation to another. On the other hand, under similar circumstances, a character-rooted disorder tends to behave in a more fixed pattern which is typical of a child's basic problem and his usual mode of adaptation to stress.

Latency-age children with character disorders are excellent clients for activity groups. Their personality defenses become ameliorated through a long-term, positive transference relationship with the therapist, and they also respond favorably to peer role models in gender-homogeneous groups. Also helpful to them are activities and games which foster gender identity. This is particularly efficacious with problems of sexual identity. Also eminently suitable for activity therapy are immature children, but not ones who are markedly anaclitic in their dependency needs. In the therapy group immature children become blocked by other group members from narcissistic self-indulgence and from monopolizing the attentions of the therapist. The group, as a social unit, in balking a child's dependency, forces him to find gratifications on appropriate, more mature levels through creative opportunities in crafts work and through games.

Neurotic and Other Problems

In addition, activity group therapy is successful with children possessing neurotic traits (but not psychoneuroses), with mild latent schizophrenics, with some schizoid personalities, and with children who suffer from situational anxiety, as distinguished from others who have already developed pervasive anxiety.

Excluded from activity groups are constitutionally atypical and organically defective children, borderline and full-blown schizophrenics, children with psychopathic characters, and those with a latent homosexual tendency, which tends to generate anxiety in latency-age children.[7]

The Question of Diagnosis of Young Children

It is true that sharply delineated diagnoses of young children's emotional problems are the exception rather than the rule, except in the cases of blatant pathology such as psychoses and neurogenic disorders. Moreover, the personality and character of young children are still formative and incomplete. Their emotions are labile; ego defenses may be rudimentary; discrete symptoms may be present, but often they are incipient. Habits, conduct, and general behavior are subject to change. A careful study of presenting problems, including developmental histories and analyses of family interactions, can elucidate elements of the nuclear problem and prognosticate more definitive diagnoses in the future given the absence of any therapeutic interventions. A therapy group is also valuable in formulating differential

---

[7] For more comprehensive references to the indications and counterindications for activity groups, see Slavson and Schiffer, *Group Psychotherapies for Children,* Chapter 6.

diagnoses. Observations of children in action in the special setting are quite revealing. They provide demonstrated evidences of strengths and weaknesses.

Composition of an Activity Therapy Group

A factor that is critical for accurate diagnosis and choice of treatment is the composition of groups. Incorrect placement of a child in an activity group may do him a disservice and possibly disrupt the group. Any question as to the suitability of a child for a particular group should be decided on the side of caution; the use of a group method may need to be eliminated, or possibly the child could be included in a differently constituted group. The effectiveness of an activity-therapy group has, among other considerations, a direct relation to the care taken in selecting candidates and blending them into a psychologically viable group.

Meaningful changes can be brought about in children in the climate of freedom that is a strict requirement for activity groups and that can only be maintained in a balanced group. Such a climate allows for a free flow of interpersonal interactions without unnecessary interference by the therapist. Interventions that are brought into being because of group imbalance vitiate the possibility of corrective therapy.

A group should be so constituted that its members will exert corrective reciprocal effects on one another over time. In the beginning, and for a period of approximately six to eight group sessions, the best-constituted group goes through a phase of testing the therapist's intentions and forbearance. Episodes of negative transference behavior occur, often consciously intended by the children, sometimes surreptitiously carried out in the case of an insecure child. During this time it might appear to an untrained eye that the acting out is extraordinary in degree and haphazard. This is a transient, evolutionary part of a therapy group's longitudinal progression, and in a properly composed group, the acting out does not become entrenched. It is a phase of *acclimatization*, an initiatory stage in the *gestalt* that constitutes activity therapy.

Group Balance

A well-chosen complement of child-patients has the capacity to reestablish its equilibrium following incidents of excitement, sometimes of a hypomanic nature, without the need for external (therapist's) controls. For therapeutic evolvement to take place, a group must be, in a sense, "master of its own destiny"—amenable to intrinsic, reconstructive forces. Such psychologically corrective influences are inherent in the ego strengths of individuals and also in the aggregate group (social) controls which, while dormant at first, become activated and maximized in time. A group capable of restoring itself to a state of therapeutic homeostasis following episodes of aggression and conflict possesses dynamic equilibrium, a vital quality of a properly composed activity therapy group.

In a gross sense, for good balance, a group should have a suitable mixture of active and passive personalities. These have been characterized according to their modes of behavior as *instigators, neutralizers,* and *neuters.* Instigators have catalytic influence on other children, which may be positive in effect (producing beneficial results in the group as a whole) or harmful (as would be the case if an "ego-weak" child of the type described in Part IV was included in the group). Neutralizers are children whose personalities and behavior act to lessen aggression and discord. Neuters are more ineffectual children who are easily influenced by others.[8]

Gender Composition of Activity Groups

The latency stage of development accelerates various tasks, chief among them being a child's need to affirm his identity.[9] As is well known, children of latency age tend to seek the company of others of the same gender, which provides them with substantive role models. Thus, in activity groups with older latency children, homogeneous gender grouping is necessary, including a therapist of the same gender. However, in the cases of younger children, gender homogeneity, while helpful, is not strictly essential as with older children. In the former, budding identification processes can be abetted by the presence of members of the opposite gender who serve as contrast models against which idiosyncratic characteristics of each gender are brought into sharper relief.[10]

Elements of Psychotherapy of Children

The primary aim of psychotherapy is to eliminate patients' emotional problems or to alleviate them to such an extent that individuals are better able to cope with situations and feelings that plagued them before treatment. Successful therapy aims at altering elements of the psyche. The extent to which this is feasible depends on the nature of the problems, the ages of patients, and other factors. Adult patients can be *helped* to cope better, but the essen-

[8]Ibid. pp. 113–115.

[9]S. Scheidlinger, "The concept of Latency: Implications for Group Treatment," *Social Casework*, June 1966.

[10]In *analytical* group therapy with young latency children, gender hetrogeneity, which is recommended, fosters discussions about sexual differences and related matters that help the process of active inquiry.

tial nature of personality and character remains mostly unchanged because ego-defensive mechanisms, idiosyncratic behavior, social adaptations, and basic identity have become well habituated. However, with young children, whose personalities and characters have not yet fully evolved, successful therapy can effect actual *changes* in their psyches.

Resistance and Resistivity

Children in latency are generally reluctant to participate in psychotherapy, which is at first perceived by them as utterly foreign. This reaction is quite pronounced, especially when a dyadic, analytical method is attempted. Skilled therapists, mindful of this initial defensiveness, are often able to dissolve it through sensitive, patient ministrations.

The psychology of latency development is of a nature to seal off intrusions that threaten to uncover emotionality and subject it to study and introspection. Rather, latency is a time for elaboration of ego-defense mechanisms. With all latency children, and especially so with emotionally troubled ones, one mechanism, repression, is vital in protecting the ego while there is further refinement of other defenses. The repressive force arises from a need to submerge cathected emotions associated with the oedipus complex in an attempt to resolve this crisis. Normal growth and development are greatly enhanced by the acquisition of compensatory behavior patterns and effective sublimations. The ego "demands" efficient performance from its defenses. Characteristically, much neuromuscular activity comes to the fore during latency, which serves as a partial outlet to alleviate tensions, ambivalences, and conflicts.

A distinction is necessary between *resistivity* to the implementation of treatment and children's *resistance* during treatment. The latter results mainly from elements repressed into the unconscious, whereas resistivity is conscious, aim-directed, and opposed to the idea of psychotherapy. In practically every instance, children are not motivated, self-declared patients. It is a rare child, usually one beset by neurotic anxiety and fears, who will acknowledge and freely accept psychological intervention. And in such a case an analytic dyadic method is employed.

When parents become sufficiently concerned with their child's behavior, habits, or perhaps symptoms, they may seek professional assistance. The child, however, usually rebels at being hauled off to a "doctor," "psychologist," or some other specialist. Almost reflexively, the therapist becomes identified with the parents and incorporated in the child's resentment. As the child perceives it, if anyone needs to be helped, it is the parents.[11]

---

[11]This may account partially for some of the success claimed by those who practice what has been termed "family therapy." A participant child feels that he alone is not responsible for the difficulties besetting a family.

Young children are normally egotropic—narcissistic and self-centered. They perceive the "outer world"—parents, siblings, and others—as agents of frustration and as the sources of their discomfort and disappointment when their demands or needs are unfulfilled. They project blame easily, feeling themselves to be undeserving victims. What is an acceptable defense for them, because of juvenescence, in older individuals could be diagnosed as paranoid. Their logic is notably syncretistic, capable of reconciling and rationalizing standards of conduct which differ from theirs. This serves well to limit a sense of culpability. Young children can, and do, harbor feelings of guilt due to super-ego strictures that become enhanced in latency. However, the nature of children's psychology is not such as to readily permit guilt feelings to convert to calm reflection and objectivity. Ergo, children's resistivity to the introduction of psychotherapy: someone else must be responsible for problems, not they!

Resistivity and resistance are negligible factors in activity therapy groups. The group is perceived by children more as a "club," an interesting physical setting for play and work activities in the company of peers, not as a clinical instrument, since it is not initially presented as such. Moreover, an activity group presents no aspects that are typical of analytical groups. No one questions the children's motivations and behavior nor seeks to engage them in discussions. When a child is first introduced to an activity therapy group, it is described as an opportunity to be with some other children, to "play," to "make things." Even in analytical groups, used with children with more internalized neurotic problems, where children soon become aware of the therapist's exploratory procedures, resistivity and resistance are minimal because of the social opportunities that the children desire.

Another factor that is operative in both activity and analytical groups, one that renders children accessible to treatment and diminishes resistance, is *universalization*. Children are eased when they discover, often for the first time, that others possess similar interests and needs.

Activity Contra Verbalization

Children are impelled by fear, anger, anxiety, and tension to express emotionality through actions, particularly when they are frustrated, although there are some children with more passive temperaments who tend to bottle up their feelings. Young children are usually restricted in the ability to describe ambivalences and deeper emotions verbally, except for impulsive utterances of discomfiture and complaint. More revealing comments, of which they are capable, await the therapist who can skillfully "unlock" the resistance against disclosure of what, to the children, constitute dangerous, forbidden thoughts and fantasies. Melanie Klein described the young patient as a "willing guide" to the unconscious once a therapist has made him cognizant of a latent meaning, affording him a basis of understanding and some relief. Anna Freud stressed the need to help a child establish a trust in the therapist, actually for the therapist to *assist* the process of fostering the positive transference.

Even with an acquired sense of freedom in the treatment situation, a young child still "converses" much in the language of play and through symbolic actions. In purely activity groups, the children's problems are of a nature to yield to the corrective influence of solely interpersonal interactions. Reflection and analysis of behavior are not a part of the treatment.

With adolescents and adult patients, on the other hand, the process of psychotherapy has to enable them, eventually, to become cognizant of the relatedness of earlier, psychomalignant experiences and their current emotional difficulties. The extent to which this is accomplished varies with different patients, depending on age, diagnoses, the goals of treatment, and other personal factors. Successful treatment leads first to knowledge, which deepens into understanding and later, hopefully, into insight. Along the way patients must be helped to penetrate the resistances that block recall of repressed material.

As already noted, young children do not apply themselves to the psychological tasks inherent in analytical psychotherapy in the same manner as do adolescents and adults. The procedures used with them—either individually or in groups—are simpler, less demanding, and geared to children's intellectual capacities. Nevertheless, despite their less complex nature, these procedures can *enlighten* children sufficiently about the etiology of problems, provide relief from psychological stress, and effectuate changes in them, including alterations of their characteristic behavior. Such outcomes are accomplished through play enactments and verbalizations encouraged by the therapist. Wishes, fantasies, and feelings, some of which the children may have previously been unaware of or unable to express, can be sensitively elicited by a therapist. In analytical groups, children become quite cooperative in exploring inner feelings as soon as they discover, for the first time, that much of what bothers them also concerns other children.

All methods of psychotherapy consist of the following components: transference, catharsis, insight formation, reality-testing, and sublimation. The variable influences of these components in different psychological treatments depend on diagnoses and the methods employed. Some of the components are discussed below.

Transference

The degree of transference between patient and therapist is appreciably different in individual as compared to group therapy. The latter method offers advantages of multiple transferences to other patients and the therapist, but the *intensity* of transferences is diluted. Moreover, in noninterpretive activity therapy, transference toward the therapist is not as penetrating as in analytical group therapy with children of the same age. In the latter, the therapist's active probing for the underlying meanings of children's behavior, fantasies, and interactions with others tends to evoke affective reactions from them, including, at times, more frequent negative transference expressions that have the effect of deepening the symbolic transferences.

Both forms of group psychotherapy—activity and analytical—offer children equal freedom for cathartic acting out. Also, as mentioned earlier, both group methods provide another special benefit as compared with dyadic treatment: the group serves as a therapeutic instrument at the same time that it is a social milieu providing many opportunities for immediate reality testing and for forming social sublimations.

Catharsis

While children are more limited than older persons with respect to their powers of conceptualization and reflection, they do more readily discharge feelings cathartically than older patients. The world allows children the privileges of childhood, one of which is freedom to *act* like a child. The unusual tolerance in psychotherapy for cathartic emotionality has remarkable therapeutic value for children. Truly, nowhere else can they express their conflicted emotions in utter safety.

Sloughing Off and Working Through

It has been determined in activity therapy groups that children's problems can be *sloughed off*. This differs from what occurs in the therapies of adolescents and adults and, to some extent, in analytical therapy with children, where problems have to be *worked through*. In the cases of children in early latency, habit and conduct disorders, neurotic traits, incipient symptoms, and some character problems can yield to the noninterpretive activity methodology. It is when genital primacy becomes established in puberty and adolescence, with its attendant sexual problems, that symptoms and behavior become more deeply entrenched and difficult to modify through purely activity methods.

The etiology of a primary behavior disorder, for example, suggests that when the environment and the handling of a child are altered in a sanguine, consistent fashion, as in activity therapy groups, changes will occur in children. Essentially, what has been "imprinted" in a behavior disorder can be reversed, given the appropriate treatment procedure and sufficient time. Initial relief is felt by such a child as soon as he finds it safe in an activity group to discharge feelings. Continuing gains become manifest after he forms a positive transference relationship with the therapist. To start with, a child with a primary behavior disorder resists the positive affect-tie because of a general suspiciousness of adults. Such a child does not possess the same quality of anxiety that exists in others with problems of neurotic etiology. Consistently benign experience, without searching analytical procedures (which behavior and character disorders resist obdurately), is sufficient to effect changes in personality and character structure.

Insight—Its Nature in Children's Therapy

Insight results from inductive discovery over an extended period of time. Its acquisition in therapy is a complex process. It develops in patients as they gain understanding of their emotionality, behavior, and symptoms, and how these relate to antecedent experiences that occurred during early development in the family and later. Young children, regardless of the differences in their presenting problems, cannot achieve the same *degree* of insight that adult patients are capable of, because their cognitive capacities are not equal to the task. It is true that in analytical treatment, children, with the assistance of a therapist, are quite capable of learning how emotionally charged experiences with parents and siblings have bearing on their conscious and unconscious play enactments in treatment. However, while such "revelations" elicited through therapy can reduce or entirely eliminate children's anxieties, guilt feelings, symptoms, and ambivalences, they are not the same as the more global awareness that occurs with insight formation in adults.

The nature of children's insight and the process of acquiring it differ even more in activity therapy, where interpretations from a therapist are entirely eschewed. In activity therapy insight is *derivative*, not ideational. It is a consequence of significant interpersonal interactions between children with each other and with the therapist, experiences that can change them without their having to reflect about underlying psychological meanings. As time passes and the ameliorating effects of treatment become assimilated, a child *senses* change in himself.

Another factor in children's treatment that is relatively unique is their need for enlightenment about the human body and physiology. Parents either avoid these subjects entirely because of embarrassment or give inaccurate information. Thus, many children remain ignorant of matters about which they are inordinately curious.

The Role of the Therapist[12]

While the approach used in an activity group differs from the analytical methodology, both are derived from the same fundamentals of dynamic

[12]The therapist's role is described here in general terms, in its fundamental, qualitative aspects. In Chapters 1 through 4 the reader will find definitive descriptions of the therapist's role, procedures, and techniques, including accompanying explanations in the protocols of group sessions. The author believes readers will become better informed through this practical approach. Additional references can be found in footnotes and in the Bibliography.

psychology. The absence of interpretations and other active, verbal inter-ventions in an activity group in no way diminishes its complex dynamics, nor does a noninterpretive method render a therapist's role simpler than that in analytical psychotherapy. In an activity group, while it is not incumbent on a therapist to explore with children their behavior and emotions in a search for latent meanings, the multiple interpersonal interactions in the group do impose extraordinary demands upon the therapist. He or she must be able to perceive and comprehend all that transpires in a group, with each child in separate focus and with regard to the group as a whole. At one and the same time it is necessary to discern the interrelatedness of cause and effect against the larger context of each child's early history and life experiences, including the exceptional circumstances in his family that were responsible for causing the present problem.

It is a pervasive positive transference relationship to the therapist that supports the children while mediating, reconstructive forces within the activity group come into being. After the initial acclimatization period in the group, during which the therapist's permissiveness is subjected to testing to verify its actuality, the children develop a durable, positive transference bond. Of course, during the testing phase there are many negative transference expressions, which is a "natural" way in which children ascertain the true attitudes of adults. A therapist's general demeanor and his actions must be sanguine in effect at all times, even in the face of children's acting out. Once again, this differs from what occurs in analytical groups, in which a therapist may see fit to induce negative transference behavior and interpret it (see Chapter 5). This is an important facet of analytical therapy since it provides opportunities to explore children's feelings and fantasies.

Countertransference

A therapist has to anticipate an arousal of countertransference feelings, especially during the initial testing period by children. The propensity for easy regression in young children, once they are assured of safety, tends to challenge the efficiency of the adult's ego defenses, let alone his professional knowledge and skills. Any spontaneous, reactive behavior induced by countertransference would be countertherapeutic. Recognition of the potential for countertransference and avoidance of its pitfalls are of more critical concern in activity group therapy than in other forms of treatment because the therapist cannot discuss with the children the motivations of their acting-out behavior. Because of the nature of the therapy in activity groups, he is constrained to a *performance role*, one in which permissiveness and acceptance of children as they are, are the essential elements. In analytical methods—*with a different patient population*—a therapist has the latitude to openly address himself to children's expressed feelings, including their reactions to occasional countertransference responses of the therapist.

In activity therapy, therefore, it is imperative that a therapist be cognizant of his conscious and subliminal feelings so that he can maintain a non-interfering, neutral,[13] and supportive role. It has been affirmed by persons with expertise in activity group methods that no other form of psychotherapy of children—individual or group—can be as demanding.

The therapist's role and other requisites for activity group practice are precisely determined and are less subject to modification than in analytical treatment. In the latter, a therapist may, at any time, talk with the children about limitations in the meeting room; the children's abuse of furnishings and materials; interindividual conflicts, or acting out by a group or a child; and other significant behavioral phenomena. In an activity group, however, substantive changes in the fundamental role of a therapist, or in the design of a meeting room and its necessary paraphernalia, obstruct the therapeutic experience. The inadmissability of verbal, interpretive interventions allows little room for modifications in the setting, and practically none at all in the necessary performance role of the therapist.

Experience with many therapists in activity groups has revealed that when they depart substantially from the basic role of unconditional acceptance of children, neutrality, and noninterference, and employ techniques that are explicitly counterindicated in activity therapy, this departure is due to one or more of the following: (1) failure to comprehend the principles underlying activity groups; (2) countertransference reactions to children's acting out; (3) lack of training and/or inadequate supervision; (4) the error of including in an activity group one or more children who tend to activate others excessively and for whom the method is counterindicated; (5) and, related to the latter, a group lacking psychological balance.

The Early Sessions

When children enter a play room for the first time, they usually occupy themselves with crafts and other materials that are openly displayed on shelves and tables. The therapist volunteers no instructions but responds to children's questions if they arise, and then only to assure them that they may "use everything." Thus, children discover the unusual nature of the special setting immediately.[14] It could be anticipated that in an environment of almost total freedom, some parts of the setting and its furnishings and equipment might be abused by the children while testing the therapist's seeming forbearance. In order to preserve the therapeutic intent and role,

---

[13]*Psychological neutrality* means that a therapist is available at all times for each child to "make use" of him in terms of the child's unique requirements. For each child, the therapist is, in a sense, a *tabula rasa*.

[14]Informing children that they may "use everything" is not equivalent to saying that they may "*do* everything" they please, which might be misconstrued by some children as a *laissez-faire* suggestion.

this testing cannot be prohibited. The therapist tolerates a range of *nodal, anti-nodal,* and *supernodal* behavior, allowing sufficient time for the building up in the group of intrinsic social controls. Nodal behavior is a transitory period of hyperactivity and disequilibrium caused by a group's acting out in unison. Anti-nodal behavior usually follows nodal activity and is quiescent. Supranodal episodes, which may occur early in treatment when children are actively testing the therapist, is typified by hyperactivity of the entire group. Such hyperactivity may exceed the children's capacities for self-regulation and may require the therapist's intervention. Supranodal intensity is a temporary condition that ordinarily occurs as a group's "last fling" in affirming the reality of the permissive adult. It could also take place later in a group because of unusual circumstances—excessive scapegoating, for example.

Even in a well-balanced group a therapist is mindful of the proclivity of young latency children to become hypomanic through mutual catalysis and "infection." At such times a therapist uses special but fairly standard intervention techniques to dissolve a supranodal state. For example, the therapist might extend the invitation "Come sit here; I'm going to read a story" or "Let's all play this game." Such interventions appeal to young children and usually suffice to moderate their agitated state. Another standard procedure used in time of need is to serve the refreshments (which are part of all group sessions) earlier than the usual time, a method that seldom fails.[15] These are examples of interventions through substitute gratifications.

Corrective Influence of the Group as a Whole

While the therapist's accepting and helpful attitudes are responsible for creating the necessary therapeutic climate of an activity group, and his ministrations support and encourage the children as they become engaged in significant ways, the group itself evolves as a social *gestalt*, and it exerts corrective influences on its component members. Increasingly, the group begins to impose limiting, social constraints against the acting out of individuals. Because recognition from peers is of paramount importance to latency children, with social status as a much sought-after goal, they respond to social "rules and regulations" imposed by the group—the social mores of latency. It is a rare child who can resist the unitary criticism and social judgment of a peer group.

In response to these influences, the salutary effects of activity therapy deepen. Children become more self-assured; they feel stronger and more capable; their sense of identity becomes firmer. These outcomes are rein-

[15]These and other procedures will be described at many points in the group protocols of Chapters 1 through 4.

forced through creative accomplishments with arts and crafts media, proficiency in active games and sports, and other activities that have special meanings for latency children. Recognition and praise from other group members and from the therapist confirm a sense of social status, which has extraordinary strengthening influence. In addition to a child's becoming increasingly conscious of such improvements within himself, he experiences them sensately as derivative insight.

The Setting for Group Therapy

Room Size, Furnishings, and Materials

One might anticipate the design of the physical setting for activity groups from what has been described thus far: the general reluctance of children to verbalize about inner feelings; the necessity during latency to formulate adequate ego defenses; and children's natural energized behavior and propensity for spontaneous acting out; which suggest a need for sufficient space free of encumbrances to facilitate movement, for opportunities to exploit their innate curiosity and creativity, and for opportunities to convert some of their extraordinary physical energy into tangible, gratifying end products through arts and crafts projects. Such needs require a setting that most children would find interesting and stimulating at first glance. A properly designed and equipped activity therapy meeting room meets these requirements.

Children find the group setting familiar because many of its available materials and game equipment, as well as the functional quality of its appearance, are known to them. The standard furnishings—tables, chairs, open supply shelves, and so forth—are of plain, unpainted lumber. The entire meeting room lacks an upholstered appearance, which would tend to discourage children's free use of it. The overall appearance suggests to children that it is a place for free movement without need to be unduly concerned about marring, soiling, or breaking objects. Restrictions against mobility and the free use of materials, accompanied by adult demands for order and neatness, are already familiar to most children in their respective homes and classrooms. The group meeting room, on the other hand, is immediately perceived by children as utilitarian, accommodated to their physical size and interests.

Meeting rooms vary somewhat in dimension for children of different ages. An optimal floor area can be determined by multiplying fifty square feet by the number of group members. Children who are approximately five to seven years old require less space and fewer and simpler materials; older latency children are exposed to a broader range of supplies. (See Appendix II for lists of supplies.) Young children should have available play items that tend to be more projective in a psychological sense, engaging them in individual play and interactions with others in episodes reminiscent of actual situations in daily life. Examples are family dolls, dollhouses, blocks, and finger paints.

Some work and play items are used equally by all children regardless of gender, others more selectively. Despite the cultural thrust of present times, which has had some impact on what some persons consider traditional stereotypic gender differentiations with respect to interests and occupations, latency children apparently still manifest focused interest in work and play activities which, for them, help to define their gender identities. In treating children, by whatever method, it would be unwise for a therapist to impose his or her philosophical convictions about homogenizing gender interests or proclivities. Only a *patient's* feelings, thoughts, and behavior are relevant in the treatment and should govern a therapist's thinking and interventions.

Thus, in an activity group composed of boys, in addition to the more plastic media that attract children's attention regardless of gender (crayons, paints, clay, and like items), there are available more resistive crafts media such as carpentry and metal work for older boys. Also to be considered are active, aggressive games such as Nok-Hockey and ball playing, which are usually considered by children as masculine activities. Girls' groups should have available, in addition to the standard items, some activities identified more with a feminine role—sewing and weaving, for example.[16]

To a casual observer, a group treatment setting would give the impression of a simply furnished play room with arts and crafts materials and games. It is actually, however, the end product of a careful design. Nothing is permitted within the setting that is without bearing on the therapeutic procedure.[17]

Room furnishings and equipment are deliberately located in a meeting room in terms of *function-relatedness*, not haphazardly. Examples of this are: easels placed in close proximity to a source of water; tools and other implements near the raw materials for which they are intended; one small table (called an isolate table) placed in an inconspicuous spot removed from areas of traffic in order to provide a safe haven for a withdrawn child who may insulate himself from contact with others in the beginning of treatment.

---

[16]These suggestions should not be considered as absolute desiderata. They are recommendations predicated solely on *clinical* considerations, particularly as they concern the treatment of emotionally disturbed latency-age children. They should not be construed as principles concerning general *education* for all children. Normal children share many interests and activities in common.

[17]In some schools where activity groups have been conducted, the unavailability of optimal conditions has necessitated the use of less desirable settings. This has always made the therapist's role more difficult. Readers will discern this in the meeting reports of several groups in Chapters 1 through 4.

Children perceive the meeting room as a place to play and make things. Sometimes they look upon it as a "club." The initial invitation to a child to join a group is couched in terms that support this; he is told that he will meet with others in a "play group" or a "club." The therapeutic intent of the group, including the professional identity of the therapist, is never stated as such. Professional and other stigmata would obstruct the therapeutic processes in activity therapy groups.[18]

PROTECTING CHILDREN FROM PHYSICAL INJURY

Situational restraints are built into the meeting room to prevent children from injuring themselves and also to spare the therapist from needlessly interfering with their activities, thus preserving this permissive image. One example is the use of cleats in a window frame that will keep a child from opening it widely, an act that might endanger him. Without such a built-in obstruction, a therapist could be put in a position of having to warn a child or actually prohibiting him. Glass panels in doors or supply cabinets are avoided to prevent the possibility of shattering. Standing structural columns within a room should be padded, as in a gymnasium. Protruding encumbrances—radiators and other fixed obstructions to free passage—should also be enclosed. Simple wood barriers can be built to prevent children from accidentally running into potentially harmful obstructions.

Frequency of Group Sessions

Activity groups meet once weekly for approximately one hour. If possible, it is advantageous to extend the meeting time to one and a half hours for older latency children. Two group sessions per week are preferable if it is possible to arrange this. These recommendations, based on empirical findings, are subject to the therapist's judgment as the final determinant.

In most groups, sessions are discontinued during the summer vacation period and resumed with the start of the school year. Whenever possible, activity groups are maintained for two years before termination. In actual practice, the author has been able to continue some activity groups in schools as long as four years because of the exceptional needs of some seriously troubled children. Since not all children will be equally ready for ter-

---

[18]In analytical group therapy, there is an advantage in the children's knowing the exploratory and interpretive aspects of the therapy, including the professional identity of the therapist. However, these disclosures should evolve as a consequence of children's interactions with the therapist. Children's awareness of the special nature of an analytical group will develop rapidly, as soon as the therapist begins to make inquiries and offer observations, explanations, and interpretations.

mination at the same time, some may be transferred to other therapy groups, or other dispositions may be made depending on individual circumstances.

Summary

In summation, the outcomes of activity therapy groups are determined in the main by the following conditions:

1. Children's discovery of a "new" kind of adult—a benevolent, understanding, tolerant, helpful person who represents the ideal "parent" symbolically and is a consistent source of emotional nurturance over an extended period of time.
2. A carefully designed environment that provides extraordinary opportunities for corrective reexperience.
3. A peer group offering opportunities for significant interpersonal interactions, recognition, and social status—important components in the process of identity formation during latency.
4. A setting that offers immediate opportunities for reality testing and the formation of sublimations.

CHAPTER 1

William and Cary

MORTIMER SCHIFFER

William

> William has not spoken at all to adults in school. He has not uttered a single word to his present teacher this year, nor did he last year. It is reported that he may whisper occasionally to another child.

The foregoing is from a referral to a guidance counselor made by a second-grade teacher when William was seven years, nine months of age. William behaved passively; he was never spontaneously active. He followed instructions mutely, always conformed, and never caused trouble. Classmates sensed his need for isolation and for the most part respected it. William's face was mask-like, practically expressionless at times. He was not learning and for some time had been visiting a remediation teacher for special instruction, but with no success. His teachers in first grade and kindergarten had reported much the same picture.

William's family was intact; he was the second oldest of three children, the consequence of an unwanted pregnancy, born nine years after his sister.

Names of all persons appearing in the cases and protocols have been changed and the content has been otherwise modified to conceal true identities. This has been done without sacrificing the accuracy of the presented information.

Matters were further exacerbated for his mother by the birth of another son, ten months after William, also an unwanted pregnancy. Child-rearing was particular difficult for her, especially with William, who, almost from birth, was compared unfavorably with his younger sibling. William's development was slower; he presented difficulties with respect to feeding and toilet training, which was not completed until age four. He could not walk unaided until seventeen months; speech started at age three, and was halting and sparse for a considerable time. William was ill frequently and often had high fevers.

The mother became depressed with the burden of simultaneous care of two infants, and her resentment became expressed on both conscious and unconscious levels. Her fundamental rejection of the mothering role was demonstrated when she quickly returned to her job, from which she had taken only temporary leave after the births of the two infants. She left them in the care of her husband, who worked evenings, and also of her young daughter, who obviously resented the premature role imposed on her. The father, although well intentioned, was strict in his manner of handling the children, particularly William, who imposed a heavier burden. All the children, including the daughter, were obviously overawed by the father's direct, sometimes threatening manner, and they were compliant.

William's separation from his family to attend kindergarten was accomplished with great difficulty. It was only when his younger brother became eligible to attend, a year later, that William could be induced to accompany him to school. His attendance in kindergarten and first grade was marked by many absences, which were ostensibly because of illnesses but were undoubtedly aggravated by phobic fears of leaving his home.

William was referred for evaluation when in kindergarten because of persistent muteness in school. The parents were not cooperative despite their obvious need for help with the boy's special problems. They resented the time lost from employment. Their economic circumstances were limited, despite the fact that both were employed. They responded only to the extent of allowing a psychological evaluation and a psychiatric examination. Because of William's failure to talk, the psychologist could not assess the boy's emotional state, intelligence, or learning skills. The psychiatrist was also blocked in his examination by William's intransigent resistance.

On the basis of information gleaned from direct observations of William in class, the parents' statements, and other observers in school, several elements were considered as possible causes of his muteness. Since William spoke at home, albeit in a limited fashion, it was thought that his inhibited speech could be a silent rebellion, perhaps an indication of repressed rage, particularly against his parents. William's bouts of crying and whining as an infant were responded to by the father in a loud voice and with threatening gestures, which eventually squelched the infant's tears but may have left him mute and fearful. The mother's failure to provide sufficient care and nurturance impeded his early emotional growth, resulting in weak ego development. In addition, it was thought that William's massive suppression of feelings, even his failure to vocalize infant sounds and later words, represented self-protective, defensive adaptations. Verbalization, in particular, became cathected with anxiety. The question of secondary gain through muteness was also considered.

This was the situation, with little change in William's manifest behavior, after two years in school. The parents consented to his participation in a "play" group when it was offered in second grade, with the suggestion that it might help William to talk, make friends, and "become happier." William attended a therapeutic play group[1] for approximately seven months, being present for twenty-seven of the twenty-nine group sessions—almost perfect attendance considering his previous history of absences caused by illnesses. Evidently the group became a significant experience for him almost immediately, increasing his motivation to attend school.

The treatment goals were as follows: to free William from the constraints that inhibited his speech; to help him become less fearful; to foster in him confidence and an improved self-image; and to enable him to ventilate cathartically what was deemed to be strongly repressed anger. If the therapeutic experience was successful, the supposition was that freer speech would result.

The use of a therapeutic play group was deemed proper for several reasons: (1) William would find a dyadic treatment relationship threatening, and it would tend to reinforce his withdrawal. (2) The presence of other children in a group would initially act as a buffer against too close proximity with the worker. (3) The testing and acting-out behavior of other children in the permissive group setting would enable William to study the demeanor and role of the accepting worker. William would feel safe in a "spectator" status. (4) The other children would demonstrate for him that aggression can be safe; it does not necessarily destroy its object, nor does it necessarily invoke retaliation from the adult. Eventually William would be brought to a point where he might be able to act similarly. (5) More pertinently, it is important that William express his essential hostility toward his parents and siblings through displacement in the group, using the worker and groupmates as substitute objects. (6) Finally, if William acquired a freedom to act without abject fear, it is probable that his inhibited vocalization could be decathected and he would speak freely.

The worker's[2] role with William had to be carefully planned in advance. While a worker is generally peripheral to interactions in a therapeutic play group, in William's case she needed to be particularly alert in avoiding

---

[1]The term given to activity therapy groups in school settings. See M. Schiffer, *The Therapeutic Play Group*, Grune and Stratton, New York, 1969.

[2]The term "worker" was used instead of "therapist" in activity therapy groups for two reasons: first, to sensitize the therapist to the nonanalytic, functional role in purely activity group therapy; secondly, to objectify the recording of the group sessions.

direct contact until he demonstrated a tolerance for it. Above all, William must not be forced into a situation of having to answer responsively in words. Also, the composition of the group had to be such as to provide him with a tolerable modicum of stimulation from more aggressive group members and a supportive relationship with at least one nonthreatening, passive child with whom William could identify and play with (actually there were two such children—Cary and John).

Cary

Cary was eight years old when he was referred. He had been phobic about attending school since he started kindergarten. At that time, in addition to frequent absences from school because of a variety of "illnesses" that were probably due to his phobic anxiety, he complained daily about stomach pains when he came to school. The pattern then was to send for someone to take him home. Cary was nervous, he twitched, he was generally fearful and timid, and he related to children and adults in immature ways. He had pronounced infantile speech that was difficult to comprehend. Given the slightest pretext he would cry. Cary was preoccupied with thoughts of illness and death and made frequent morbid references about both.

The parents were employed and Cary was left in the care of a grandmother who hovered over him overprotectingly, further exaggerating the child's already immature dependency. There was one sibling, an older brother who attended secondary school. The brother was often in conflict with his demanding younger brother, who was always supported by the grandmother. Cary's intelligence was within normal range, his learning fair. Cary attended twenty-one of the twenty-nine sessions of the group, with most of the absences attributed to sickness. He was highly motivated to attend the group, practically from the beginning.

The presenting problem was that of a latency-age child who was developmentally immature, excessively dependent, and had neurotic features, notably phobic reactions to school and a marked tendency for somatization. He had been treated unsuccessfully in individual play therapy during the past year. This was the situation when it was decided to accept Cary for the play group.

The choice of group treatment for Cary was based on the following reasons: (1) If his initial response to it was favorable, it could reduce his reluctance to coming to school. (2) A positive transference relationship with a female worker (maternal substitute) might alter the neurotic constellation typical of the relationship of a phobic child and his mother. (3) The climate of freedom in the group might lead him to convert phobic and somatic symptoms into cathartic acting-out behavior, through sloughing off. (4) Such a change could be motivated through a supportive ego relationship with a stronger child. (5) Creative accomplishments through the arts and crafts activities will improve his self-concept. (6) Group (social) pressure may act as a restraint against infantile behavior and direct him into more acceptable social patterns.

The group worker had to be mindful that Cary would need support, perhaps protection, if stronger boys threatened him. If this came about, she would have to intervene carefully so that others would not consider him favored. On the other hand, the worker must allow him sufficient latitude to experience reasonable degrees of frustration, even threat, from group members, so that he may learn to cope without the dependency ploys he presently uses so effectively. Finally, regressive behavior, if it eventuates, must not be permitted free reign, because it would habituate further the present infantile adaptation. Any extraordinary dependency demands made on the worker should be carefully monitored to foster autonomous growth.

The Other Group Members

The play group was composed of five boys. While the body of this report will focus on Cary and William, the events to be described will become more meaningful with short descriptions of the remaining three group members. Following, in condensed form, are brief vignettes of the others:

Mitchell, eight years old, was described as being very aggressive, although he tended to be a loner. He was often truant from school and disobedient in class. In appearance he was morose and defensive, as if anticipating censure from adults. He had been discharged from a parochial school prior to his attendance at this school because of severe acting out. Despite his tendency to truancy, Mitchell became so motivated to attend the group that he missed only three out of the twenty-nine sessions.

George, eight years old, was referred because of temper outbursts, aggression, underachievement, truancy, and poor peer relationships that were mostly caused by his intransigent behavior. He attended twenty-three of the twenty-nine group sessions.

John, eight years old, was shy, fearful, nervous, and restless. While attentive in class, he did not learn and was still at a pre-primer level in second grade. He liked his teacher and sometimes brought little gifts to her. John chats with his classmates but has no friends to speak of. He attended 21 of 29 group sessions.

At its inception, this small group appeared well balanced psychologically. Three of the boys—William, Cary, and John—were passive, recessive types, tending toward social isolation and all apparently lacking in aggression. Mitchell and George, on the other hand, were overaggressive, sometimes obstreperous in behavior and defiant. The psychological balance of the play group was maintained fairly well during its existence so that the interpersonal interactions among the group members were self-regulating for the most part, rarely requiring direct interventions by the worker. When on several occasions she found it necessary to do so, in almost all instances indirect measures were used that adequately limited conflictual situations without the children's experiencing them as reproof or denial.

It is interesting to note that in a relatively short time after the group started, the school attendance of all the boys, including the two notable truants, improved significantly. Also, at no time did either of the acting-out boys, Mitchell and George, manifest in the play group the intensity of angry, aggressive conduct that was described when they were referred. This despite the fact that the climate of the play group was one of almost complete freedom, created by the permissiveness of the worker.

What follows are records of group sessions describing the major events that transpired, focusing on incidents involving William and Cary. Following each group session, the worker wrote from memory a detailed record of what took place. This was used in weekly supervision conferences with the author. No notes were taken during sessions, which practice would distract a worker's attention from ongoing activities and also make her less accessible to children should they need her. Interspersed in the records are comments and interpretations by the author.

The first six sessions constituted a "warm-up" phase during which the boys became accustomed to the play room and its games, crafts materials, and selected, simple play items. The boys were particularly conscious of the worker, trying to fathom her permissiveness, the fact that she never initiated or interfered in their activities, and most of all the extraordinary freedom, to which they were unaccustomed. At first they were disconcerted by the absolute lack of direction from her, including the freedom to use everything in the room. Such initial bewilderment is characteristic of children in a therapeutic play group. It represents a period of discovery of an altogether novel kind of adult, one who accepts children without reservation or question; does not interfere in individual or group activities, and accepts without comment behavior that is limited or altogether forbidden by parents and teachers.

Toward the end of each play session the worker prepared one of the tables for a small repast, using decorative settings with placemats and other paraphernalia to accommodate the food that was served. For the children the repast always had the semblance of a "party" and they eagerly shared the treats, usually cookies or cake with a beverage. Surprised by this offering at the first session, the boys slowly partook of the refreshments, shyly and embarrassed. There was little said at the table. In the next several sessions it was evident that they looked forward avidly to the "treat." They directed no questions to the worker as to the reasons for their attending the play group, but they did ask whether they could meet more than once weekly. Routinely the boys were brought to and from the play room by two older children acting as escorts. The same escorts were used throughout the existence of the play group. Definite emotional ties were formed between them and their young charges.

Group sessions were scheduled for approximately one hour, timed to end just before regular school dismissals in order to preclude the possibility of carryover into the classrooms of any activated, stimulating behavior that could have disruptive effects.

During the first six group sessions, William and Cary were mostly passively involved in separate play, seldom communicating with the others—William not at all, because he remained mute. Yet, both boys gave visible evidence as the weeks passed that they looked forward to attending the group sessions and, despite their shyness, they sat with the others at the refreshment table. During this period of acclimatization, the overall behavior within the group was modulated, with no episodes of conflict or acting out by anyone, including Mitchell and George, the aggressive boys. By the time of the seventh session, Mitchell and George, as anticipated, began actively to test the worker's forbearance and permissiveness. The fact that they had not done so for six sessions was surprising. They asked for more frequent meetings, requested additional materials and special foods, and solicited the worker's attention by involving her in their games and crafts work. The worker, without comment, calmly met all requests, except for increasing the number of sessions, which she explained she was unable to do. By the seventh session, the first to be reported here in detail, the acclimatization was essentially completed; the boys were assured of the reality of this "special" setting and the worker. Of course they continued to act out episodically as the months passed, but this later behavior was more spontaneous and uncalculated, and it represented for each boy a measure of catharsis, relieving inner tensions. The opportunity for catharsis and the ego-strengthening experiences related to the positive transference with the worker were the corrective influences that eventually modified the children's behavior.

William and Cary had become more relaxed by the seventh session, although they were still reserved in manner. William was more so than Cary, with the latter demonstrating a greater capacity for making contact with the other boys and the worker. William maintained both physical and emotional distance from her.

It was during the seventh session that an incident occurred which was of much import with respect to William's muteness. It took place almost at the onset of the session.

Session No. 7, Excerpts: Present—William, Mitchell, George, John

William and Mitchell entered the play room. Mitchell started to play with blocks on the floor. William observed him quietly, not participating. Suddenly William burst into loud crying, almost screaming. He grasped his neck with both hands, as though he was choking himself. For a moment the worker was concerned that he had been hit by a block, although she had not seen this happen; it had all occurred so quickly. The worker said, "Are you sick?" William continued to cry, without replying. The worker then asked Mitchell if anything had fallen on William. He replied, "No." The worker turned to William, saying, "Come sit here with me and rest a while." He looked unhappy but complied. Soon John and George entered the play room. By that time William was visibly calmer. He took the box of plastic blocks and quietly played alone with them on a table.

Comments and Interpretations

In supervision conference, the worker was asked to *reenact* William's behavior as exactly as she could reconstruct it. In doing so she gave the unmistakable impression of William's attempting to prevent vocalization, as if trying to strangle sound. At this point the worker recalled something she had not recorded in the protocol of the session. *She said that William had distinctly uttered the word "Mommy" twice amidst his sobbing.* It was the author's feeling that a spontaneous break had occurred, somehow induced by a momentary weakening of the boy's defense against speech. Instantly William tried to suppress it by "choking" it off, as if the utterance had fearsome consequences. It was apparent that his first blurted-out word, "Mommy," was associated with the transference to the worker that had developed during the initial six group sessions. Prior to this there had been no overt evidence of transference bonds to the worker.

Earlier in the session, when George and Mitchell had entered the room, George yelled, "Kool-Aid!" Both boys asked the worker if drinks were to be served again and she replied affirmatively, adding that she would serve as soon as she finished making placemats. She was cutting these out from oilcloth, one of the activities she busied herself with during sessions. (Workers have to occupy themselves during sessions in tasks related to the group. In this fashion they set an example of purposeful work and, at the same time, they may observe the group unobtrusively.)

George and Mitchell reminisced happily about last week's "party," telling William how much he had missed. (William had been ill the preceding week.) John began to paint at the easel. George took a puzzle; then he drummed a loud rhythm using two blocks, saying this was how he used to beat time in Canada, where he used to live. John said, "Indians do that." George nodded. He continued to hum a tune as he banged the blocks. Then he ran to the window, looked out, and commented on the newly fallen snow. He called the others to come look, and they did so, all commenting about it except William, who merely watched. Soon William went to the easel and began to paint. John and Mitchell went to the block corner, where they played together.

Comments and Interpretations

Despite William's tendency when referred to isolate himself from other children, in the play group he had begun to move into contact with the boys, joining in some of their activities but always silent. This is an open indication of a loosening of the self-encapsulation that was characteristic of him heretofore. Also, painting at the easel was a first such attempt for him and another sign of greater mobility, which for him represented manifest aggression—a voluntary exploration and "touching" of the setting.

Note also that John joined Mitchell in block play. Here we see the positive influence of a stronger boy, Mitchell, acting as a supportive ego to a shy, frightened child who had already begun to share in the activities of others without displaying his usual timidity.

George kept asking about when the "party" was to start. He went to the round table where the worker was and voluntarily assisted her in setting out placemats, cups, and saucers. The four boys assembled at the table and sat with the worker. They drank juice and ate cookies in good humor. George spoke of a club he belonged to that met after school. John said he, too, went to the club meetings. They described one meeting in a graveyard. (In fact there is a cemetery close to the school, and children occasionally congregated there during lunchtime.) George went on to describe how the boys "dug up" a grave and saw a body "with a cross and things on it." John said they often went there. George said it was "scary." Mitchell and William just listened, saying nothing, but evidently quite interested.

Comments and Interpretations

Assemblying for a repast tends to promote conversation between members of a group, and the topics are usually about events in their lives outside the play group. Proximity in the group during refreshments is psychologically analagous to the congregation of a family at mealtime, with conversation about events of the day. In a therapeutic play group the worker listens so as not to interfere with the spontaneous, sometimes associative flow of conversation. Much factual information and also fantasies and other wishful productions emanate from children which prove informative to the worker. It is probably true that the therapeutic impact which is inherent in group psychotherapies of various types with child-patients becomes maximal during refreshment periods.

George's comments about digging up a body in the cemetery are apocryphal, a braggadocio denial of fear: "scary," as he put it.

With respect to William's vocal outburst at the beginning of the session, nothing else took place during the rest of the session that cast further light on what had provoked it; nor were there any subsequent evidences that William was perturbed about its having happened. In its context it remained a sudden, dramatic event, seemingly unrelated to overt stimuli, with no aftereffects as far as the worker could determine.

Session No. 8, Excerpts: Present—George, William, John

Note: The worker was concerned about two consecutive absences of Cary and wondered whether this was related to the meeting day, Monday, which tends to be a day of absence for phobic children—a prolonged "weekend."

The three boys entered the play room together. George and John immediately began a make-believe fight using hand puppets. William joined in. They continued this goodnaturedly for a brief time. Then George took a puzzle, singing as he put it together. He said to the worker, "I'll fix the others for you." The worker thanked him. While this was going on, William walked over to watch George at work with the puppets on his hands.

George asked, "Are we getting Kool-Aid again?" (It was the boys' favorite beverage.) William and John stared at the worker, awaiting her reply. "Yes," she said. George asked, "When?" and she answered, "Soon." Meanwhile a child knocked at the door with a message for the worker. The children were interested and the worker explained that it was from the office, informing all school personnel of an early dismissal. The worker then told the boys that she had arranged to have their meetings from 1:30 to 2:30 in the afternoon in the future so that they could have minimally a full hour. George and John said, "Great!" William smiled.

The worker set the table and the boys had their drinks and cake. George took several pieces from the serving plate, crumbling them into bits. John took three. William drank two cups of Kool-Aid, but he had only one piece of cake, this before George confiscated the remainder. John pointed this out to the worker, saying, "He [William] had none." The worker replied in a modulated voice, "I brought enough for everybody." No further reference was made to the cake. Soon there was a knock on the door. The escorts had come to take the boys back to class because of the early dismissal.

Comments and Interpretations

With regard to the absentees: as a regular practice, the worker mailed postal cards to children who were absent, informing them that she and the other boys missed them and hoped to see them the following week. Such mailed reminders have proved very meaningful to children, for obvious reasons.

In this session, William's participation in the sparring with the hand puppets was another "first" for him. It was an innovation of much import since it was a direct, physically aggressive act. It is interesting that when the others ceased to play with the puppets, William still kept them on his hands, an indication, perhaps, of the unusual effect on him of such an open demonstration of aggression. This short episode illustrates the catalyzing effect of child upon child in group therapy. What an acting-out, ego-strong type of child like George is capable of without apparent concern tends to mobilize weaker children like John and William to dare attempt similar behavior. This is another example of the supportive ego influence. Further, in this incident, George served the role of a positive instigator, a necessary component in group composition.

The worker's reply to George's query about when the group could have refreshments was ill-advised from a technical point of view. A better rejoinder when children ask such a question is, "Whenever you want to." Such a reply further reveals her to be a totally giving, responsive adult—dramatically so. However, soon thereafter, the worker more than substantiated her global "love" by telling the children she had voluntarily made a change in their meetings to extend the amount of time they would be able to spend in the play room. The boys were delighted.

In therapeutic play groups, refreshments are served family-style, on a serving plate, with the children free to help themselves. In the beginning sessions there is usually some disparity between what the different children get, the more aggressive ones taking the lion's share. When this is verbalized by a child, as John did, when he incorrectly stated that William had gotten no cake, the worker either says nothing or makes an entirely neutral comment, such as she did. Another kind of response by the worker, when children point out what they consider to be negative behavior on the part of others, is merely to acknowledge the remark with a brief nod, with no verbal response. The meanings of such rejoinders are implicit: the worker is not oblivious but choses not to interfere; it is up to the group to settle such affairs. In effect this conveys: "I trust you."

When some children with oral cravings, or strong sibling-rivalry feelings, engage more persistently or vigorously in grabbing food and thus depriving others, the worker may use other interventions to help the group remedy such a problem. However, she still avoids comments or maneuvers that would arouse feelings of guilt; nor does she ever deny food following episodes of a group's acting out. One technique is to supply a cake that has to be cut. The worker does this and carefully portions out a separate serving for each child. Thus, the group is assisted in learning to share by an indulgent "reward" the following session.

Again in this session we see other "beginnings" for William. Still silent, he nevertheless moved into aggressively physical interaction. While the "fight" with puppets was rather innocuous, for him—to whom such behavior was entirely foreign previously—it represented an event of major importance. William was also becoming more expressive facially, as the worker described in supervision. The effect was rather pronounced because he was formerly mask-like. It may be of significance that these events occurred after the vocal "breakthrough" of the prior session.

Session No. 9, Excerpt: Present—William, John, Cary, Mitchell

This session was relatively uneventful, with an exception. At one point during the meeting, John quietly reported to the worker that William had *whispered* to him: "Wanna play checkers?"

Comments and Interpretations

Two points deserve comment. John's reporting to the worker about William is an indication of his—and the group's—awareness of William's characteristic mode of silence, so much so that even a whispered comment was something impressive to them. Secondly, the incident represents the second evidence of speech by William in the play group. He was certainly capable of speech; his mutism was selective.

Session No. 10, Excerpts: Present—Mitchell, John, Cary, William

The boys appeared at the play room door almost simultaneously. Mitchell began to build with blocks. John joined him. They built a tall tower that fell over, making a loud crash. Both boys jumped and looked toward the worker guiltily. The worker neither looked back nor made any comment. Then the boys again built a tower, but this time they deliberately threw it over. Once again they glanced toward the worker to see whether she would react to the noise. John announced: "She'll holler." He and William studied the worker, who was engaged in hanging the children's finished paintings on the wall, evidencing no concern for the noise made by the crashing blocks.

William wandered about the room, his hands in his pockets. He then joined John, who was putting together a jigsaw puzzle at the table. Cary came over also. It seemed that two jigsaw puzzles were mixed together, and Cary and John argued loudly about which pieces belong to each. William became openly excited. From time to time he would object strenuously, wordlessly, *shaking his head violently* whenever he thought a piece of the puzzle was incorrectly placed. At one point he disagreed so much that he uttered "Uh, Uh!" negatively and strenuously.

Comments and Interpretations

Events and changes occurred rapidly during this session. This is not uncharacteristic of the momentum of behavioral changes with even severely disturbed young children, once they have become assured of the essential safety of the environment, especially the accepting, helpful adult whose attitude and behavior have allayed their doubts and fears. Young children are emotionally labile, capable of being quickly brought into spontaneity and interaction given the proper therapeutic climate.

Noteworthy is the incident of the crashing blocks, a truly evocative "accident." The worker continued hanging pictures, apparently unmoved by the commotion. So the children repeated the act, deliberately, with John "announcing" it to ensure that the worker was aware; he was apparently delighted with her forebearance. Once again the worker passed the "test"; she did not even pause in her work. Also, a partner in this destructive, loud play was Cary: phobic, timid, and immature. As is usual with such children, he was supported in the play by a stronger child.

Following this we find all three of the passive-type children joining in activity. This again is typical of the direction of social involvements that are characteristic in group therapy. First John and Cary came together; then William joined them. Of interest is the degree of active disagreement and the vocal expressions by these boys, William's being the most dramatic. He became so overwrought that once again there was a speech "breakthrough." His sudden, unexpected blurting of words or sounds was the third time he had vocalized since being in treatment. As perceived by the worker—and sensed by the boys—William's rare vocalizations occurred as if impulsively released from stringent controls against expression. This would imply some conscious withholding of sound, a factor that is related to selective mutism.

John began to paint, and now Mitchell helped with the puzzles. William painted on the other side of the easel. Next, Mitchell took the small plastic blocks to the corner. Soon thereafter he put the crow puppet on his hand and threatened Cary with it. Cary did not appear frightened, but he was excited and more animated than usual. (His classroom teacher had reported before the session that Cary had complained of stomach pains in the mornings and his grandmother had been taking him home. This day, however, while he again said he felt ill, he told the teacher that he *had to stay* for the afternoon because he wanted to attend the play group.) Cary went to play with the wood blocks, building a tower as before and deliberately crashing it. William covered his ears to block out the noise, watching the worker for her reaction. He then put puppets on both hands and stared at them reflectively.

John and Mitchell played checkers as the worker began to set the table for refreshments. Immediately the four boys pulled chairs over to the table to watch her. Cary spoke excitedly, "Cwackers! Kool-Aid!" adding something incomprehensible that the worker thought had to do with stomach pains. His speech, which was usually infantile, was so much so then that John and Mitchell laughed uproariously after each of his comments. William smiled broadly. Each of Cary's remarks continued to evoke gales of laughter, but Cary continued talking as if oblivious to the boys' responses.

The boys ate happily. William refilled his cup three times. Mitchell asked the worker whether he could put one cookie aside for later so that he could take it with him. The worker said he could. He wrapped it carefully in his napkin. Everyone but William groaned aloud when there was a knock on the door, which meant the escorts had arrived to return them to class.

Comments and Interpretations

William was continuing to congregate, more and more, as indicated by his joining another boy at the easel. He was still mindful of the acting-out activities of others and concerned about how the worker would react, as when he watched her to see if she would do something when Cary crashed the blocks. The other children were no longer apprehensive about how the worker would behave. It is interesting that William momentarily put puppets on his hands, this time not using them but staring at them. This was evidently a conscious act in which he reflected on his earlier "daring" participation in the "fight" with the other boys. Later, William joined the others when they made fun of Cary's infantile speech, but only by smiling broadly, not uttering sounds.

In sum, in this session William continued to behave in increasingly centripetal fashion, making contacts with others and once again vocalizing.

Cary also showed diminishing self-restraint and, with the support of more assertive boys, became aggressively involved. The crashing of blocks was a dramatic experience for him, so much so that he repeated it later alone. His marked immaturity, expressed in one aspect through his infantile speech, was apparent to the others. Another aspect of immaturity was Cary's apparent obliviousness to their laughter, a narcissistic character trait. He merely continued to chatter on. Cary's growing interest in his membership in the play group was amply demonstrated by his decision to remain in school for the afternoon to attend the group—this despite his avowed "bellyache" in the morning.

Session No. 11, Excerpts: Present—John, George, Mitchell, William

John and George entered the play room first. The worker said to George, "We missed you last week." George replied, wonderingly and surprised, "You did?" The worker said, "Yes. How do you feel?" George: "I wasn't sick. I didn't have shoes. See, my mother bought me these," pointing. The worker continued, "Did you get my postal card?" George: "Card? No. You sent *me* a card! Just for me?" He was amazed, almost overcome. The worker answered affirmatively. At this point William and Mitchell arrived.

William took the plastic blocks to the corner isolate table, where he played alone. Mitchell painted at the easel. George took the pool game, placed it on the floor, and played with it, singing and humming happily. John painted.

George announced to the room in general, "Let's play puppet show." He took the alligator and crow puppets in hand, singing still. John joined him at the table. George said, "This is the stage" (indicating the table). The two boys stooped up and down, waving the puppets, and sang some patter songs. Then George took two wood blocks and beat them together, marching to his own rhythm. John followed, albeit less demonstratively.

During this time William continued to paint at the easel. George joined him at this activity later. Then William went to the other end of the room where the blocks were, and piled them high as he had observed others do in the prior session. William deliberately made them crash, looking toward the worker. She gave no indication of noticing this. William rebuilt the blocks, then wheeled a toy truck into them, once again crashing them to the floor with a loud noise. He then pointed to the fallen blocks as if to enunciate what he had done. Mitchell, who observed this, seemed to understand what William meant.

Almost from the beginning of the session, George had been inquiring about the nature of refreshments, which he often did. Once he reminded the worker, "When is the party?" He did this momentarily, interrupting this singing: "Come little ducky, come, we'll march. . . ." He was making up nonsense rhymes, with John following his lead. As soon as the worker began to prepare the table for refreshments, the four boys immediately ran to seat themselves, watching her with interest. Cookies were snatched by all rapidly, leaving none on the plate. George, noticing this, said, "What about her?" (indicating the worker). Silently William placed a cookie on the serving plate. George did likewise. John said, pointing to William, "He never talks, even in class." George said, directly to William, "Why don't you talk?" William just stared back at the two boys. George said, "His brother don't talk either. I don't know what's the matter with them." (William's brother was timid and quiet, but he did speak in school.)

The boys refilled their cups. William was the first to leave the table, going back to the blocks, where he again built a tower. Again he rammed it with the toy truck, this time scattering the fallen blocks indiscriminately.

When a knock sounded at the door, George said, "So soon." He wanted to stay after the others left, saying his teacher wouldn't mind if he came a little later. But he left with the waiting escort.

Comments and Interpretations

George's amazed and pleased response to the worker's inquiry about his absence, and her remark about the mailed card, are typical of children's reactions to such evidences of interest in them and affirm the correctness of the procedure of writing after each absence. Of greater import is George's reactions when considered in the context of his problem when he was referred. He was exceedingly aggressive toward peers, defiant toward and difficult to manage by teachers. During the remainder of this session one notes his freedom of expression, open happiness, and reluctance to leave the play room after the others did. This desire to be alone with the worker was his unconscious wish to be the "only" child. George had formed a strong, positive transference relationship with the worker.

William again showed his reclusive tendency when he took the small table blocks to play alone at the isolate table in the far corner of the room. This small table was placed there purposely to accommodate timid children, who, in the beginning of a play group, protect themselves from contacts with others until they are ready for such experience. William's stay at the isolate table during this session was short, and he soon replicated the aggressive block play of the other boys that he had carefully watched the week before. It may be that he was working up to this brave attempt, first pondering it at the isolate table. It represented for him a *critical event*[3] because not only was it loud and destructive play, but he chose to do it alone. This was even "braver" than Cary's aggressive block play the week before, supported as it was by a stronger group member. Further, note William's more complex experimentation, as when he used a truck to demolish the tower. Finally, this "release" activity must have been very meaningful to him, because he could barely wait for the end of refreshments to return to the blocks and the crashing.

Two of the boys focused on William's failure to talk, without William evincing any response to their direct questions. It is true that William's younger brother was reticent, but this did not represent the severe problem that necessitated William's treatment.

As was noted earlier, when children assemble for a repast, it has symbolic meaning characteristic of a personal gathering of a "family" and

---

[3]A critical event is an episode wherein a child, either verbally or through an enactment, demonstrates a turning point in his basic problem. It usually occurs after a series of tentative "experiments" in new ways of behaving by which he slowly builds up enough confidence for a "major" act of strength.

tends to evoke conversation on personal levels. The references to William's failure to speak are an example of such an interaction. Episodes of this kind have therapeutic leverage, stemming as they do from such a symbolic context, in addition to the fact that peer assembly is a potent, social catalytic force.

The incident of the worker's being deprived of food is meaningful for several reasons. She made no comment about it, merely accepting the situation, thus not fostering feelings of blame or guilt. Further, the incident generated constructive ego responses in the children, who made accommodations to show their liking for the giving adult. Also, the occurrence illustrates the growth of a group *gestalt*, inasmuch as it reflects the beginning influence of member upon member, as witness the denoument when two boys replenished the empty plate from their respective hoards of cookies.

Rivalry also grew, and it was responsible for some children seeking preferential status. George used a device that is common with children in groups, as demonstrated by some children who contrive to arrive early at the start of sessions in order to be "first"—perhaps *more* than first, really to be the "only" child.

Session No. 12, Excerpts: Present—Cary, Mitchell, William, George

All four boys arrived together, excited. They became involved right away. George took one of the hand puppets and hit Mitchell with it. Mitchell fought back, but both boys were playful and not intending to hurt. William watched this and then suddenly joined them. The three tussled good-naturedly. Meanwhile Cary set up blocks, humming to himself as he did so. Mitchell said to Cary, "What are you mumbling?" Then Mitchell kicked over the tower. Cary objected, "Stop!" Both boys continued as before: Cary set up the tower; Mitchell kicked it over. Cary again yelled, "Hey, don't!" He went to the worker, who was opening paint jars at the easel, and said, "Make him stop it! He's bweaking up my house!" Mitchell ran off to the easel and began to paint. The worker did not interfere at any point. A bit later Mitchell returned to Cary and joined him in the block play.

William now played alone on the floor with the pool game. Mitchell explained to him, "This way. No! Here." William accepted the advice good-naturedly. George painted. Soon William walked about the room, at one point stopping to examine his paintings on the wall where the worker had hung them. Each time he located one, he stole a sly glance at her. He had puppets on his hands during this wandering about the room. Finally he joined the others at block play. William placed small father and mother dolls on the top of the tower structure just before the boys destroyed the tower in the usual noisy fashion. After the crash, William restored the same dolls at the top of the next completed tower.

George said, "I'm thirsty. Can I go out for a drink?" The worker replied, "There's a sink here." George: "Where's a glass?" The worker obtained a cup for him from the refreshment supply shelf, and he drank. Mitchell also wanted a drink. George said, "The water is too warm. Can I go outside to the fountain?" The worker replied, "Yes." George ran out of the playroom, followed by Mitchell, who called out, "Me, too!" as he left. William also went out, without a word. The boys returned almost immediately. George and William began to work on puzzles, separately.

George: "No Kool-Aid today?" Worker: "Sure, there's Kool-Aid." Sensing the boy's need to be fed at this point, she began to set the table even though it was earlier than usual. As usual, the boys assembled to watch her. George spoke, "I saw the man who saved my life." The worker looked at him inquiringly, without comment. George continued: "From the fire. We had a fire last year. He saved me. My mother said that's why my skin is so dark, on account of the fire burning me." Mitchell said, "Oh, yeah!" as if doubting the veracity of the story. Cary said, "I like these cwackers." Mitchell and George laughed at his baby talk. Cary asked the worker, "Where did you buy them?" Worker: "In a grocery store." George asked, "How much did they cost?" Mitchell: "Maybe about twenty cents." George to the worker: "Is that right?" The worker replied, "A little more." Cary asked her, "Write down on a paper the name of the cwacker so my mother could buy it for me."

While drinking, William had been fingering a small plastic figure he had taken from his pocket. He filled his cup again and again. He was the first to leave the table, as in the prior session, pausing this time at the supply shelves. George said, "Whose is this?" holding up the little figure of William's that had been left on the table. Mitchell said, "It's his." George: "Hey, William, here's your toy." William walked back to the table and *said, "Thank you."* He spoke in a barely audible whisper as he took the object.

Cary and Mitchell involved themselves with painting obviously aware that it was time to return to class since the escorts had just knocked at the door. However, they asked the worker if they could finish. The worker promised to hold their papers for the next meeting.

Comments and Interpretations

In this session William joined two of the boys in direct, aggressive play—hitting one another with the puppets. He was increasingly mobile as he walked freely about the play room, this time spotting all his paintings on the wall and gazing at the worker who was responsible for hanging them up for display among the other boys' productions. The children had the privilege of taking the paintings home whenever they wished to. In his peregrinations about the room, William held the puppets on his hands. This was in consonance with his growing aggressiveness, since the puppets were symbols of aggression that he had participated in. Moreover, he now used dolls in more focused ways, in that he placed the parent dolls on the tower to be destroyed. And he repeated this. This act was not fortuitous with respect to his selection of "victims." There was a complete set of small dolls available—other family members (including grandparents), a policeman, a doctor, a nurse, and other less-related representations in a child's life. William *intended* to do injury to his parents—symbolically, but quite directly to judge by the method of choice. As a further indication of the boy's growing self-confidence and ability to discharge repressed feelings, he ran out of the play room with the other two boys, ostensibly to get a drink but actually to retest the worker. Children in a school-based therapeutic play group inevitably do this. "Outside" the play room is the world—a constricting, forbidding school world, now ideationally separated from the uniquely free quarters of the play room.

Psychologically, it is as if a play room becomes placed in limbo, conceptually and emotionally divorced from the larger, authoritative setting. Leaving a play room obstreperously, as the boys did in this session—with the worker's permission or sometimes without—represents a test of the worker and also an example of newly discovered ego strength. In numerous play groups that were conducted in public elementary schools with hundreds of children, only two children were motivated to leave the play room repetitively for other reasons. One, a boy of seven, could not tolerate the climate of freedom because it fostered anxiety in him, and other treatment measures were employed. The second child, a girl of ten, used her time out of the play room to steal objects from unoccupied classrooms. In both cases there was deeper pathology, and more intensive treatment plans were instituted.

Significant interplay occurred during refreshments in this session. The positive transference to the worker was expressed in the queries about the cookies: her paying for them—which symbolized that she loved the boys; her choice of cookies, which pleased them; and Cary's demonstration of the maternal transference when asking the worker to write down the information about the cookies.

Cary was now going home less during school hours. He was not altogether without phobic anxiety but was evidently more capable of coping with it. This dilution of anxiety was due to the transference, which, in a symbolic but functional way, placed his real mother proximal to him in school. The worker had become partially a maternal libidinal object fused with the actual mother. Cary's aggressive behavior incorporated the worker in its sphere, since the play room in its psychological dimension was an extension of the worker. It may be that the expression of repressed hostile impulses originally intended for the mother through displacement against the psychological "mother" was responsible for decathecting the unconscious emotion which created phobic symptom formation. Several school-phobic boys who were treated exclusively in therapeutic play groups in different schools have shown definite loss of phobic anxiety. More experience is necessary to confirm the therapeutic efficacy of this group modality of treatment for children who have essentially psychoneurotic problems.

In this session William spoke again, directly and appropriately to the situation. He said, "Thank you," albeit in a whisper. However, this was the first "normal" speech rejoinder since the start of the group. Psychologically it undoubtedly was related to his demonstrable aggression—having puppet fights and smashing blocks, including destroying the parent figures. If all such activities are safe, as he experienced them, then speech may also be safe—at least in this setting in the presence of an adult who was a more benign superego representative.

Session No. 13, Excerpts: Present—William, John, Cary, Mitchell

When the boys entered, Cary went to the block corner; Mitchell played the pool game at the same table with William; John painted. Mitchell threw over Cary's block structure. Cary yelled at him, "Stop it!" He rebuilt the structure, and again Mitchell knocked it over. This time Cary said, "No, no! Wait 'till it's bigger!" William watched this from his position at the table. Occasionally the boys looked toward the worker, who was engaged in replenishing the paint jars.

John sang happily as he washed his hands at the sink after painting: "This is the way we wash our hands, wash our hands. . . ." Cary took the same refrain and sang, "This is the way we kill ourselves, kill ourselves," banging blocks together as he sang. Now Mitchell said to him, "Stop that." Cary stopped banging but still sang, "This is the way we kill ourselves. . . ."

William now took a jigsaw puzzle and moved from the round table to the isolate table. Cary continued to build with blocks, singing and mumbling to himself unintelligibly. Mitchell was at the easel. He made a hodgepodge of many colors, smearing over the whole paper. Cary came to the easel to watch, then he painted on the other side. At one point Cary deliberately let the paint drip from his brush to the floor, all around the easel, not on the newspaper that was there to protect the floor. The worker said to him, "Keep the brush here at the easel." He stopped dripping paint and now painted on the paper. Cary said, "Have you got paint remover?" The worker said, "No." Cary then said, "I'll pour powder on it." He took the container of scouring powder from the sink and sprinkled it over a spot on his painting, ostensibly to obliterate it, because he then attempted to paint over the mess. John accidentally spilled a jar of water near where the brushes were soaking. He began to wipe it up. The worker went over and helped him, without speaking.

William and Mitchell now sat together at the table. Mitchell suddenly laughed out loud, as though in response to something William had said to him. The worker had heard nothing. John now sat with them as well, singing, "This is the way we throw the sticks," as he threw squeegee darts at the dart board. Hearing this, Cary again sang, "This is the way we kill ourselves." Cary started another painting. He said to the worker, "I can imitate very well. Wanna hear me imitate a rooster?" He made rooster sounds. Then, "Wanna hear the bird sounds?" He made several other sounds. All this was done in an immature way. Mitchell and John laughed at him.

The worker began to set up for smacks. William was the first to sit down, followed by Mitchell and John. Cary rushed to finish still another painting, stopped to wash his hands, and also seated himself. Mitchell, John, and William grabbed all the cookies that had been set out on a plate. John said, "What about her?" Mitchell and William each returned a cookie to the serving plate. When Cary came to the table, John gave him a cookie. Cary asked, "Where are all the cookies?" John replied, "You came late." Cary to the worker: "Do you have more?" The worker said, "No." John was eating his "loot" very quickly. William nudged Mitchell silently, pointing to what John was doing. They both laughed. Soon the escorts came and the boys left the play room.

Comments and Interpretations

During this session, and for the first time, acting out took a markedly regressive tone, as noted by Mitchell's smearing and Cary's deliberate "soiling" with paint. Such acting-out apparently started with the block crashing, which had been happening for several sessions and had activated Cary's impulsive and immature tendencies. He began to chant aloud his anxiety, which had been aroused by the fact that he was acting-out aggression much more earnestly. He did this chanting with references to death—"kill ourselves," certainly a bizarre utterance. William evidently could not bear the intensity of this, as he twice removed himself into isolated positions, only later moving back into contact with others. Cary's speech, which was infantile to start with, also reflected the regressive shift, becoming even more infantile and unintelligible at times.

With such children, who tend to become unbridled in regressive acting out, careful restraints may be necessary to prevent altogether chaotic behavior, which can catalyze an entire group to act similarly. The worker sensed these factors but, perhaps because of her own anxiety in the face of primitive behavior, erred in intervening in the manner she did. Her implicitly prohibitive choice of words with Cary was unfortunate: they were directing and limiting. The result was to immediately stop Cary and make him feel guilty, and he tried to compensate. However, as an index of his immaturity, even in compensating he was highly regressive—using scouring powder to "correct" a painting blot, smearing over that mess with more paint. A better intervention in such a situation—a standard procedure—is for the worker to spread even more newspaper around the easel, without comment. This is almost always sufficient in itself to limit smearing, while at the same time it does not convey an element of censure.

Even John was affected by Cary's messy activity, because he spilled water close by, perhaps accidentally. The worker had now recovered the situation at the easel, and she wisely and silently assisted John in mopping up the mess. Such behavior was perceived by John, and by the group, as tolerant, helpful, and understanding. Such interventions preserve and foster the positive transference ties. It is clear how Cary's ability to act-out was due to stimulation in the supportive ego relationship with Mitchell, who had repeatedly acted as a model for Cary, without intending to. Cary also got courage episodically from fluctuating supportive ego ties with other group members.

Evidently the pace of regression during this session was too "rich" for William, who retreated several times. However, it was not without value to him, ambivalent though he may have been, because it influenced him. He did communicate somehow to Mitchell at the table, when they observed Cary's antics, which made Mitchell laugh in response. Also, there was more seizing of food, now with William an active participant. Yet, note how several of the boys still voluntarily made accommodations and shared, without intervention from the worker.

Session No. 14, Excerpts: All Present

George and John entered. George immediately rushed to the worker and told her an involved story explaining his absence last week, something about his brother being ill and his mother in the hospital. (In supervision conference the worker described this rambling story, wondering how much of it was reality-based and how much elaborated. George had some preoccupation with "dramatic" events, so perceived by him because of a tendency to worry about himself and others in his family.) Meanwhile, John took plastic blocks to play with at the isolate table.

The other boys entered. William started with a jigsaw puzzle; Cary immediately went to his regular "game" at the blocks. He kept on mumbling to himself, letting out an occasional little scream as the blocks were knocked over. The others eyed him with annoyance following each scream, but they did nothing more about it. Then Mitchell idly began to toe the blocks. Cary yelled at him to stop, but to no avail. Mitchell continued, obviously teasing.

Cary finally seized a block and threatened Mitchell with it. The worker said from a distance, "Don't throw blocks." Cary still held onto the block, obviously angry with Mitchell. Then he let the block drop and it fell on Mitchell's foot. Mitchell took a block and tapped Cary on the head. The worker said, "No hitting with blocks." They wrestled on the floor. Mitchell seemed to be pummeling Cary. The worker hovered nearby and said, "No punching." The boys separated and Cary returned to building with blocks. Once again Mitchell threw them down. Now Cary put hand puppets on and hit Mitchell. Mitchell also donned hand puppets and did likewise. Cary was angry and red-faced. The worker intervened again: "I have a new game, it's fun." She sat down at the table with the new game—Chinese checkers. Mitchell immediately left Cary and came to her. He asked, "You're going to play?" He seemed surprised that the worker was going to participate. He sat down, joined by William. As the worker explained the game, John also joined the others, and all four played.

Cary came over to watch briefly but then returned to the blocks. He was still flushed and excited. He continued building structures and knocking them over. He took a block and banged it against a wall.

George had been painting and singing, as he often did. After a while John left the game to join Cary at the blocks. They built separate squares, closed-in areas on the floor. Occasionally, when Mitchell was between plays at the table with the worker and the others, he would run over and try to stand in the "yard" built by Cary. Cary yelled, "Hey, get out!" When Mitchell wouldn't, Cary built his square higher to fence him in. William walked over and nudged Mitchell to inform him in this way that it was the latter's turn at the checkers game. Mitchell returned to the table.

George asked about refreshments, Mitchell adding that he was thirsty. The worker said, "Maybe we can finish the game later. Let's leave it here." She set out the small table, leaving the unfinished game on the table usually used for refreshments. The boys all sat down promptly and partook good-naturedly of the cake and milk, without any conflict over sharing. When it was time to leave, they departed in a good mood.

Addendum: Two days later Cary came to the worker's office accompanied by his grandmother. She usually appeared in school to take him home at dismissal time. Cary had complained to his grandmother about Mitchell's hitting him on the head with a block: "That Mitchell 'cwacked' my head! I heard it 'cwack!' I felt it and heard the noise when it 'cwacked'!" He also accused Mitchell of pushing him against the wall after the session. It was obvious to the worker, who had observed the incident, that Cary was not in fact hurt. He showed no marks of injury, and her observation of him during the group session did not indicate the possibility of injury or real pain. It was equally obvious to her that other motivations were responsible for Cary's involving his grandmother. She habitually supported Cary's infantile appeals and maneuvers. The worker was able to calm the boy and reassure Mitchell, who kept protesting that he really had not meant to hurt Cary (Mitchell had accompanied Cary and his grandmother to the worker's office).

Comments and Interpretations

Increasingly Cary was ventilating aggression, through building and destroying. Now, however, he was more able to initiate and carry on this activity without support from others, especially Mitchell, whom he now threatened and resisted. This was direct aggression against the strongest boy in the group. The worker intervened prematurely, perhaps because she knew Mitchell's strength and the nature of his anger when provoked, one of the reasons for his referral. In acting too soon, she was prompted by her own fears. At no time in the play group had Mitchell demonstrated the quality of hostile behavior typical of him elsewhere. Further, it was revealed in supervision conference, from information further elicited from the worker, that Cary was only threatening Mitchell with the block and apparently would not have thrown it. Even when Mitchell tapped Cary on the head, this was done with deliberate restraint, not in anger, and it could not have pained him as Cary protested it did. Again, an unnecessary intervention followed when the boys were wrestling on the floor. The worker failed to estimate the situation correctly and invoked a "rule" about "no punching." Finally, in her attempts to deflect Mitchell, who was the real cause of her undue anxiety, she properly used a new game to capture his interest. This is a technique that can be used, with others of similar nature, to interfere with activities that require limitation. Children enjoy new games and also like being read to.

For Cary's sake, the worker should have allowed more latitude in these aggressive episodes. Such activities represented for him critical events, despite whatever reservations and temporary fears his participation may have generated in him. The fact is, he was now strong enough to initiate his anger *directly* against a person instead of repeating his usual infantile, dependency appeals to the worker. In all likelihood, in view of Cary's capacities and Mitchell's exercise of reasonable restraints in teasing him, the encounter would have worked itself through. In any event, should matters have gotten truly worse without the worker's intervention, she could then have introduced the new game to impede it.

Parenthetically, on the basis of the author's experience with many such treatment groups, male workers more accurately assess the seriousness of physical encounters between children than do females.

Note that Cary observed the interesting new game that involved all the others, but he chose to continue *his* "game," which was more important to him psychologically. And he again demonstrated growing strength by trying to "wall" Mitchell in with the blocks. At one point Cary banged a block against a wall. This was a symbolic assault on the person of the worker, because the treatment setting is a symbolic extension of the worker. Thus, Cary was retaliating against the worker. Two days later, he tried in his usual manipulative fashion to use his grandmother to further establish his grievance against Mitchell, and possibly against the worker. This was a negative transference maneuver, but a weak one. Banging the wall was certainly more assertive.

Session No. 15, Excerpts: Present—William, Mitchell, George

. . . William was restless, flitting quickly from one thing to another. He started weaving, then took the pool game, then the Pick-up-sticks, finally dominoes. He accidentally spilled the contents of the Pick-up-sticks box and carefully picked them up. Finally he took weaving materials to work with at the isolate table.

. . . William played with puppets. He held the father puppet on his left hand, the alligator on the right. He kept snapping at the father puppet, catching it between the jaws of the alligator. Over and over the father puppet was caught in the teeth of the alligator. Then William did the same with the mother puppet. At times he would grimace as if sneering, baring his teeth. He stood at the isolate table during this enactment, completely absorbed.

. . . William made a clay base and stuck Pick-up-sticks around the edge, with the points of the sticks up like a picket fence. He then placed a boy figure inside the fence, and continued to surround it with sticks. He also thrust sticks through the clay across the base. When finished, the structure looked as if the boy was captive, caught in a trap.

Comments and Interpretations

In the first series of episodes, William displayed an uncommon restlessness, as if uncertain about how to involve himself. The succeeding episodes illuminate the cause of his initial restlessness: William was really inclined to continue previous play scenarios wherein he had been ventilating his hostility toward the parent dolls. Evidently he still needed a "warm-up" interval before his anxiety would abate sufficiently that he dared again discharge inner feelings. Once again he "destroyed" his father and mother, this time with cannibalistic fervor using the alligator as a foil. For the first time since William was in the play group, the worker was able to detect a facial expression that mirrored the intensity of his feelings. He had never shown such an expression of violence. Later he was himself imprisoned behind a symbolic barricade—or if not imprisoned, then perhaps safely guarded from retaliation for his "desperate" violence committed in play. In either case, the clay representation was a defensive and/or retributive reaction to what was essentially an intended destruction of his parents. This enactment was a critical event brought about through a loosening of ego defenses and a resulting cathartic discharge of repressed feelings. The worker, sensing the deeper implications of William's enactments during this session, preserved the clay work that he left behind.

Session No. 16, Excerpts: All Present

All the boys arrived at once. Cary ran to the worker and said, "Here's a pwesent for you." He handed her a piece of candy. She said, "Thank you," immediately placing it in her pocket. Cary added, "It's salt-water taffy." Cary then walked over to watch Mitchell, who was fashioning figures from pieces of Tinkertoys® and clay. William spotted the clay project that he had made in the last session. He worked on it, merely rearranging the sticks.

George asked, "Where's the thing that I began to do last time?" The worker procured the loom with his partially completed work, which she had saved for him. John, who watched, also took a loom. George made a mistake and asked the worker to correct it. She helped him for a while until he could manage by himself.

Cary went to the shelves. This time he shoved the blocks from the shelves to the floor unceremoniously so that they scattered about, making a loud noise. Some of the boys were startled by the noise; they all turned to look. Mitchell rolled a piece of clay and threw it at Cary. Cary threw it back. They continued this back and forth. George now retrieved a piece of clay from the floor and threw it. John did likewise. William watched from the small table. Once Cary threw a piece up in the air, at an angle, running to catch it. A piece hit the worker on the shoulder as she was engaged in moving some items. She looked up but said nothing. Cary gave no evidence of dismay. Now William left the table and threw clay at Mitchell. John helped Cary in throwing and catching the clay. George said to the worker, "They're throwing things." Then he himself threw clay toward the ceiling.

After the clay throwing had persisted for some time, the worker silently obtained a small wastebasket, propped it against a wall, and from a distance threw clay pellets into it. George asked, "What are you doing?" She replied, "I'm aiming for the basket." He and the others immediately came to watch, and then each grabbed pieces to do the same. George lined up the boys to take turns. George, Mitchell, John, and William all stayed behind the table where the worker had stood, but Cary remained in front of the table, hurling larger pieces of clay into the basket vigorously. He yelled, "I can get it in every time!" The others told him he had to stand where they were. Mitchell tried to push Cary back, but Cary stayed in front. The four boys kept count of the pieces that successfully entered the basket. At this point Cary grabbed a big chunk of clay and threw it wildly across the room. No one was standing in the area where he aimed. Cary screamed childishly and ran about. Mitchell took a stick and threatened Cary; Cary screamed. He grabbed a stick also, and now both boys chased each other about the play room, Cary screaming in glee and excitement. His zipper was open. Mitchell pointed his stick at it threateningly, saying, "I'm gonna get a bull's-eye!" The worker silently put her hand out for the stick, and Mitchell released it to her. He then went to the blocks. Cary, on the other hand, continued to chase him with his stick. The worker said, "Let's have our Kool-Aid now." She obtained Cary's stick and set the table for refreshments.

The boys' general boisterousness was maintained at the table, where they laughed and pushed each other, with all participating. Cary jumped up with a cookie that had fallen into his cup of juice. He threw it at Mitchell, who retaliated by throwing a piece of clay. Cary grabbed the butter knife and threatened him with it. The worker said, "Leave it here," implying that they needed it at the table. Cary put it down and initiated a wrestling match with Mitchell. They fell to the floor on top of the widely scattered blocks. Cary screamed, and held his side. The remaining boys watched this as they continued eating.

After the escorts had returned the boys to their rooms, the worker received a note from Cary's teacher, who reported that Cary had told her his head had been hurt.

Comments and Interpretations

In this sixteenth group session we see mounting excitement characterized by much more activated individual and group behavior. A manic quality was detected in the behavior of some, Cary in particular. Even George, who was usually more restrained and seemingly conscious of the intensity of the acting out, first informed the worker about what was generally known to all—that "things" were being thrown—and in one and the same breath he continued to do it.

As noted earlier, in the longitudinal development of a therapeutic play group, the first phase is one of *acclimatization*, during which children experience an entirely novel and extraordinary freedom, becoming accustomed to a "new" adult who is amazingly tolerant. A period of testing out the soundness of these first perceptions follows, after which the children become more spontaneous in their activities and interpersonal enactments. What follow in subsequent sessions are vacillations between nodal and antinodal states. Supranodal behavior characterized the play group in its sixteenth session, having been preceded by nodal and anti-nodal phases. As a group progresses, rehabilitative and reconstructive influences become maximized. It is during this time that the children's original symptomatic and behavioral patterns are subject to much change.

For the most part the worker allowed the children to act out despite her anxiety, which she acknowledged during supervision conference. At one point when she was struck by a piece of clay thrown by Cary, she did nothing. Finally, to abate the extraordinary hyperactivity, she intervened by converting the wild clay throwing into a game. This is a good technique, but some question could be raised as to whether it was premature. In most groups, fluctuations between nodal and anti-nodal activities are allowed without interference, with the group remaining free to develop limits against its acting-out. Clay "wars" between children are always occurring at some point in group development, and they are more useful as cathartic experiences than they are potentially injurious. True, they do test workers' capacities for tolerating nodal interactions.

While these boys at first submitted to the worker's introduction of the game, Cary resisted and continued his excited clay throwing, which for him was psychologically more important than having his behavior constricted by intervention. The worker again revealed her anxiety and again limited the aggressive interplay between Cary and Mitchell, this time, surprisingly, initiated by Cary. She then offered refreshments as a further inducement. But Cary was too "high" to be restrained by even this maneuver and continued to behave impulsively and regressively, using a smeary cookie. Yet, despite his evident enjoyment in acting out during this session, he had to tell his teacher about his "wounds." But this was a superfluous complaint, as in the prior session, when he reported similarly to his grandmother, Evidently, following periods of excitement, Cary's neurotic preoccupations with accidents and "death" come to the fore momentarily.

As for William, he first observed the heightened acting out of the group from the safety of the isolate table, then quickly participated. He threw clay at the boys, played the "game" with the basket, and joined in the general merriment during refreshments. With each succeeding group session, William revealed growing spontaneity. In this session it reached the highest point of direct expression so far.

Session No. 17, Excerpts: Present—Mitchell, George, Cary

. . . Once again on entering the play room Cary shoved all the blocks from the shelves to the floor with a crash. This time he said, "Let's play war! Here are bombs. And more bombs!" and shoved checkers and dominoes to the floor. He told Mitchell, "You'll be on my side. He's the enemy." Mitchell painted instead. Cary persisted, nagging Mitchell to "play war," tossing "bombs" at him. Mitchell refused. When Cary persisted, Mitchell began to throw pieces of clay back at him.

. . . Cary and George grabbed most of the cookies. Mitchell took the rest, placing one on the worker's plate, however. Cary demanded, "Where are the chocolate cookies? I like them. I want to bring one home for my mother." Cary said, "I can walk like a duck" (he demonstrated). Then: "I like coming here. Could my friend come, too?" . . . George said, "Can't we come every day? You can fix it so we come every day, can't you?" Cary: "Are we going to come next year, too?"

Comments and Interpretations

Cary's excited behavior had grown apace. This time he again initiated the boisterous play, first by making a racket with throwing blocks and other items to the floor, which had become a self-stimulating act for him. And he wanted "war." Note how he interacted persistently, or attempted to, with Mitchell, the stronger boy, with whom Cary had initially started to display such behavior some time before. Mitchell, who could easily have hurt Cary and stopped his instigations, demonstrated a degree of mature tolerance for the impulsive behavior of a much weaker boy.

The import of the play-group experience as it affected Cary is revealed in his open statements of how much he liked the group and how he wished to bring a friend. Such requests often indicate a child's wish to demonstrate his social success to a friend in the setting that gave it birth.

Session No. 18, Excerpts: All Present

. . . Cary rushed to the worker and shouted, "Here's a pwesent for you!" He gave her a box of cookies, which she placed on the shelf.

George asked, "How come we are coming on Wednesdays now? Are we gonna come Monday *and* Wednesday?" The worker replied, "I had to go to a school meeting on Monday and I don't want you to miss coming, so I changed the day." Mitchell said, "We won't meet Mondays now?" Worker: "We'll meet Mondays like before. Only this week was different." George said, "Oh, boy!" Cary echoed, "I'm glad." When John rushed into the room late, he said, "I was in the bathroom when the monitor came. I didn't know it was today. How come?" George answered him, "She wanted us today because she had a meeting Monday. So we wouldn't miss it." John looked pleased and surprised.

While they were busy working, John sang, "Hello, Dollie." George took up the melody, singing, "Hello, Charley." Cary sang: "Go kill yourself," over and over.

Comments and Interpretations

Once again Cary brought a gift to the worker—the "giving" person, another indication of his appreciation for the group experience. Positive transference to the worker built up rapidly now. More importantly, with Cary the transference was of a different quality, lacking the marked dependency appeal that had characterized it in the beginning. From a technical point of view, the worker was right to merely acknowledge the gift briefly, then promptly place it on a shelf out of sight. This was done so as not to aggrandize the act of gift-giving, and to prevent rivalry with other children who may have observed the gift. Further, the implications of a child's gift may be other than apparent, and in a nonanalytical form of therapy such as the therapeutic play group, in which examination of motives and interpretations is eschewed, it would be counterproductive therapeutically to do more than merely accept a gift with a brief acknowledgment.

The change of meeting day to accommodate the boys is standard technique. Actually, an interruption of a session such as sometimes occurs because of an unanticipated school meeting, becomes an opportunity for the worker to demonstrate further her consideration for the children by substituting another day. Obviously this impressed the boys, to judge by their happy remarks. Several seemed altogether amazed that the worker had shown such concern.

Again Cary paraphrased the boys' melody with a theme of death, revealing one of his inner concerns.

Session No. 19, Excerpts: Present—George, John, Cary, William

Cary ran in first, breathless. "I'm first!" he said. As usual he shoved all the blocks to the floor. "Atom bomb!" he yelled. And again: "Atom bombs are falling!" John told him to cut it out. George said, "It's enough already." They were annoyed with Cary. But Cary continued.

William withdrew to the easel. He silently offered a jar to the worker for refilling.

Later Cary put clay on the floor, put blocks on the clay, and then jumped on them to flatten the clay. He offered George a "pizza pie."

Cary rolled clay into a hot dog shape, with a clay "roll" around it. He urged it on George and John, saying, "Here, eat it. It's a hot dog with 'puztis'" (mustard).

During refreshments—consisting of cookies, bread and peanut butter, and juice—George began to tell a story. He liked to do this. Cary kept interrupting with piercing screams. George looked toward the worker, who did not interfere. George told John to take Cary out of the room. John laughed as he himself tried to tell a funny story. William grinned widely, with his hands covering his ears because of Cary's screaming.

Addendum: Cary's teacher reported markedly improved attendance. *Also, Cary had not had stomach upsets for the past several weeks.* George's teacher reported improvement in his work and general attitude.

Comments and Interpretations

Cary's acting out was both aggressive-destructive ("atom bombs") and regressive (the clay "hot dog" that he wanted the others to eat). Such play items sometimes have unconscious homicidal meanings—here, to poison. Cary enacted these "play" scenarios in a manic way; his screaming was shrill, without words, possessing a hysterical quality. His need for attention was apparent, as when he rushed ahead of the boys to be "first" in the play room. Objections to his behavior, made by several of the boys, were increasing, and this was to eventually become a limiting social pressure against his immature ways. For the first time his teacher reported a change for the better with respect to Cary's phobic patterns and the somatization.

William was observing everything. In recent weeks he had opted for the safety of the isolate table for a brief interval, perhaps because of the manic quality of Cary's behavior. This withdrawal was only temporary, because William shortly moved into activities and contact with the others. William was able to enjoy Cary's antics, as witness his grinning—even as he covered his ears against Cary's shrill screams. This may be further evidence of how loud noises were still cathected for him with anxiety.

Session No. 20, Excerpts: Present—George, Mitchell, William

. . . George threw down the blocks from the shelves and began to build a structure. William joined him. The structure became very tall, and William touched Mitchell to call his attention to its height. The structure collapsed with a crash. George: "It scared me!" They looked toward the worker for a reaction. George then went to the puppets, but William continued to build alone. Mitchell and George began to tussle with puppets on their hands, playfully. William joined them. Shortly thereafter, William and Mitchell wet the puppets with water and splashed each other.

William laughed aloud. Mitchell said, "Hee, haw." William repeated these sounds. Mitchell then said, "Haw, haw, ho-ho!" which William also repeated, loudly. It was a childish game, repeated about ten times, each time William mimicking aloud. Both boys laughed because of their nonsense behavior.

At refreshments, William coughed. Mitchell said, "He can talk." George added, "If he can cough like that, he can talk."

Addendum: The escort later reported to the worker that William had voluntarily spoken aloud when she asked him and Mitchell a question on the way to the play room.

Comments and Interpretations

In Cary's absence, William moved immediately to join the play, behaving in a mildly provocative way. Apparently he hoped that Mitchell would involve himself also and crash the block structure. Without any hesitation he engaged in tussling with the other boys and, following that, joined in the nonsense vocalizations many times, each time enunciating the sounds clearly. Note the perceptiveness of the other boys when they commented "diagnostically" about William's speech and the direction it was taking. Finally, older children who are used as escorts become sensitive to their young charges and alert to changes in their behavior. This is shown in the report of one of them about William's vocal answer to a question.

Session No. 21, Excerpts: Present—William, George, John, Mitchell

. . . Mitchell and William teased each other, laughing as they did so. This was much like their behavior in the last session. They built a tall block structure, which George promptly knocked over. Mitchell got furious, turned red, and motioned threateningly with a block at George. He looked so funny that George and William burst out laughing. This reaction surprised Mitchell and he laughed also. He still held the block, now uncertainly. George seized a block and said, "If you throw, I will too." The worker said mildly, "No." Both boys immediately put down the blocks.

Mitchell and William now built an elaborate block house, yard, tower, and so forth, using all the blocks. Mitchell kept directing, telling William, "No, not there. Over there." They worked well together.

Later, Mitchell and William donned hand puppets and began to wrestle with them. Soon all the boys were engaged in throwing the rubber puppets at each other across the room. The throwing stopped when the worker was setting the table for refreshments. This time they cautioned each other about grabbing, but to no avail, because they did just that as soon as the cookies were put out.

Later the puppet throwing was started again. At one point, George stretched out on one of the supply shelves and said, "Time for bed." He urged Mitchell to do it also: "Come on, time for bed." Mitchell lay on another shelf.

Comments and Interpretations

A moderate amount of aggressive interaction continued, again with William actively participating. The worker prematurely intervened when indications were that the boys would not throw the blocks. For the first time block play became constructive, when the two boys built a complex settlement. In group therapy, acting-out by children through aggressive use of the supplies eventually ceases, and they become engaged more creatively. We see a beginning of this in the session. However, there was still an ebb and flow of impulsive aggression in the mock play, followed by more constructive group play, followed again by regressive acting-out by grabbing food. Free to do much as they wished, the boys unconsciously revealed the transference bonds to the worker when, after a repast, they went "to bed," an act common with young children after the evening meal at their respective homes. This example of young children acting as if they were going to sleep—either on shelves or on the play room floor—has taken place in almost every play group the author has supervised. Its transference meaning is irrefutable.

Session No. 22, Excerpts: Present—William, Mitchell, Cary

. . . Cary immediately knocked the blocks to the floor after he entered the room. William took the plastic blocks to the isolate table. Later Cary and Mitchell built and destroyed structures. Soon William joined in. Once Cary said, "Stop. She has a splitting headache!" But they continued, now with Cary and Mitchell building and William destroying. William placed the father and mother dolls within the building.

Cary said, "I've got a better idea. Let's make it higher." They built the structure up, using all the blocks. They decorated the structure and made separate rooms, using plastic parts and variously shaped other objects. Cary painted a block red and used it on the roof. When the worker set the table for refreshments, the boys left this structure intact—for the first time. It was only when the boys prepared to leave the play room that Cary ran against the blocks to crash them.

Comments and Interpretations

William initially moved to isolation when Cary was present and acted boisterously. Again William had to "warm up" before joining the others. Cary manifested concern for the worker, surprisingly. Also, for the first time, with Cary participating, block play that started out destructively became converted into cooperative, constructive building. The children's freedom to use the therapeutic setting as needs dictate was seen when Cary painted a block to make it a colorful roof, without the worker intervening. Impressed with their handiwork, the boys left the structure intact, except at the end when Cary destroyed it. In circumstances like these, should children leave standing such a creative fabrication, instead of destroying it, the worker allows it to remain until the next session, if her use of the play room permits this. The purpose of preserving such a structure is to reinforce the children's perceptions of their socially cooperative engagement. Often children will ask a worker to make sure that "no one" touches the work. If this is not possible and they do not find it intact the following session, the worker merely states the reason for this.

Increasingly in succeeding sessions we see creative and sublimative play activities. The children's energies were becoming available for more healthy, substantive endeavors as they relaxed. Inner turmoil was beginning to give way through repetitive cathartic discharges of repressed feelings. For all individuals—children and adults—creativity comes into being spontaneously as psyches are freed from debilitating forces. Characteristically, in all forms of children's group therapy, more mature social interactions and creative work and play activities increase in direct proportion to the diminishing of individuals' emotional problems. While in this particular play group this positive growth was only now palpable and had to go much further to consolidate itself, the pattern of change is quite evident.

Session No. 23, Excerpts: Present—Mitchell, George, Cary, William

George ran into the room, soon followed by the others. He asked, "Can I eat my candy here?" The others surrounded him asking for some, and he divided it among all. He said, "I was very sick last week. I had the flu. I almost died. *Did you miss me?*" The worker said, "Yes, we did miss you."

William began to paint at the easel while Mitchell and Cary threw the blocks from the shelf and built structures. Cary mumbled, "I'll put 'beople' in my house." George asked, "What's 'beople'?" He laughed as he mimicked Cary.

William took one of the Pick-up-sticks and threatened Cary with it. Cary shrieked, running away, but not in real fear.

William took two blocks and just banged them together to make noise. Mitchell joined him in this random activity.

Cary volunteered, "Someone is dying in my house [of blocks]. Someone was killed in my house!" Later he decorated the house and asked, "Isn't this beautiful? It's going to be beautiful."

Later, when Mitchell and William were chasing Cary, he went to hide behind his block structure. Mitchell said, in mock threat, "It's gonna fall. The monster is coming to make it fall!" Cary hit the building, knocking it over, but then immediately tried to keep it from falling, yelling, "Don't let it fall! Don't throw it down!" He seemed to panic as it fell.

Comments and Interpretations

George had a propensity for dramatizing events in his home life, as we have seen earlier. While he was explaining the reason for his absence, he affirmed the freedom of the play room as opposed to the atmosphere of the school proper by eating his candy "here." Almost poignant is his query as to whether he was "missed."

The change in the nature of Cary's block play continued, as he elaborated the structure using doll figures. Yet, he momentarily alluded to his phobic anxiety about illness and death. It is significant that these remarks were made associatively with the play structure and its family dolls, which were symbolicaly representative of a family. Thus, one may surmise about the psychological relationship of homicidal and retributory guilt meanings of his play. These are probably elements of his school phobic anxiety, which is etiologically related to the mother. It is such cathartic play, accompanied by a new capacity to act out hostility in this and other ways, which is responsible for decathecting neurotic elements of phobic symptomology with young children. It has been demonstrated that, given a sufficiency of such abreactive expressions in a therapeutic play group, some neurotic patterns can be sloughed off.

Cary was becoming proud of his construction work, attempting to prevent its destruction in the very act of destroying it.

The manner in which William was now playing aggressively is interesting in that it follows the scenario of behavioral aggression demonstrated by other boys in early group sessions. His behavior pointedly demonstrates that isolative-type children, who protect themselves from interacting with others for considerable lengths of time, are, in fact, silent but close observers of all that takes place in a play group. As they become emboldened to make contact with others, and finally to express their formerly repressed hostility and anger, they use the channels for such expression that were demonstrated by others. Psychologically, this comes about for two main reasons. First, if the isolate-type child views enactments by others as safe by virtue of the worker's having allowed the behaviors without comment, then it should be safe for him to do likewise. Secondly, first attempts at demonstrable aggression are more easily consummated through mimicry. Later, when ego strength is further enhanced, more spontaneous, idiosyncratic manifestations of inner feelings become possible. It is as if first attempts at hostile expression by recessive, well-defended children are "exercises." What follows later in acting out is a *direct* expression of hostility against individuals—usually parents and siblings—and symbolic representations of the hostility in the playgroup. Actually, the first episodes of such newly found freedom are initiated in the group.

Session No. 24, Excerpts: Present—William, Mitchell, George, John

John arrived first. (Earlier in the day he had come to the worker's room several times to ask if it was time for the group.) John followed the worker as she moved about and asked about the whereabouts of the other boys. George rushed into the play room. He spotted a typewriter that was there for the first time. "Can we use it?" he asked. When the worker nodded, he asked for paper and became engaged happily in typing. When William and Mitchell entered, they came over to watch, then pushed George mischievously to keep him from typing. Mitchell got a sheet of paper and asked to type, but George would not relinquish the machine. William also obtained a sheet of paper. They continued to tease George, trying to get at the typewriter.

Later Mitchell grabbed John and pushed him against the other boys, who were crowded around the typewriter. All the boys then pushed George, who was still typing. Finally George left. William laughed aloud more heartily than usual during this activity.

Now Mitchell started to type and William leaned over the machine trying to interrupt him. Mitchell kept saying, "Stop it, William!"

At one point, while Mitchell was spelling out the words he was typing, William said aloud as he pointed to a key, "Y." He quickly looked in the direction of the worker, guiltily.

George said to the worker, "You give out the cookies. They grab!" As the worker put out the plates with refreshments, all the boys grabbed. John and Mitchell laughed at how quickly the cookies disappeared.

When William finished eating, he left the table to type. Mitchell joined him, both of them taking turns. Mitchell gave William one of his cookies.

Comments and Interpretations

John's eagerness to attend was shown when he visited the worker's office prior to the session. For him this was a new expression of interest; he was much withdrawn when first referred.

An old typewriter was introduced by design, as are all new play, craft, and other materials, in accordance with their therapeutic value. This was done mostly to experiment with another communicative medium, with the hope that it would further elicit vocalization from William. It did exactly that, for a brief moment. Still notable is the extraordinary cathexis related

to his speech. William almost furtively looked toward the worker as if anticipating some sort of reprisal from her after daring to utter: "Y."

As for the request to the worker that she distribute the refreshments,
this represented one child's avowal—and perhaps the avowals of others—
that they could not yet resolve the conflict over food. However, the worker
still allowed them to grab, without intervention. Her judgment was that the
rivalry was not of a nature to merit her intervention—the group had shown
a capacity to settle this problem for itself.

Session No. 25, Excerpts: Present—William, Mitchell, Cary

The moment they ran into the play room, William and Mitchell struggled
for possession of the typewriter. Even when Mitchell successfully sat on the
chair before the typewriter, William continued trying to stop him. . . .

Cary, in typical fashion, threw the blocks to the floor and began to
build. At one point he brought the Pick-up-sticks to the worker and told
her, "Throw these away. They tried to kill me with them." (He was referring to an earlier session, when William and Mitchell had playfully teased
him with the sticks.) Cary was building a house, humming to himself. He
asked Mitchell to help him. Mitchell refused. Cary kept bothering him and
William to help him. He whined, "Come on, help me build a 'ouse." William and Mitchell pushed him away and finally threw single blocks at his
structure, more to keep him away than to demolish it. Cary screamed and
squealed at them and continued building alone. He said to the worker, "I
like coming here. We can talk here. The teacher won't let us talk in class."
Mitchell, overhearing this, said, "William doesn't talk here or in class."

. . . Mitchell obtained a piece of cloth felt and asked if he could use it.
The worker nodded. He took scissors and cut out a square, which he then
stapled into a small purse. Cary asked Mitchell to make one for him. Mitchell pushed him away. Cary persisted, "Where's the 'tsiders' [scissors]?" He
finally found a pair and tried to cut a square. Failing to do this, he asked the
worker to do it for him. She did so. Cary asked Mitchell to staple it for him.
He also added small, decorative strips as Mitchell had done to his.

At refreshments, Mitchell and William got all the cookies, leaving none
for Cary. Cary whined and tried to snatch one from Mitchell, crushing it in
the attempt. William's soda was spilled in this scuffle. He looked worried.
The worker silently obtained paper towels and wiped the table in front of
Wiliam, as well as his chair. Mitchell ran for towels and assisted.

Comments and Interpretations

It is notable that William's aggression was directed against Cary and also
against Mitchell, who was strong. Mitchell, as noted earlier in this docu-

mentation, at no time displayed the intensity of aggression in the play group that was characteristic of him at the time he was referred and that was the main reason for his referral.

Cary's remark about the freedom within the play group, in contrast to the restrictiveness of the school and classroom—"the outer world"—is typical of such comments made by many children in play groups. The author has elsewhere described how children unconsciously separate the special setting of a therapeutic play group from the larger structure, the school.[4] For a time the play room is cast into psychological "limbo," so to speak, and the children perceive it in a light entirely different from their view of the larger superstructure, which for them symbolizes uncompromising authority. Much later in treatment, as a consequence of successful changes in them, the children perceive the school itself as a more pleasant place. It has become ideationally less authoritative and now is more acceptable to them because of their profound experiences in the play group. The "part" modifies the "whole."

Another outcome which has been noted in therapeutic play groups in schools is that as the global image of the school changes to a more benign one in the children's minds, they become more responsive to educational influences that they had previously resisted and more inclined to strive for goals that they had previously failed to achieve. The school and classroom, of course, remain intrinsically the same as before, except that the children are more permeable to their influence. This phenomenon has been termed the *halo effect*.

In a therapeutic play group, the children's increasing motor activity becomes channeled into more productive crafts work. Suitable new materials with the necessary tools are added to the general equipment from time to time to exploit the children's growing interests and their capabilities to use these items creatively. The end products of such work are taken back to classrooms and to their homes, where they elicit positive comments from teachers, friends, and family members. Such comments are dramatic acknowledgments for children who formerly were more used to criticism and scoldings, perhaps no praise at all. The psychological consequences are to enhance the children's self-images and generate much confidence.

Session No. 27, Excerpts: All Present

William, Mitchell, and George dashed in; John and Cary arrived somewhat later. William and Mitchell scrambled competitively for the typewriter. While William succeeded in getting on the chair first, he had no paper. Mitchell ran to obtain a piece, and William had to yield the typewriter to

[4]M. Schiffer, *The Therapeutic Play Group*, Grune & Stratton, New York, 1969, pp. 124–125.

Mitchell while he went for paper. George tried to push Mitchell off the chair in order to type, but Mitchell held his ground.

The worker had placed out several magnets and a container of iron filings prior to the boys' entrance. John and George spotted it and asked if they could play with it. They were fascinated with the magnet's properties. William, who was standing directly behind the worker, let out a scream. The worker turned and caught his eye, smiling as she did so. William now joined the two boys at the table who were playing with the magnets. *Throughout the session he screamed aloud every few minutes, at least a dozen times in all.* As far as could be determined, this behavior was unrelated to any ongoing activity, neither his nor that of any other boy.

Cary asked the worker for paper and crayons. They were easily available to him, as were all the items openly displayed on the shelves, but he requested them nevertheless. He told her he wanted to draw a tree. He actually drew a spring scene with a large tree in the center. He kept mumbling to himself, also emitting little screams now and then, but not as frequently as William had been doing.

Mitchell worked laboriously at the typewriter, bending intently over the keys. Finally he brought his finished work to show to the worker. He had typed "I love you" on it. The worker smiled, and he returned to the typewriter happily.

William now played with the plastic blocks at the table. Then he took crayons from Cary's box and threw them across the room. One hit Cary as he got up to obtain scissors. He yelled, "Stop! Mrs. B., look what he's doing." The worker did not comment. George also got a crayon, but did not throw it. Now Cary threw one at William. Mitchell joined the "battle." The three boys were now throwing crayons at each other. The worker began to weave a lanyard with the plastic material she had brought to the room for this session. George saw this and asked her if he could make one. John and Mitchell were also attracted by this new activity. William took two spools of lanyard plastic and cut two lengths. He attached them to a nail on the shelf's edge near where the worker was and attempted to braid. Cary asked, "Make one for me?" George replied, "She can't do it for you. Make it yourself." Cary then unwound a long piece of braiding. The worker helped him to measure the proper lengths and cut them. Cary wound several long pieces, put them in his pocket, and said, "I'll do this at home." Mitchell also cut excessively long strips and the worker helped him cut shorter lengths, showing him how to braid them so they did not twist unnecessarily.

William *continued to let out little screams* as he worked at the lanyard. He could not braid well, and began to wind the threads by twirling the parts into a sort of braid. The worker, seeing this, *addressed him directly* for the first time: "Want to see how I braid?" He came over to her eagerly and watched her intently. Later he returned to his own work and tried to copy what he had seen her doing.

Mitchell inquired about refreshments. He looked for the cookies, standing on a chair and searching all the shelves. Others joined him. It was a game to see who would find them first. The worker was setting the table. Finally the boys seated themselves. They pounced on the cookies when the worker served them, crushing most of them in their fists as they rivaled each other to obtain the most. Some of the juice spilled from cups as they tangled with each other. William kept pouring juice into his cup even after it was filled to the brim, so that some spilled on the table. Mitchell flicked juice at Cary. Cary almost cried, but quickly rallied and splashed back at Mitchell, dipping his fingers in the cup to do so. Then William and John began to throw pieces of crayons at each other, playfully. Mitchell and Cary joined in this. George did not. Soon the escorts appeared at the door and the boys left to return to class.

Comments and Interpretations

The worker had introduced new materials, magnets and iron filings, which the boys found fascinating. This is another instance of the technique of introducing new materials and crafts work to promote sublimation by enhancing curiosity and engaging children in meaningful exploration and creative endeavors. This technique also fosters greater socialization because group members are drawn together from common interest and the need to learn to share the purposely limited new items.

Except for intervals of playful "war" with crayons, maintained throughout on a rather good-natured level, the boys were busy with constructive activities during this session: Cary drawing a bucolic scene, which for him was an entirely new development; Mitchell at the typewriter, typing out his "message of love" for the worker; and the general weaving of lanyard material that was brought into play by the worker to interfere with the crayon throwing. This intervention was successful, at least until after refreshments, when the "battle" was resumed for a short time.

The search for the cookies by the boys had to do with the fact that the worker had concealed them in a drawer, to prevent premature grabbing at the table. This was not her usual practice, and it was an error. It reflected her own anxiety about the continuing hassle over food. Essentially it was overmanipulative, and the boys' acting out over the food in this session was in response to their own anxiety and perhaps guilt, which the worker heightened by use of this questionable procedure. When a therapeutic play group of young children continues to demonstrate difficulty in resolving a problem of sharing food, several procedures can be used to assist them. One is for the worker to serve a cake or pie, which she then carefully cuts and serves individually. Another method is for her to hold the serving plate as she offers each child in turn a serving, whatever the food item may be. In such ways she gently demonstrates other, socially acceptable ways.

Procedures such as the ones just described are not instituted in the beginning phase of a therapeutic play group, but only after a group has been given sufficient time to experience the feeding process with its aggressive and regressive interactional permutations. A worker constantly evaluates the children's tolerance levels and growth before attempting to introduce *education* procedures to assist their further improvement.

Behavioral changes were evident in Cary and William this session. Cary's interest in higher-level work activities, which appeared spasmodically in earlier sessions, was being maintained and further improved. Moreover, the quality of his social interactions improved. As for William, he no longer needed a "warm-up" time before becoming involved with the other children. His aggressive participation was spontaneous and consummated without apparent concern with respect to the "authority" figure—the worker. As a matter of fact, he was able to act-out almost directly his formerly suppressed anger against adults (parents by displacement), as shown when he quite deliberately spilled juice on the table. This "accidental" episode of hostile intention is quite dramatic in its implication when one considers the original referral picture. Such an episode involving more aggressive children carries much less significance. The import of negative transference behaviors varies in consonance with the personalities of children.

William's screams, uttered periodically throughout this session, seem to be spontaneous, experimental vocal "assaults" against the "world," albeit a special therapeutic world. The screams represent an experience in two dimensions. First, his formulations of sound—initially as brief, guttural exclamations, then as screams and cries, finally as single words—are all, in developmental sequence, a decathexis of the basic fear that was associated with vocalization. William had learned, literally in the cradle, that sound evoked the presence of a forbidding, angry father. A second dimension of sounds is that they can be used to aggress against the outer reality, as William had learned to do in the group. It was shortly after this group session that William, *for the first time*, spoke in another setting within the school. More about this later.

The worker, who sensed the changes in William, ventured direct verbal contact with him, also for the first time in the play group, except for the incident reported in Session Seven. This registered fruitfully; William displayed no anxiety. He remained relaxed and interested.

Session No. 29, Excerpts: All Present.

This was actually the last session of this play group, because, unknown to the worker at this time, she was about to be transferred elsewhere.

The last play group session prior to the summer vacation hiatus is always a "party" time. The meeting room is set gayly for the event before the children arrive. More elaborate party-type refreshments are already in place at the decorated settings: cookies, a cake, ice cream, soda, and a small gift for each child, packaged in party wrapping paper with each child's name on it. The meeting is shorter than usual, with the children returning to their classes after partaking so as to terminate the sessions with a generalized feeling of happiness, allowing for no conflicts between children.

The boys were thrilled with the surprise party. They spoke loquaciously, several asking whether the group would continue when they returned following the vacation—"next year," as they put it. The worker assured them of this. They left happily, carrying their respective presents, including the colorful placemats and napkins containing cookies and cake not completely consumed.

Addendum: Before proceeding further, a brief statement needs to be made about the circumstances following the unforeseen transfer of the worker, which led to termination of the group. When the children returned in the fall, each received a personal letter from the worker in which she explained what had happened. In language carefully couched to their level of comprehension, she told them that the "Board of Education" (outer authority) had "sent" her to another job and that *she would rather have remained with them*, but she had no choice in the matter. She "hoped" to visit the school someday to say "hello." Meanwhile, she sent along with each letter a small present.

The context of the message was true: Its format was designed to convey the worker's personal feelings for each child and to dilute their disappointment about the unexpected termination of the play group.

It would be unwise, probably counterproductive, for a worker to maintain further correspondence or episodic contact with the children. This would tend to maintain the transference without an opportunity to utilize it therapeutically. Hopefully, the gains made by the children will prove lasting and enable them to cope better with reality. In cases where other personnel are used to replace the worker, they can be informed as to the histories of each child and their involvements in a special group procedure. If it is possible to continue a therapeutic play group with a second worker, it would be best to do so.

Note: On the day of the last session, William engaged in speech at great length. This is detailed in the following memo:

> Mrs. B., the remediation teacher who had worked with William unsuccessfully for a long time, reported that she had sent for William to try to test him for a remedial reading program for the coming fall. At first William just stood silently, pointing to words. She began to read aloud, and urged him to do so. *Suddenly he read aloud, continuing for three pages* in the pre-primer. Then she took another reader, and he read an entire page aloud. She praised him highly. Mrs. B. asked William whether he would like to be in her reading club next year. He replied, "Yes." She then inquired about what he liked to do at home

to help his mother. He replied, "Clean." When she asked what else, he replied, "Sweep." She accompanied him back to his classroom, and on the way he repeated some of the things he had told her.

Summary

William, seven years, nine months of age when referred, had never spoken to adults in school. There were unconfirmed reports that he may have whispered to children. He was passive, generally inactive, unemotional, and mask-like in expression; he followed the teacher's instructions mutely; he conformed at all other times; and he had practically no involvements with peers. At home William spoke sparingly.

From available information, a reasonable premise can be established to account for William's selective mutism. His mother had surrendered maternal care of two infants to recalcitrant supervisors—the father and a teenage daughter. The former responded peremptorily and angrily to the plaints of the infants—William and his brother, nine months younger—scolding and overwhelming them. The ministrations of the daughter were evidently no more sympathetic. The babies' crying was met with special sternness, which would be reacted to with frustration of basic wants at first, and then probably by fear. When infants' needs are repetitively denied, partially fulfilled, and, as in this instance, accompanied by severe scoldings, the infants—and later, young children's—accommodations may eventually include a blocking off of sound. Thus, sound and vocalization of any sort become suppressed, wholly or partially, and cathected with anxiety and fear. It is significant that William's younger brother also spoke little.

Inhibition of speech may thus become a defensive adaptation to start with, with other permutations developing in time. A conditioned inability to communicate with a threatening "outer world" can later extrapolate and be displaced to the world in general. In addition, it can add a quality of negativism, a modulated, devious form of aggression. Finally, withholding speech can produce a secondary gain which—as in William's case—gave him special attention in school.

It is conceivable that William did whisper to children on occasion. In kindergarten and first grade, young peers would not be perceived by him in the formidable image of adults. However, as noted by remarks of children in the play group, he was considered to be a nontalker for the most part.

To recapitulate pertinent episodes in the group bearing on vocalization: In the seventh session William tried to "choke" off the unexpected utterance, "Mother." We cannot determine what stimulated this, but the word has undoubted transference meaning in the context of the treatment situation. Ninth session: John reported that William had whispered to him, "Wanna play checkers?" Tenth session: The boys crashed blocks; there was much noise; William was concerned about the worker's reactions; he also smiled broadly because of Cary's infantile speech. Eleventh session: William built blocks and deliberately crashed them (made a noise). Twelfth session: William mouthed "Thank you," to Mitchell. Fifteenth session: He made the alligator puppet eat the father and mother dolls, while he grimaced in expressed rage; he also created a clay tableau of himself behind a picket fence. Nineteenth session: William was pleased with Cary's screaming, although he covered his ears. Twentieth session: William laughed aloud and said nonsense words, mimicking Mitchell; the escort reported he had said, "Yes," in reply to a question. Sessions 21, 22, 23: William continued to laugh aloud, tease, crash blocks, and bang blocks together; he made his first direct contact with the worker. Twenty-seventh session: William emitted sounds (screams) standing *directly behind the worker*, repeating this many times. Twenty-eighth session: Following the play group meeting, William read extensively for the remediation teacher and answered her questions.

The foregoing episodes reveal a definite pattern of change from mutism in the play group to speech. The broader, longitudinal description of his demeanor and behavior in the group parallels the developmental sequence resulting in speech. From a passive, withdrawn state, William slowly came into contact with others and participated more frequently and freely as the weeks and months passed. Had the group continued for another year, it is altogether likely, on the basis of his change to this point, that spontaneous, meaningful speech in the group with both the boys and the worker would have come about. At the end of the school year his teacher reported definite improvement in his school achievement, particularly in spelling and penmanship. He played more with other children, but he was still quiet in his manner.

Cary, an eight-year-old boy in second grade, was very immature and demandingly dependent, with infantile speech and mannerisms. Of greater concern were several neurotic manifestations: he was phobic about coming to school, starting in kindergarten and continuing into the second grade; he also had conversion symptoms, notably stomach pains, which necessitated his leaving school to return home during or after morning sessions. He was preoccupied with thoughts of bodily injury, accidents, hospitalizations, and death, and he often made references to these. Cary was slight physically, with nervous mannerisms. Information relevant to his early development and family data was bleak. It was known that there had been some agency contact in the past and that Cary had not responded. A maternal grandmother was responsible for his supervision because both parents worked. She indulged Cary, favored him over an older brother, reinforced his somatic complaints through her indulgence, defended him against other children, and, in all, proved to be a supportive foil for the boy's symptomology. Cary's peer relationships were limited and inadequate. He tended to complain at the slightest touch of another child. The presenting problem was of an immature, infantile, and infantilized child, who was insecure, demanding, and dependent, with somatic complaints and phobic fears.

The group session protocols describe a distinct evolution of Cary's behavior. In the beginning he was subdued, watchful, and observant of the worker's responses to the testing by others. By the tenth session Cary engaged with several boys in an argument over puzzles. Typically, he joined the more passive group members in this—for him—initial aggressive exchange. In the same session, he was able to participate in throwing over a block structure, a destructive play enactment that became his pattern for many succeeding sessions. At this session it was learned from Cary's teacher that although Cary had complained of typical stomach pains in the morning, he nevertheless refused to go home as was his wont, because he did not wish to miss the group session in the afternoon.

Cary became more impulsive in succeeding sessions, acting almost without inner restraints at times, with a manic quality typifying his behavior, facial expressions, and speech. Such physiological manifestations are common with children possessing anxiety when they first become free to act out. In the twelfth session the worker avoided helping Cary when he cried out to her to stop another group member who was teasing him. But Cary was able to handle the situation, nevertheless. He formed a supportive ego relationship as the dependent, weaker member with Mitchell for a long time, while he experimented aggressively. Fortunately Mitchell tolerated this dependency, only occasionally teasing Cary or limiting his infantile ways. Cary's immaturity was reflected through his behavior during refreshments, when he showed his oral preoccupation with food, in the manner in which he used materials, and, of course, through the infantile speech that drew upon him some teasing.

Repetitively, Cary recounted episodes of injury and death, or he made general comments on these themes, evidences of phobic concern. Some of his comments were pointed references to "killing ourselves," perhaps an indication of savage intent and/or expiation to allay guilt feelings. In an experiential, noninterpretive form of treatment, as is the therapeutic play group, such material cannot be explored by a therapist with a view to establishing its historical references and fostering insight. Instead, it is hoped that derivative insight predicated on ego reinforcement and improved self-image will eventually enable such a child to slough off neurotic symptomology. This is feasible with young children. Corrective reexperience in a therapy play group has demonstrated that some neurotic features can be dissipated if the neurotic cathexis is not yet crystallized into a psychoneurosis—which is relatively rare in young latency children. However, with children whose inner anxiety is too deeply entrenched to respond sufficiently in exclusive activity therapy, both individual and group analytical methods of treatment may be indicated.

In the course of the sessions, more favorable socialization developed between Cary and the other boys, his chaotic, cathartic play lessened, and there was a concomitant growth in aim-directed activities and crafts work. At this point the observant worker, voluntarily and sometimes by request, assisted him in furthering his skills in these areas. Heretofore, in accordance with the original treatment plan, she had given him almost complete exposure to the strains and threats exercised against him by events in the group. Had he not been able to tolerate these, with the essential, occasional "assists" from the worker, it would have been necessary to remove him from the group. In such a case as Cary's, the reader can appreciate the critical element of group balance so necessary for corrective interpersonal interactions.

Meanwhile, Cary's school attendance improved and his somatic complaints diminished, even at home, as confirmed by the grandmother. She also reported his playing more and more outside the home.

Several times Cary demonstrated his appreciation by giving little gifts to the worker. This probably represented symbolic reciprocation for her allowing him to grow independently. With such a child, the multiple interpersonal contacts with other group members are important as limits against excessively immature behavior and as opportunities for enhancement of social capacity, but it is the positive transference relationship with the worker which forms the supporting structure that carries the child through his "trials." Our knowledge of the etiology of phobic patterns in young male children points up the extraordinary libidinal ties to the mother, in particular. This implies that in therapy, either group or individual, such a child would develop similar transference bonds to a female group worker. The psychologically corrective influence of the transference to the therapist, which results in transformations within a child's psyche, can modify the nature of the transference relationship to the mother, in a sense "detoxifying" it. This phenomenon has been termed *transference in reverse*.[5]

To sum up, the transference to the therapist, in this case the worker, has the potential for effecting psychic changes. The group serves as a limiting, redirecting, conditioning social force.

The end-of-year evaluative report from the teacher noted improvements in both Cary's academic work and his social relationships.

A few comments about the other group members: Mitchell had been discharged from parochial school to the present public school because of

---

[5]S. R. Slavson and M. Schiffer, *Group Psychotherapies for Children: A Textbook*, International Universities Press, New York, 1975, p. 465.

aggressive misbehavior and truancy, which patterns continued in the public school at the time of his referral. A the end of the school year his teacher reported, "dramatic, remarkable improvement in every area. He began to read, scored 2.0; attendance now excellent. From a hostile, belligerent, unhappy child, he has become happy and cooperative."

George was referred for very aggressive behavior, temper outbursts, underachievement, and truancy. The teacher reported he has settled down. He was trying to learn and was paying more attention to his work. His attendance had improved and he now had friends in class. His relationship with his teacher was good, although other teachers occasionally had difficulties with him.

John was referred as "shy and fearful, underachiever, nonreader, restless." A final report stated: "John has become much less timid; has made more social contacts and plays better with others; is more confident; not much improvement academically; excellent relationship with his teacher."

CHAPTER 2

Santa and William

Mortimer Schiffer

The transference relationship of patients to therapists is a fundamental element of psychotherapy and, with particular respect to children, has bearing on the nature of the transference relationships with parents.

During infancy and early childhood, the libidinal tie to the mother is preeminent, with the father having a lesser psychological influence on a child's maturation. While the father may perform nurturant tasks, in comparison to those of the mother they are episodic and are perceived and assimilated psychologically by children as ancillary experiences. They lack the same penetrating psychic imprints of the mother's influence. It is with the onset of the oedipal phase and during its resolution that the father becomes vastly more enhanced as a significant libidinal object affecting children's development.

When a young child requires psychological treatment, especially at a time prior to the onset of the oedipal complex, a female therapist is usually preferable because the child relates more readily and the necessary positive transference is more easily forthcoming. However, during latency the effectiveness of a male therapist becomes potentially much greater because the libidinal cathexes relating to the father (and males) have increased greatly, reinforcing the child's attendant feelings specific to the child-father dyad. Also critically involved in personality development at this time is the further evolution and crystallization of the superego, in which process the father exerts major influence. This applies to children of both genders.

In treating children approximately four to six years of age, such factors should be considerations in determining the choice of therapist according to gender. These general principles do not necessarily negate other possibilities with respect to gender of therapists in individual cases. Much can be written on this subject, but considerations of space and subject priority do not allow for it here. The point to be made is that in the psychological treatment of young children the gender of the therapist may be a factor of significant proportion, sometimes as important as an appropriate diagnosis and the correct choice of the treatment method.

The standard methods of activity and analytical group therapy of children are usually conducted by an individual therapist. However, there are special circumstances in group treatment wherein the use of cotherapists—male and female—is indicated. Such worker-teams in therapeutic play groups have had particular success with children who experienced traumatic conditions caused by the permanent loss of one or both parents, or the frequent, intermittent separations of parents. Also included are children who have never known one parent—in most cases the father—due to death, desertion, or other reasons. Similarly affected are children who live in households with changing "fathers," individuals who stand *in loco parentis* psychologically, regardless of the information given to the children to account for their presence. Finally, there are foster children, some of whom have been shifted frequently between different "families."

In intact families there can be circumstances with respect to parental relationships comparable in their psychological effects on children to those caused by "broken" families. In our experience this was seen in cases where there exist radical departures from the customary male-female parent roles. In some instances, relatively uncommon, the father remains at home fulfilling the role usually carried on by the mother, while the latter is the regular wage earner. In one case this was the result of a chronic illness of a nature necessitating the change of roles. In other intact families, the personalities of the parents may be such as to alter significantly the parenting roles, with the mother in an ascendant, dominating position and the father in a passive, perhaps feminized role vis-à-vis his wife.

In elementary schools in socioeconomically "disadvantaged" communities, where the author conducted therapeutic play group programs, there was a considerable number of non-intact families.[1] Worker-teams were used in therapeutic play groups with children who had suffered from the loss of a parent, and with some children, in intact families, who had been adversely affected developmentally because of idiosyncratic features of the

---

[1] One study revealed that more than 50 percent of the resident families in the community were non-intact, with one parent, the father, absent.

parents' roles. The use of co-workers was predicated on the premise that the influence of dual transference relationships in such play groups would be even more penetrating than would be that of an individual worker and thus more able to bring about sanguine changes in the children. In essence, the presence of male and female workers would create a psychological surrogate "family," and the children would have an opportunity for corrective reexperience of a holistic nature to offset the psychomalignant effects of their earlier life experience.

It was anticipated that the psychodynamic nature of a therapeutic play group with co-workers would be different from one conducted by an individual worker, not so much in the nature of the children's experiences but in their intensity. Almost from the outset we discovered that our expectations were understated; the effects generated by co-workers were dramatic. This was due partly to the children's transferences to a pair of workers but, in addition, to a vastly more complex pattern of interpersonal interactions that developed between group members. Another factor that was more intensified in the co-worker groups was the feelings induced in the workers in response to the complex and more intense transference bonds that developed. Facets of both negative and positive countertransference were prominently involved for a while, and did affect the functioning of the workers. Countertransference reactions were dealt with in regular supervision conferences with both workers present.

Theoretically, a co-worker team in a therapeutic play group should be an "ideal parent" combination. This posits the need for an optimal psychological "marriage" of co-workers—a pairing of individuals whose temperaments blend and would register in sanguine fashion on the children. Children have an extraordinary capacity to sense the permutations of feeling tones (especially negative ones) of individual parents—or their surrogates—and the reciprocal effects of one upon the other.

It was also rapidly observed that young children whose character defects were primarily related to sexual identity were influenced in greater psychological depth by virtue of co-worker leadership. This was attributed to the fact that children's perceptions and experiences, which are intricately involved with their own expanding sexual identities, become more sharply polarized and defined in the presence of optimal models of both sexes. Further, since boys and girls were included in these play groups by design, the mix of sexes further reinforced sexual differentiation on a peer level. The presence of both genders in the persons of the workers and also the heterogeneous group not only provided appropriate gender models but they also served as *contrast* models, which tends to further delineate the differences between genders. The foregoing were some of the more important considerations that were recognized and dealt with in managing therapeutic play groups with co-workers.

The record that follows is of a therapeutic play group conducted by a male psychologist and a female guidance counselor, both trained in the play-group method and both experiencing for the first time a co-worker relationship. The elementary school was located in an area populated mostly by black and Puerto Rican families who lived under depressed socioeconomic circumstances. The play group had a time span of more than two years—sixty-three sessions in all. Of this number, forty-five sessions were held with the co-workers and the remainder were conducted by the male worker because the female counselor was transferred.

In the content of the records, it will be noted that the composition of the group changed somewhat, first in the beginning sessions and again much later. Most of these changes were due to children moving from the neighborhood and then being transferred to other schools. But in two instances children were removed from the play group for reasons concerning personal treatment needs, and other arrangements were made for their continued help.

Under ideal conditions it is better that young children's therapy groups—of whatever nature—be maintained intact from start to finish. Moreover, as far as possible, groups should be *closed* as opposed to *open*.[2]

The two children who are central to this study, Santa and William, presented nuclear problems related to sexual identity and other behavioral difficulties. It was fairly clear that in the absence of therapeutic intervention both children would continue to develop atypically, each crystallizing feelings, attitudes, and character structures more characteristic of the opposite sex. The multiple activities and interpersonal interactions in the therapeutic play group eventually brought all group members into contact with one another and the two workers, but there was a definite dyadic attraction which drew Santa and William into more frequent interaction with each other. The contacts that took place between them were significantly linked to the commonality of their respective problems.

Santa

Santa, six years, five months old, was referred by her first-grade teacher. She was a sturdy child, with a masculine quality in both physical appearance and mannerisms. Santa always wore dungarees and blouses, never feminine attire. She was attractive, but when angry, as she often was, she looked grim and threatening. Her teacher was concerned about Santa because she was aggressive and sometimes bullying. Her classmates did not like her because she always attempted to dominate them. She could manage quite well in boys' games and often fought with them, frequently emerging the victor.

[2]A closed group is one whose membership is kept constant; an open group allows for modifications in composition at any time. The latter practice is more easily tolerated by adolescent and adult patients, although it can create special management problems even with older groups.

Santa spoke in a deep voice, was energetic, and was not much interested in learning. She liked her teacher and could respond positively if the teacher gave her individual attention. Study of the school record cards and a conference with Santa's former kindergarten teacher confirmed much of the referring teacher's observations. The kindergarten teacher added that Santa had constantly sought attention from her. The teacher felt Santa was "starved for affection." While neither teacher used the term, they evidently considered her a "tomboy."

It was difficult to ascertain the relationships between Santa and the persons with whom she lived. An elderly woman claimed to be her grandmother, although there was no confirmation of this on record or from other sources of information. It was known that Santa had been born in Puerto Rico and that, somehow she had been "given" to the elderly woman at the age of two and raised by her since. There was no evidence to indicate whether Santa had ever known her father, and her mother's identity and whereabouts were unknown. Furthermore, there was no male adult living in her household presently nor in the past. There were several other young children being cared for by the "grandmother," and Santa addressed them as "cousins." Santa called the elderly woman "mother," although they had different surnames. As far as could be ascertained, from age two until the present, Santa had been raised in a household devoid of a male adult.

Information was elicited from the "grandmother" that shed light on Santa's growth and development from age two. Santa was walking and talking at that time. She was not fully toilet-trained, however; she still wet the bed often. As punishment she was whipped on the legs with a strap. She sucked her thumb when she was upset and during sleep, at which time she was restless and cried out or spoke aloud. Santa was in rivalry with her "cousins," and when she was compared unfavorably with them she became angry and threw objects. Despite this obstreperous behavior, the "grandmother" denied that Santa presented exceptional problems at home. Her "formula" for rearing children was simple: when they disobeyed they were beaten. Yet, she did show warmth also. When Santa was disinclined to eat the "grandmother" would spoon-feed her, which Santa enjoyed. The "grandmother" was concerned about Santa's wild behavior in the streets, where she played after school hours, because of her habit of running between automobiles. For this reason she would often forbid her to go out.

After evaluation of the information, it was decided to place Santa in a therapeutic play group with children a year or more older than she, who would be better able to manage her aggression.

William

William, seven years, nine months old, was referred from second grade. He was the only child of elderly parents—they were, in fact, old enough to have been his grandparents. The mother, who was interviewed, gave sparse information with respect to her son or the family. One element was prominent, however: She was the employed provider for the family. Her husband could not work, according to her, because of some obscure ailment that prevented it, about which she was reluctant to elaborate. He remained at home, did the cleaning and cooking, and also shopped while she was at work. Evidently this arrangement had existed for a considerable time. The family had originated in New England. William, later, made references to an earlier residence outside New York City. Whether he had actually lived there or was recounting information culled from his parents could not be ascertained.

The teacher described William as "nervous, tense, restricted in his physical motor movements, highly verbal. William loses self-control easily. He also has a habit of shrugging his shoulders, almost involuntarily, similar to a 'nervous tic.'" She was unable to make personal contact with him; he resisted her efforts. The teacher reported also that she found it impossible to gauge how William really felt about anything. He did his assignments and tended to intellectualize a good deal, but did not respond to her praise. He never smiled or initiated conversation with her. Evidently William did not know how to make friends. While not deliberately provocative, he did bother other children somehow, because they wouldn't accept him. They complained sometimes of William's strange attempts to intrude in their groups; "clowning" would be one way of describing his manner. Initial observation of William in the period of time during which children were under consideration for the group revealed a driven quality, almost a compelling need on his part to make contact with other children.

On the basis of teachers' reports and direct observations by the group workers, a diagnostic impression was gained of a possible character disorder, with strong ambivalence related to sexual identity, and an extraordinary amount of anxiety for so young a child. It was felt that William's problems stemmed from the unusual conditions in his family: old parents, the role reversal of the parents, being an only child.

William was a member of the therapeutic play group for twenty-two sessions, then he was removed because of his acting out. Following this he was seen individually. More details on these developments will be provided in the record.

The Other Group Members

Carmen, seven years, five months of age, was referred from second grade as timid, quiet, and lacking in social participation. She was a pale, thin child, physically immature for her age. While she tended to be reticent, she did like her classmates and was accepted by them at the times when she behaved responsively. She spoke softly and, when she wanted the teacher's attention, would repeat her message quietly but insistently until the teacher responded. She enjoyed games but, when something proved beyond her capacity, would isolate herself. It was thought that she was dull-to-normal intellectually. Carmen was always obedient. In her quiet way she often attempted to be first in the line-up when the class moved out of the room. This placed her in a position where she could hold the teacher's hand.

The mother was interviewed through an interpreter. The family consisted of the mother and five children, Carmen being the second oldest. They occupied a one-room apartment under extremely crowded, uncomfortable conditions. There was no present contact with the father, who had been away for several years and prior to that was in and out of the home periodically. Carmen made no inquiries as to the whereabouts of her father, nor did the other children. Carmen used a nursing bottle until five years of age, just prior to entering school. She walked at age one and resisted toilet-training, which was accomplished at age three. She ate and slept well, sharing one bed with her siblings. She listened to her mother, but it appeared that she did this out of fear of punishment. In contrast to Carmen's more passive demeanor and behavior in school, at home she would have temper outbursts. She kicked and screamed when frustrated, argued with siblings, was noisy, and competed to hold the youngest child, an infant. Carmen was sickly and tended to have colds, although the doctor otherwise gave her a clean bill of health. The mother saw the need for special help for Carmen and agreed to her inclusion in the therapeutic play group. Carmen remained in the play group during its entire course.

Maria, age seven years, six months and in second grade, was referred for extreme shyness, timidity, and failure to make friends. She was immaculate in appearance and very anxious about getting herself dirty. Her physical movements were markedly rigid. Maria never spoke with adults in school. She may have had limited communication with children, but this has not been definitely determined. She would sing in chorus with the class or recite in group readings. There were pronounced compulsive qualities, particularly with respect to cleanliness and orderliness. Maria had nervous mannerisms, such as touching her braids and straightening her dress constantly.

At home, according to the mother, Maria spoke freely. Strangely, when other adults were present she spoke to her parents in Croatian, never in English. Maria had an older sister, older brother, and younger sister; she argued mostly with the younger sister. She cried easily when reprimanded and listened dutifully to her father when he disciplined the children. She went to her mother more readily than to her father. Maria read a good deal at home and played "school" with her younger sister. She was not permitted to play outdoors unless accompanied by her mother. The latter kept her children neat and clean and seemed unaware of the compulsive concern that Maria exhibited with respect to cleanliness. She could not account for Maria's shyness and isolation in school, although she was aware of it. After one visit to a family agency in the community, the parents discontinued because the father professed to see no need for treatment for Maria. The mother, however, was anxious because of the social problem in school. She said she would like Maria to have friends and participate more. She agreed to have her join a play group.

Maria started in the first session of the therapeutic play group and remained for the next twenty-one sessions, when the family moved out of the state. When this occurred, her mother evinced interest in having the receiving school made aware of the special help given to Maria. She had been impressed with the changes that had taken place.

Note: With respect to other children who were added to the group during its second year, referral information will be provided at the time of their entry.

The children selected for this play group all had emotional problems of different kinds, with a majority of them possessing one feature in common: They had experienced traumatic effects of the loss of a parent—the father. The exceptions were Maria and William, whose families were intact. However, as was described earlier, William was included because of the unusual quality of the parents' roles and relationships. When it started the group had six children, three boys and three girls. After the first session one boy was removed because his behavior indicated that the group as constituted was not in balance psychologically. Another boy moved away from the neighborhood. These boys' names (Stanley and Perry) appear in the protocols of the group sessions for a short time.

When changes are made in the composition of a therapeutic play group during the early sessions, this does not generate anxiety in young children, including those for whom separations and disappearances have become associated with fear and anxiety because of former events in their lives. The reason is that inconsequential degrees of transference have been established, if any, in so short a time. However, changes in a group's complement that take place after transference bonds have become substantially formed do elicit anxiety responses. This phenomenon in children's groups will be amply and dramatically illustrated in the records of this play group. For reasons mentioned elsewhere in this book, in some public elementary schools in "disadvantaged" neighborhoods, there is often much moving about of families with a consequent shifting of pupil populations. This accounts for both administrative and technical problems affecting some therapeutic play groups. However, despite the unforeseen changes that took place in this group, the events that transpired demonstrated unmistakably the extraordinary emotional impact of a surrogate "parent" worker-team.

To recapitulate: The group started with equal numbers of boys and girls; lost two boys almost immediately; remained stable in composition for approximately twenty-two sessions with four girls and one boy; and during the following sessions continued with three girls and two boys. Two girls—Santa and Carmen—were in treatment for the entire sixty-three sessions.

It was planned that each worker would document the group sessions independently. It was considered likely that some events might be perceived and interpreted differently by them and also that one worker might observe incidents the other might fail to note. The workers were to read each other's reports, which would then be examined in simultaneous supervision conferences with the author. Later in the group's history, the workers took turns in writing the protocols, and the nonrecorder of a particular session would study the other's report and add his or her observations. Experience confirmed, in time, that the workers varied in their documentations, including the interpretations they attributed to the children's behavior. These not unexpected variances became part of the search for meanings in supervision.

In this chapter, sequential excerpts are extracted from the sessions that provide the historical continuity and highlight the significant events and interactions involving the children and the co-workers. Attention will be directed to the special psychodynamics created in the group by virtue of dual transference relationships with the workers. The author's comments and interpretations will also focus on the special problems of the target children—Santa and William—and on other psychological permutations inherent in a group with co-therapists.

Session No. 1, Excerpts: All Present

. . . Most of the children were around the table playing with clay. There was some talk about William being "a girl," but male worker (MW) was unable to ascertain who had said this. William told Santa she was a "boy," and the others laughed. Maria smiled. Stanley and William went to build with blocks on the floor, playing somewhat apart. The girls were around the table. Perry grabbed an ottoman and started to slide on it.

. . . Maria was pressing clay with a tongue depressor. Perry crashed into the blocks, and Stanley protested mildly. Female worker (FW) and MW sat together talking while a good deal of this feverish activity continued. Perry initiated most of it. William and Perry took turns pushing each other across the room on the ottoman, while Stanley looked on and the girls smiled. Perry said, "I'm playing trains," and was using tongue depressor sticks as his "tickets." Santa and Stanley tried to join but were not able to break in. Perry then brought the ottoman and a chair into the small closet. Stanley gravitated to the closet, and then all three boys went into it and closed the door. There was much play involving entering and going out of the closet. Santa tried several times to get in, but Perry said, "Only boys can come in." Carmen stayed near and opened and closed the door several times.

. . . MW and FW were seated on the couch. Santa went to the round table and put her head down on her crossed arms. She looked both sad and angry. There was much in-and-out of the closet play, and William was finally ejected by the others. He started to hit Santa, lightly tapping her, and Santa hit back with all her strength. William then picked up the broom and other cleaning equipment and played with Carmen for a short time, making believe they were cleaning the play room.

. . . Perry grabbed three pretzels and laughed. He also drank his milk quickly, spilling it over his shirt. He asked for more food all the time. Santa took the remaining pretzels, leaving none for Stanley. Perry said that Santa had taken Stanley's pretzels, and Carmen and William joined in accusing Santa. There were no pretzels left for MW and FW. Cupcakes were also distributed with additional servings of milk. Perry said he didn't like them but he ate one anyway. Santa asked for more and was given it by MW. William and Perry wanted to play and began throwing clay at each other. FW picked up a large piece from the floor. Eating time was rather hectic. MW felt frustrated and at a loss to control what was happening. When the escorts appeared, all the children left except Perry. He asked MW to play with him; he meant to test him again. He also told FW that he wanted to stay. He finally left after a short while.

Comments and Interpretations

As is the practice in forming a therapeutic play group, the children had met each other a few times prior to this session during short "pregrouping" meetings held for the purpose of evaluating their suitability for the group. Even such brief initial encounters do not account for the nodal level of activity that occurred in the first session. It is not typical of a therapeutic play group; children usually require some time to become acclimated to the permissive group experience. It was deemed necessary to remove Perry from the group. He was a decided instigator, impulsive and hyperactive to a degree exceeding the author's initial expectations. On the basis of prior experiences in groups with many acting-out children, it has been ascertained that those who act impulsively from the start and do not apparently require a "warm-up" period covering at least several sessions minimally, are not good candidates for a group. If such a child is tried in a play group, he or she is best placed with children several years older, who will be less amenable to instigation and can limit his or her behavior.

Even in the beginning session, a comment was made about William being a "girl." While the workers could not ascertain who had said this, the finger of suspicion pointed to Santa, if we are to draw meaning from William's teasing rejoinder that Santa was a "boy." Regardless of the origin of the remark, what became apparent to both workers was that some of the children early recognized a "different" quality in William, and in Santa. This was the beginning of much focused interplay between William and Santa.

Also noted were the initial assembly of the group as a unit at one table and then the separating of the boys from the girls into subgroups. This was pointedly made clear by Perry at the closet, when he announced that "only boys" could play there. This and subsequent events show a tendency in heterogeneous play groups for subgroup formation according to gender. Part of the division into subgroups is attributable to normal developmental tendencies in latency, when children seek out peers of the same gender for play. In therapy groups also, such tendencies help foster sexual identity, particularly so with children for whom this constitutes a central problem, such as William and Santa.

In the excerpts there are references to an ottoman and a couch. There was also an upholstered easy chair in the play room. These items of furniture, and several others, were purposively used to create an atmosphere reminiscent of a home setting. In most therapeutic play groups, such furniture items are not used. It was thought advisable to include them in a cotherapist-led group to enhance the formation of transferences.

Maria, the compulsively clean child, was drawn to a regressive medium—clay—from the outset. But she handled the clay with a wooden spatula, carefully avoiding it with her fingers. In subsequent sessions we will see a gradual drop in her need to maintain absolute cleanliness.

Santa pressed to join the boys, particularly in the closet play. She made forceful attempts to get in but could not, because Perry was strong enough to block her. Santa did feel rejected by the boys, as evidenced by her momentary retreat when she appeared sad and angry, and sat with her head on her arms.

Carmen and Maria, both recessive children, nevertheless showed mobility, albeit minimal, in making peripheral contact with the others. This was a promising sign, occurring as it did so early. Both girls momentarily went to the closet door, attracted by the hullabaloo being raised by the boys.

The closet was a small one, with a standard-size door. Places for concealment—a closet or alcove—are desirable physical features in a therapeutic play group because they invariably induce a wide range of play activities. The children may hide (sometimes in the dark, with attendant symbolic meanings), trap other children, or enact immature or regressive behavior (in one play group a boy would crawl into a small alcove and lie there silently in foetal position for several minutes).

MW became a bit distraught because of the minor hysteria of some children when they grabbed food during the repast. They sat only momentarily and then some sprang up, especially Perry. MW stated in supervision conference that he had a general feeling of "abandonment" which bothered him. This was his first experience in a therapeutic play group, which generally evokes affective reactions in beginners. FW had become inured to the acting out that took place because she had had much prior experience with other such groups.

Perry was evidently anxious about some of the events that took place and perhaps about his part in setting them in motion, and he sought reassurance by remaining after the others had left. It was the consensus that Perry should not remain in this particular play group. After this session he was seen individually. It was not known at this time that Stanley's family was in the process of moving and that he would appear only once more in the play group. After his departure, William was to be the only boy in the group. It was decided to continue the group as constituted and to observe the interactions. The presence of another male, MW, would support a single boy. Were the group to be conducted only by FW, it would have been necessary to add another boy. After studying the play group during the next several sessions, it was decided to continue it as structured.

Several times the workers sat together, conversing, first at a table and later on the couch. During supervision the implications of such proximity were considered. The workers stated that they had felt awkward, quite conscious of each other's presence, and unsure about when and how to communicate with each other. They felt it would be strained and unnatural to maintain an "artificial" distance between themselves, so they simply allowed themselves to be together a good deal of the time. The author pointed out the possible effects of this should it become their pattern of accommodation in the future. Some children, more passive than others, would hesitate to approach the workers when they were together; or, wishing to make contact with only one of the workers, would be inhibited by the presence of the other. Such close pairing of workers might not deter more aggressive children. However, it would militate in a general way against the workers being used as separate libidinal objects at times when the transference bonds of individual children dictated a primary affiliation with one worker as opposed to the other.

Another question was presented to the workers for their consideration: Could their close pairing represent an expression of insecurity? Resolution of these questions and others related to their roles—individual and together—represented a significant problem because of the many permutations affecting the children. The workers would have to be sensitive and alert to the special implications of dual transferences as a combined influence, and also to the idiosyncratic effects of each worker's separate influence on each child.

The workers were advised to become involved in separate, routine tasks having to do with maintenance of the setting; to have *occasional* contacts with each other, but not sustained ones; to converse in moderate tone at such times when they were together; and never to discuss openly the ongoing behavior of the children. There would be "natural" times for convergence, such as for the regular repast toward the end of a session. Finally, they were reminded to reflect on their different responsibilities as these related to specific chores and their larger roles. Thus, MW was to be responsible for "heavy" tasks, such as shifting furniture and other heavy objects, and was participate in active games, particularly when the boys so involved him. FW was to assume major responsibility in preparing food, setting the table, serving, and clearing the table; putting smocks on the children; cleaning them; and so on. The workers found it easier in time to adapt to their roles and still maintain a natural, easy flow of communication. As will be seen later, some children needed to bring the workers together at times for reasons unique to the children, or because of an immediate situation in the interactions.

In this supervision session, the author made no direct reference to countertransference or to feelings that the workers might have had about each other's actions. When such factors have to be dealt with, it is accomplished best in the context of real episodes, not theoretical possibilities. Affect responses on the part of therapists are not unknown, and their implications in treatment are significant. In co-worker therapy they are more prominent, especially in a group such as the one under consideration, where a psychological "family" had been constituted.

Session No. 2, Excerpts: Present—Carmen, Maria, William, Santa

Santa, Carmen, Maria, and William entered the play room together. Santa sat on the armchair with Carmen for a moment. Maria and William went over to the couch and sat. Soon both stood up. William whispered something to Maria. She smiled, without replying. William then went to the large blocks and built a well-constructed building with train tracks, trestle, and a bridge. Maria sat on the ottoman with Carmen, and Santa pushed them for a moment or two.

. . . Santa took the can with Play-Doh® and brought it over to FW to open the lid. She was unable to and asked MW to open it. Santa said, disdainfully, "Mrs. M. doesn't have muscles!" MW opened the can and gave it to Santa.[3] She proceeded to use all the Play-Doh, refusing to relinquish any to Carmen, who wanted some. Carmen would get some and then Santa would take it from her, making angry remarks like: "It's all for me! None for you!" Santa then took all the wooden wedge figures and used them to

---

[3]The professed inability of FW to open the lid was intended to fortify symbolic and functional role differences between genders. As stated earlier, most of the children comprising this therapeutic play group presented problems attributable to the absence of fathers or a reversal of traditional parental roles during the children's early developmental years. This factor produced serious character problems in sexual identity with Santa and William in particular. The FW's *technique* in this instance should not be construed by the reader as recommended behavior with normal children in other settings, particularly in the family. Actions by adults that constitute a deliberate stereotyping of gender differences are inimical to spontaneous child-adult interactions in normal, emotionally healthy settings. Also, note how Santa retrospectively and unconsciously revealed the nature of her original problem and compared it unwittingly to her new perception of herself (p. 132).

make imprints on the clay. Next she took all the jars of paint from the easel and proceeded to paint the impressions she had made in the Play-Doh. She was not pleased with the results, as the smears were indistinguishable. While Santa was doing this, Carmen took pieces of the Play-Doh, but again Santa took them back. Carmen finally was successful in obtaining some, and she too pressed the wedges into it. At one point Santa spoke aloud: "I'm making a giant man."

. . . Maria was using the plasticene clay (clay with oil—more plastic than Play-Doh, and messier). She was rolling tiny balls and a larger object that resembled a head with a hat. She worked fastidiously, taking care not to soil herself. She looked around frequently, and smiled once when Santa put a slab of Play-Doh on her own head and walked about the room, saying, "I'm wearing a hat in the rain." Maria would look often toward the workers, with a half-smile.

. . . MW had molded a clay ashtray. Santa walked over and took it from him, without saying anything, and placed it on her backside as if she were going to sit on it. She laughed, went back to clay modeling, and placed her completed objects on the shelf to dry. She then said she had to go to the bathroom and left the play room.

. . . Santa took the box of napkins, folded them, and set the table, taking full charge. She then placed the ottoman at the table alongside a chair and gestured that she wanted FW to sit beside her on the ottoman, MW on the other side. Maria was the first to take a cookie; Santa grabbed several. William and Carmen helped themselves quietly. William drank quickly and replied, "No, thank you," when MW offered him a large pretzel stick, another part of the snack food. William got up from the table and started to pace quickly about the room. Carmen left the table and followed him. William beckoned her to enter the closet with him. Carmen kept closing the door to the closet, saying, "No, you're not allowed."

. . . During the snack Santa picked up two long pretzels and pretended she was fencing; they fell to the floor and broke. She placed the pieces on the table. Taking one that was unbroken, she said to MW, "Close your eyes and open your mouth." He did so and Santa laughed as she put the pretzel piece in his mouth. She did the same with FW. She called them "cigarettes" and imitated a smoker, holding her own pretzel as a cigarette. Then she opened her personal box of raisins and gave a handful to FW, a handful to MW, and one to Maria. She went to give one to William, but he ran away saying, "I'm strong enough." He then proceeded to have a game of "tag," running about the room, going behind the table where the others were still seated for snacks, and grabbing hold of both workers as he passed them. Now Santa and he kept chasing each other about the room, and they took turns hiding behind MW. Santa slipped on the floor and William mounted her back, pumping as if riding a horse. They giggled; Carmen and Maria looking on and smiled.

Comments and Interpretations

As soon as the children entered the play room, their first positioning was on the armchair and the sofa; then they moved to the ottoman to play with it. This became a pattern for future meetings. There is significance to this assembly of the children at the "home" furniture items, which were becoming symbolically identified with the co-workers. On occasions when the workers did sit together, they used the sofa and easy chair. The children's coming together in this fashion signifies symbolic contacts with the workers. In later meetings we will see how the children began actually to sit there in close proximity with the workers.

William was imaginative and skillful in building with blocks, his favorite choice of play item. Maria was less rigid than before and joined in play on the ottoman, obviously enjoying it but still not making a sound. Santa's reference to FW not having "muscles" was a manifestation of her preoccupation with qualities and abilities reflecting differences in gender. FW's behavior in not being "able" to open the lid of the Play Doh can was not fortuitous. She could have managed the task but professed inability to do so and deferred to MW, who succeeded. Santa's perception of this incident was to deprecate the FW. As far as she was concerned, females are entitled to have "muscles." Nevertheless, it was important that Santa be exposed to experiences in which definitive discriminations were clarified. In this way, aided by the transferences to the workers, which did include gender differentiations, Santa's identity could become oriented more to her own gender. Her aggression and overbearing attitude toward the other children were shown typically in her control of all the Play-Doh, when she refused to let Carmen have any.

In this session Santa began to use some materials regressively, as did some of the other children. First she chose Play-Doh; then she smeared paint over the impressions she had made, a truly messy procedure. Carmen, who finally succeeded in getting some Play-Doh, followed her example. Maria voluntarily chose the plasticene clay, probably because she was afraid to challenge Santa's possession of the Play-Doh. Since the plasticene clay was softer and potentially messy, Maria very carefully molded with it. Yet, this was a departure from the prior session when she used the Play-Doh with a wooden spatula, not touching it with her fingers at all. We shall observe in succeeding sessions how her fastidiousness and compulsive cleanliness succumb to a real desire to smear, and she eventually dirties herself. Herein is depicted an advantage of group therapy over individual, with respect to the *momentum* of behavioral change. Children like Maria become more readily mobilized toward regression—and aggression—both of which are necessary in treatment, through catalysis, one child affecting another. The interpersonal effects of suggestion and universalization are preeminent in group treatment.

The quality of Santa's regressive play became further explicated when, without permission, she took the flat slab of clay that MW had been working on and placed it on her backside. The hidden anal meaning of this "play" was substantiated when she immediately thereafter had to use the bathroom. The incident may also have had unconscious erotic significance.

Santa soon "took charge" by setting the table for refreshments, instructing the workers to sit on either side of her. In a sense she was supplanting FW by assuming the latter's usual role, but yet, at the same time, Santa was enacting her more basic dependency role when she became the "only" child in closest contact with the workers. For Santa, who to our best knowledge had not experienced an intact family, her compelling need to manipulate the workers from the very beginning was tantamount to assuring herself that they are "hers." Her game with the pretzels is another example of bidding the workers to satisfy her unconscious needs. This latter interpretation flows from feelings that both workers sensed within themselves in response to Santa's persuasive demands, feelings that they identified during supervision conferences.

William barely joined the group at the snack table, a pattern of avoidance that was to continue for many sessions. He seemed to be defending against contacts with the workers. Evidently he tended to become more anxious when events brought him within a closer context of the "whole family," which is the psychological state when a therapeutic play group assembles for a repast. Yet, William did sometimes make direct physical contact, albeit momentarily. This was mostly with MW, as when William touched him or swung behind him during a game of tag. In conference, MW described a manifest resistance on William's part to accept him, almost a warding off. William had strong ambivalent feelings toward MW.

William definitely selected Santa as the focus of his interests. In "play" he actually mounted her on the floor, "pumping" on her. There was little if any resistance to this on Santa's part; she evidently found this sexual play stimulating. She need not have been compliant had she wished otherwise, because she was physically strong and not afraid of William.

Session No. 3, Excerpts: Present—William, Carmen, Maria, Stanley

. . . Maria sat quietly, working with the plasticene clay and molding it with the animal wedge figures. Stanley said to her, "Can't you talk? You don't have a tongue or teeth?" She looked at him, said nothing, and then seemed to ignore him. William was building with blocks, not as elaborately as in previous sessions. He would periodically brush by and jostle Stanley, pushing him about, and provoke him to laughter. Also, William ran in and out of the closet.

. . . William drank his milk very quickly, in gulps. He then got up from the table and dashed around the room, resuming the same kind of running about he had done earlier in the session.

. . . Carmen and Maria were working together at the clay table. The workers were seated at both sides of the same table, discussing the clay objects, when Stanley came over evidently wanting to work with clay also. He said to FW, "Is he your husband?" FW replied, "What?" (In conference she said she had not been sure she had heard the question correctly.) Stanley smiled and said, "Oh, nothing."

Comments and Interpretations

We now observe another phenomenon typical in group treatment of children, namely how one child perceives and verbalizes about another child's idiosyncratic behavior—here, Maria's failure to speak. The reader may recall an almost identical episode in the case of William (Chapter 1), who was mute. When one child focuses on another's symptomatic behavior, the latter becomes more apparent to the entire play group, and there is certainly increased social pressure on the child in question. In time this does have some effect in altering the behavior.

William was impulsively hyperactive in almost all the things he attempted to do, as noted by his trying to provoke Stanley into joining him. He had behaved similarly with others. Once again William seemed unable to remain seated during the snack period and moved about the play room almost compulsively. There was a quality of anxiety in this behavior, as is often detectable in hyperactive children. Motor activity serves to diminish the quantum of anxiety, particularly with children who are capable of such release behavior. There are others who are physically immobilized by anxiety. In William's case it is questionable whether motoricity did any more than momentarily assuage his anxiety, leaving its causative basis untouched. It was becoming increasingly apparent that William might require more intensive treatment.

Stanley's inquiry about the relationship of the workers, directed to FW, was not unexpected. Such personal questions indicate incipient positive transference. Young children in treatment inevitably ask such questions: "Are you married?" "Where do you live?" "Do you have children?" However, they do not persist in such questioning. FW'S failure to respond to Stanley's question may have been due to the suddenness and unexpected nature of the question, but more probably stemmed from her indecision as to how to reply. Answers to queries about the workers' personal lives should be given directly and simply couched—in this case: "No, we are friends." The author assured both workers that children would not pursue this subject in depth. To do so would be antithetical to their need to have the workers joined ideationally as "parents." At this stage in treatment, children require the fantasy more than accuracy of information. The latter tends to diminish the needed transferences.

Session No. 4, Excerpts: Present—Carmen, Maria, William

. . . Carmen put her feet on the ottoman and settled back on the couch. She then rose, walked over to the shelf, and took the can of Play-Doh. She could not open it and brought it over to MW to do so. . . . Maria put the wedge people and animals on the block shelf, neatly in a row. . . . Maria played for a short time with clay, using a flat circle top of the can to flatten the clay. . . . Carmen used her hands as a rolling pin, rolling out several "snakes" and making them into balls. . . . Maria seemed restless and walked about the room, touching the doll, the telephone, the cleaning brush, and other equipment in the corner. . . . William, who had been playing with the rubber horseshoes alone, said rhetorically that he had played horseshoes in Maine when he was there last year. . . . When William needed the stick and base of the game attached, he went to FW and asked her to fix it. She made an attempt, unsuccessfully, then asked MW to do it. He did and gave it to William. . . .

Comments and Interpretations

Again a child used the "family" furniture to relax. Opening the clay can was almost a ritual, a task that the girls now brought to MW. William, who was still resistive toward MW, did not do so; he brought his problems to FW, who managed to divert them to MW.[4] William's aloofness from MW may have been characteristic of his relationships at home. In the absence of confirming information, we may assume that William was accustomed to having his mother take care of such problems.

Maria was again attracted to the clay, touching it with implements once more. She was more ambulatory now, exploring the play room. This was a good sign, indicating her need to know more about a setting that was beginning to affect her.

William made several remarks about experiences in Maine, where he was said to have been born. It is possible that his remembrance of that location was a happier one because circumstances in his family with respect to his parents' relationships may have been different then, more to his liking.

[4]Ibid.

Session No. 5, Excerpts: Present—Maria, Santa, Carmen

. . . FW was seated at a table when the children entered. She was working with finger paints (introduced for the first time, particularly to move Maria toward using them). Santa sat down immediately. She squeezed more water from the sponge to further wet a sheet of paper. She then found it too wet and said so, but she continued to work at it, smiling and enjoying the new experience. Carmen and Maria stood by, both smiling. Maria then sat down on the sofa, near the table where finger painting was going on. She showed much interest in it. . . . Later, Maria walked over to watch FW as the latter smeared with her fingers. Maria kept her hands locked behind her back; there was a half-smile on her face, her eyes wide open, and once her mouth opened in astonishment. She then sat down at the table opposite FW. Next she walked over to a chair at the other end of the room, watching FW at all times. She walked back, again standing close by FW. Santa noticed this and said to Maria, "You can paint, too." No response from Maria. Later Santa looked over to Maria, who was on the couch, and said, "Why don't you play a game?" Again no response. . . . Maria stepped over Santa's block structure two or three times as if she were playing hopscotch. . . . Before Santa started to build with blocks, she left the play room for the bathroom. Maria walked over to the door and waited patiently for her to return, opening the door for Santa when she did. . . . Santa finished painting, brought a game to MW, and said, "You've got to play with me!" . . .

Comments and Interpretations

The introduction of finger paints gained immediate attention from the children, especially from Maria, who seemed almost shocked with amazement. Yet, she was also a bit distressed over the sight of smearing, as shown by her restless movements to and from the table where the finger painting was going on. FW had introduced this new activity correctly, by silent demonstration.

Finger painting is an excellent medium for children like Maria, but it can be excessively regressive for others, and its use should be carefully considered before adding it to a play group's materials. Maria's ambivalent, strained response to smearing was further demonstrated as she clasped her hands behind her back, an unconscious gesture against such "dirty" play. Note how children can be perceptive to the exceptional behavior of others, which we have seen repetitively in this play group and others reported on. Santa identified the "holding back" tendency in Maria and encouraged her to participate. Santa was catalytic in influencing Maria; she demonstrated for the latter a freedom to use the setting, which has begun to take effect.

Despite her own reticence and mixed feelings, Maria followed Santa to the door when she left the play room and waited expectantly for her return.

Once again Santa "demanded" compliance to her needs from MW, literally ordering him to play with her.

Session No. 6, Excerpts: Present—Santa, Maria, William, Carmen

. . . Santa went directly to the table set up for finger painting. She saw the new colors and said, "I'll paint with this red." . . . At one point Santa pretended to feed the scooped-out finger paint to Maria, on a spoon. Maria had been watching Santa use the paint intently, almost from the beginning of the session. . . . Maria walked from one finger painting to another as FW removed them from the table to dry. She looked for some time at the wet imprint left on the table. . . .

William was building a long railroad track with MW. . . . Santa moved quickly, stepped over William's building, and broke some of it. William playfully made a dash to grab Santa. She fell to the floor purposely, and both children tussled and wrestled. Santa broke away and ran to the easy chair on which Maria and Carmen sat.

. . . MW helped William push the ottoman on which Santa and Carmen were seated. At times William also got on the ottoman, and MW pushed it alone. Maria laughed aloud but did not get off the armchair while the ottoman pushing was going on. . . . Santa hopped off and ran around the room, screaming in a high pitch and pushing aside blocks, tables, and chairs. . . .

Santa rolled on the floor again with William on top of her. She called out, "Mrs. M., help me!" but laughed and screamed as she did so. William said, "You're my horsey now!" Santa asked FW if she could go to the bathroom.

. . . FW served cake and candy. Santa grabbed two cupcakes and two candies, saying, "One is for my brother." William asked, "Your brother?" She replied, "No, my cousin." William refused a cake. Santa wanted to wrap a cupcake in a napkin. It was wet, so FW offered her a paper towel. Santa punched the towel and said, "Look, it's got no muscles!" When FW addressed MW as "Jerry," asking him to bring some more napkins, Santa looked at William and repeated "Mrs. M." aloud, looking at FW. Then Santa turned toward MW and said, "Jerry." . . . Santa noticed that MW had no candy. She took one of her own and gave it to him.

. . . At one point in the session, MW had pushed all the furniture to the side so that the children would have more space to play with the ottoman. Also, he tried to engage William in minor conversation as they worked with blocks, but William did not seem interested in talking. A good deal of the time, FW was cleaning the play room and picking up strewn items.

Comments and Interpretations

Maria continued to be intrigued with finger painting—but still from a safe distance. William permitted MW to help him build a track. This was promising; it showed some diminution of his defensiveness against MW. Still, William refused to engage in talking with him. And once again William and Santa were involved in what was obviously a form of sex play. Immediately thereafter Santa had to go to the bathroom, evidently stimulated by the play. This had happened following other incidents of a similar nature.

During the snack Santa referred to a "brother," which she corrected to "cousin." As noted in the referral, there were many children in her home whom she identified as "cousins." And again, repetitively, Santa was preoccupied with "muscles," another reflection of her confused identity. Her bids for attention from MW were more frequent and more open. She was somewhat taken aback by hearing FW address MW by his first name, and she repeated it.

MW correctly picked proper moments to participate with the children, notably those requiring strength, as when he pushed several children on the ottoman. Also, he recognized the need for more open floor space and accommodated the children without being asked. FW complemented her co-therapist's assistance to the children but at a different level of ministration. Much of her activity was geared toward what the children would see as a traditional maternal role: cleaning and food preparation, and like tasks. As noted previously such role definition isolates and emphasizes gender qualities of the co-therapists and serves to further substantiate the children's perceptions of the differences in genders.

Sessions Nos. 8–11, Excerpts

. . . Again Maria watched Carmen with interest as she used finger paints.

Santa completed a game she was playing, put away the pieces neatly, jumped up with exuberance, and grabbed MW around his waist, suspending herself for a moment with her feet off the ground.

. . . William built a high wall of blocks and proceeded to high jump, doing it very well. He gradually added to the wall's height. Santa said, "I can do it too," but continued to draw. William said to MW, "Girls can't do it as well." He added that his father used to be "champion high jumper at Maine State."

. . . William had been running around the room, tussling with Carmen on the couch, who laughed and pushed and pulled with him. At one point Maria went over to the play telephone and began to dial intently, but spoke no words.

. . . Santa said she had to go to the bathroom. She returned quickly, carrying a copy of a *TV Guide*, and showed William a picture in it. Later, at snack time, she said, "Stanley moved away." No comment from the others.

. . . Santa told MW he "had to play" with her—the Chick-in-the-coop game. MW complied. Santa did not play according to the rules and looked at him smiling whenever this happened.

. . . William again built blocks to jump over. Both workers were seated near each other at the table close to the girls. William asked MW what he thought the height was. MW said the blocks were "close to championship" height. William tried to jump over the structure but knocked it over. He built it up again and asked MW if he thought that he (William) could do it. MW said he thought so. William did jump it successfully.

. . . Santa got up from the table. MW and FW were standing. Santa put her arms around MW, with her head on his chest. She laughed and broke away shortly.

. . . Maria remained seated on the ottoman. MW pushed her gently along the floor. She looked up at him and smiled, without a word. This happened twice during the session.

. . . Carmen and William were wrestling on the couch and on the floor. Santa was running around throwing the couch pillows. Carmen and William joined in.

. . . Santa came over to MW and held his hands for a moment.

. . . Carmen used MW for a shield during the pillow throwing. Maria picked up one pillow and put it on the easy chair. FW prepared the refreshments and called the children to the table. Santa remarked again that Stanley had moved. FW confirmed this. William drank milk, refusing other snacks. In helping FW serve, Santa spilled milk on the floor. FW silently mopped it up.

. . . William and Santa ran after each other with the puppets on their hands and ended up in a tussle, with Santa saying, "I'm not playing anymore." Maria stayed close to FW during this excited play.

. . . Cookies were served. William read the print on the cookie package, ate one cookie, and seemed to like it. This is the first time he seemed satisfied with food of a non-liquid variety.

. . . Santa asked MW to join her at another table and draw with her. MW drew a tree. Santa drew a house and the people who lived in it. She then added MW to the picture; the figure had a dunce cap on it. Then she drew FW. This figure had tiny feet, which Santa laughed at. Santa then drew herself and William in her picture. William came over to see what she was doing. Santa said William was an "egg."

. . . Santa started to finger paint as FW brought over smocks. MW took one smock and offered it to Maria, who allowed him to put it on her. She then sat down with a sigh, took some finger paint, and began to use it.

She kept on, looking frequently up at both workers. MW commented about how nice the paintings were, making it a point to include Maria's.

. . . During the snack FW told the group that the next session would be the last until after the summer, when the group would resume. The workers talked with each other about planned activities for the fall.

Comments and Interpretations

The workers finally manipulated Maria into using the finger paints after having for weeks studied her avid interest in this activity and her uneasiness about attempting it. She literally sighed, as if in finality or gratified relief, now that she had been helped to do what she in fact had been yearning for. Overcoming this child's compulsive patterns of order and cleanliness, to the point where she actually touched a highly regressive substance, was in itself a most important experience, since these traits were already characterologically habituated. The advance took place after only three months of treatment, which represents rapid change. This occurrence points up the advantage of group treatment, for reasons already enunciated.

Santa made many physical contacts with MW. This was a promising sign, pointing toward a growing oedipal involvement. She took him around the waist; another time she hugged him and placed her head on his chest. She continued to use the bathroom after such physical contacts with males, including with William.

Twice Santa referred to Stanley's absence. (His family moved from the neighborhood unexpectedly.) Her comments reflect anxiety about loss and separation which are common feelings in children who have experienced traumatic breaks in the family constellation. In a treatment group sudden changes are reacted to as personal losses because of a felt threat that a similar experience could happen to the anxious child.

Maria also tolerated closer proximity to the workers, without demonstrating preference for either one. She enjoyed this but still without verbalizing. To recall: It was known that she spoke at home and possibly sometimes to children in class.

William demonstrated athletic prowess and commented about his father as a "champion" jumper, a type of remark he had made before. This seemed to express a wish rather than the fact of masculine achievement by his father. Such remarks emphasize what was deemed to be his sensitivity to the idiosyncratic roles of his parents, a reversal of what William perhaps wished to see. MW supported William's growing estimation of his prowess by confirming the "championship" height of the obstacle. The sexual interplay between William and Santa continued from week to week, to a heightened degree as described by the workers. Evidence of this was the manic quality when Santa and William ran about with more and more abandon,

Santa shrieking loudly. Evidently the sexual nature of their activity generated anxiety in her, and perhaps guilt feelings as well.

William accepted solid foods now. His refusal to do so before, coupled
with his usual brief stay at the table when the repast was served, is still believed to be a reflection of momentary anxiety, and perhaps negative transference. The group's coming together for a repast is reminiscent of what
takes place in a real family, and William's behavior probably reflected
something about how he felt. After all, the matter of eating in his family
carried different connotations: His father did the shopping and cooking.

Several times William used Carmen instead of Santa in rolling on the
floor and the couch, and she was not resistive to this. Rather, she evidently
enjoyed such play.

The reader has undoubtedly noted by now that in the content of the
protocols more references are made to MW than to FW. Since the documentation was done by both, it is apparent that the selectivity of the children as far as the workers are concerned has more than incidental meaning.
It became obvious to both workers that on an observable level, MW was indeed more heavily weighted in transference relationships with the children.
This is in consonance psychologically with young children's emotional development, especially with children such as those in this play group. They
have lacked the influence of male adults in earlier years and at present and,
as a consequence, have been deprived of libidinal experiences in the oedipal
phase with a male parent. Except in the case of William (where role reversal
occurred), this applied to all the children.

In children's experiences during the oedipal complex phase the father—or a surrogate, as in the play group—has a dominant psychological
impact on both male and female children. For girls he represents a desired
sexual object; for boys, mainly a rival and prohibitor; but for both genders
he represents a focal libidinal object. For these reasons, it is expected that in
a therapeutic play group with co-workers, the male would be cast in a central position vis-à-vis the female worker. This tendency has been confirmed
in this and other co-worker groups. Much later in the development of such
play groups there is abatement of the oedipal drive, accompanied by ego
strengthening, improved superegos, and other maturational outcomes. At
such time the interactive patterns between the children and the workers
change. The co-workers are perceived and responded to more equally, not
as separate libidinal objects with varying intensities of transference, as they
were earlier in a group's history.

Session No. 12 (Last in June): All Present

Carmen entered the play room first. MW said, "We missed you," welcom-
ing her return. Carmen had been ill for several weeks. She smiled shyly but

did not say a word. She had brought some papers and other items with her, which she placed on the couch. Meanwhile, MW brought paper to the round table and set it up for finger painting. The play room had undergone some structural changes since the last session, although the furnishings were the same. This involved removal of temporary partitions that had been present since the beginning and the erection of permanent ones. Carmen walked about looking at the changes. MW remarked that the room was being "fixed."

Santa, Maria, and William appeared together with their escorts. FW was engaged in cutting drawing paper and making place mats for the snack table. Santa rushed up to her and said that she would not be able to do much playing because her foot hurt. She went into details, but FW could not quite make out what she meant. William picked up a rubber puppet and began kicking it. Maria immediately sat down at the finger painting equipment, although without touching it. MW was seated near FW. Santa and Carmen were also there. FW went to Maria with a smock. Maria stood up soundlessly and put her hands into the outstretched smock. FW returned to the other table. Maria just continued to sit without starting to paint. MW noticed this, went over, and told Maria to wet the paper first with the sponge, which she did, slowly and laboriously. Carmen then sat next to her and MW brought a smock for her. The two girls began to use the finger paints.

FW told MW that Santa had a nail in her shoe. This had been determined when Santa again complained of a pain in her foot. FW asked MW if he could remove it. He tried to, without success. He returned the shoe to Santa, saying that he would try again after the session when he could get other tools. MW sat down next to Maria and commented favorably on her finger painting. There was no perceptible difference in Maria's facial expression.

William asked what time it was and fixed the face of Carmen's toy clock, which was one of the articles she had made in class and had brought with her. William was surprised at the hour; he thought it was much later. MW put Carmen's completed finger painting on the radiator to dry. William kicked the puppet, which went over one of the construction screens. He went to get it. MW tried to stop him but William went anyway. Santa observed this and also went behind the screens. Carmen wanted to, but she did not when she heard MW mention that they should not go there. William and Santa remained behind the screens for a while and played with a portable blackboard that was there. Finally the children came back into the play room proper. MW suggested that William kick the puppet in the other direction so it wouldn't go over the screen. Instead William chose to chase Carmen with the puppet for a while. He then went back to kicking it.

Carmen asked MW for the time, cuddling up to him in the process of doing so. This was the first time she had done this. Santa picked up a block and played "batter" with William as the "pitcher," using the rubber puppet as the "ball." MW cautioned Santa about the long block and the possibility of its hitting someone when swung. He added that it was "fun" but not in the play room. Santa refused to put the "bat" down, even when MW put his hand on it. He suggested that they could play catch with the puppet instead. Surprisingly, William agreed to this but Santa did not. She swung the "bat" a few more times. MW suggested again that all three of them play catch. He threw the puppet to William, who threw it to Santa. Santa then threw it back to MW, angrily.

Maria and Carmen went behind the new partition, as the others had done earlier. MW went there to get them. William again picked up the block to use as a bat, and MW reminded him that batting in the room was not allowable. William put down the block. Meanwhile Santa began finger painting, and William now kicked the puppet. The other children were seated with FW. Santa asked MW to hang her painting on the radiator to dry.

FW left the play room to get the refreshments. Since it was the last session, there was to be a special treat. Carmen asked MW to give her a ride on the easy chair. Maria quickly got on the large chair with her, with William and Santa soon following. They played a game: William said he wanted to ride to Maine; Santa said that she'd like to go to 91st Street first, then Cuba, and then Puerto Rico. The children were laughing and excited as MW pushed them (which was a feat, since the chair was heavy with children). FW reentered the room carrying soda and ice cream, which had been kept in a nearby room under refrigeration. William asked why they were having these to eat. MW said it was because this was the last meeting. William asked, "Forever?" MW replied that they would meet in the fall, when they returned to school.

Just before the group sat down at the table, which was gaily decorated with place mats, napkins, and cutlery, Maria picked up two puppets and made their mouths move. When they all sat, FW said to MW that Carmen did not know it was the last meeting because she had been absent the session before. FW informed Carmen that the group would resume in the fall. She had felt it necessary for Carmen to be reassured, in the event she had not followed MW's explanation.

FW asked the children which sodas they preferred. William chose a fruit soda, as did Santa; Maria and Carmen chose cola. The children were much quieter than usual during the snacks. William engaged in conversation and did not get up from the table as in prior sessions. He showed MW his thumb, saying it hurt him. MW told him that it was probably a sprain and the pain would go away. William spoke of going on a cross-country trip with his parents instead of spending the summer in Maine. Then he said, "I'll put ice cream in the glass and make an ice cream soda." The other children liked this idea and, following his lead, put ice cream in their glasses. Both FW and MW tried to elicit some feelings from the children about their coming to the play group, but the children did not say much beyond the fact that they liked it. At the end the workers distributed wrapped gifts. All the children were pleased and all said "goodbye" except Maria, who had not spoken at any time although she appeared happy with the occasion.

After the group left, MW accompanied Santa to the custodian's room to obtain a tool to remove the nail from her shoe. Santa smiled and quietly said "goodbye" to MW as they went upstairs.

Comments and Interpretations

When entering the play room, Carmen placed the objects that she had brought from her classroom on the sofa. This is not usual for children when they have things with them: There are other places where they are accustomed to storing objects. As noted previously, the couch symbolizes the persons of the workers. Carmen's behavior is another manifestation of "touching" significant libidinal objects. Carmen, who was passive and withdrawn when referred and remained essentially quiet for some time in the play group, especially with respect to MW, had moved into easier relationships with the workers, particularly MW. Later in this session she actually cuddled close to him. She had observed Santa do this and thus had become emboldened to show oedipal "love" for the first time.

The play room was being altered with minor construction changes, which accounted for the new partitions. It would have been better not to have this done at this time, but school administration is not always in a position to accommodate to psychological considerations. Emotionally troubled children, generally speaking, have suffered from inconsistencies in their lives and in the ways they are treated. For the majority of the children in this particular play group, there were additional trials, such as unexpected changes in family constellations and movements from one residence to another. When treatment is instituted it is necessary that *consistency* and *constancy* typify the therapeutic experience, which includes the setting. When there are unexpected alterations in conditions that have become familiar and comforting to children, they become uneasy and sometimes anxious. The physical setting for a play group should be maintained in its beginning state—in a condition of *fixity*—as much as is possible. If circumstances make it necessary to change the setting, or to use a different one—as will happen with this group—this is best done at a time of natural change, perhaps in the fall when children return to school. Children are accustomed to changes at such times.

In this session Santa sought nurturant attention from FW. There was indeed a nail protruding into her shoe, but the workers deemed her complaint to be out of proportion to her discomfort. Yet both workers, sensing her need, ministered to it. Also, Santa had recently been making more direct overtures to FW, a signal of increasing interest in her. She had previously shown almost open preference for MW and was challenging and negativistic toward FW.

William continued his athletic games, first kicking the rubber puppet about, then later, with Santa participating, using it as a ball to be batted with a block. Both workers were rightfully concerned about the real possibility that a long block would accidentally strike another child, and they intervened. Young children are not sufficiently aware of the inherent dangers of some physical actions. William, however, resisted MW's interventions several times during the session, as did Santa. MW then converted the game into a threesome, a better technique than direct intervention. MW should have used this approach to start with instead of prohibiting the batting. True, it may not have been successful with the two children, who had a need to act out negativistically, but an indirect attempt should have been used first.

Maria was immediately drawn to the finger paints upon entering the room, but she remained "frozen", unable to start. MW engaged her directly and sensitively, levering her just sufficiently to bring her to use the paints. She was in an ambivalent struggle between her desire and her obsessive inhibitions about cleanliness. Maria was only too happy to have been assisted in resolving her anxiety. The fact that Carmen was using fingerpaints made it easier for Maria to do so, another example of catalysis in group therapy.

Maria was unable to respond to MW's verbalized praise; she sat masklike. In supervision conference, MW was questioned as to what had prompted him to try to evoke conversation from Maria. His feeling was that since she had on a number of occasions given *expressive* evidence of pleasure by smiling and laughter, she appeared ready to speak. Generally, when speech is cathected in children to a point of noncommunication—in this instance a selective mutism—it is better procedure not to "force" vocalizations. Such efforts tend to reinforce defenses against speech, which may have become loosened as a result of treatment. Deliberate withholding of speech—as in Maria's case—may be an unconscious form of hostility, despite her timidity and isolation. If so, it begins to dissipate at a point when the transference is sufficiently established.

Given the support of the positive transference, such children become strengthened to express repressed aggression. They may first do so through enactments with dolls, puppets, and falling blocks, then commit mild infractions (such as Santa's going behind the partitions), and also express aggression in other non-verbal ways. After a sufficient period of time and repetitive cathartic behaviors of this nature, a child like Maria becomes capable of expressing her anger more directly. This is done first through mild, then stronger, forms of negativism. Following this development, the characterological "symptom" of withheld speech weakens. In a regressive

sense, Maria's refusal to speak, a hostile behavior, may have an anal reten-
tive meaning.

Both Maria and Carmen showed their aggressive potential by going behind the partitions *after* they had observed MW caution William and Santa.
Whether this represented for these two timid children a subdued form of defiance or a less than conscious ploy to solicit MW's attention is a matter of
conjecture. In either case, the children's actions do depict a growing confidence. Carmen was speaking more often now, more to MW than to FW,
and, as noted above, she cuddled him once.

William was amazed by the party. For the first time he sat still throughout the snack period, more relaxed and not perspiring, as was reported in
prior sessions. He even evinced anxiety when the worker spoke of this as the
"last" meeting, with his query: "Forever?" All the children were pleased
with their gifts. The workers had prepared the play room in advance for a
short, party-type meeting, with the table already set and refreshments and
party favors out. This is the usual procedure. It avoids the possibility of unpleasant interactions between children, ending the session on a sour note.

With respect to interruptions of group sessions for intervals of vacation, short or long, it is advisable that workers speak about this subject, to
reassure children about continuation of the group. Otherwise, some children for whom the play group has become a vital experience may spend a
long summer worried about the future. This principle accounts for FW's
repetition of the announcement of temporary termination to ensure that
Carmen "got the message." In case a child is absent for the last session, it is
imperative that a note be mailed informing him or her of the fact of temporary termination; the gift should be mailed to the child or presented when
school reopens. Further, if it appears likely that a particular child may not
be continued in the play group in the fall, he or she should *not* be so informed in June, prior to vacation. One cannot assess with certainty the level
of disappointment such information may generate. It is not advisable to run
the risk of spoiling a child's vacation needlessly. Alterations in treatment
plans can be better accomplished in the fall.

When the children returned to school in the fall, the play group was
partially reconstituted with the addition of two boys. Gerry, one of them,
appears in the records for only a few sessions because he became hospitalized for illness. The second boy, Hector, was present in only one session and
then removed; he did not fit well in the group. *Carmen R.* was added in the
twenty-fifth session and remained until the group's termination. Two other
boys were added: *Alfonse* in the twenty-second session and *Michael* in the
thirtieth session. Both remained in the group. Referral information on these
added children will be supplied at the time of entrance.

Another change also took place: the group was now meeting in a new
location, much superior to the original one. It was more suitable in size and

design, and had a toilet facility directly accessible from the play room. All furniture and other equipment were the same as in the prior room. The children liked the new setting.

Session No. 13, Excerpts: All Present

Somewhat before the meeting time, Santa came to the play room door and peeked in. MW saw her and said, "Hello." She then left. Later she came with the other children and their escorts. Gerry, the new group member, sat on the couch with Carmen. Santa took the Candyland game, brought it to the round table, and asked Maria to play with her. Maria acquiesced but did not speak. Carmen joined the game.

. . . William obtained puppets and went to Santa, who was still playing the Candyland game, wanting her to "fool around" with him. She was annoyed and said, "Go away, I don't want to play with you." William continued to touch her and push her, then proceeded to mess up her game. She turned from the table, put her head down for a moment, and cried, apparently out of anger and annoyance.

. . . The new boy, Hector, had been fighting with William using the rubber puppets as boxing gloves. Earlier, when Hector had entered the play room, Gerry said, "I know him. He fights all the time!" William said he knew Hector also. Hector started to throw toys, wooden figures, and other items across the room. One hit Maria in the face as MW was about to intervene. Maria looked startled, then sat without moving or changing her position at the table where she was playing with a puzzle. FW applied a cold compress to Maria, above her left eye. William told Hector to sit down in a very firm tone of voice.

Comments and Interpretations

Santa visited in advance of the session to assure herself, perhaps to see the new play room. William immediately provoked Santa, trying to involve her in familiar interplay. It has been noted in many therapeutic play groups that, following a long interlude of vacation lasting more than two months, children will promptly engage in activities characteristic of them in past sessions, as if no time had intervened. A moving example occurred in another group: A young child entered the play room for the first session following the summer and immediately asked the worker: "Did you bring the clay you promised me *last week*?"

Hector quickly showed his unsuitability for this play group. He was impulsive and provocative, and if he had remained, the workers would have had to use extraordinary degrees of intervention to contain him and protect the others. This would have vitiated their meaning to the group members, who would then have perceived them as prohibitors. Children such as Hector can sometimes be helped in play groups with older boys who can limit their aggressiveness. When Hector was being considered for this group, it was not thought he would act-out so severely.

When a child is removed from a play group, the remaining members may become upset, especially in well-established groups. This is a reflection of anxiety about sudden changes in psychologically meaningful groups. The children seek assurances that provision will be made for the missing child, even though they may be privately gratified by his absence. Also, they are concerned that "disappearance" may happen to them. Should children inquire about the missing group member, the correct rejoinder is: "He/she comes another time." This always registers favorably with those who seek the information. Should a child leave the group by virtue of having moved to a new residence, the worker so informs the group.

It is truly dramatic how Maria became immobilized, not even expressing pain when struck by the small object thrown by Hector, so great was her guardedness and timidity. This despite the fact that she showed considerable relaxation in many other ways. One can anticipate more expressive and aggressive reactions from Maria only after she has herself become enabled to act out her repressed and suppressed feelings. At such time, given the realization that releasing anger is not in itself disabling, she may then direct her hostility against others at times when she feels like it. (In Chapter 1 we observed such changes in William and Cary, both of whom were formerly incapable of expressing themselves aggressively.)

Session No. 17, Excerpts: All Present

A new play item, an inflatable plastic Joe Palooka, was introduced. This was done to help some children in particular: Maria, to induce her to hit a "safe" object; William, to displace some of his mounting aggression.

. . . William became very excited with the large Palooka. He used it vigorously, punching it, his face becoming red and perspired. At one point William grabbed Maria around the neck, standing behind her, and then threw her to the floor. She quickly pulled her dress down, turned red in the face, and moved away from William *with apparent anger*. Later in the session William perched on Maria's back, even straddled her once.

. . . Santa was monopolizing the Palooka, even took it into the bathroom. She permitted Carmen to come with her but not William, who was locked out. When Santa carried the Palooka back into the play room, she lay down on it and hugged it. William tried to lay on it alongside of her. Santa allowed this. William put his arm around Santa affectionately for a moment.

. . . Santa called out to FW, "Mother," apparently without realizing what she had said.

Comments and Interpretations

The reasons for the use of the inflated figure were detailed earlier. William quickly used it with extreme aggression. Less often, some children will use the figure erotically. Santa, for example, lay prone with it in close embrace. It is important to mention that the plastic figure is adult size. This lends more significance to the ways in which children make use of it—aggressively and libidinally. In another such group, a six-year-old girl would straddle the figure and rhythmically move up and down upon it, her facial expression further emphasizing the blatant masturbatory nature of her actions. In this instance it was contrived to have the plastic figure "broken" and removed from the play group for a considerable time to get it "fixed."

William joined Santa in lying with the Palooka, even embracing Santa. It was Santa who was William's sexual object, not the plastic figure, which only served to mobilize the libidinal play. Earlier, William, who became very excited while battering the Palooka, threw Maria to the floor. Later he did it again, this time straddling her. Maria showed anger for the first time but could not act on it. It appeared that she was red in the face not because of anger but because of her extreme discomfort over the sexual connotation of William's act. This is why, despite her mixed feelings, she took time out to carefully pull down her dress.

Santa's "slip" conveyed an implicit meaning. In supervision conference, FW stated that Santa was unaware of the fact that she had called her "Mother." This incident further illuminates Santa's growing transference to FW.

Session No. 18, Excerpts: Present—Carmen, Santa, Maria

Carmen and Santa entered first, soon followed by Maria. Both boys were absent because of illness. Santa went immediately to the Palooka and organized taking turns with it. Maria took her turn quietly, gently tapping the Palooka, but she increased the intensity of her blows as she went on.

. . . Santa came over to the table where FW was setting up for finger painting and asked FW to paint with her. FW did so, setting out enough paper and materials for any of the other girls who wanted to join. Maria did come over and proceeded to finger paint. Her designs were freer than heretofore. She mixed paints on the paper to make it muddy, then threw it into the wastebasket and painted another picture with a free-form design. While this was going on, Santa told FW about a movie she had seen: Shirley Temple wanted to wear a uniform like a boy in the army. Her father was in the army and she did not have a mother.

. . . Maria was moving the Palooka closer to the table. She pushed a chair that was in front of Santa out of the way. Then Maria started to tap the Palooka so that it would manage to hit Santa on the shoulder as it veered toward her. Maria smiled as she continued this. Santa said nothing, nor did she even look toward Maria.

. . . Santa became involved with the Candyland game. She let MW and FW join her. Santa set it up favorably so that both MW and FW could advance quickly in the game. She said she was doing it for her "friends." Maria came close by, possibly to play, but Santa said, "No," gently.

Comments and Interpretations

Maria actually hit the Palooka, soon managing a few strong blows. Later she deliberately contrived to have the figure hit Santa. These pallid initial aggressions were "firsts" for her. As anticipated, the aggressions were experimental, tentative, and enjoyable. Also demonstrated in this session is the capacity of many needful young children to sense personal qualities of other children that can assist them in assaying new directions. Whereas Santa had shown many times that she could immediately react when others aggressed against her person, in Maria's case Santa actually tolerated the aggression, not even bothering to look at Maria. This amazing tolerance for the needy peer was again shown when Santa *gently* denied Maria entrance to the game with the workers. The relationship between the two had much earlier been identified as a *supportive ego relationship*—one in which each child derives therapeutic benefit. In this example Maria is both stimulated and supported by the stronger Santa; the latter derives a better self-concept as the helpful person.

Maria's experiments with the Palooka served to relax her further in other respects. Her use of finger paints in this session was markedly freer than all previous attempts. FW remarked about the easier physical motions she employed and the open, flowing lines of her paintings, as contrasted with Maria's exact, linear productions in earlier sessions.

Santa recounted the dramatic story about Shirley Temple to FW. In supervision conference, FW enlarged on this: Santa was truly impressed with the heroine's attempts to join her father by dressing in male uniform. And she had "no mother," something which Santa emphasized in the telling. Recall that in the prior session Santa unwittingly addressed FW as "Mother."

Session No. 19, Excerpts: Present—Santa, William, Maria

Santa entered first, went to the doll bed, and looked towards MW. She asked him, "Can I play house?" MW nodded. William and Maria then entered. William went to Santa, who asked him to play with her but received no response. William instead went to the blocks, trying to build with the long ones and knocking them over several times accidentally. MW tried to build them up with William, but they were not steady enough. William then played with the rubber ring toss game, saying that he had one like it at home and that he played with his father. Santa wanted to play with him but he pushed her aside. She insisted, so he went after her. William pushed and pulled her, shouting hysterically in a loud voice. Santa ran to MW and FW in turn for protection, although she was laughing and yelling. William threw her to the floor, sat on her back, and pulled her arms back as she yelled. He yelled louder, imitating her. He said, "Let me get you down and *you* sit on *me*, just to see how it feels. You feel like a cushion!"

. . . During this time Maria had been walking about, skipping, very active. She picked up the sweeper, tried to clean the floor with it, and then took it into the bathroom and did the same there. She went to the table, took crayons, and drew a picture rather hurriedly. She used the crayons with aggressive motions, slapping them down noisily on the table and holding them bluntly, not in the usual manner of holding a pencil or crayon. She completed the picture—a large one of stars, varied in size and shape, with many colors superimposed one upon the other, not in a particularly neat or orderly design.

. . . Santa had spilled a jar of red paint. FW helped her wipe the paint and also cleaned Santa's sweater, which had been spattered with the paint. Santa took the small mop, brushed the floor thoroughly, and proceeded to mop up the bathroom also.

. . . At snack time Santa grabbed the cookies, putting them in her lap. When she saw that MW did not have one, she broke one in half and gave it to him, saying, "For my friend."

Comments and Interpretations

The workers noted that Santa had begun to play with the furniture items—an open-front doll house, a baby crib large enough to hold a child, and a baby carriage. Santa knew she could use these items without the workers' permission, yet she asked MW if she could "play house." This can be understood as another evidence of the oedipal transference. Of pointed meaning is Santa's suggestion to William that he "play house" with her. This would indeed make the "house" symbolically complete in a gender sense. If this was Santa's unconscious motive in asking William, it implies a deepening feminine identity.

It required little provocation for William to again engage Santa in their sexual "game." While Santa sought the protection of the workers, this was only apparently so; her "teasing" of William was exciting and stimulating for them both. During supervision conference, the author evinced some concern about the varying meanings and the effects of such libidinal play for the two children. It was felt that Santa definitely benefited from it psychologically in that it fostered appropriate feminine identity, which was essential in order to correct her character defect. On the other hand, the author detected a manic, slightly hysterical quality in William's behavior at such times, probably due to the heightened anxiety such play aroused in him. This was deduced from the workers' elaborations about the way William screamed when chasing Santa. Further, for the first time, William sought to reverse roles in this thinly disguised sex play: Santa was to sit on him, just so William could find out "how it feels" (to "feel like a cushion"). Such an experience was not good for him psychologically in view of his problem. In effect, in such play he was assuming a feminine role. The workers were instructed to intervene indirectly should such episodes be repeated.

Maria was surprisingly active; she skipped about, a pronounced evidence of freedom. Also, she explored the entire setting with ease, as noted by her playing with the cleaning implements. As for including the bathroom in her cleaning activity, this is another example of her acute awareness of what other children had been engaged in previously, especially Santa. This, plus other observations of Maria's behavior, revealed a definite patterning after Santa. The two children in their supportive ego relationship were drawing different psychological benefits: Maria quite obviously was getting more support from it, and Santa the feeling of security. A question can be raised as to why Santa became Maria's unconscious choice for such a supportive relationship rather than Carmen, who had personal qualities similar to Maria's. While Carmen was like Maria in some respects, she did not fulfill the latter's inner needs, which Santa did. Santa represented a model for emotional release, a catalyst who loosened Maria's rigid character defenses.

Maria's manner of drawing with crayons in this session was much like Santa's, vigorous and free.

FW cleaned up Santa's accidental mess, without comment. Such acts represent continuing reaffirmations of "love." Neither by word nor implication do workers manifest displeasure with children's accidents, either real or, as sometimes happens, contrived. In response to FW's caring gesture, Santa reciprocated "lovingly" by voluntarily cleaning the setting. Later, Santa did not forget her particular "friend," who received half a cookie from her.

Session No. 21, Excerpts: All Present

. . . Santa had visited FW's office at 9:00 A.M. FW told her the escort would pick her up later.

William seemed to concentrate on Carmen during this session. He was quite rough with her, throwing her to the floor, sitting on her back, holding her arms, and firmly demonstrating much strength.

Santa's hair was combed neatly into a braided pigtail. She sat at the table and crayoned with interest and eagerness, intent on doing a "good" drawing. She discarded two drawings into the wastebasket. Maria joined her at the table, did one finger painting, then drew a crayon picture of three figures that looked like colorful clowns with definite expressions centered around their eyes. She looked up at FW rather furtively several times. William tried to get Santa to play with him several times, but she refused. He went toward Maria, who also ignored him. At one point he pulled the table and Maria *uttered a hissing sound*, annoyed.

. . . Santa tried to get away from William and went into the bathroom. Carmen followed her. She tried to close the door, and William forced his way into the bathroom saying, "I want to kiss you." William left when the girls pushed him out. He used some blocks near the couch, creating a barricade and saying he was making boundary "lines" to keep himself in. He used part of the couch and the blocks in fabricating the "lines." He was restless throughout the session. He kicked the puppets aimlessly into the air near where the girls sat. At one point he also kicked the rubber horseshoes into the air; then he stood on the table for a moment.

Comments and Interpretations

Once again Santa came to the worker's office early, in advance of the session. This was her special bid for "only" child status. It is common behavior with emotionally deprived children, and it is observed frequently in therapeutic play groups. Both her manner of dress and her physical appearance had changed perceptibly, evidences of important modifications in her sense of identity. The workers were beginning to report increasing signs of this from week to week. When Santa was referred, she always wore dungarees, rejecting feminine attire.[5]

Maria moved about apace, increasingly freer. She chose to use finger paints first, then crayons. Her drawings were of clowns, which had been the recurrent theme of Santa's drawings not long ago and occasionally at

---

[5]This play group was conducted in 1958, at a time when wearing slacks or dungarees was not as common with girls as today.

present. Here again Maria was "modeling" Santa. In her record, FW made special note of the clown's expressive eyes, as Maria drew them. Maria, like other quiet, self-effacing children, was a "looker," alert to all that went on. Well-defended children become habituated in such self-protective behavior, which is essentially the intent of the "observer" status. In group treatment of such children, when they become sufficiently relaxed to interact with others and are more mobile, they replicate activities that others have shown to be "safe" (acceptable to the workers). Emboldened by such experience, they then engage in more spontaneous behavior.

William "picked on" Carmen, more roughly than usual. His behavior had largely been tolerated by the girls, but there were episodes recently when MW had had to intervene to deflect his aggression, usually by moving him into a game activity. It was becoming increasingly evident that a noninterpretive form of therapy such as the therapeutic group might be insufficient for this boy. While the group served to encourage cathartic activity, which did help William to discharge tension, some of these activities—especially the sex play—seemed to generate further anxiety.

Another child, Alfonse, was added to the play group at this time. Alfonse was eight years, six months of age, in grade three. The original members of the group were now a year older than when referred. Alfonse started in the twenty-first session and remained with the play group for twenty-three sessions, following which his family was referred to a community agency for more comprehensive treatment. His referring teacher described him as "immature, inattentive, 'clown-like' in seeking attention, confused when reprimanded." He was jumpy and nervous and tended to daydream. Alfonse walked haltingly, with an uneven gait, sometimes in a mincing fashion. He was well-groomed, immaculate, and much concerned with his appearance. He could be aggressive and antisocial; and was inconsiderate of other children, pushing and tripping them. He sometimes defied the teacher, and former teachers found him to be extremely troublesome.

The mother was interviewed. Alfonse was an only child. The mother said he had been born in Italy, but she was vague about details, evidently not wishing to confide more. She herself was American-born. There was some inference that Alfonse may have been a child from a marriage to an army man stationed in Italy, from whom she was later divorced. Little information could be elicited about when Alfonse had last seen his father. Two years ago his mother had remarried. She claimed that Alfonse got along well with his stepfather, who, she added, was less restrictive than she in handling Alfonse. She worked during the day and was interested in a suggestion that Alfonse might join an afternoon center until she returned from work. She was quite willing to have him included in a play group. She proved less cooperative in the future, however, failing to keep appointments.

Session No. 24, Excerpts: Present: William, Santa, Carmen
(Alfonse attended session 21; he was absent this week.)

. . . William and Santa came in quietly. William sat on the couch; he said he had been sick during vacation (Christmas recess). He looked pale and thin. Santa was smiling. She wore a new dress that she said she had gotten for Christmas. She went to the easel, said she wanted to paint, took red paint from the supply shelf, and proceeded to paint the jars red. She then painted a picture of a house, for the first time since she had been in the group; usually she painted clowns or designs. She then walked to the round table and wrote some words from the reader that she used in class. William wrote a note to her that stated: "From William to Santa. I have a girlfriend." He showed it to her, and she pretended to read it but was largely unable to do so. William became quarrelsome, tried to push Santa, and pulled her hair. Santa cried and said, "I don't want to play." She rushed to MW, who was sitting on the couch next to Carmen, and jumped into his lap, whining like a baby. William crept into the large doll crib and then pushed himself back and forth across the room. Santa pushed him, called him "baby," and pushed him over to FW, saying to her, "He's my baby. Merry Christmas and Happy New Year!" She also took a turn getting into the crib.

. . . MW was reading a book to Carmen, who was most interested in it. William joined them for a few minutes. Then he became restless, took several rubber animals, and threw them at the dog puppet that he had placed on the table as a target.

. . . William pulled the doll away from Santa, and she went after him trying to get it back. She said, "You're a girl!" He rushed into the bathroom saying, "Yes, I'm a girl!"

Carmen was very helpful at snack time. She set the table and helped bring the milk tray.

. . . In the first session attended by Alfonse, no. 21, William had been very aggressive toward him, but during snack time he put his arm around Alfonse when the latter seemed shy about helping himself to food. William said to him, "I used to be shy."

Comments and Interpretations

Santa's "grandmother" had reported that Santa was now very much interested in wearing dresses and liked to have her hair combed out. More of this in a later evaluation report.

There had been a progressive alteration in Santa's appearance, which was becoming decidedly feminine. Also, the nature of her work in the group had changed, as indicated by the first drawing she made of a house. Her repetitive paintings and drawings of clowns in the past may have had some bearing on her ambivalence or confusion about sexual roles: clowns are masqueraders, and thus they are symbolic of multiple roles (sexes?). However, Santa was to show deeper regressive movement in the near future, heralded this session by her infantile whining in the lap of MW. There was plenty of room on the couch for her to sit *beside* MW, as did Carmen. The latter child had also become much more confident, and she too sought out MW more frequently than FW. In this session she asked him to read to her.

Carmen now assumed a providing role, perhaps in competition with FW, by setting the table and serving the food. This was exactly what Santa had done in a session much earlier, at a time when she was manifesting negative transference toward FW. For both children, this behavior was an expression of oedipal rivalry. To recall the referral information with respect to both children: Santa altogether lacked a male person in her family; Carmen had had little contact with her father, who left the family many times.

William vacillated greatly during the session. First he was "man" enough to "have a girlfriend"; then he was a "baby" in a crib; and finally, he confirmed Santa's ridicule by agreeing, "Yes, I'm a girl!" A further measure of the boy's insecurity, ambivalence, and anxiety, expressed unconsciously through the mechanism of denial, was his attempt to encourage Alfonse by reassuring him that he (William) had also been shy at one time.

Maria's family had been contemplating moving. This was not known at the time of group organization, and her leaving the play group was unanticipated. Her mother asked FW whether the latter could send a report to the receiving school, in another state. She was pleased with Maria's changed behavior, particularly her social growth. It was this request which first apprised the workers of the fact of Maria's leaving the play group. The mother was assured that whatever records she wished forwarded to the new school would be sent.

From a final evaluation report: Maria was referred because she never spoke to adults in school, though she may have whispered to children, and because she had very limited contacts with peers. She was orderly, was obsessively preoccupied with neatness, and avoided activities in which she might soil herself. She attended twenty-one group sessions, being absent only once because of a cold. She told her mother she liked the group and loved to play with finger paints. She also described some of the "bad" things other children did in the group. She never spoke to either worker, although she did smile frequently and began to utter reproving sounds when annoyed by other children. She became much freer physically and used the play room setting and materials readily. She definitely became more relaxed and expressive.

Maria's teacher described her as still a bit shy, but no longer isolated socially. She was generally accepted and liked by her classmates and now had several friends. She was invited to parties but limited her contacts only to girls. She participated in all class group activities and projects. She helped her teacher with various chores, and also was responsible for the class library.

It is unfortunate that Maria left the play group. There had been moderate improvement with respect to some characterological (possibly symptom) aspects of her problem. We can only surmise about what was psychologically nuclear in this case. More comprehensive information about Maria's pre-oedipal development would have been useful in establishing a definitive diagnosis and thus in further illuminating the meanings of events occurring in the play group that led to changes in her behavior and manner. Associated with her obsessive concern about cleanliness was a mild obduracy, which was interpreted by the author as negativistic hostility. Since such feelings are etiologically related to the development of obsessive character traits and compulsive symptoms, one of the primary goals of treatment is to enable the child to express openly her underlying hostility.

The play group experience would have eventually enabled Maria to act out aggression directly and more forcefully, which she was only beginning to do. But this would have required much more time. She would also have begun to talk in the group; there were beginning signs of this. While Maria liked to tell her mother about what the "bad" children were doing, she really enjoyed what she observed and was gradually working up to similar acting out. However, children who are initially as immobilized as Maria require two years *minimally* in a therapeutic play group before significant personality and characterological alterations can be accomplished and more healthy adaptive patterns established.

Another girl was added to the play group. Carmen R., seven years, nine months old, was in the second grade. Her teacher described her as "shy, quiet, fearful of new places and new experiences; she does not play with others." Carmen R. was physically slight, smaller than the average child her age. Her body movements were fluid, although she became rigid and tense in situations where she was confronted by something new. She would not hold hands with other children, keeping herself aloof from them. She responded moderately to the teacher's attempts to reach out to her, through the use of praise, for example. She resisted organized class games strongly, to the point of physical withdrawal when urged to participate. Once her teacher insisted that she join in a game and forcibly took her hand and pulled her into the game. Carmen R. relaxed a bit and appeared to enjoy it. She had fingered the teacher's dress when seated near her, yet, on another occasion when the teacher tried to pressure her into involvement, she said, surprisingly, "I'll tell my mother on you!" The teacher added that Carmen R.'s mother brought her to school, insisting on taking her directly to the classroom despite the fact that school regulations decreed otherwise. The teacher's impression was that the mother overprotected the child.

The mother was interviewed. The family consisted of three children, with Carmen R. being the oldest. The father deserted the family more than two years before, but he did visit occasionally and Carmen R. looked forward to seeing him. The mother said Carmen R. was not so quiet at home and sometimes argued with her siblings. However, the mother confirmed that outside the home Carmen was very quiet. She reported that Carmen was sickly, having many colds, fevers, and earaches. She helped the mother in household tasks, sometimes caring for the younger children when the mother went out to shop. The mother offered no additional information with respect to her husband or the reason for the separation. She agreed to Carmen R.'s participation in a play group when it was recommended on the basis that it could help her develop friendships.

Session No. 25, Excerpts: All Present

All the children arrived at the same time. William was particularly noisy and quick to fight today. He and Santa played with the Palooka. They sat on it and rocked it back and forth, playing seesaw, and did not permit any of the others to play with them. Alfonse was interested in playing with the Palooka, but William pushed him away at every attempt. He went after Alfonse to fight with him. When Alfonse said, "Why don't you let me alone?" William replied, "I want to fight with you." When Alfonse was pushed to the floor, William said he was playing football. MW intervened each time when it appeared that Alfonse might be hurt.

. . . Santa had taken the Palooka to the couch. She lay down on it and called William over to lie with her, addressing him as "Willie." He lay next to her and she rocked him back and forth, singing "Rock-a-bye baby." William left and went over to destroy Alfonse's block building. He then stood on one of the tables and dropped a block on the floor.

. . . Santa kept calling to William to get Alfonse off the couch. He wanted to join her in sitting on the Palooka. William came over each time she called and pulled Alfonse away. At one time he asked Santa if he should also take Carmen away. She replied, "No, only Alfonse."

. . . MW read to Carmen while they sat at the round table. The new group member, Carmen R., was sitting there also and was listening as he read, showing interest. She smiled shyly and frequently at FW, looking to her for support. She looked at the books, played alone with the doll family for some time, then walked over to the couch. FW spoke with her over the toy telephone. Carmen R. spoke quietly and with good English. She said, in response to FW's questions, that she had a brother and sister and mother and father—five members in her family.

. . . Santa sat in the doll crib with the Palooka, which had lost most of its air. Alfonse pushed her and so did William. The boys took turns getting in and out of the crib.

Addendum: Mrs. L., Carmen R.'s teacher, said that the child seemed to have had a good time, judging by her reaction when she returned to class following the group session. The teacher had had to escort Carmen R. to the play room earlier because she had started to cry when she was told about leaving the classroom to attend the group.

Comments and Interpretations

William continued his aggressiveness with Alfonse, who was now a focus of his anger. At least part of his behavior can be attributed to resentment against a new group member. Alfonse was no match for William, and MW had to intervene. A worker cast in a prohibitive role, no matter how subtly he may implement it, eventually becomes counterproductive if circumstances continually warrant his so acting. This relates not only to the child who is being limited—in this group, William—but also to the others in the group, who did not previously perceive the worker as a denying person. In a well-balanced therapeutic play group, it is the group itself that develops into a source of social restraint upon recalcitrant members. Once having acquired this capacity, a play group is able to reconstitute its sanguine nature following episodes of severe acting out by individual children. The present concern was whether this group could accomplish this without repetitive interventions by the workers.

Santa played with the Palooka using the couch, by choice. Most times previously she had played with the Palooka on the floor. Since the couch is identified with adult imagery, her play was taking on libidinal meanings related to the workers, particularly MW. This interpretation finds validity in Santa's bringing William into the scenario, nurturing him, not the Palooka, in "maternal" fashion. However, this "play" conveyed much the same sexual meaning of their previous engagements. William became palpably anxious as a result. He left and destroyed Alfonse's building, and he also "bombed" with a block from a standing position on the table.

Carmen R., the new group member, carefully observed the workers, in particular their behavior with the children. Carmen R. was another typical "looker." Evidently, despite her trepidations about coming to the play group, she became sufficiently assured that she was able to engage in a phone conversation with FW. Carmen R. denied the absence of her father when she conveyed the family constellation.

FW deliberately engaged Carmen R. with the toy phones. It is not generally acceptable practice in a therapeutic play group for workers to initiate activity with new children until they have become acclimated, and until other children have had an opportunity to work through their feelings about new members. There are attendant risks in so doing. First, the receptivity of the new child to the worker's overture cannot always be correctly assessed, and a frightened child may be driven further into isolation by even the mildest attempt. Also, in advanced play groups, the addition of a new member generates sibling rivalry that produces resentment and possibly aggression. When the group observes a worker selectively engaging a new member, this tends to mobilize jealousy.

Santa again reverted to "babyhood" in the crib. Thus, we observe discordant elements in her regressive recapitulation of emotional development: at times she acted "maternal," as with William on the couch; at other times she competed with FW in oedipal rivalry; then, in the same session, she whined like an infant in MW's lap or was trundled about like an infant in the crib. This inconstancy in role enactment has its own logic psychologically. In the throes of characterological and personality imbalance, which is brought into being during therapy by the penetrating influence of transferences, it is understandable why there can exist an ebb and flow of affective expressions—some highly regressive, others less so. It is the gratification of basic developmental needs, through repetition, over a considerable time, which creates a gestalt of maturational consequences and sublimations of infantile "residues."

Sessions Nos. 27–29, Excerpts

. . . Santa called the Palooka "Baby," and went over to hug it. William grabbed Santa with his legs around her head, on the floor, calling this maneuver a "headlock." Both tussled. He picked up her dress and pretended to spank her, hitting her once on the buttocks. She yanked away, looked at her dress, accused him of tearing it, and showed a little hole in the hem.

. . . Santa drew a picture of a clown, this time dressed like a girl.

. . . During most of the session, Carmen was playing with the doll and crib while sitting on the couch. She undressed and dressed the doll, once asking FW to help put on the apron. When Santa and William came over separately to take the crib from her, Carmen put her leg in the crib and held on tightly. She succeeded in holding it.

. . . William and Alfonse were getting uncontrollable; they took little blocks and started to throw them at each other. William stood on top of the table with Santa. Santa called to MW and jumped into his arms. William followed suit and so did Alfonse, each in turn. When William did so, he held MW's neck and then said, "Let me go. Don't hold me!" However, he came back several times to do the same thing. MW tried to limit the children's hyperactivity, but it was difficult to calm them. Observing this, FW began to set the table for snacks and called the children.

. . . William entered the play room with his arm around Alfonse. Alfonse seemed to be enjoying the "roughing up" that William handed out. Alfonse was always the one down on the floor, with William straddling him and bouncing up and down on him. Once William said, "I enjoy this." Alfonse most often smiled in response.

. . . Carmen took the lotto game and asked MW and FW to come play with her. She took the workers' hands, directing them to the table.

. . . Santa seemed disgruntled this morning. She took FW's smock and said, "That's mine!"

. . . MW intervened in the activity between William and Alfonse, as William was getting out of control. Alfonse was brought to the table to join in a game. He did so reluctantly. FW asked William to join in the game but he refused. Instead, he tried to break up the game. FW said that if William was unable to calm down, he might have to leave the room. He said, "O.K., I'm going," but made no attempt to leave. He came back to the game table and tried to sit down on the same chair as Alfonse, who was willing to let him, but FW brought another chair over. William was restless and did not accept the invitation. He walked away, climbed up on the other table, and proceeded to throw the puppets around.

. . . During the activity between Alfonse and William, William kept patting Alfonse on his back and face, calling him "My baby," and pretended to slap him whenever Alfonse whined.

. . . Santa spied the Palooka, which had been repaired since last week. She rushed over and grabbed it by its neck gleefully. She then put it between her legs and walked a few steps, awkwardly.

. . . At one point William grabbed Alfonse around the neck and said, "You're my girl, darling." Alfonse looked up at FW, which he did frequently, and said, "He's crazy," pointing to William.

. . . At one point William took one of the puppets and kicked it so that it hit FW. She said, "It hurt. And people . . . I . . . don't like to get hurt." She went over to William and tried to restrain him, holding both his arms. He then went to the table, climbed up, and tried to jump into MW's arms. He did so, then said, "Let me down." When he tried to jump on the Palooka, MW said, "It might break open." William said, "I'd like to break *you* open!" He added, "I'll build a fortress." He meant with the blocks.

. . . Carmen R. was weeping. It seemed she had misplaced her dime. Santa pointed it out to her on the table. FW said she would hold the dime until it was time to leave.

. . . William threw the Palooka at Alfonse. William said, "I like him, but don't like his friends." MW took the Palooka and said, "The sand might come out the bottom." William then took a rubber doll and threw it, and kicked and punched it several times.

. . . At snack time William wanted to sit next to Alfonse. FW said, "Here's a chair for you," pointing to another chair away from Alfonse since the one William wanted was occupied. William tried twice to get near Alfonse, and when he was not successful he said, "I don't want any milk," and sat down on the couch. He took the tall chair and tried again to sit next to Alfonse, during which he spilled the milk on Carmen R.'s lap. "I don't like girls anyway," he said. MW took William to the door and said, "We'll see you next week."

Comments and Interpretations

William wrestled Santa to the floor then picked up her dress and pretended to spank her. This was an open display of sexual curiosity. Santa drew another clown, for the first time identifying it by gender—female. Prior to this, her many clowns were gender-amorphous and undefined. This present drawing was another evidence of further crystallization of feminine identity.

Carmen had now become more capable of withstanding aggression and demonstrated her own growing capacity for it, when she managed to withhold the crib from both Santa and William. Carmen also openly made contact with both workers, actually drawing them by hand to play with her. She recreated her "family" intact.

As described in several separate excerpts, both William and Alfonse became hyperactive, with William usually the instigator in the interactions. While Alfonse complained periodically about William's roughness and MW had to intervene to protect him, Alfonse nevertheless seemed to derive pleasure from physical contact with William. This homoerotic experience may have been an indication of latent homosexuality in Alfonse, possibly also in William. To recall an earlier episode: William had straddled Alfonse and rocked on him, then had ordered Alfonse to do the same with him so that he (William) could find out "how it feels." And William could not keep from saying he enjoyed this activity. The boisterous hyperactivity accompanying such play pointed toward its sexual overtones. Another time William patted Alfonse, calling him "My baby," another spontaneous libidinal gesture, more maternal. These observations underscore the strong ambivalence and confusions associated with William's problem. MW sensed the sexual context of this play, as well as its manic quality, and he intervened. In response, Alfonse, more passive, allowed himself to be drawn into a table game; William refused defiantly. However, at another moment William did participate in the game of jumping on MW's back, an unusual type of contact for him. This contact made him anxious—he quickly wished to be let go. "Don't hold me," he said, but it was he who was doing the holding. This again revealed anxiety, although William seemed also to be struggling with a desire to claim MW's attention.

In yet another session, William held Alfonse and said, "You're my girl, darling!" As has been seen, Alfonse did respond to Wiliam's physical handling of him in a passive, receptive manner, which had the effect of further stimulating William's ardor. At the present time we could not be sure to what extent Alfonse's role vis-à-vis William represented identification of a feminine, homosexual nature. Whatever the underlying meanings, the interactions between these two boys were symbiotic and reflected marked ambivalences in their sexual identities.

A degree of homoerotic attraction between children in latency is normal. However, in William's situation, such additional factors as the nature of his interchanges with Alfonse, and the frequency of these episodes over a period of time indicated more than a normal degree of homoerotism.

Both workers attempted to limit William, ostensibly mindful of his excessive boisterousness and the possibility of hurtful consequences to other children. However, countertransference-induced reactions are evident, probably stemming from the sexual quality of the boys' interactions. FW told William that he might have to return to class if he could not "calm down." Another time she was "accidentally" struck by a rubber puppet. Her attempt to be neutral—"people . . . I . . . don't like to get hurt"—instead revealed by its tone her anger. When MW cautioned William about the possibility of the Palooka breaking, William blurted out, "I'd like to break *you* open!" Such strong negative transference acts toward the workers—really displacements from William's parents, against whom he presumably harbored extreme rage—do tend to assault the workers' own sense of security, and they tend to invoke reactive countertransferential responses that can lead to technical errors. However, it was necessary in William's treatment that he experience catharsis through negative transference expressions, and it was inevitable that these would occur in the transferences once established. The author anticipated having to explore countertransference-induced reactions in supervision.

By now a serious question had arisen as to whether the play group should continue with its present composition. The advantages for William were mixed; the group had become unbalanced and therefore was less efficient, and the workers' roles were in some jeopardy. The author concluded after these sessions that it would be better for William if he were seen individually. More of this later.

The denouement of William's hyperactivity, and the workers' inability to manage him, came when MW took William directly to the play room door and sent him to class. MW attempted to diminish the effect of the rejection by saying, "We'll see you next week."

A few comments about the others:

Santa's placing of the Palooka figure between her legs, an unusual, awkward maneuver, has copulative meaning.

Carmen R., the recent addition to the play group, appeared fragile, as implied in the referral. She wept easily, as when she thought she had lost her dime. The workers both felt she might need active support.

Another boy, Michael, was added to the group at this time. He was nine years, one month old, in third grade. He was described as defiant and sullen; he refused to conform and frequently abused his classmates. To quote directly from the referring teacher: "Michael's behavior is intolerable at times. He refuses to obey and is absolutely unmanageable in the class line. I have filled a truant slip for absence (possible truancy) and lateness and as yet have heard nothing from his parents." Michael's behavior was erratic; there were days when he acted out less. His teacher reported that he was not learning. Michael was receiving special speech correction lessons, and the speech teacher reported that his behavior in her room was acceptable—also that he was more responsive to her than to his classroom teacher. Michael was lean, well-built, and strong. His weight and height were commensurate with his age.

Michael's mother did not respond to an invitation to come to school while Michael was being considered for the play group. FW was able to reach her by phone. She offered little information at that time, and it appeared to FW that the mother was generally resistive. She agreed to have Michael join the play group, perhaps because she did not want to become personally involved. Also, she had had many communications from the school and knew of the difficulties her son was encountering. From later contacts with her it was learned that the present family consisted of herself, Michael, and his two sisters. The father was not at home, and it could not be ascertained how long this condition had existed or the reason for his absence. Michael did make occasional references to him in his class, and later in the play group. Michael said that his father took him on excursions and also on visits to relatives. Michael spoke of these events with evident feeling for his father; he seldom spoke of his mother. It could not be ascertained how factual were Michael's statements about the contacts with his father; it was felt that some of what he said may have been wishful thinking.

Evaluation of the submitted information about Michael, particularly his teacher's strong complaints about his aggressiveness, raised some question about his probable influence in the play group. However, on the basis of a continuing conference with his speech teacher, it was concluded that Michael had good potential for positive transference to adults and that, as a consequence, his deportment in the play group would not necessarily parallel that in his class. This assessment proved valid later.[6]

Session No. 30, Excerpts (Michael Added to the Group)

. . . Michael came into the play room happily. He went over to the Palooka immediately and sparred with it for a few moments. Alfonse entered, saw Michael, and said to him, "I know you." They greeted each other with smiles. Alfonse joined Michael in hitting the Palooka.

---

[6]Some teachers' referrals frequently reflect highly subjective reactions to children and do not necessarily prognosticate how children will comport themselves in a special therapeutic milieu. Often, a child's purported "extreme" behavior in school is actually negative transference behavior caused by a teacher's mishandling of the child. When a child is troubled to start with, such reactive misbehavior to unsympathetic adults is easy to understand. In some therapeutic play groups, children of this type have been successfully treated—this despite the referral descriptions of extraordinary acting out. See particularly the cases of Wayne and Frank in Chapter 3.

. . . Carmen entered with Carmen R. Her arm was around the latter, protectively. Carmen R. told FW that she had just had her picture taken and showed FW her comb. FW proceeded to bring the animal puppets from the closet and placed them on the table near Carmen R. The latter smiled at MW, who happened to be seated at the table. At one point Carmen took the crow puppet and plucked at MW's shirt and laughed.

. . . William was blasting away furiously at the Palooka. Santa wanted to hold it, but William pulled it away from her roughly and she dropped to the floor. She tried to get it again but was unsuccessful. William punched at it again, furiously, and then pretended that the Palooka was hitting him in retaliation. At one point he grabbed it and put it over himself, lying down.

. . . Alfonse and William hit the Palooka, but soon Alfonse left and got into the doll crib. William pushed him around the room, with Alfonse pretending to be a baby and talking in a whiny voice. MW persuaded Alfonse to build blocks with him, which he did readily. William was left playing with the Palooka.

. . . William paced around the room, bothering each member of the group. He grabbed and pulled at Carmen R., who was at the round table. When he was restrained by FW, he pulled doll figures off the table and went toward FW with his hand raised in the air, pretending to frighten her. He went over to Carmen, who was painting, and tried to distract her. She seemed annoyed and called out, "Mrs. M." William then went over to the block building that Michael was working on and destroyed it. Michael insisted that William rebuild it, and William said he didn't remember how. Michael insisted again, and William began to put a few blocks in order. MW was building with Alfonse. William took the dog puppet and placed it on MW's head.

. . . Because William was getting so excited and lashing out at all of the group, FW said, "You're losing control. You had better go back." He walked to the door, moved back into the room once more, and then dashed out to return to his classroom. Later, at the snack table, Santa asked FW, "Why did William go away?" FW replied that he was too excited.

Comments and Interpretations

Michael wasted no time in becoming involved; he required no "warm-up" period. Despite his tendency to act out in class and elsewhere, for which reason he was referred, he seemed relatively intact and adapted quickly to new situations. Later in the session, he reasonably insisted that William rebuild his block structure after the latter threw it down. The differences in the interactions between Michael and William, as compared to those between William and Alfonse, emphasize the important factor of psychological balance in groups. It is unlikely that an aggressive, angry, but essentially symptom-free boy like Michael would lend himself to the "neurotic" interplay that was characteristic of the other two boys. Rather, in a dynamic sense, Michael could be instrumental in interfering with excessive regression in the group. Michael contributed to the "checks and balances" that are vital as regulating social interventions and as reconstructive influences in group therapy. Further, his behavior helped obviate the need for a worker to intervene inappropriately. In order for group therapy to be maximally effective, the group itself must become a monitoring social influence. Michael would have been a better first choice for expanding the play group's complement than Alfonse. Unfortunately, even with the best forethought and planning, it is not always possible to prognosticate how certain children will affect the homeostasis of a therapy group.[7]

Both Carmens were doing well. Carmen R., recently added to the play group, was less fearful, perhaps because her namesake, Carmen, and, previous to her, Santa, were protecting her. The first Carmen had become more bold in her advances to MW.

William was now even more agitated and uncoordinated in his behavior. He was undoubtedly reacting to the presence of Michael. William apparently found it difficult to adjust to the presence of other boys in this group. While he had been much involved in various ways with Alfonse, he nevertheless was initially distressed with his being added to the group. And now he had to accommodate to still another boy, Michael. This was evidently more than William could do. He was an "only" child, confused and anxious because of the anomalous relationship of his parents. The psychological meanings of transference relationships with the co-workers were central and constituted the primary influences in his treatment, such relationships appeared to be dynamically interfered with by the presence of the other boys. We have noted that his interplay with Alfonse was mostly libidinal, reflecting part of William's inner problem, and such interactions had not been helpful. On the other hand, the presence of girls, particularly Santa, had been of value. He had been able to experience the girls as psychological "foils" with whom to affirm his difference gender-wise. William required individual therapy in which he could be helped to verbalize about some of the deeper implications of his feelings and behavior.

William's play with the Palooka is very interesting. It fuses libidinal and aggressive feelings. One can only speculate about whom the figure represented in this session, since William was still reacting to the direct interventions recently employed against him. In any case, after symbolically destroying the Palooka, William contrived to have the figure "hit" him in retaliation. He was then "vanquished" in punishment when he placed the

---

[7]An example of such group imbalance and of the need to modify the structure of a treatment group is seen in a film, *Activity Group Therapy*, that is available from the film library of New York University, Washington Square, New York, New York.

Palooka over himself on the floor. The Palooka's striking back is retributive; the Palooka's straddling him on the floor is libidinal, a further example of such spontaneous erotic enactment as we have witnessed at other times (as when William acted similarly with both Santa and Alfonse). One wonders whether William had actually witnessed the primal scene at home, so great was his need to indulge in erotic interactions. Much has to be surmised, because the mother was very resistive in the interview. Another theory may be ventured: William's assuming a position beneath the Palooka figure may represent a negative oedipal expression in relationship to his father.

It would have been better for the workers to have kept William for the balance of the session, without subjecting him to the sense of rejection he must have experienced. The workers had come to represent vital individuals for him. Some of Wiliam's acts were directly related to the countertransference-induced behavior of the workers during this and the preceding session. William's placing the dog puppet on MW's head—gently—was less retaliative than it was a bid for support. William had had more direct contacts with MW during recent sessions than at any previous time.

Prior to this session—the last one for William—the author had arranged for him to be seen in regularly scheduled individual sessions with MW.

Santa, who knew why William had to leave the play room, inquired about it nevertheless. It is rare that a child has to leave during a play group session. This procedure is invoked only in a dire emergency, which was not the case here. When evaluation of a child's behavior indicates the need for a change, the alteration should be made between group sessions to avoid placing the worker in the role of "punisher." Even when such a change is correctly implemented, other children will still inquire as to the whereabouts of the missing child. The indicated reply is: "He/she comes at a different time to play." Should the inquirer persist, seeking the reason for the change, a worker should reply, "It is better for him/her." These statements are true, although simply formulated. They are also reassuring to others—Santa in this case. Breaks in the continuity or composition of a group induce anxiety in young children, particularly in this group, where all the children had already experienced the traumatic effects of separation in their families. Anxiety induced by such events has the following connotations: "If it happened to him, will it happen to me?" Also: "Can it happen to me again? Are these grown-ups (workers) like my parents?"

When children question the loss of a group member, particularly when this follows upon obstreperous behavior by the absent member, the correct answer provided by the worker implies that the removed child has not actually been "punished" or cast out; rather, he or she is still being provided for. Thus, by identification, the questioner learns that he will also be assured of continuing protection under any circumstances.

Individual Sessions with William

MW continued with William on a once-weekly basis, in another, smaller treatment room that was also equipped with play materials, mostly of a psychologically projective nature. The treatment procedure used was analytical play therapy. The therapist more actively pursued underlying meanings, occasionally offering the child explanations and interpretations at proper intervals. As a follow-up, it is informative to study the content of several individual sessions held with William that show the boy's responses to the dramatic change in the nature of the therapy.

In the first interview, William was patently resistive to MW. MW attempted to explain to William the reason for the change to individual treatment along these lines: "I think it is better for you to come alone. Sometimes the group made you excited, which isn't good for you. Here you can play by yourself, or we can play together, and sometimes talk about what you do here and how you feel." William replied to this: "How long do I *have* to stay? Two minutes?" The worker replied that William *did not "have" to stay*, but that the worker would like to be able to be with him. Prior to this exchange, the worker had asked him, "How are things?" to which William replied, "It is not good for me between leaving school and going home. I get into too many fights." The worker sensed William's tenseness and kept him for only a short time.

For the second session, worker picked William up at the school library to escort him to the treatment room. William walked rather stiffly in the halls, hands at his side, until they arrived at the entrance door to the room. He then turned, jumped toward the worker, and said, "Boo! We're going into the haunted house." He was hyperactive during almost the entire session (fifty minutes). He jumped on and off a table, making as much noise as he could. Other times he simply ran all around the room without looking at the worker. He inspected all parts of the room and its equipment, and hid in the clothes closet for several minutes. One time he threw an alligator hand puppet about the room. The worker retrieved it from a ledge where it had landed and gave it back to him. William continued, kicking it instead. Then he sat down and wrote with a crayon, "I am a pig and cow—me, William," while laughing. He then drew a picture of the alligator and said: "This alligator is all tied up, but it can get away anytime it wants to." Next he wrote the following words: "I, WHO, IS, THE TALE," with his name following. He then spoke of a little girl whom, he said, he had known for seven years. Associating further to this, he added that he remembered her from when he was quite young, even before he was "one year old." The worker queried him about this. William said he had been in a carriage being wheeled by his mother in a park. He recalled green leaves being there, saying the park was "cool and shady."

William asked the worker many times about his (William's) ability to kick and jump. The worker praised his ability, which William liked. The worker observed that while William was almost as physically active as he had been in the play group, it was noticeable that he perspired less. He remained throughout the full session, without commenting about its length.

William was next seen two weeks later, having been away visiting his grandparents. The worker had a stack of playing cards on the table, and he and William played a game that William had suggested. William spoke little while playing, although he was excited about winning a game by a large margin. At one point he volunteered something about being "afraid" to play with his father. When asked why this was so, William replied that his father won all the time. When the session was over William lingered, reluctant to go.

William was seen in individual sessions for a considerable time.

Comments and Interpretations

William was manifestly tense during the first session; the dyadic experience, coming immediately after the play group, in which he had had opportunities to insulate himself from contacts with the workers when he felt it necessary, was responsible for the tension. His verbalizations were definitive in meaning: Did he have to stay, or was he priviledged to leave should he chose? The worker correctly informed him that he had a choice; William could determine whether he would choose to be a "patient." Also correctly, the worker added that he would like to be with William. Dismissing William early was also indicated.

In the second session the interaction was entirely different, dramatically so. William's stiffness in the authoritative setting of the school could barely be maintained until they reached the worker's room, when it disappeared immediately, to be followed by a frenetic exploration of the setting. William had to reassure himself of the permissiveness of the treatment experience, somewhat in the same testing manner as in the play group when he first started. Except now there was additional reason for his acting out in this way: He had to ascertain whether the worker would limit him as he had done in the play group only recently.

Of interest are the boy's level of verbalization and the content of his volunteered information, factors of much importance in analytical treatment. Children who communicate readily with respect to events in their lives, past and present, and who are intellectually bright, are admirable candidates for individual therapy.

William first derogated himself: "pig and cow—me, William." He insisted on being understood—*he* is the animal, or animals. He then carried this theme further, identifying himself as an alligator, a wild creature, "all tied up." The last comment indicated his suppressed rage. Yet, in the permissive treatment atmosphere, he could "get away anytime it wants to." The worker missed an opportunity for reflecting in a catalytic fashion: "Yes, I know. Here *you*, too, can act the way you feel." Such allusions by a therapist give substance to allegorical, symbolic projections of children's play, enabling them to make more open, personal disclosures of feelings. In analytical play therapy with young children, it is important early in treatment, at opportune moments, to give correct "samples" of the analytical procedure. This acquaints the child with the purpose of therapy and its direction. Melanie Klein has pointed out that the child-patient becomes a willing "guide" to the unconscious when he comprehends for the first time the accuracy of a therapist's interpretation of a play enactment that affords him some relief.[8]

William further revealed his suitability for analytical therapy when he free-associated from a girl he had known for a long time to an earlier recollection of himself as an infant in a carriage. The transference to the worker had readily carried over to the dyadic treatment. William volunteered significant information, and he was also responsive to sensitive questioning and explanations. In retrospect, it can be stated that an optimal treatment program for this boy from the outset would have been combined therapy— membership in a therapeutic play group composed of boys and conducted by a male worker, and individual play therapy with a female therapist. In such a play group he would have had more opportunity for male identification, more freedom to discharge his conflicted emotions in interactions with other children through "release" games, and more ego-strengthening experiences. This would have enabled him to deal better with the more penetrating inquiry of individual treatment, speaking as it did to his confusions, ambivalences, fears, and anxiety. As matters turned out, the play group did loosen his defenses, making him readily accessible to the worker, to whom he had already developed positive transference. The decision in his case to have MW continue with him in individual therapy instead of FW was predicated partially on the fact that MW, a psychologist, was more skillful in this treatment modality.

Sessions Nos. 31–42

Following the removal of William from the play group, it consisted of the three girls, Alfonse, and Michael. The group now proved to be in much bet-

---

[8]M. Klein, *The Psychoanalysis of Children*, W. W. Norton, New York, 1932.

ter balance, and the workers were able to maintain their accepting roles without the interventions that they had used in the recent sessions.

In order to abbreviate the record, without substantial sacrifice of informational content, the following material is focused on each child in turn during the next twelve sessions, bringing the play group to its usual annual termination in June.

Sessions Nos. 31–42, Excerpts

Santa: She became anxious over William's "disappearance" from the play group, and in the following session was agitated and hyperactive. Making no further references to William's whereabouts after her first inquiry, she nevertheless acted out in the very manner that typified much of William's recent behavior. It was as if, by depicting his behavior, she was reconstituting his presence. Seeking reassurance, she repetitively involved both workers. Often she called upon MW for the "game" of jumping into his arms.

Santa provoked Michael many times, interfering in his activities. Michael, however, was not like William, and he limited Santa, sometimes physically. More and more, Santa dressed in a feminine way. In one session she arrived wearing a new dress, her hair tied neatly in a braid. However, there were still episodes in which she acted regressively. There were also times when she saw fit to retest the workers to assure herself that she was still "loved"—that they would continue to accept her regardless of occasional acting out. Oftimes Santa showed her real progress by voluntarily cleaning up after making a mess accidentally with paints. In session 34, after again jumping from a height into MW's arms, she inquired about the relationship of the workers. . . . She pointed to FW and said, "Are you his sister? Cousin? Is he your father?" She smiled in a mixture of embarrassment and sheepishness.

At a following session she was dressed very prettily, with a bright yellow ribbon in her hair. She was unmistakably pleased with her appearance. At that session she told FW, in detail, the story of Rapunzel, the maiden with the long golden hair who was imprisoned in a tower. There were further evidences of improved sexual identity. Several episodes occurred wherein she again behaved like an infant, in MW's arms; once she lay in the crib. These acts were now short-lived, but still were evidence of the deep regressive pathways to which the transferences had led her.

MW conducted one session alone when FW was unavoidably detained at a meeting. The real depth of the transference bonds between Santa and the workers, and her still-present anxiety about separation—an experience that was responsible for the psychomalignant effects during her early development—were revealed in her immediate reaction. She asked, almost frantically, "Where is Mrs. M.? Where is Mrs. M.?" When informed, she then asked, "When will she come back?" Then she cried out, "Mommy, Mommy!" She looked at MW and smiled.

Once FW was offering a smock to Santa, who had indicated she wanted to paint. Santa refused it, adding that she wanted a "lady's" smock. The smocks available were made from discarded men's shirts with sleeves cut short. Later, when she wanted to remove the smock, she went to MW and said, "Poppa, take it off."

Santa once brought a piece of birthday cake from her home to the group. This gift represented, in essence, a psychological joining of two primary, familial influences. In succeeding sessions, Santa began to refer frequently to events in her home, and she spoke of "aunts, cousins," and others with whom she conceived herself to be meaningfully related. This development implied a beginning of transference dilution to the workers, which necessarily has to occur in therapy—regardless of the method used. Weakening of the transference and its eventual dissolution is one evidence of successful treatment.

Meanwhile, Santa continued to be moderately rivalrous with the other children. She showed this variously: She attempted to have the workers play with her alone, occasionally intervening when the workers were giving attention to others; she fluctuated between helping to support Carmen R. and then resenting her; she teased Alfonse a good deal (Alfonse had become increasingly infantile in his behavior); and she sometimes teased Michael and at other times joined him in acting out. However, in all these interactions with others, Santa's behavior was reasonably tolerable, and she was able to respond more acceptably to the denials and resistances of the other children.

Alfonse: He behaved in a babyish manner, whining or asking others to indulge his whims. He used the baby play toys and furniture in a regressive way, placing himself in infantile roles. He developed a pattern of pretending to phone his mother on the toy phone, speaking in a dependent, whining way. The cross-transference situation was apparent: mother equaled FW. In the play group he "phoned" his real mother as an unconscious enactment of his regression. His mother was known to be very impatient with him and physically punitive. In a sense, Alfonse's phone calls were pleas for her to nurture him in a dependency position, accepting his infantile behavior as the group generally did. The workers remarked on the intensity of his dependency needs in the play group and were concerned about this behavior becoming habituated. For this reason, both workers—more MW than FW—tried to divert Alfonse from his "baby" play into other activities and games. Such interventions did move him to higher-level involvements, but it was questionable whether they had lasting effects. As might be expected, Alfonse became the occasional butt of ridicule from other children. This did not change his ways essentially, which was another evidence of his fundamental immaturity. Alfonse displayed passive qualities that had first been observed earlier when he permitted William to manhandle him. This persistence of passivity further indicated the possibility of homosexual tendencies.

Michael: He attended ten group sessions between the time he was admitted to the group and its seasonal ending in June. As noted earlier, Michael participated actively from the outset. He was vigorous and interested in everything the play group had to offer. At first his behavior was reasonably acceptable—this during the early sessions when he seemed to want to take advantage of all the activities available. Then he began to test the latitude of permissiveness, spoiling things made by others, bothering some of the children physically (although not excessively so), teasing Alfonse, and in other ways. Occasionally the workers—mostly MW—limited this carefully, and Michael accepted their restrictions without a sense of rejection. Children new to a play group necessarily have to test the workers' permissiveness in ways reminiscent of the original members' early patterns. Michael manifestly enjoyed every minute of his participation in the group and looked forward each week to the next session.

Michael worked creatively with clay and received praise from the other children and from the workers. He would occasionally act to restrain Alfonse's infantile play, and he also braked Santa's provocations when she was so inclined. Michael served as a group neutralizer in these ways, exerting a moderating influence on the children's interactions. He was less aggressive with both Carmens, in a way sensing their vulnerability. Occasionally he would tease them. The boy's essential intactness was shown in many ways, particularly in the manner in which he accepted indirect interventions when these became necessary to direct him into other activities. His rivalry feelings were not extraordinary, nor did he make excessive bids for the workers' exclusive attention. He liked to recount experiences he had had with members of his immediate family—mostly his father—and with relatives. Some of this was undoubtedly exaggerated, if not altogether wishful. Nevertheless, it was evident that Michael did experience some positive relationships at home and elsewhere. All in all, Michael moved into the play group easily and demonstrated resilience, in sharp contrast to the more obstreperous behavior in his classroom that had led to his being referred. He proved a good addition to the play group and his presence, more than any other child's, restored the balance of the group.

Michael's adjustment to the play group supports the principle in group therapy that when children are added to a group in an advanced stage, it is best to consider more ego-intact children than those who are immature, overly dependent, passive, or neurotic. It is much easier for the child who is emotionally stronger, despite his presenting problems, to "catch up" psychologically with the group. Moreover, such children complement the progress that the group members may already have made, whereas more seriously troubled children who are added late would tend to hinder the play group. This latter effect derives from the group members' desire not to re-linquish their growth gains—not to have these further challenged by regressive and other immature behavior patterns of new members.

Carmen: Carmen became increasingly involved with the crafts media. She painted and used clay, fingerpaints, and other media. She was very happy in this work. Carmen was no longer shy and continued to make contact with the others, notably with Carmen R., with whom she maintained a protective relationship. Both girls were often together when they came to sessions: They worked together and left that way at the end of each session.

Carmen's bids for MW increased. These were solicited unaggressively, with shy smiles, whenever she sought him out. She still liked to sit on the couch while MW read a story to her. While she also had contacts with FW, they were minimal as compared to those with MW. She obviously was in an oedipal relationship with him. This occasionally brought Santa down upon her because of jealously. If Carmen was jealous, she lacked the aggression to demonstrate it strongly. She spoke more often but still was generally limited verbally, a characteristic quality from the beginning of treatment. Typical of her present behavior is the following excerpt from session 37.

. . . Carmen entered the playroom. She wore a new dress, also pretty new shoes and blue tights to match the dress. She was carrying a little purse and opening it, showed FW the contents. She told FW that she had more pretty dresses at home. Then she walked to MW, plucked at his sleeve, and asked him to read some books to her. Later she asked that he play a game with her. . . .

This modulated behavior was typical with Carmen through the sessions ending in June.

Carmen R.: She was markedly timid. From information gathered at the time of referral and subsequently, it was learned that her mother "babied" her, overprotected her, and at the slightest sign of illness kept her home for protracted periods.

Carmen R. was no longer fearful of coming to the play group, as she had been when she cried when the teacher brought her to the first session. Carmen R. responded well to Carmen's protective ministrations; both children established a tight supportive ego relationship, with Carmen R. the passive, receiving member. Despite Carmen R.'s timidity, it was obvious to both workers that the child enjoyed her membership in the play group. She continued to glance at the workers shyly, and when she caught their encouraging, responsive smiles, she would smile in return. FW sensitively engaged her from time to time in simple crafts or games, which Carmen R. liked. MW also did this, and Carmen R. seemed to respond as positively to him as to FW.

One thing was evident with respect to the other group members: they sensed Carmen R.'s essentially passive, retiring quality and left her to her own devices, though sometimes they helped her. Even Santa, who was sometimes jealous of the workers' attention to others, saw fit to help Carmen R. Only Alfonse, who was indeed very immature, seemed oblivious to Carmen R.'s vulnerability and, in his generally immature way, sometimes bothered her. When this happened, Carmen R. showed her lack of aggressivity and her inability to tolerate aggressivity in others. She immediately became frightened and looked about for protection. Despite these trials, Carmen R. was profiting from contact with the children and was beginning to show signs of spontaneity in her behavior, which had been altogether lacking before.

Resumption of the Group in the Fall

When school resumed in the fall, FW was no longer there; she had been transferred elsewhere by the Board of Education. Both workers had known of this as a possibility, and tentative plans had been made to deal with it if it eventuated. Alfonse no longer attended the school; his family had moved, without informing the school as to their new residence. This is not altogether uncommon with families living in marginal circumstances who are subject to sudden moves from one location to another on short notice. The play group was reduced to Carmen, Carmen R., Santa, and Michael. MW met with the group for the following ten sessions, after which it was decided to form separate play groups, one for girls, the other for boys. Thus, within a short space of time, Michael became a member of an entirely new play group. Also, a new child, Evelyn, was added to the girls' group. MW conducted both groups on different days.

The children's adjustments to the various changes, particularly the loss of FW, are significant and will be described in more detail. The following events are extracted from sessions 43 through 55, at which point the division into two play groups was made. As might be expected, the departure of one worker had immediate impact, for several reasons. First, all the children had experienced such "losses"; second, despite their individual improvements in response to treatment, the transference bonds to both workers were still pregnant with meaning.

When the children assembled for the first session without FW, MW explained that FW had been "*sent by the Board of Education*" to another school and that *she had wanted to remain but could not*. Such information, accurate in substance, is phrased so as to have the children understand that another authority was the agent of their loss, not FW. Thus, she did not "desert" them; she was "taken" from them. This helps perpetuate the children's ideation of FW as they knew her.

Sessions Nos. 43–46, Excerpts

. . . Michael and Santa were the first to inquire about FW's absence, both appearing visibly alarmed by it. They asked whether she would "ever come back." MW replied that he did not know. They then asked where she was, and MW replied, "In another school." Carmen and Carmen R. did not inquire; both sat close to MW.

. . . Again Michael and Santa inquired about whether FW would come back. Santa asked also if they were going to have "bread" to eat that day. By this she meant sandwiches. She reminded MW that FW had on occasion supplied sandwiches for snacks. MW said he had none that day but would bring them next time. Santa then asked him about a doll, whether she could use it. She had a play washboard and said, "I want to wash the baby's clothes." Michael asked MW to paint a boat for him. MW told him that he would bring tools and wood, and that they would build a boat together. Michael was pleased.

Carmen was absent. Carmen R. frequently smiled at the worker. At one point she brought some books to him. The worker picked one, sat on the couch with Carmen R., and read to her. Several times Michael and Santa came over quietly to listen. . . . Carmen R. got on the hassock several times and moved it gently toward the worker. She obviously wanted him to push her.

. . . Carmen R. took male and female hand puppets, pressed them together face to face, and smiled at the worker. Santa saw this and laughed aloud. Michael and Santa climbed up on the low cabinets. . . . Carmen had taken the Candyland game and asked the worker to play with her. Santa came to join the game; Carmen R. came only to watch. . . . Santa did not leave the play room with the others at the end of the session. The worker had to leave for a moment to go to the office. When he came back, Santa was still in the play room. She left, saying that she would see him next week.

Comments and Interpretations

The insecurity caused by the absence of FW was openly manifested and was also seen in subtle ways. First, the children directly inquired as to why FW had had to leave, repeating this in a following session, as if the event were altogether incredulous. Further, the children congregated near MW, unconsciously expressing their anxiety about the loss and seeking reassurance through contact with him. Both Carmens were only able to express themselves silently, remaining close to the worker. Carmen R., who was markedly shy, nevertheless was capable of seeking out MW, bringing books to him and silently managing to have him give her a "ride" on the hassock.

For several sessions all the children were quite subdued in manner.

Their behavior was equivalent to "mourning" reactions after the loss of a loved one.

Several other incidents are laden with meaning:

Santa acted in a mixed dependent and assertive fashion. For example, she sought permission to do things with the doll, permission that she knew from the past she did not have to solicit. This play affirmed several needs: to be reassured by MW that he would still allow her to do as she wanted; to reconstitute the "family" via "mother play"; and also, perhaps, to supplant the missing FW entirely.

Carmen R., a silent child, created a play scenario of a complete family when she brought the mother and father puppet dolls together. Perhaps she too, as she shyly smiled at MW during her play, unconsciously revealed that she herself might act as a substitute for FW.

The true depth of Santa's sense of loss and her anxiety is revealed by her remaining behind after all had left the play room. Moreover, she awaited the return of MW, who had had to leave the room momentarily. And it was Santa who told MW that she would see him "next week." This was an exact rendition of a phrase used repeatedly in the past by both workers when the children left at the termination of a session.

Such were the manifest and subtly poignant expression of the children's sense of loss, an experience which, in their own families, they had earlier suffered the consequences of. Our present concern is to observe how they managed this present crisis.

Sessions Nos. 47–53, Excerpts

. . . The worker felt a small hand in his and, turning to see, realized that it was Carmen R.'s hand. Santa asked Carmen R. something, speaking in Spanish. Carmen R. replied in Spanish. Santa said to the worker, laughing, "I asked her if you were her father, and she said, 'Yes!'" The worker looked at Carmen R., who smiled up at him and then turned her face away shyly.

. . . Michael and Santa were pleased with the new workbench (added that session, particularly for Michael). Santa made a cross of wood; Michael, a ship. He asked the worker's help frequently . . . Carmen R. and Carmen both climbed up on the low cabinet and sat there, with their feet dangling. Then Carmen called to the worker, who was at the woodwork bench, to tell him that Carmen R. had jumped to the couch from the cabinet. (This was a common play activity of other children in the past and occasionally in the present.) The worker moved over and sat to watch. Carmen R. did not jump. The worker stood, opened his arms, and then she did.

. . . Later, Carmen R. grabbed a chair to sit next to the worker at snack time.

. . . Carmen R. started to saw a piece of wood at the workbench. There was little wood available; the children had already used much of it. Michael grabbed the saw from her. He then ran about the play room chasing Santa and Carmen. The worker tried to distract him by suggesting that they build something together. He and Michael started to build a fort with blocks. Santa sat at a table, crying. Michael had hurt her during the chase. The worker walked over and held her in his arms without saying anything. She continued to cry for a few moments. She didn't appear angry.

. . . Both Carmens were playing with clay together. Carmen R. spoke to the worker directly, for the first time since she had been in the group. She said, "I'm making a house." She repeated this for Carmen. This was the first time the worker had noticed her speaking to another child in the group, except for the query she had answered in Spanish.

. . . Santa said she wanted to help the worker clean up before she returned to her classroom. She had earlier asked who was going to clean up the room, and the worker had told her he would. Carmen R. left the play room with her escort, but she quickly returned saying that she wanted Santa to take her to her room. Both joined in cleaning up.

Note: Santa's family moved and she was transferred to another school nearer her new residence. The worker arranged with the principals of both schools, her new school and the former one, for Santa to continue to attend the play group. Santa's "grandmother," who was pleased with this arrangement, said she would escort Santa to and from the old school.

Comments and Interpretations

Carmen R. was now making direct contacts with the worker. Santa expressed the libidinal attraction that Carmen R. felt toward the worker when she playfully asked Carmen R. if the worker was her father. Thus, both children expressed their oedipal attachments—one directly, the other teasingly. Further, the rivalry feelings of Carmen R. become manifest at the end of the session when she returned to the play room supposedly to have Santa, rather than her escort, return to the classroom with her. However, Carmen R. revealed a hidden motive: jealousy. She remained with Santa and the worker to help clean up.

The worker had introduced woodwork for Michael in particular. When it is indicated, new materials are added to the available supplied to accommodate special needs and growing interests and capabilities. Woodwork is a resistive medium, even in its simplest forms, and an excellent activity for sublimating aggression and encouraging creative output. It is classified as a *libido-binding* material, in contrast to other *libido-activating* supplies.[9]

_____
[9]See Glossary.

Carmen R. experimented with aggression: she dared to jump from the low cabinet to the couch, an activity that she had studiously watched other children do. When the worker walked over to watch, Carmen R. became embarrassed, but then, encouraged by his extended arms, she jumped. Emboldened by such successes, she contrived to sit next to him at refreshments. In still another session, she tries her hand at woodwork, a further expression of her growing confidence.

It is questionable technique for the worker to have voluntarily comforted Santa as he did—holding her in his arms after Michael made her cry. Affective demonstrations of this nature can increase anxiety in children who are working through oedipal feelings. Further, such demonstrations tend to foster rivalry feelings in the other children. As we have seen, children do seek physical contacts with workers in various ways—by sitting close to the worker, jumping into his arms from a height, and so on. At such times the worker should merely *allow himself to be so used*, thus momentarily gratifying the child's need. However, it is quite different to "sponsor" libidinal feelings in children by deliberately touching them. In the earlier instance, with Carmen R. hesitating to jump from the cabinet, it was acceptable technique for the worker to encourage her with his open arms. However, it was altogether different when he placed his arms around Santa. This act is an example of positive countertransference; in its effects upon the child it may be as obstructive to the purposes of psychotherapy as would be an act stemming from negative countertransference.

Carmen R. was progressing well in the relatively short time she had been in the play group. She now spoke out, first in Spanish and then openly in English, and addressed the worker.

Santa's transfer was effected unbeknownst to the worker or to the author. Such occurrences create problems in school-based treatment programs. They happen quickly—as when a parent merely informs a school secretary or teacher that the family has moved or is in process of moving. A school secretary is usually unaware of the implications of such transfers. A child's teacher, who should know better, may also routinely go through the motions of filling out transfer records, forgetful of the possible dramatic effects such a separation may have. In this case, Santa found herself "cast out"—it was as if no one cared about her anymore. When the principals of both schools were apprised of the circumstances and the probable traumatic effects of such a sudden termination, they agreed promptly to Santa's continuation in the play group through visitations to her old school in the company of "grandma." As noted earlier, the "grandmother" was eager to have Santa continue in the play group. A simple woman, she was nevertheless aware of the progressive improvements in Santa since her start in the play group. As for Santa, what could have ended as a psychological disaster was converted through this special arrangement to an important substantiation of therapeutic commitment: she was "loved" so much that the worker ensured that she would remain in the play group.

Parenthetically, it is obviously important that those who are involved in therapeutic programs within public schools inform administrative and clerical personnel of the need to consult with clinical practitioners before administrative actions that could in any way interfere with ongoing counseling or therapy are set in motion.

Something should be said about children's use of foreign language in therapeutic play groups. To start with, bilingual children rarely speak in their primary language in the group. Such behavior is most often a form of negative transference, when it is deliberately employed to keep a worker in the dark regarding the meaning of a communication. In our experience, when this is done, it is with hostile deliberateness on the part of the child. It is rare in a play group, since much of negative transference, which is necessarily part of any form of psychotherapy with children, is enacted spontaneously and behavioristically, not through *deliberate* use of a foreign language. As we have seen in this group and in other chapters, positive transference to the worker is the pervading relationship, with negative expressions occurring only episodically and transiently. The positive relationship to the worker is fundamental and omnipresent, even at moments when negativism is evident. It is this sanguine relationship which blocks children's use of language incomprehensible to a worker. In some play groups the common language of the children was Spanish, and, moreover, they were more facile in that language than in English. Nevertheless, children have been known to scold another group member who may have used a Spanish word or phrase even unwittingly. "Don't speak Spanish! He/she [the worker] doesn't know it." Santa's question to Carmen R., about the worker being her father, was couched in Spanish. In this instance the "concealment" had libidinal context that may have momentarily led Santa to disguise it. Yet, a moment later, she openly revealed the oedipal "secret" to the worker, although with some minor embarrassment.

Sessions Nos. 54 and 55, Excerpts

. . . Carmen R. was absent. Santa met the worker outside the play room door and shook her fist at him playfully, saying, "I'm going to beat you up!" Michael and Carmen came in later with Michael stating that they had been there earlier but the worker was not there so they had left. The worker thought Michael was concerned that he (the worker) might leave as FW had. He said, "I'm not going away, Michael." Carmen sat on the couch with a book for the early part of the session.

. . . All three children asked for the worker's attention an inordinate number of times during the session, probably due to the length of the intervening holiday, Christmas recess. Santa asked the worker to bring the paints to her where she was seated, and she remained there for most of the session, painting. The worker placed some paper on Santa's lap and a piece of oilcloth around her dress so that she would not spatter herself. She obviously enjoyed this, although she shook her fist again playfully a few more times, as she had done at the beginning of the session. . . . Carmen asked the worker to cut out a horse for her, and she then made a card of it, giving it to the worker as a gift at the end of the session. Michael saw this and also asked the worker to cut out something for him.

. . . Santa asked the worker if he had any little girls. The worker replied by asking her if *she* wanted to be his little girl. She smiled and said, "I'm going to beat them up!" (referring to the worker's "girls," about which she still had not received an answer). Santa remained behind for a short time after the session to clean up. . . .

Comments and Interpretations

The worker felt that the holiday intermission had caused the children to feel insecure again, with this accounting for the many requests made of him for assistance. Moreover, he felt that Michael's initial statement about the worker "not being there" was actually a fearful expression of the possibility of termination of the group. These episodes still reflect the anxiety initially generated by the "loss" of FW, which had increased the children's sensitivity to absences and time lapses. Whatever the underlying reason or combination of reasons, the worker correctly reaffirmed the continuity of the group and his own presence through words and actions.

The worker protected Santa's clothing, a reasonable act. However, even such superficial touching was sufficient to mobilize libidinal and rivalrous feelings in the child. She wanted to know whether the worker had children of his own. The worker's response to this was an error: in this activity method of therapy, interpretations of a child's behavior are incorrect; in fact, they may interfere with the therapy. As indicated elsewhere in this book, in activity therapies there is no psychological gain for the client when information or interpretations are offered that cannot be utilized profitably in the treatment. In analytical group therapies, on the other hand, explanations and interpretations of children's unconscious intent may be made part of the interchange at appropriate times. In these procedures it is incumbent on the therapist to help his clients grasp more than the manifest meanings of their expressions and behavior. It should be borne in mind that the analytical group therapies are used with different types of clients. Santa can only enact mock anger (real jealousy) by stating how she would hit the worker's "girls"—if in fact he had them.

Note: At this point the planned changes into two play groups were made. Michael and Alfonse (who had been absent for weeks because of illness) were placed in a new boys' play group. Another girl, Evelyn, was added to the girls' play group. Evelyn was referred because of extreme shyness and a need to provide her with social experiences.

The documentation that follows will deal with the girls' play group, in order to continue our focused study of Santa.

The time was considered opportune to effect the changes. The children seemed to have managed the "loss" of FW fairly well. Changes in the group would not be reacted to as additional separation experiences, since the children would continue with the same worker. Moreover, it would be of some value to test their resilience under new circumstances.

Psychologically, a number of factors indicated the desirability of homogeneous groupings from this point on. For Alfonse, a group of boys would tend to place more limits on his immature behavior and would provide more suitable identification models. With regard to the children as a whole, they were at an age where they tended to gravitate more to peers of the same gender.

Session No. 56, Excerpts (First Session with Evelyn Present)

The worker introduced Evelyn to Santa, Carmen, and Carmen R. Immediately, Carmen asked about Michael, as did Santa. The worker explained that there was going to be one group for girls and one for boys. They seemed pleased. Santa said that she knew Evelyn. Santa asked the worker for her paint set. A few sessions earlier she had asked the worker to hold it for her. The worker replied that he had given it to someone for safekeeping but had forgotten to bring it today. Santa was pleased because he had seen fit to "protect" her paint set. Santa bossed Evelyn about for the entire session. She told Evelyn to build with her and directed her as to which blocks to get.

. . . Carmen R. went to the low cabinet and started to jump down to the couch. When Carmen saw this she also went on the cabinet, but instead of jumping, she asked the worker to take her down. Actually, she jumped into his arms. Santa then asked the worker to help her build a house. Carmen came over to show the worker a reader and asked him to read it to her. They sat on the couch near where Carmen R. was seated. The latter snuggled up to the worker as he started to read.

. . . Santa was talking a lot about her new school. She said she liked it because boys did not hit her now. She *called Carmen "tomboy," adding, "That's why boys hit you!" She spoke for several minutes without letting up about the subject, repeating that Carmen was a "tomboy." Santa added, "I play with girls. I'm not a "tomboy." She also called Evelyn "tomboy"* later in the session. The worker asked Santa if she was "worried" about being a "tomboy." Santa laughed but said nothing in reply. Just before snack time, Santa picked up a book and said she was a teacher.

She asked the girls if they wanted to play games, and they all came over for a few minutes while Santa sat at a table acting like a teacher.

Comments and Interpretations

The children showed some concern about the changes. While Santa appeared to welcome Evelyn, she placed her in an inferior position, bending her to her will. This was her way of establishing primogeniture. Rivalry for the worker's attention is obvious in the interplay between Carmen, Santa, and Carmen R.

Santa's comments about "tomboys" are fascinating, since they bear on her nuclear character problem, for which reason she was referred for treatment. Her remarks reveal open awareness of basic changes in herself, her new self-perception. This is an excellent example of derivative insight.

The worker's question to Santa as to whether she "worried" about being a "tomboy" was a blunder. Actually, the question was entirely gratuitous and may have been obstructive to the interchanges taking place between the children. Santa could not possibly have replied to the question, the answer to which is based on subtle and complex unconscious factors, much beyond a child's capacity to formulate meaningfully in words. Analytical techniques are not fitting in activity-group therapy. The modifications and strengthening in Santa's character structure with respect to her sexual identity were the consequences of penetrating psychological influences stemming from deep transference relationships with both workers, as well as arising from other complex psychodynamic factors inherent in the long-term corrective reexperience in the play group. Fortunately, the changes in Santa were by now well crystallized and could not be undone by chance technical error. One could further surmise that Santa's teasing the other girls as "tomboys" was an unconscious projection on her part, a form of denial of masculine qualities within herself. As such, her behavior points to *residues*, not *essential* character. Santa had been helped reconstructively. While there may have been character residues reminiscent of the past, they were not in psychological ascendance.

Sessions Nos. 57–63 (Termination of the Group), Excerpts

. . . Santa was pleased to see that her paint set had been placed out for her. She quietly took it and asked the worker for drawing paper. Carmen sat at the other end of the table from where Santa painted. She gave the worker a picture of herself, and another which she identified as her brother. Santa said she didn't believe the person was Carmen's brother. The worker put the pictures in his wallet. Santa commented on this and said to Carmen, "I'll beat you up!"

. . . Santa asked the worker to open a paint jar, calling him by his first name. Carmen asked the worker if that was his name. He confirmed that it was.

The worker had noticed when Carmen R. entered the play room that she was in distress; her eye was red and she may have had a cold. He suggested to her that she see the school nurse later about her eye. Carmen overheard this and said that the worker was a "doctor" and he could take care of Carmen R. The worker replied that he wasn't "that kind" of doctor. Santa said the worker was the kind of doctor who took care of you when "you're nervous." (Evidently some of the children had heard the worker addressed as "Doctor," meaning Ph.D., elsewhere in the school building.)

. . . Carmen R. brought a book to the worker, sitting next to him on the couch. Carmen had taken out the domino game and tried to get Carmen R. interested in playing with her. Carmen R. would have none of it, so Carmen also brought a book over to the couch and started to ask the worker questions about it. The two Carmens started to fight with each other. Carmen chased Carmen R., who frequently sought the worker's protection.

. . . Carmen R. was absent. The session was extraordinarily quiet, with the three girls painting silently through most of it. Carmen asked the worker to read to her. He did so and then went to Santa, who had asked for help. Santa asked if the boys' group had used her paint set (which she still had the habit of leaving behind). The worker told her that he had not left the set out when the boys' group used the play room. Santa was pleased. Emily shyly smiled at the worker during the session, but she did not speak.

. . . A teacher informed the worker that Santa had inquired about the worker's whereabouts the previous week. The worker had been ill, which had necessitated cancellation of the play group session. When informed by the teacher that the worker was ill, Santa said she wanted to see him. On the day of the present session, Santa met the worker as he entered the school building. She shyly asked whether he had a picture of her. When told the obvious answer, that he did not, adding, "But I would like one," Santa gave him the picture that she was holding in her hand. She also asked whether the worker had seen "Mrs. M." (FW), because Santa wanted her to have a picture also. The worker told her that he spoke with FW occasionally by phone and would be glad to see that she got the picture of Santa.

. . . There was much running around by both Carmens, with Carmen R. hiding behind the worker many times. Santa told the girls that the worker had a picture of her; Carmen replied that the worker had one of her. There was a good deal of competition between Santa and Carmen for the worker's attention.

. . . Santa said she wanted to protect Carmen R. when, at the beginning of the session, Carmen started to run after Carmen R. . . . Santa did not want to let Carmen on the low cabinet, but she allowed Evelyn to get on it. Carmen R. jumped into the worker's arms, and all of the others followed. Santa jumped with abandon, leaving herself completely free to be swung around when caught. Earlier, when Carmen was caught by the worker, Santa said, "Carmen's your baby!" and laughed.

. . . When all the girls were on top of the cabinet, there was much talk in Spanish in relation to the worker. When Carmen R. once pulled her dress down below her knees, Santa laughed. Santa interpreted for the worker that Carmen R. had said the worker could see her panties. Santa and the others laughed, and there was continuing talk in Spanish that the worker could not understand. Evelyn told him that what Carmen had actually said was that Santa wore panties and that the worker could see them when she jumped.

. . . Santa picked up the worker's jacket and wore it for a few moments before returning it to him. She and Carmen R. played the Candyland game. Santa played honestly this time. Evelyn and Santa had a fight with pieces of clay. Santa said that her hands hurt her when Evelyn gripped her. Carmen R. took the worker's hand in hers and asked him to read a story. She sat down next to him on the couch. Evelyn sat on the other side; Santa pushed her away, sitting between Evelyn and the worker. Carmen brought over the hassock to sit on, and all the girls were then around the worker as he read the story to them. Santa commented that the worker had read the story to her "a long time ago." Carmen said that Santa was the father (bear), Evelyn the mother, and Carmen R. the baby bear. Santa objected to this, saying that the worker was the father, she the mother, and Carmen R. the baby. After the story had been read, Santa and Carmen R. each repeated that the worker was the father. They both put their heads on his lap, and the worker placed his hands on their heads. It was a very quiet session for the most part.

The worker happened to meet Santa in front of the school following the last group session in the month of June, which was a party. When he separated from her, saying "goodbye," Santa asked teasingly, "You're not going to take me with you?" The worker told her he would see her in September.

There were to be no more group sessions. In the fall of that year the worker left the employ of the Board of Education. He and the author composed a short letter to be mailed by the worker to each child in both play groups, informing them that the worker could no longer be in the school, that he had enjoyed meeting with them and that perhaps "some day" he might be able to "visit" them in school. A gift was enclosed with each note.

Comments and Interpretations

Santa was pleased that the worker had kept his promise about her paint set. It is very important in group practices with children that promises made to individual children, or to the group as a whole, be scrupulously kept. The perception of the worker as a consistent helper and a reliable person fortifies the *gestalt* image of a perfect "parent." In essence, this typifies the technical role of therapists in activity-group therapy.

Santa was jealous of Carmen's now open bids for the worker. Carmen had been transformed from the shy child at referral to an open, seeking little girl, relaxed in her approaches to the worker. Having more assurance, she was less dependent on the supportive ego relationship that she had been mostly instrumental in establishing with Carmen R. when the latter was introduced into the play group. In the foregoing excerpts, the reader will note how Carmen literally chased Carmen R. for weeks, now in anger and rivalry, as she had also entered in rivalry with Santa. This dissolution of a supportive ego relationship is typical. When such a relationship is in force, it provides psychological nurturance to both participants. But when the idiosyncratic needs of both members for mutual support are dissipated—as when the children become more confident and independent—then individual needs predominate in the interactions between the children. Thus, at a latter point in the development of the group we have been studying, both Carmens reacted to the larger interactive influences in the play group.

The episode identifying the worker as a "doctor" is interesting by virtue of Santa's comment on the true nature of the worker's doctorate: He helped those who were "nervous." It has been observed in almost every therapeutic play group that children eventually verbalize their awareness of the special nature of the group, even though they have never been informed of this. Also noteworthy is that when a child refers to the play group as a special experience—implying its intention to "help" them—as Santa did, the subject is quickly dropped. For the children to do otherwise would be to threaten the transference meanings. Children prefer not to think of the play group as a specialized experience. This tends to vitiate their more vital perception of the group as a happy place, perhaps a "club." In the analytical group therapies on the other hand, it is otherwise: The children become aware early in treatment that the therapist, and the group, have special purposes. Yet, even in these groups, it would be unwise for therapists to continue to delineate and stress the special clinical nature of the proceedings. Children do not relish being reminded that they are being "helped." They would prefer to experience the help but not have it set forth repetitively.

Relating to the foregoing, it is best that when conducting therapy groups of any sort, all professional stigmata identifying therapists as such be eschewed. This would include such titles as "doctor," "social worker," "psychiatrist," "psychologist," and "counselor," as well as titles of ministers of various faiths. No aspects of dress should indicate professionalism or religiosity. It is best for therapists who are conducting groups to dress casually. In sum, the best presentation of a practitioner with groups of children is a normal one, one that promotes relaxation on the part of children and is not oppositional to the formation of transference relationships.

The children's brief colloquy in Spanish was obviously intended to cover up the libidinal implications of their comments to each other. Such concealments of communications from the worker are rarely sustained.

The last excerpt, with its references to the family of bears, is touching. The children gently tease each other by identifying themselves in the family roles. Santa, who recalled that the worker had read the story to her "a long time ago," placed herself once again in senior position—in the psychological dimension of "mother." In so doing, she not only asserted her precedence over the other children but unconsciously replaced the missing FW. In a sense, Santa was defining a rather complete, acceptable sublimation for the original "tomboy."

The standard procedure was used in termination: the worker sent letters and gifts to the children, mailed to their schools.[10] This personal procedure reinforces the significance of the relationships between the children and the worker and tends to soften the reality of termination.

Summaries

Santa: She was referred at age six because of behavioral difficulties, but the nuclear problem was characterological: Santa was confused as to her sexual identity, being decidedly masculine. Evidences of this were observable in her speech, physical carriage, and preference for the company of boys, with whom she acted aggressively and participated in their games. The identity problem was attributed to the absence of a father during formative years. Actually, she had been deserted by both parents and was raised by a purported "grandmother." No substitute adult males were present during the years she lived in this woman's home.

Santa was in a therapeutic play group for a period of over two years. Her attendance was almost perfect, so great was her desire to attend the group. Because the group was conducted for most of its existence by a worker-team, it constituted a psychological "family" providing sustaining transference relationships with the workers, who served as psychological surrogates for her missing parents. The other children represented surrogate siblings. Regression in Santa's behavior occurred in response to the nurturant influences provided by the group. Over time, she was enabled to experience greater fulfillment of her early developmental needs, and the group provided nurturant experiences of which she had earlier been deprived. Further, Santa was able to experience the oedipal conflict in the context of a psychologically complete *gestalt*—the intact "family." The group provided all necessary libidinal objects required for the resolution of oedipal stresses.

[10]In many urban neighborhoods, mail sent to children's homes, especially as a boxed gift, does not always reach the persons for whom it is intended.

Thus, Santa had a reconstructive oedipal experience that acted as a more appropriate mutating influence affecting her sexual identity.

It was very helpful to Santa in reestablishing a firmer identity to have been able to interact with William for the entire first year of the play group's existence. Because his nuclear problem was similar to Santa's, in that his own sexual identity required masculine affirmation, the two children served as psychological foils for each other's needs.

The presence of other children dramatically increased Santa's "sibling" rivalry, which had the effect of further deepening the transferences to the workers. With the passage of time, the group acted oppositionally to Santa's dependency needs, and the influence of the group was to foster sublimations. The group induced maturation, distancing Santa from her libidinal ties to the workers, which helped further crystalize the alterations in her personality and character structure. Evidences of these changes in Santa were reported in the terminal evaluation by the workers and were substantiated by observations of teachers in several grades and reports from Santa's "grandmother."

Michael: He was referred at age nine, at a time when the play group was well advanced. Michael attended the play group for one year and seldom missed a session. In his classroom, Michael was defiant, negativistic, noisy, and belligerent, often engaging in fist fights with peers. The children, in fact, had nicknamed him "Punchy." Only limited contacts could be held with his resistive mother, and those by telephone. More complete information about the boy's early development and his present situation in the home could not be obtained for some time.

At no time in the play group did Michael behave in a manner comparable to what was attributed to him elsewhere. This is not intended to imply that the description of his deportment elsewhere in the school building was other than described. Rather, his responses in the permissive group setting indicated a firmly intact ego and a capacity to respond favorably to sympathetic handling.

Michael enjoyed the play group experience immensely. He did test the workers' forebearance for a while to convince himself that their accepting attitude was indeed true. Occasionally he acted out more aggressively, but he did exhibit fairly healthy guilt reactions and also responded well to the interventions from the workers. When the play group was reconstituted and he was placed in a boys' group with the male worker, Michael adjusted easily to the change and continued to respond favorably. In both play groups he played a central role. He was a child with leadership capacities who often tended to invoke good social interventions when such were needed in the group.

Michael made occasional references to "outings" and "visits" with his father and other relatives. The workers detected a quality of fantasy in these productions, perhaps childish exaggerations of events. The most that could be drawn from this, in the absence of consistent communication with his mother, was that the boy's family was not intact and that contacts with his father were limited in number.

Michael's behavior in class and elsewhere in the school changed for the better. He was less obstreperous and more responsive to teachers and to authority in general. His happiness in the special setting of the play room modified his perception of the larger school environment. This has been described as a halo effect. What he formerly saw and reacted to as onerous, namely the teachers and the authoritative structure of the school, he now dealt with more favorably. However, the actuality of such a larger setting is relatively fixed; it is the child who, following changes in himself, becomes better able to cope.

Carmen: She was referred at age seven as timid, shy, and lacking in social participation. Carmen was pale, thin, and physically immature. She was isolated, although other children liked her. She was affect-hungry, eager for attention from the teacher. While Carmen was a recessive, frightened child in school, at home she was capable of more aggressive behavior. However, she was fearful of her mother, who could be punitive with her. Her father was away from his family for several years, and Carmen had seen him only episodically prior to that.

The protocols of the play group sessions show a progressive improvement in this child, slow to start with but increasing rapidly as she relaxed in the free environment. The group tolerated her aloofness for a considerable time without bothering her. As the others sensed her growing confidence, they made more contacts with her, and the subsequent interactions no longer spared Carmen from teasing and other provocations. This is a subtle sign of a group's perception of a member's increased tolerance for the "give and take" of peer interaction. At first needful of support and acceptance from both workers equally, Carmen later began to show preference for contacts with the male worker, a sign of oedipal involvement. At this time she began to experience more rivalry with others, with Santa in particular. However, Carmen was now more capable of competing for the worker's attentions and resisting her more aggressive "rivals." While she was never combative, Carmen nevertheless demonstrated a strength which, in contrast to her original disposition, was rather dramatic. Her assuming a protective role in the supportive ego relationship with a new group member, Carmen R., was important in that it made her feel stronger.

The changes that took place in Carmen were described also in the evaluations made by teachers and her mother. From teachers' evaluations: "Carmen speaks clearly now; will talk of her work; a noticeable increase in the volume of her work; relationship with the teacher is normal but she can be negativistic at times; no excessive attention seeking; girls accept her readily; short attention span; no special academic interests."

Carmen's mother described her daughter's increased interest in schoolwork. Carmen was also not fighting with her siblings as much. She was "more grown up" and wanted to help her mother with household duties and chores. She spoke often of her play group, commenting once to her mother that the male worker "loved her more than any other girl." Both group workers described Carmen as more outgoing, participative, and assertive. The play group experience helped further this child developmentally by improving her self-image, strengthening her ego, and enabling her to acquire social skills. It is more difficult to assess the extent to which her libidinal needs, particularly with respect to the transference to the male worker, enhanced her identity. The oedipal expressions became open and persistent, and there were definite evidences of the gratification she received from the male worker's responses to her.

Carmen R.: She was almost eight years old when she was added to the play group, which was then in its second year. Of all the children, Carmen R. was the most shy, for which reason her teacher had referred her. She was physically slight, a sickly child, fearful of new experiences and other children and changes in school routines. Carmen R. resisted her teachers' attempts to encourage participation. Her father visited the family infrequently, having lived apart from them for more than two years. Carmen was not quiet at home, according to her mother. However, the mother knew that Carmen R. was quite shy in school and was eager to have her in the play group.

Carmen R. was accepted by the group from the beginning, despite the fact that she entered late. She represented no threat to the others. The children were impressed by her marked shyness and protected her. This was particularly true of Carmen, with whom Carmen R. formed a supportive ego relationship. Once emboldened by her observations of the workers' permissiveness and helpfulness, Carmen R. began to move out of her shell. In a manner similar to that of her namesake, Carmen, she first related equally to both workers but then moved into more frequent contact with the male worker in response to oedipal strivings. She, like Carmen, expressed preference for MW without at the same time demonstrating negativistic feelings toward or rivalry with FW. Santa, in contrast, was able to fortify her identity using both workers—MW as a desired libidinal object, FW as a rival.

Carmen R. became more assertive, eventually engaging in aggressive play with others, including her supportive ego, Carmen, from whom she began to separate. Further, she became more productive creatively and eventually spoke to others, which she had been unable to do for some time.

From teachers' evaluations: " She is now not as shy; is active in class programs; not tense; was silent at first, but now raises her hand; quite normal in responding to questions; sometimes talks of visiting her father; likes to be near the teacher; a great difference in teacher's relationship with Carmen R.; she is a 'different' child; is well liked." The mother reported improvement also. She now permitted Carmen R. to supervise the other children while she went shopping and would send her out on little errands.

From a closing evaluation report from the male worker: "Carmen R. has progressed from an infantile, dependent, frightened little 'baby' to a much more assured little girl. She has begun to assert herself and enter into activities quite vigorously. Her relationship to MW has developed to one in which she actively bids for his attention."

As in the case of Carmen, one cannot assess the true depths of psychic changes in Carmen R., lacking a more complete developmental history. Obviously Carmen R. was immensely more assertive; she had gained greater self-confidence and an improved self-image.

Evelyn: While there were palpable changes in this shy child, her stay in the play group was too short to warrant evaluation.

Alfonse: As was noted, Alfonse was added to the new group of boys. MW continued to report immature, masochistic behavior on his part in the play group, and the teacher said that Alfonse continued to tease and provoke his classmates. Efforts continued in referring the mother to a community agency: Both the boy and his mother needed more intensive help. Because of the mother's resistance in the beginning, the probability of her following through was minimal.

William: William continued in individual therapy on a regular weekly basis until the end of the school year. He became increasingly relaxed and communicative with the therapist, tolerating more exploration of his ambivalent feelings about his parents. He would refer mostly to his father whom he still tried to aggrandize as a strong, masculine libidinal object. The therapist chose not to expose William's unconscious denial of the anomalous circumstances in the family, realizing that the boy had great need to preserve the idealized image of his father. Instead, the therapist used a positive, more relaxed transference to himself to foster compensatory ego strength in William, which was successful to some degree.

When it was known that the therapist was to resign his position in the agency, a further attempt was made to refer the family to a community agency for continuing treatment for parents and child. It failed. The therapist terminated with William as he did with the other children in the two therapeutic play groups—with a letter expressing regrets about his having to do so and a modest gift.

The indications were that William required analytical therapy, probably of long duration. Also, this treatment would have to become more penetrating as the boy became fortified to deal with it in order to have him verbalize openly his repressed anxiety and anger against his parents. As for the parents, even if they had accepted referral, it was unlikely that they would have allowed themselves to engage in exploration of their roles and emotions. They were markedly resistive. However, they could have been guided in child management to afford William some relief from a truly difficult situation.

Addendum

The reader will have noted that this therapeutic play group and the one in Chapter 1 were terminated by reason of transfers of group workers to other schools by administrative order. Such changes were not typical of the many play groups that were conducted in a large number of public elementary schools. In some schools the groups were continued for three years, sometimes longer, with the same group workers. No group was maintained for less than one year.

A public elementary school represents an unusual setting for clinical programs, especially ones that employ a highly permissive group methodology. Successful administration of a school is predicated on definitive organizational structure and regulations. In such a rigidified environment, the more personal needs of troubled children, which are implicit in the helping psychological procedures, are viewed by many educators as "foreign" intrusions. As a consequence, unforeseen hindrances (such as the automatic transfer of Santa) may arise to encumber therapeutic procedures. This would not be the case in a community agency.

In maintaining a school-based clinical program, of whatever nature, it is helpful to first prepare the ground before implementing it. Conferences should be conducted with school administrators and faculty—including the school custodial helpers, who are closely concerned with physical maintenance—to explain the nature of the intended clinical efforts. Such communication must be maintained, particularly with the teachers of the children involved, to ensure that important information is readily shared between the professional disciplines. In these ways, the continuity of the therapeutic endeavor can be assured, with fewer interruptions and interferences.

Despite the exceptional circumstances associated with conducting a therapeutic play group in a school, a vast number of children have been helped in this way. Considering the great demand for therapeutic services, particularly in large urban centers, and the comparatively restricted availability of community resources in proportion to the need, it is imperative that these special helping procedures be utilized in schools.

CHAPTER 3

Wayne and Frank

MORTIMER SCHIFFER

WAYNE AND FRANK were pre-delinquents, children who, although manifesting the qualities and behavior associated with delinquency, had not as yet been subject to police or court action. Incipient delinquent behavior can readily be detected in young children. Some of its characteristics are: a defiant, rebellious attitude toward parents, teachers, and authority in general; aggression in the forms of bullying and fighting; stealing and insufficient guilt responses; minimal anxiety in situations that ordinarily elicit such a response; boastfulness and bravado; truancy; and fraternization with other children who manifest similar attitudes and tendencies.

Studies of delinquent children reveal strikingly similar psychonoxious conditions in their families that predispose them toward delinquency and other emotional problems.[1] Delinquency itself should be looked upon as only one aspect of an individual's emotional maladjustment and not as a nuclear personality disorder. In this sense it is akin to a symptom. One does not treat delinquency; rather, one treats a child who presents this behavior pattern among other emotional disabilities.

Pre-delinquent young children perceive school as a hostile environment and learning as an onerous task, with the result that they are typically below their grade in achievement. Teachers, administrators, and other school per-

---

[1]Gleuck, S., and Gleuck, E. T., *Unravelling Juvenile Delinquency*, Commonwealth Fund, Harvard, Cambridge, Mass., 1950.

sonnel are viewed as "persecutors," and the children react to them sus- piciously and defensively, even in the absence of cause. Such generalized distrust ofen makes it difficult for guidance counselors and clinicians to ini- tiate contact; the children tend to resist helpful overtures. Their prior expe- riences with adults have instilled a paranoid quality in their defensiveness. In most instances, having been deprived of a trusting, nurturant relation- ship during early development, such children become uneasy and suspicious when attempts are made later to involve them in a dyadic relationship in counseling or therapy. The libidinal implications of a positive transference, especially in a dyadic relationship, make them anxious. These children are more accessible through the various methods of group therapy.

In treating pre-delinquent children in therapeutic play groups, early in their school careers, one should anticipate unusual management problems with them at first because of their idiosyncratic features. They display a heightened sensitivity to the extraordinary amount of freedom that is typi- cal of a therapeutic play group, particularly the permissive demeanor of the worker. Such an atmosphere is entirely alien to their prior life experience. They are unaccustomed even to "reasonable" treatment from adults, let alone the complete acceptance of children that typifies the group worker's attitude. Their initial reaction is open disbelief. They then engage in repeti- tive testing to determine both the reality and the consistency of the novel en- vironment. Such testing by them exceeds, in quality and duration, that of the average child who is suitable for treatment in a therapeutic play group. It is reasonable to assume that such initial testing will impose more than the usual strain on the therapist, and also sometimes on other group members who are less aggressive. The first, difficult task for the group worker is to foster the formulation of a positive transference at a rate tolerable to the "too well-defended" child. This is essential before there can be any thera- peutic outcomes.

After years of working with many such troubled children in school- based therapeutic play groups, a significant finding was made. At no time did it become necessary to remove a child from a group because of extreme acting-out behavior comparable to that which led to the initial referral. The obstreperous, defiant, and negativistic behavior that characterized these children at referral was not replicated in the play group. There were aggres- sion, anger, provocation, and impulsiveness, but these were directed mostly against group members and, in almost all cases, were within tolerable limits. The retaliatory "punishment" that pre-delinquent children usually visit on adults whom they consider authoritative and inimical to their interests never occurred in play groups.

When such children are faced with the unbelievable presence of an "ideal" worker in a play group, their defensiveness becomes thrown into disarray. Their testing behavior, which is always obstreperous, is set in mo- tion by their uncertainty and doubt. But, because of the worker's consistent acceptance of the children as they are, the acting out is more modulated and rarely comparable to the nature of their actions in other settings. As a consequence, many pre-delinquent young children, who might otherwise have been cast out by administrative procedures instituted for serious misbehavior, have been successfully treated in therapeutic play groups in schools.

It needs to be emphasized that the foregoing statements apply specifically to *young children* who are placed in treatment early, at approximately six to nine years of age. If these children are not given psychological assistance early, by the time they reach pre-puberty the pattern of delinquency becomes habituated, sometimes characterological, and remedial measures to modify it must needs be more intensive and of longer duration and, all too often, in residential settings.

Two of the young children we are to study in this therapeutic group, who were in the third grade, were pre-delinquent. At the time of referral both were faced with a serious threat of suspension from school. It is questionable whether they could have survived in the normal school setting without the intercession of the meaningful group experience. The record that follows describes a long, dramatic, often stressful (for the worker) struggle before these two youngsters could tolerate the bonds of positive transference to the worker and respond to the mutating influences within the play group, including the socializing influence of other children.

Four children comprised this group, which met for a period of two-and-three-quarter years, during which time eighty-eight group sessions were held. The play group started with five children, but one dropped out after a few sessions because his family moved away from the area. Following this, the play group remained intact almost to the end. An extraordinary statistic: the average attendance for eighty-eight sessions was 95 percent!

The elementary school in which the play group was conducted was located peripheral to the city, bordering the suburbs. While most residents lived in private homes that had been built for single families, many were occupied by several families to share the financial burden of maintenance. Most of the parents earned marginal incomes; many had only recently lived in central urban neighborhoods. There was much delinquent and criminal activity within the community.

The group was the first one conducted by a female counselor who had been trained by the author. She received supervision on a weekly basis throughout the life of the group. The composition of the group was kept small, primarily because of the limited area of the only available room in the school. While this limited the size of the play group and affected some aspects of the play, the interactions between children were not deleteriously affected in the main.

Following are summaries of the referral information concerning the four group members.

Frank

Frank was nine years old, in the third grade. His teacher described him as "sullen, nervous, aggressive with peers, not learning." Other children complained about Frank "shaking them down," extorting money from them in the bathroom. The teacher said Frank was extremely "touchy"; he started fights with little or no provocation. He barely acknowledged the teacher's attempts to reason with him. If ignored by classmates, Frank disrupted their activities. Because of his behavior he had no friends. Frank was often reported for infracting school rules and was well known to the principal and assistant principal.

Frank was well built, large for his age, and in apparent good health. He was usually neat in appearance, with his clothing reflecting care at home. Frank lived alone with a maternal aunt; both his parents were deceased. He never knew his father. His mother, prior to her death several years after a protracted illness, had had considerable trouble with Frank. He was disobedient and wandered from home many times. After her death, Frank's maternal grandmother cared for him until she passed away, which occurred shortly after she had taken him into her home. Following this, Frank lived with his aunt, with whom he had been for the past three years. She found it difficult to control the boy. She was employed and left Frank to be "minded" by a neighbor until her return from work. The neighbor complained that Frank did not respond to her.

Frank's aunt resorted to physical punishment when his behavior became bothersome. "Some days he hardly talks to me at all," she commented. Moreover, she added, "I'm stuck with him!" implying that there was no one else to care for him. Despite these remarks, she worked hard at trying to maintain the boy in her home, and she did comment sympathetically about his reactions to the deaths of both parents and his grandmother, which experiences she said left deep impressions on the boy. Frank's first volunteered remark during his initial interview with the worker was, "I've no mother or father. They're dead." Frank's aunt was very appreciative of the school's interest in her nephew, being especially pleased with the plan to help him in a special group.

Apart from the concern about his deceased parents, Frank revealed no unusual fears or other symptoms of a neurotic quality. He seemed relatively ego-intact, resilient, and well-defended, albeit in a brash, pre-delinquent way. After initial doubts expressed in his first interview with the worker, he seemed responsive, which pointed to a potential for forming a positive relationship. It was felt that this highly active, aggressive boy had good potential for transference, but that such a relationship would be forthcoming only after a considerable period of time. Significantly, Frank attended all eighty-eight group sessions during the two-and-three-quarter year period.

Wayne

Wayne was eight years old, in second grade. He was referred because of severe aggression, manifested mostly in frequent fights with other children. He had a constant "chip on his shoulder" and never would acknowledge blame in starting fights, always pointing to others as instigators. Wayne knew that other children disliked him, and he used this fact to rationalize all his behavior. All previous teachers described the boy in the same way: "restless, defiant, unresponsive, morose, seldom happy. He cannot tolerate praise; he suspects adults who pay attention to him." There were, however, some times when he did make persistent (though unreasonable) demands upon his teachers, an observation that was one of the considerations for accepting him for the play group. It was felt that beneath his air of defiance and bravado there were a child's need for adult support and a hunger for affection. Wayne was a strong, robust boy with no physical defects.

In an initial interview with the worker, Wayne boasted about his prowess in fighting, implying that he could take care of himself if others bothered him. The worker felt that the boy constantly needed to prove himself, evidently in order to compensate for an essential insecurity.

Wayne was bright; he scored an I.Q. of 129 on a group intelligence test. He read at grade level but showed disinterest in academic work. At no time did his performance reflect his capabilities.

Wayne lived with his mother and a brother who was one year his senior. His father was not living at home, and there was little information as to whether he had any contact with the family. The mother was hostile and defensive, resentful of the many complaints received from school about Wayne's misbehavior and the need to visit the school to speak with teachers and administrators. She, like her son, never acknowledged the possibility of Wayne's responsibility for the escapades charged to him. In many respects, Wayne's aggressive mannerisms reflected the open hostility of the mother. She always blamed teachers and the school in general for her son's difficulties. She was equally defensive and recriminatory with neighbors who had occasion to complain about Wayne. While she gave grudging consent to her son's possible inclusion in a play group, it was evident that she did so merely to spare herself continuing interviews with school personnel. At no time during the ensuing years did her attitude change perceptibly; very little contact could be maintained with her.

The general impression about Wayne was similar to that about Frank. While Wayne was very combative, he appeared relatively ego-intact and asymptomatic in other respects. Central to his problem were the belligerence, defiance, aggression, and defensiveness that are characteristic of the acting-out, impulsive, pre-delinquent child. There were some evidences of a capacity for a relationship with an accepting adult, and, as with Frank, this was one of the reasons for including him in the group. It was estimated that it would take considerable time for Wayne to accept and respond to therapeutic intervention, even more so than Frank. He, like Frank, possessed a resolute defensiveness against well-intentioned adults, developed to defend himself against anticipated "injury" by the adult world. Wayne attended all but five of the eighty-eight group sessions; each absence was accounted for by illness or another event that prevented his attendance.

Ronald

Ronald was also considered for play group because of his pre-delinquent behavior, although it was not as severe as with Wayne and Frank. Unfortunately, Ronald's family moved from the neighborhood after he attended a half-dozen group sessions. His name appears briefly in the records.

Two other boys completed the group's composition: Norman and Michael. In balancing this group it was essential to pick a reasonable number of more passive children. A group composed entirely of "tough kids" would have been difficult to maintain. Group (social) controls had to be inherent in the mixture of different presenting problems. On the other hand, consideration was given to the possibility that passive, unaggressive children could be exposed to levels of acting out by others that they might find difficult to tolerate. Given such an eventuality, the neutral, permissive role of the worker would be jeopardized. The worker would have to intervene excessively in the absence of compensatory balance in the group. On the basis of experiences with similar groups elsewhere, it was decided to include the two recessive-type group members and make changes in the group early if it was necessary to do so.

Norman

Norman was nine years old, in third grade, in the same class as Wayne. He was extremely shy, practically uncommunicative in class. There was some question about whether Norman was moderately retarded intellectually, because he scored an I.Q. of 77 on a group test. He had attended a parochial school until grade two, at which time he transferred to the present school. At that time it was recommended that he repeat a grade because of his immaturity.

Norman was the only child of elderly parents who had married late in life. They lavished attention on him; he was markedly overprotected. Norman was fearful of strangers and new experiences. At such times he "won't say a word," according to his mother. Norman was indulged to the extent that a large portion of the family's finished basement was set apart for his exclusive use, filled with toys and games. His mother complained that her husband was sometimes "too harsh" with Norman and she had to protect the boy. "Yet," she added, "My husband *wants* Norman to love him. He sometimes cuddles Norman in his lap and gives in to him if he screams and has a tantrum." When Norman was frightened she permitted him to sleep in her bed. Her main concern was his poor schoolwork and the fact that he had no friends. She was pleased that Norman would be seen, either individually or in a play group.

The teacher described the boy's utterly compliant manner; it was as if he lacked volition altogether. Rarely did he react to the teasing of his classmates, and then only by "making faces" or name-calling. Norman daydreamed in class, probably because he found the work difficult. He never presented a problem in discipline.

It was apparent that Norman was very immature, "smothered" by the emotionally debilitating nurturance of both elderly parents. Obviously they were using their only child unconsciously to gratify their libidinal needs, with the net effect that the boy was fixated at infantile levels. More seriously, the mother's behavior—and perhaps the father's at times—exerted pronounced seductive influence upon him. It was thought that the group experience might help Norman experience a corrective relationship with an adult who would give him a chance to grow independently. It remained to be seen whether this could offset some of the effects caused by destructive overprotectedness and emotional seduction.

It was possible that a group composed only of boys would further Norman's masculine identification, direct him into more appropriate social activities, and motivate him to repress his infantile ways. The serious question was whether Norman could hold his own against the likelihood of teasing and aggression from the others. It was decided to try him tentatively in the play group. It was conceivable that since he and Wayne knew each other, some protection might be offered him by Wayne. Such symbiotic relationships are not uncommon in therapeutic play groups. Individual sessions with Norman were considered less promising inasmuch as they would tend to complement the dependency bonds that already existed. Subsequent events in the group indicated that Norman could remain, with occasional interventions and encouragement from the worker.

Michael

Michael was almost nine years old, in third grade. He was referred for shyness, social isolation, and underachievement. His lack of success in learning was surprising in view of the fact that he scored an I.Q. of 115 on a group test. It was considered that emotional factors interfered with his application to his work. In class he was passive, never a problem. Classmates showed him tolerance, but he formed no friendships. He was the first to comply when the teacher asked the class to do something; he was anxious for approval. Only recently had he felt secure enough to bring lunch to the school lunchroom. Prior to that he was too frightened to attempt it, because there often were arguments and fights between children in the crowded, rather noisy lunchroom.

Michael had been absent many times in the past because of asthma, a condition that subjected him to constant medical attention. He received injections weekly for the asthma. His mother could anticipate Michael's attacks of asthmatic wheezing, "especially when he's scolded." Michael was also allergic to many substances.

The family was intact; Michael had two older brothers and a younger sister. He was the only "sickly child," according to the mother. She was aware of his shyness in school and his lack of friends, but she reported no unusual difficulties with him at home, other than the need to monitor his health carefully. Michael attended eighty group sessions, an extraordinary record in view of his frequent earlier absences from school.

Michael was more ego-intact than Norman, and more independent. However, it was felt that he, too, might require special support from the worker if he was exposed to strong aggression. Moreover, in view of his medical condition, there was some concern about triggering respiratory distress under circumstances that might make him anxious. This concern proved illusory; at no time during the group's existence did Michael suffer a wheezing attack or any other physical response associated with asthma. This, too, was in contradistinction to the mother's initial description of Michael as suffering attacks under slight provocation—"scolding," as she put it.

It was thought that the group experience would enable Michael to become more outgoing, increase his confidence in himself, and perhaps enable him to discharge the aggression that was undoubtedly bottled up. The author had particular interest in whether a growing capacity to assertiveness and aggression would influence the manifestations of asthma since it has been shown that emotionality can be one predisposing element in the incidence of asthma.

Session No. 1: All Present

Frank arrived at the play room first, unaccompanied by his escort. He said that his teacher had sent him because it was time for the play group. He asked if the others were coming also. (There had been two short, pregrouping sessions before this one, in which possible candidates for the group were observed.) The worker explained that the escorts were bringing the other boys. Seeing paints at the easel, Frank said, "I'll paint. No, first I'll finish my drawing from last time." He found it where the worker had stored it and started to color.

Ronald arrived next, entering with a grin. He was followed by Norman and Michael. Ronald spoke to Michael about boats and complained about the orange paints. Wayne sauntered into the play room. Ronald asked the worker why the paint "runs." She said, "Maybe it's too thin." Wayne wandered about, studiously looking over the room and the equipment. Frank found a small plastic boat and played with it in the sink. Norman joined him. They dumped rubber puppets into the water—first Frank, who used a mother puppet, then Norman, who had taken a boy puppet. Frank said, "She can swim. Yours can't. You'll drown."

Ronald said, "I'll sew" (weave). He asked the worker for wool and mesh. Michael followed him. Ronald asked the worker to start his weaving for him. He was happy; he sang, "It's easy if you use your brain." Michael joined the refrain. Both boys weaved and sang. Wayne played alone with blocks. Frank took over an available side at the double easel. Norman watched him. When the other side became available, Wayne walked over. Norman said quickly, "You paint. I'll go next." Norman listened while Frank and Wayne discussed "monsters" in movies they had seen. Occasionally Norman joined in.

Ronald spoke: "You could use a bigger room." (The room that was used adjoined the stage in the school auditorium. It was sometimes used as a dressing room.) The worker agreed. Ronald went on: "If we could use the auditorium, the whole school could come and play!" Michael and he discussed whether or not this would be possible. Michael said, "Only third and fourth grade would fit in."

The worker had set a table for refreshments and she called the boys. Ronald came first. All sat down, except Frank and Norman. Then Frank came over. Ronald said, "There's no more chairs. Yes, there's one! Norman, you take it." Meanwhile, the worker poured milk for each boy. No one touched it. Finally Ronald drank, and the others followed. The worker said, "The cookies are for you." Ronald took one, followed by the others. Ronald said, "We should have washed." Frank noticed a spot of paint on his trousers. He went to the sink to wash it off. Meanwhile Ronald continued to help himself to more cookies. Michael followed suit. Frank returned and took another cookie. Then he asked the worker how many there were. She replied, "Twelve." Frank: "I only got two."

The boys left the table. Ronald and Michael returned to their weaving, and Norman asked whether he could paint. The worker nodded. Frank also continued to paint. Meanwhile, the worker was assembling a ring toss game. The escorts knocked at the door. Wayne asked whether he could stay on, but was told that it was time to leave. He said, "I'll come next Wednesday."

Addendum: While at refreshments, Wayne said, "When my mother sees this paint on me she'll ask if I stole it from the garage." This started Ronald on a story about cars, concerning boys who "steal" them and how a certain boy had "crashed" a car. He and Wayne laughed and exchanged similar stories. The others merely listened.

Comments and Interpretations

All the boys had been in the playroom before for preliminary sessions, some once, others twice. Other children had been present who were not included in the final group. This was the first session attended as a unit. From the manner of their entrances and their immediate reactions, it is evident that the boys were happy to return. Frank, Ronald, Norman, and Michael all became involved in activities, but Wayne spent a good deal of time carefully studying the setting and, more pertinently, the worker. He was guarded and unable to engage himself freely, as did the others. Michael and Norman, surprisingly, worked at various enterprises throughout the session. It was thought initially that the two shy boys would be more aloof and observant, which typifies the behavior of such children in early group sessions. However, both Michael and Norman paired themselves to the two outgoing, aggressive boys—Norman with Frank, Michael with Ronald. All during the session Norman and Michael were involved in work and play activities, initiated mostly by the boys with whom they had respective supportive ego relationships. For the most part, Wayne was a "loner." Characteristically, children with aggressive temperaments require less acclimatization to new experiences, including the exceptional climate of a therapeutic play group. They are less dismayed, or hindered by novel experience. Wayne, as we know, could be quite impulsive and aggressive, but he, of all the boys, was the most suspicious and distrustful of adults' intentions. This accounts for his initial wariness.

The personal variables that distinguished the relative strengths and weaknesses of the boys were openly revealed in this first session. Wayne, for example, approached the easel where Frank was already engaged in painting. Norman, who had previously come to the easel after Frank, whom he had been following about, observed Wayne's approach. Without a comment from Wayne that he intended to paint, or any other such indication, Norman quickly submitted, saying, "You paint. I'll go next." This brief scenario vividly illustrates the differences between the two.

Ronald was open, observant, and vocal enough to spontaneously remark about the size of the play room, which led to the discussion about the auditorium. This simple comment captured Michael, who had been duplicating Ronald's involvements, and Michael engaged in the conversation.

Herein, one can observe the extraordinary effects of supportive ego relationships in modifying children's typical behavior. In class, Michael was entirely different.

When a snack was offered for the first time, the group became temporarily immobilized. The boys had observed with curiosity the worker's preparations for refreshments. However, they were so irresolute that even when invited to partake the boys became "frozen." A "treat" seemed incomprehensible to them. The worker had to reassure them that it was all right to participate. When the moment of indecision thawed, a more intact child, Ronald, became the first to demonstrate the "safety" of responding to the unusual kindness.

At the end of the session, when the escorts knocked at the door, Wayne made his first—and a significant—comment, asking whether he could remain after the others left. In a sense, his request was a challenge. He was openly questioning whether the worker would do what it was rather apparent she could not: permit him to remain after the others were gone. In some instances such a request indicates an unconscious desire to be the "only" child. In this case it is unclear whether this was Wayne's primary motivation or whether he was deliberately testing the worker. In either case it was a good portent, indicating the boy's potential for a relationship.

Noteworthy is the brief exchange between Wayne and Ronald about car thefts and their sophisticated manner of talking as they expressed their knowledge about such events. Whether their stories were true or apocryphal, they nevertheless typify the unusual interest such children have in delinquent and criminal activities in the community.

Session No. 2: All Present

Frank arrived at the play room alone, about fifteen minutes before the scheduled meeting time. He said, as he had last week, "The teacher said I should come." The play room was still in process of being prepared for the group by several of the older escorts. The worker told Frank that the play room was not yet ready, but that he could sit in the auditorium until it was. The escorts finished pouring the paints and left to get the other boys.

Frank returned with Wayne. Both decided to paint. Frank ran to the open door to look out. The worker said, "We're keeping the door open for the other boys, but we stay inside." Wayne and Frank started to paint lines on the sheets of paper, using different colors. The worker was holding two smocks, looking for a place to hang them. Frank said, "How about us wearing them?" He put one on, as did Wayne.

Ronald, Norman, and Michael arrived with the escorts. Ronald took the Candyland® game, and Norman and Michael joined him at the round table to play. Ronald directed the activity. Ronald won the game. Michael said, "I don't want to play." Frank, who had continued painting at the easel, kept running back and forth, "kibitzing" the game. Meanwhile, Wayne found the ring toss game and played with it alone. Michael joined him later. Ronald, still at the table, asked aloud, "Who wants to play Candyland?" Frank called out, "I will. See, Mrs. K., I made brown by mixing the colors. I'm finished. I'll play." Wayne left the ring toss to join the Candyland game. He soon drifted away and again played alone, with the blocks this time, rolling down a slide he had built.

The worker was occupied with decorating the walls, hanging up designs she had cut from colored construction paper. Michael came to her and asked, "Can I paint?" The worker gave him a large sheet of paper for the easel. Frank was still wearing the smock. Michael looked at it. Worker: "Frank, do you still want to wear the smock?" He answered, "No. Here, Michael. Wayne, take yours off." Wayne did so. Norman took it and also began to paint. He covered the entire sheet with red paint.

As they played Candyland, Frank and Wayne laughed. They talked about "candy." Frank then went to the ring toss, managed to get a hoop on the target, and looked toward the worker, obviously seeking approval. She nodded and raised her eyebrows in "amazement" because of his prowess. This exchange was repeated several times.

The worker watched Wayne and Ronald at the round table as they played Candyland. When they had finished, she put milk and cookies on that table, with placemats and napkins. The boys took their game to the other table. Ronald watched the worker as she set the table. The worker announced, "Time for refreshments." Frank sat down, then Michael. Norman looked, came over, and sat next to Michael. The worker carried over a chair and sat. When she did, she observed that a cookie had been set out at each plate. She said, "I wonder how I got a cookie?" Ronald said, "Frank gave it to you." By now all were seated. The boys drank the milk. Ronald then grabbed four more cookies, which he ate quickly. Wayne grabbed another. Frank asked, "How many did you have, Ronald?" "Four," Ronald replied. Frank: "You don't get anymore!" Frank grabbed the last one. There was no other conversation during the repast.

While the worker was clearing the table, Wayne and Ronald played dominoes. Michael obtained crayons and paper. Norman asked the worker, "Can I color?" The worker replied, "Paper and crayons are on the shelf." Frank played ring toss and Wayne joined him, leaving Ronald. The escorts had not returned to take the boys to their classrooms. The bell rang; it was time for lunch. The worker escorted the boys to the lunchroom. On the way she dropped Norman off at the exit because he was going to have lunch at home. Ronald asked, as the group was leaving the playroom, "Can I stay?" The worker replied, "It's time to go." Ronald lagged behind as the group left the play room.

Comments and Interpretations

The general tenor of this second session was subdued, with the boys shifting from one activity to another without discord. The only manifestation of aggressive conflict, albeit a minor one, occurred toward the end, during refreshments, when there was some grabbing for the cookies. This group was in a preliminary stage of acclimatization, a phase in which they explored the setting, its offerings, and particularly the role of the neutral, permissive adult, who maintained a peripheral position with respect to the ongoing activities.

During a supervision session the worker commented about the "good" behavior of the boys, indicating that an outside observer, if there had been one, would never conclude from what was observed that three of the group members were capable of very obstreperous behavior.

Frank and Wayne arrived early at the play room, without their escorts. Somehow they had contrived to get to the play room in advance of the others. The worker was a bit anxious about procedures, as when she told Frank not to look out of the open door, in itself a harmless act on Frank's part. Frank was really watching for the other group members to show up. It is best to keep the entrance door to a play room closed and locked at all times, so that it cannot be opened independently from the outside, for several reasons. First, this avoids the problem of "strange" children walking in. Second, when late arrivals appear at the door, the worker is in the psychologically advantageous position of having to open the door, an act that is positive in meaning—a nonverbal expression of "welcome."

In this session the worker made several minor, unnecessary interventions, technical errors that were due to inexperience. This was probably because she felt that acting-out, pre-delinquent boys would replicate in the play group the behavior that was responsible for their referrals initially. An example was when she suggested to Frank that he relinquish the smock to Michael, something that group members should work out themselves. As was noted, this is the first play group the worker had participated in. Despite intensive training in the procedure, play group workers must learn the refinements of practice as they become actually involved with groups. Countertransference responses, for example, may be anticipated and discussed during the training period, but it is the actuality of interactions with the children and the workers' spontaneous affective responses that later crystallize into significant learning experiences. Time and repetition, and the input of the supervisor, can help the practitioner. This makes mandatory regular supervision conferences, especially during the first year of practice.

The reader will note a continuation of two general patterns of contrasting behavior in the group: assertive, as with Frank, Wayne, and Ronald; more passive, as with Michael and Norman. Repetitively, the former boys were the initiators of activities and games, usually without requesting permission of the worker to use various media. They had quickly grasped the significance of her permissive attitude. Norman and Michael, on the other hand, periodically inquired of the worker whether they could do something. Further, there was more mobility by the aggressive boys: they shifted easily from place to place, from one activity to another. Norman and Michael were not adhering so rigidly to their supportive egos, Frank and Ronald, as they had in the first session; they now tended to support each other. Of the two, Michael exhibited the greater capacity to move independently. It was Michael who was able to say to Ronald, "I don't want to play." Norman lacked even this degree of assertive strength.

The worker spent much time doing things related to improving the appearance of the setting, mindful to remain tangential to the group so as not to get in the way of the boys. Such concern for the setting is eventually perceived by children as dedication to their interests. At the same time, the worker made herself readily available should any child require her help. Moreover, while the worker was occupied with matters affecting the group's general welfare, she was also alert to all that was going on between the children, without appearing to be an active observer.

Wayne was more "into" the group this session, making contacts mostly with Frank and Ronald, and he was also verbalizing more. Yet, he still occasionally removed himself into isolated play, as with the building blocks, a pattern of shifting that was to continue for some time. Frank betrayed a need for positive transference, an example being his open nonverbal solicitation of approval when he successfully rang the target with the hoop. Both he and Wayne had confirmed the validity of impressions gained when they were initially being considered for the play group: they did possess potential for transference. They were yet to establish this bond, however, and in the near future were to test the worker's forbearance severely. Nevertheless, one critically important factor that is essential for successful therapy had been affirmed through the early behavior of the two boys.

The worker erred in her choice of the table to be used for refreshments, and also lost an opportunity to further fortify her role as an accepting person. Without speaking openly, she nevertheless dislodged Wayne and Ronald from the round table that was ordinarily used for the repast. She should have used the other table. Children will note such a sensitive accommodation to their needs and will inevitably question the worker openly. Her rejoinder then becomes another affirmation of her therapeutic role. She would reply, "You were playing and I didn't want to stop you. So I used another table." A bit later in this session the worker "wondered" aloud how a cookie had come to be on her plate. It is better to avoid gratuitous statements of this type or questions that have no meaningful relationship to ongoing situations. Such an utterance as the worker's could be used properly under different circumstances—for example, if two boys are about to engage in an actual fight. At such a time, a mild comment—perhaps made in levity—could dissolve tension.

To the extent that is possible, workers who conduct therapeutic play groups in schools should avoid accompanying group members beyond the confines of the play room. Doing so can place the therapeutic relationship in jeopardy, especially when the children become obstreperous in the "outer" environment. It is better to dismiss the group without escorts. Should they act out in the corridors, teachers and administrators will surely act as the authoritative prohibitors.

In the following four sessions, the group's behavior continued as before, within reasonable bounds. All the boys enjoyed the new experience; even Wayne began to display more positive, open signs that the experience was something he liked. Occasionally there took place small tests of the worker, again to ascertain the degree of her forbearance. Subgrouping became more apparent, yet without crystallizing into fixed patterns. Wayne and Frank were often together as a unit; so were Norman and Michael. Ronald, who was to leave the group after the eighth session, continued as before, happy and active. The following excerpts will convey the general nature of events in these sessions.

Sessions Nos. 3–6, Excerpts: All Present

. . . Once again Frank and Wayne arrived at the play room without escorts, almost ten minutes before the session was to start. The worker asked them to wait in their classrooms until the escorts picked them up.

. . . Wayne joined Ronald at the Candyland game. Ronald kept laughing loudly. Wayne said, "Shush!" They argued over the game, and Wayne left. Ronald: "I win! If you quit I'm the best Candyland player!"

. . . Wayne: "Everybody is making sloppy pictures. Not me." Ronald said, "You're making a mess." A bit later Wayne said, "I *purposely* made a mess." He painted all over the paper, after first painting stripes. His picture was a smear. Wayne: "I really have a sloppy picture." Meanwhile, Norman and Michael sat working quietly at one of the tables.

. . . Wayne and Ronald put rubber puppets on their hands and boxed each other. They yelled and chased about. Frank meanwhile "sailed" a lady puppet in the sink. He kept filling the sink with water. The worker walked near and Frank said to her, "You thought it would run over." The worker said, "Yes." Frank: "See, it runs out here," pointing to a drain.

. . . The escorts came for the boys. Michael had piled up the soiled dishes after the snack. Frank and Ronald helped. As the boys began to leave, Frank ran back to let the water out of the sink.

. . . Ronald arrived and said, "Boy, that monitor passed my room three times 'til she called for me!'' . . . Later he said to the worker, "You brought the material. Good! I'll sew" (weave).

. . . Frank said to Norman: "You can't play here. Go play Candyland." Norman just moved back and watched Frank play at the sink.

. . . After spending a few minutes weaving, Ronald asked, "Mrs. K., do I have to finish this today?" The worker replied, "You may do whatever you like." Ronald said, "I'll leave it. No. Maybe someone else will want it." He took the material off the loom and replaced it in the storage box.

. . . Frank was using puppets as boxing gloves. He boxed at Michael, make-believe, not actually hitting him. Michael put on a pair of puppets and they boxed and yelled. Ronald said, "Hey, you're fighting! You're noisy!" They stopped.

. . . The escort reported later that when she was taking Wayne and Frank back to their classrooms, they had behaved boisterously and the assistant principal had taken Frank to his office. Wayne had run away from him.

. . . Michael said to the worker, "Mrs. K., how come they are here?" pointing to checkers and a checkerboard. The worker replied, "Someone asked for them." Wayne: "I did."

. . . Frank obtained a new sheet of paper. He handed his finished painting to the worker, who hung it on the wall.

. . . Wayne began block building, constructing a wall and a house. The lunch bell rang. Wayne replaced all the blocks on the shelves.

Comments and Interpretations

These excerpts reveal the equable nature of the boys' behavior during a period of more than one month. Wayne was much more communicative; he had relaxed. He had not yet expressed in any way the impulsive, aggressive conduct still being reported in his classroom and elsewhere. Once he did engage in regressive smearing, but carefully, as if monitoring himself. Another time he joined Ronald in playful "boxing." Yet, it was he who mildly admonished Ronald in another session for making too much noise.

Wayne and Frank were eager to attend the group. They contrived to avoid their escorts, continuing to arrive at the play room in advance of the meeting time. Instead of telling them to return to class to await their escorts—which is probably not what they did—the worker could have allowed them to remain in the play room. This would have kept them from mischief in the school's hallways. Later the worker could have queried the boys' teachers about how they had gotten out of their classrooms early and could have arranged to prevent this in the future. Ronald's comment about the escort passing his room "three times" typifies the eagerness of the children to attend the group.

Norman and Michael worked and sat together, although Michael demonstrated more potential for autonomy than Norman, as shown when he "boxed" with Frank. For Michael this was a surprising undertaking. Norman, on the other hand, passively complied when Frank told him to play Candyland.

The worker made some technical errors but still fulfilled her role for the most part. She tended to move into situations prematurely, without assessing the urgency or lack of it. Frank "reminded" her not to worry—the sink would not overflow. Note how sensitive he was to the worker's nonverbal communication.

Among the positive actions by the worker were the two instances when she brought special items requested by the boys to the sessions. This was immensely gratifying to them. When children make requests for special items, it is imperative that the worker satisfy them at the next session. If unreasonable requests are made, such as for expensive items, the worker should produce a letter from the "office" stating that the item was not available or attainable. This follow-up will impress a child who made the request and absolve the worker from a role of denying the item requested.

In one exchange the worker told Ronald, "You may do whatever you like," in response to his question about whether he "had" to finish his weaving "today." A sufficient response would have been, "No," without further comment. As a matter of fact, it is not true that in therapy groups children may do "whatever you want." Such a remark could lead seriously troubled children to truly challenge workers with extreme acts. A worker's understanding and forbearance are made dramatically evident by telling children succinctly that what *they* decide to finish—or not to finish—is acceptable to the worker.

Wayne built with blocks and then carefully returned them to their proper place on the shelves. This act is noted here because of a marked departure from such "model" behavior that Wayne was to exhibit in the near future. A final note about Wayne—and Frank—is the episode that took place in the school hallway, when the assistant principal apprehended them acting boisterously (according to the escort). Wayne escaped, openly defying the administrator, who, because he knew Wayne, was unlikely to overlook such an act of *lèse majesté.*

Session No. 7, Excerpts: All Present Except Ronald

Michael and Norman arrived first. They walked to the easels and put on smocks. Michael noticed the new crocodile and crow hand puppets. Both boys tried them on. Frank and Wayne then arrived. Frank asked the worker, "Is the clay ready for me?" The worker showed him where she had kept it, wrapped in wet cloth, explaining that soaking it had kept it from hardening (Frank had asked her to save his unfinished work).

Wayne said, "Hey, look at this old crow! A crocodile too!" Frank walked over to look at the hand puppets. He returned to his clay work, making an ashtray. Meanwhile, Michael and Norman continued to paint. Michael painted a rainbow, Norman a vase of flowers. Wayne ran about the room with the crow puppet, yelling, "Old crow! Old crow! He'll eat you!" When Michael finished his painting, Wayne asked him to play checkers. He agreed. Wayne said, "I'll win you." Wayne kept the crow puppet on his hand as he played.

. . . Frank finished his clay ashtray and said, "Look at it, Mrs. K., an ashtray." The worker said, "Good." Frank: "What should we do with it?" The worker replied, "You may take it home or leave it here." Frank replied, "I'll take it." He cleaned the table where he had been working, managing to splash water on the floor. He said, "I cleaned some of the mess with the rag."

. . . Wayne called to the worker, "I winned him, Mrs. K." The worker nodded.

. . . Frank took some puppets to the sink. Norman joined him. They were splashing, yelling, pushing, and chasing each other. Wayne said, "Look, they're wetting the puppets." The worker nodded, indicating she knew. Wayne repeated, "Mrs. K., they're wetting the puppets!" Worker: "I see."

. . . Frank took the remaining puppets and threw them against the wall. Now all the boys joined in this game, tossing puppets all over the room and at each other, laughing, yelling and running. The puppet throwing grew almost to a feverish pitch. The worker began to set a table for snacks. When she had done so, she sat down. Wayne immediately joined her. The room became silent. All sat. Norman giggled.

. . . The worker cleared the table and then washed the dishes. All the boys picked up the puppets again, and the throwing grew wilder; the yelling and laughing continued. The worker was now seated in a corner near the sink. Norman said breathlessly, "I quit." He sat down next to the worker, then he walked to Michael and whispered to him. All the worker could hear was her name being mentioned. Michael said, "I quit." He took out some weaving materials. Norman continued to watch Wayne and Frank throw puppets at each other, occasionally handing puppets to them when they fell near him. Frank said, "I'm through," and sat down with a book. Wayne: "Oh, books. Let me see." He took one.

. . . Frank asked, "Does anyone else use this room?" The worker replied, "No." Frank: "What about the girls?" The worker replied, "They help fix it up for you."

. . . Wayne asked, "Can't we come morning *and* afternoon?" The worker explained that the group could meet only on Wednesdays in the morning.

Comments and Interpretations

Highly motoric acting out occurred for the first time during the seventh session, first by individual boys and by the group as a whole. Prior to this, Frank, Norman, and Michael had been engaged in quiet activities. Frank showed a reasonable response to his spilling of water and attempted to clean up the mess. Norman was again drawn to Frank's water play, which for both boys was a regressive, urethral preoccupation.

Twice Wayne "pointed out" to the worker that Frank and Norman were wetting the puppets, which was not something novel, since Wayne had seen Frank do this before. Wayne was impelled to call the worker's attention to what he considered "naughty" behavior because his own impulse to act out was surfacing. It was Wayne who initiated the running about and the throwing of puppets a few moments later, which catalyzed the entire group into similar action. The worker became anxious in the face of this first episode wherein the group as a whole acted out. In her recording of the session, her choice of the term "feverish" reflected this anxiety. However, she was becoming more capable of employing interventions without acting as a direct prohibitor. She prepared a table for the snacks. During the repast the boys were quiet and orderly, a marked change from their just-terminated wild play. However, the moment the worker left the table and the refreshments were finished, the wild game started again. Note that this time Frank hurled puppets directly against the wall. This act, more focused than before, was a symbolic assault on the person of the worker. As noted elsewhere, the setting in a therapeutic play group is an extension of the worker.

First Norman, then Michael withdrew from the obstreperous play. Norman sensed the worker's distress, which led Michael to join him in stopping the play. The two boys set a compensatory pattern; Frank and Wayne then followed suit and took books to read. The timid boys had been the first to show some guilt for acting out. The fact that both Frank and Wayne settled down was a good sign of inner controls, an ability for self-limiting behavior. Such behavior is promising, particularly in the case of pre-delinquents. Frank's query to the worker about "who else" used the play room had some bearing on their hyperactivity—perhaps, "does anyone else act this way in here?" The question was followed by a request to use the play room in both morning and afternoon. This obviously was an attempt to find out whether the worker was upset—the meaning was, "Are you angry? Can we come here more than once a day?" The worker could have responded differently, thus shifting the denial to the outside source, the school office: "I'll find out and let you know next week." This is a standard technique in response to such a question. It is more effective to delay a negative response until the following session and to produce a typed letter indicating that additional meetings cannot be held.

By now the play group had, in essence, passed through an initial phase of acclimatization and had entered a nodal phase. It could be anticipated that more impulsive, even wilder behavior would occur in the future.

Session No. 8, Excerpts: All Present Except Michael

Frank and Wayne entered the play room, this time accompanied by escorts, who remained outside the door. Wayne took the crow and alligator puppets and danced around. Ronald came slinking into the play room. The worker put Ronald's coat away after he left it on the chair. Then Ronald spoke to her: "Did Mr. S. [the assistant principal] tell you about us?" (He meant his family.) The worker replied in the negative and asked what Ronald meant. He said, "We live too far from here. Now I have to take two buses to come to school. We're out of the district. We have to change schools." The worker started to respond, but Ronald spied the two new puppets and walked over to Wayne. He grabbed one from Wayne, saying, "You have to give me one." Each boy took a family puppet figure also, and they began to box with each other furiously. Ronald was knocked down. "Wait," he said, "you have to let me get up." They boxed once more. Ronald said, "I have cramps," and sat down on a chair.

. . . Later Wayne and Ronald resumed boxing, more wildly. Wayne knocked Ronald down once more. Ronald: "I hit my head in back. It hurts in front now." He replaced the puppets and went to an easel. Norman was dipping wooden figures into water at the sink. Wayne said to him disdainfully, "You still playing with water?" Norman answered, "I just started."

. . . Frank joined Wayne, who was working with the clay. Norman drifted over and watched, silent. Wayne said, "I'll have to clean the table." Frank: "It's a mess." Ronald joined the boys. All now were using blocks in working the clay. Frank said, "Here's a smashing and mashing machine!" The others imitated these words singsong fashion: "Mish-mash-smash!" Ronald tried to make an imprint of a wooden figure on the soft, wet clay. He called to the worker, "Mrs. K., I can't get this off." The worker said, "It will dry, but it can come off with water." Ronald took the block to the sink and peeled off the clay. Frank said, "How about a cup of water? We have an extra cup today. Like last time." The worker procured one of the cups and gave it to him. Frank filled it with water and brought it to the table. Since the boys were working with clay at the round table, the worker set up for snacks at the other table.

. . . Frank washed his hands. "Look, how clean," he said to the worker. The worker admired his hands and said, "Yes, very clean." Wayne also cleaned his hands. Frank, Wayne, and Norman sat at the table. Each boy took a cookie. Frank called out, "Ronald, hurry or you won't get a cookie." Ronald replied, "I'll get one. I'm coming. I *better* get one!" He came to the table and grabbed a cookie. "You had two," he said to the others, "so I get two," grabbing another. The worker offered more milk to the boys. Frank, who had started to leave the table, said, "I'll have some." Wayne: "Me, too." Ronald: "Me, too." Norman looked as if he wanted more but said nothing. Frank said to the worker, "Next time there's extras, you start with Norman. That's what my teacher does."

Frank and Wayne returned to the table where the clay was. The worker remained at the repast table with Ronald, who had not finished eating. The others mashed, rolled, and hammered at the clay with blocks. Norman held his ears. Ronald said, "They're watching T.V. out there [auditorium]. They can't hear." Frank said, "You're making a mess for Mrs. K. to clean." Ronald said, "I'll clean these" (wooden figures). The worker had collected them, preparing to wash them at the sink.

. . . The worker began to put things away on the storage shelves. Clay had spattered all over. Wayne noticed the mess on the wall. "Ooh, look at that!" he said. Suddenly Ronald asked, "Can we take it home?" (clay). "Yes," said the worker. All grabbed at the remaining lumps of clay.

. . . Ronald said, "I'll paint mine." All the boys except Norman seemed to grab for paintbrushes at once, and they began to paint their pieces of clay. "Where shall we put it?" someone asked. The worker set out pieces of newspaper on the table. All put their work on this. Norman said, "Oh, Frank, Wayne got paint on yours." Frank ignored him.

The escorts knocked at the door. Wayne ran out of the room. Norman said, "Goodbye, Mrs. K." Frank said, "Let's get out of here." Ronald: "I'm going to hot lunch." They all seemed to sweep out like a bolt of lightning, leaving the room looking as if a cyclone had struck it.

Comments and Interpretations

The hyperactivity that had started in the preceding session continued. Immediately upon entering the play room, Wayne set the tone for the session by resuming loud play with the puppets, as he had done in the prior session. He quickly moved from this to roughhousing with Ronald, and twice in their "boxing matches" he punched and shoved Ronald to the ground. Ronald who was strong and aggressive, found himself no match for Wayne, who now fully demonstrated his aggressive capabilities. The worker was concerned about the vigorous exchange, but she did not intervene. This situation subsided of itself. This is an example of a case where a worker must carefully assess events. Should intervention be used prematurely or improperly, a child may consider the worker's act as a negative value judgment. Therefore, he may feel that the worker considers him "bad." In this instance, the worker's forbearance, based on her judgment that no real hurt was being done, conveyed an entirely different meaning—namely, that she understood that there are times when children need to express themselves physically. In many instances the need for intervention—as a self-limiting force—stems from feelings of guilt or anxiety. This acts as a disciplining, internalizing force, self-generated and self-strengthening. A reasonable flow of aggressive interaction between children, within safe parameters, almost always creates its own inner pressures for adaptations to new modes of behaving. It is only when interactions are palpably destructive. hurtful, or momentarily beyond the capacities of the children to modify that assistance by the worker is appropriate. At such times, the careful use of intervention, without judgmental overtones, is usually effective. In a situation wherein the children are apparently helpless to bring about their own solution, a neutral intervention, one that places no blame, finds fertile ground. The essential positive transferences to the worker enable even recalcitrant children to yield. As was noted at the start of this report, one of the main initial concerns in working with pre-delinquent children was to determine whether they had a capacity for developing positive transference.

In this session, regressive acting out was set into motion by the wet, sticky clay. The worker allowed the boys much freedom in this activity, even coming to their assistance several times without restricting their immature play. The therapeutic value of such regressive media—also water play and smearing with poster colors—lies in loosening anal and urethral fixations. Wayne sensed Norman's need to "still" play with water. The boys exhibited healthy compensatory responses to the regressive smearing: Frank spoke of the "mess" and later showed the worker his clean hands. Ronald offered to clean off the messy blocks that had been used for pounding. Wayne became temporarily dismayed about the clay "messing" the wall.

The boys grabbed for food, but without unusual conflict. Only Norman was handicapped by timidity. Yet, it was Frank who suggested how Norman could be treated fairly in a subsequent repast. Stimulated by the supranodal activities of the session, the boys left at the end in an excited state.

This session reveals the spontaneous, supranodal activity that normally follows the period of initial acclimatization. The children had sufficiently confirmed the reality of the worker's permissiveness, and they became able to express feelings and needs without undue concern about limitations, punishment, criticisms, or chastisement, which their acting-out behavior commonly elicited from other adults in other settings. This was the beginning of another phase in treatment, in which catharsis, including negative transference manifestations, would occur increasingly. It was a critical period of therapy and one that placed much demand upon the worker's forbearance and tolerance. The durable, sustaining positive transferences that had developed acted as moderating factors that supported the group's integrity during the new phase of nodality and supranodality. In this eighth session, the worker further crystallized the positive transferences to her through her neutrality and helpfulness, including her continued food offering—a "treat" that was never denied regardless of the children's behavior.

For Ronald, unfortunately, this was the last session. His family moved and he was transferred to another school. Because the worker was unable to speak with him in person, she mailed him a letter expressing her disappointment and enclosed a small gift.

During the next two months, acting-out behavior increased, mainly involving Wayne and Frank, with the former in a leading role. Much of this so-called "play" was aimless, unconstructive, and sometimes negativistic in its implications toward the worker. The latter behavior was an unconscious displacement of anger against the parents, enacted against the worker. It was expressed in such activities as smearing with poster paints on the easel and "accidentally" smearing paints on the walls and the floor; indiscriminately splashing water at the sink; painting blocks and puppets; and throwing objects (mostly puppets) about the play room, sometimes directly against a wall—all this supposedly in the form of "games." There were other such actions: a game of "baseball" using a puppet as the ball and a long block as a bat; a game of hurling quoits toward the ceiling and striking the wall bell with them; and general carelessness with respect to maintaining the orderliness of the play room. Almost all of these activities were carried on primarily by Wayne and Frank, singly or acting together. Norman, in particular, was openly fascinated by this aggressive, assaultive behavior, despite his occasional attempts to call the worker's attention to the events. Michael observed all that went on carefully. He tended to occupy himself with crafts and other activities.

Yet, during all this cathartic acting out, both Frank and Wayne would spontaneously limit their hyperactivity when it peaked. They would then tend to compensate by blaming each other for "messing up," as they put it. At times they also made feeble attempts to put the room in order. Such acts were reassuring signs for the worker, who was truly placed in states of anxiety from time to time but managed her role nevertheless.

There were occasions when Norman and Michael were drawn into the pattern of acting out, usually when the four boys engaged in competitive "wars" using rubber puppets for throwing ammunition and moving the furniture about freely to form barricades. Interestingly, the boys created a fair balance in these engagements, with Wayne permitting Norman on his "side" and Michael joining Frank. Norman, despite his timidity and sometimes fear, became excited during the "wars" and sometimes mimicked the "tough guy" behavior of Wayne and Frank. This was so apparent that both boys began to ridicule him. Nevertheless, Norman continued his puerile attempts to behave as he observed the others do. Michael, on the other hand, despite his occasional participation with the others, showed more reserve at moments when the play became loud and boisterous. It was noted that he, too, used Frank and Wayne as supportive models.

During snack time the boys behaved noisily and there was more arguing and grabbing of food, with Frank and Wayne characteristically getting most of it. They always ensured that the worker was provided for.

Wayne and Frank constantly sought reassurance from the worker that she still accepted them, especially after fighting and other acting-out behavior. Individually and repetitively, they would request special items from her, or ask her to make various little projects for them. Lately, Frank and Wayne had begun to seek her out in her office at times other than group sessions, on one pretext or another.

Norman, surprisingly, was able to sustain being shoved about, "used," and sometimes ridiculed without the worker's having to protect him. Yet, he was too often a compliant butt, a masochistic role that did not augur well for the future. Most times when Norman felt put upon excessively, he would seek relief by engaging in quieter play or work with Michael.

The last group session of the year was set as a party. When Wayne and Frank saw the elaborate setting, with special treat foods and gifts, they became alarmed. Both were certain that this spelled the end of the play group, and they stated as much. The worker assured them that the group would continue in the fall. In that session Wayne demonstrated how much more meaningful his relationship with the worker had become. He told her, "Mrs. K., I have a problem. A boy tried to knife me. I even have a mark. I have to tell Mr. S." (assistant principal). Wayne had never before confided to the worker conflicts that occurred outside the play group. The episode he spoke of had, in fact, taken place, as was later determined by the worker.

When school opened in the fall, the boys were eager to resume play group sessions. The first session was rather modulated, with the boys making comments about the appearance of the room and recalling aloud the "wars" and other excited episodes that had left obvious marks on the walls and the ceiling. Little time passed, however, before they resumed the acting out typical of the last sessions prior to the summer. We pick this up in the twenty-third session. Wayne was absent, one of the few sessions he missed. The reader will note a difference in the tone of the session caused by his absence, and the boys' comments about it.

Session No. 23: All Present Except Wayne

The day of the session had been changed from Wednesday to Tuesday because a special Thanksgiving magic show was to take place in the auditorium and the worker did not want the boys to miss it.

Michael, Frank, and Norman entered the play room, talking about the change in meeting day. Norman said, "There's no school tomorrow." The others corrected him. Frank said, "Tomorrow's the magic show in the auditorium, isn't it, Mrs. K.?" The worker replied, "I changed the day because of the magic show, so you wouldn't miss it." Frank said to Michael, "Let's play our checker game." Michael: "Later." Frank: "Later will be too late." "O.K.," said Michael, and they began.

Norman danced around the room, throwing puppets at the wall aimlessly. Then he went to the easel and said, "I'm mixing colors." He continued: "I'll make brown." He painted lines, then blotches. He spoke aloud about his painting, but no one paid attention to him.

The worker sat at one of the tables, making a centerpiece in the shape of a turkey. Frank and Michael argued. Frank would not allow Michael certain moves in the checkers game. When Frank made the same moves, Michael said, "That's not allowed." They continued arguing; Frank won out. Michael tried to hold his own, but Frank managed to win out on every point. Meanwhile, Norman left his painting and began to throw puppets against paintings hung on the wall. Frank looked up and said, "Hey, Norman, stop hitting the pictures." Norman looked at him and deliberately threw the puppet again against a painting. The worker walked over and straightened one of the paintings without saying anything. Norman walked to the other end of the room and threw the puppets there.

The worker cleared one of the tables and prepared to set up for snacks. Norman stood nearby and watched. Frank: "Look, you better not touch anything. You either! [to Michael]. Today we're sharing." Norman: "Mrs. K., too." Frank to Norman: "Shut up!" The worker set out about ten cookies on the serving plate, including a saucer with stewed prunes at each place. Norman sat, then Frank. Michael walked to the far end of the table where there was no setting. The worker moved one toward him. Frank: "We're sharing!" Michael added, "If Wayne was here there'd be grabbing." Frank distributed the cookies as if he was dealing cards—two cookies each for Frank and Norman, three each for Michael and the worker. Norman grabbed a cookie that was on the table near Frank. Frank slapped his hand.

After finishing the repast, Michael and Norman picked up hand puppets and playfully hit each other with them. Frank took dice from one of the games and started playing "craps" against a wall. One of the escorts opened the door partially, and Frank yelled, "Get out! You're not supposed to be in here!" Frank slammed the door shut.

The worker began to wash the dishes. Norman returned to the easel and once again smeared a painting. Michael did the same at the other easel. The lunch bell rang, and the worker arose. Frank said, "I just threw a six!" Once again he rolled the dice and then gave them to the worker. Michael went to get his coat. Frank went to Michael's painting and smeared it some more. Frank said, "Look." Michael: "Thanks. You finished it. I don't care." All left.

Comments and Interpretations

In Wayne's absence there was a pronounced difference in the boys' behavior. The activities were less fragmented; nor were the boys as tense as they usually were when Wayne was present. While Frank still took the dominant role, with little opposition from the others, his behavior was much more tractable than when Wayne was present.

Once again the worker demonstrated her consideration for the boys by scheduling the session on another day so that they would not be deprived of the show. Such acts never pass unnoticed by children in such groups. They register with great effect.

Norman, independently, enacted some of the "naughty" (for him) behavior that he had seen Wayne and Frank perform at other times. While he had joined them in the past, his actions had always been peripheral. In this session he performed the behaviors spontaneously, and alone. Everything he did—throwing puppets against a wall and aiming them at the drawings—replicated the behavior of others. He also spoiled the paints by mixing all the colors together, an act that he "announced" as if to ensure that the worker noticed what he was doing. For a child whose behavior had always been characterized by a compelling need to conform, to behave, and never to defy authority, particularly in school, such behavior represented defiance of the worker—defiance of past subservience. When the worker tactfully straightened out a painting that Norman had knocked awry, he deliberately moved to the other end of the room to continue.

Michael also displayed more strength; he argued with Frank over the latter's manipulation of the rules of the game. He also smeared a painting later, this again an act similar to what he had observed others do. The reader will note repetitively, in this play group and others reported on, how aggressive children in play groups serve as models for passive children, who, once they feel secure, begin to mimic the actions they had previously observed. This group phenomenon supports the principle of heterogeneity in the selection of children, whereby children with different types of problems are chosen to ensure significant interactions between aggressive and passive types.

The boys commented openly during the snacks about how "different" it was when Wayne was absent. Michael flatly stated that the distribution of goodies would be otherwise if Wayne were present. No one disputed this. Norman "dared" to steal one of Frank's cookies.

Frank loudly affirmed the concept of "territoriality" when an escort inadvertently opened the play room door (which should have been locked). In no uncertain terms he shouted out his challenge and slammed the door shut. This firm gesture, which denied entrance to strangers (although the escort was not a true stranger), was dramatically demonstrated in a therapeutic play group in another school. One day the locked door to the play room was opened with a pass key by the principal himself. For some reason he had to talk with the worker, and when his quiet knock at the door had not been responded to, he opened it. The noise generated in the play room by a group of five- and six-year-olds had evidently muffled the sound of the principal's knock. One child, openly dismayed by the "strange" presence (not really so, because all the children knew the principal), spontaneously placed both his hands on the man's chest, pushed him toward the door, and said, *"You're not supposed to be in here!"* For children in a therapeutic play group, the play room setting becomes psychologically separated from the body of the authoritative setting—the school.

In this session Frank demonstrated the ways of the "street." He showed everyone that he knew how to play "craps" against the wall, an activity common to the gangs in the community.

Session No. 24: All Present

Frank came first. He hung his coat in the locker. (Recently two narrow clothes lockers had been installed, one to hold the boys' clothing, the other for storing supplies.) He then went to the easel and examined the paint jars. Frank said, "Mrs. K., you put fresh paint in every Wednesday." The worker replied, "Yes." Wayne burst into the room, breathless. "I beat Norman. I bet the monitors are looking for me!" Then Wayne crept into one of the lockers and closed the door behind himself. Frank went into the other locker.

Michael and Norman entered, and they tried to put their jackets into the locker. Michael said, "Hey, we gotta hang up our clothes." Wayne yelled, "Go away!" Frank also yelled: "Get out of here!" Norman hung back while Michael argued. Michael said, "I'm putting my stuff here" (on the table). Norman followed suit. Then both began to paint. Wayne came out of the locker and threw his own and Frank's coats on the same table that Michael had used. "They're in my way," Wayne said (meaning the locker). Then he returned into the locker, and he and Frank banged "messages" to each other through the walls. They also opened and closed the doors, yelling, "Blast off! Here we go! Countdown!"

Frank left the locker and began hitting a ball that belonged to him against paintings on the wall, tearing one of them. The worker, who was sitting cutting out designs, silently repaired the painting with cellophane tape.

Michael, at the easel, began to paint off the paper, on the easel itself, holding brushes in both hands; he also smeared his paper. Norman "oohed" and "aahed" when he observed this, finally saying, "Look what Michael's doing!" Frank came over to see. The worker wiped the wall near the easel. Frank said, "Look, you messed Mrs. K's wall. She has to clean it up."

Wayne began block building. Frank threw his ball into the sink, which was full of water, causing water to splash out on the floor. Norman watched. Michael joined Wayne at the blocks. The ball bounced near Wayne. He grabbed it and raised his hand as if to throw it violently. Norman ducked; Michael held his ears. Then Wayne and Frank began to wrestle for possession of the ball, which belonged to Frank. Wayne got on top of him. Frank said, "No hurting." Wayne raised his arm as though ready to punch. The worker walked nearby as if to watch. Wayne released Frank.

The worker began to set up for refreshments. Wayne and Michael continued building with blocks. Frank was punching his ball. Norman watched everything. Wayne walked over to the table and counted the items on the plate. Then Frank came over. The others stood and watched. Wayne gave half a cake to Frank. All sat. The worker poured milk. Michael said, "Last week we shared," speaking directly to Wayne. "You weren't here," he continued. Then Michael spoke to Frank, "You said we'd share sometimes." Michael said, "Frank, you made these on the wall," pointing out dirt marks that had been made by Frank's ball when it struck the wall. Frank replied, "That's not my painting." Michael spoke again to him: "*Those* marks" (pointing so Frank would know exactly what he meant). Frank replied, "Yes, I made them, last year."

Then it became quiet. Wayne returned to the blocks. "It's too quiet," he said. Outside there was singing in the auditorium. Wayne yelled, "Shut up!" Michael said, "Let's play checkers, Frank. We didn't finish last week." "Yes, we did," said Frank. Michael: "No." Frank: "Yes." Michael: "I still had two kings." Frank: "No, you didn't." They sat to play and Norman watched the game.

Wayne built a set-up with blocks resembling a cannon. Frank joined him. then Frank contrived a lever and, by striking the end of a long block, shot a smaller block up to the ceiling. Norman covered his ears, expecting the crash. "Ooh!" he said. Michael ducked. The worker walked closer. Then Wayne said, "Shoot it again!" Frank looked toward the worker. The worker merely looked back at him. He leaned on the block as if to shoot it, but he did not. Then he and Wayne began to toss blocks about the play room. The worker picked up some of the long blocks and replaced them on the shelves. Then the boys converted the game into "bowling." Each time the blocks banged together, Norman shuddered. Michael commented, "Here they go. "It's hitting!" The bell rang for lunch. "A few more," said Frank. He and Wayne "rolled" a few more.

Norman left, saying "goodbye" to the worker as he did so. He said exactly the same thing every week. Wayne and Frank left the play room last, tagging each other playfully as they went out the door. Frank said to Wayne, "I got last tag!"

Comments and Interpretations

The loud tone of this session was in marked contrast to the preceding one, when Wayne was absent. Well illustrated in this session is the effect of catalysis, with one group member, the most aggressive, Wayne, exerting unusual influence. The net effect was to evoke parallel behavior in the rest of the group. Children in therapy groups take characteristic roles depending on their personalities; as noted earlier, some are instigators, others act as neutralizers and still others are neuters. In this group Wayne and Frank were activators, Wayne notably so; Michael and Norman were at present incapable of neutralizing the intensity of the other boys' acting out, nor would they have done so if they had been more capable, since they were themselves needful of expressing aggression. As a matter of fact, we have already seen both Norman and Michael enacting roles that they copied from Wayne and Frank. Whatever neutralization that was occurring in the group stemmed from momentary guilt feelings or anxiety generated in the "perpetrators," or it was induced by careful interventions by the worker. We observe two instances of the latter, when the worker slowly moved closer to the scenes of wild behavior. Her proximity had an inhibiting effect on Wayne and Frank, although she did not say a word. These interventions were necessary because of a possibility of real injury from blocks that were being thrown indiscriminately.

Michael seemed to have "come alive" rather suddenly, although he had given earlier signs of moving from isolation. He was more verbal, even criticizing Frank for soiling the walls. Further, he told Wayne directly that food had been shared in his absence, and he also reminded Frank that he had promised earlier to share more. Yet, these comments are reflective of ambivalent feelings brought into play by his own aggressive "experiments." In this session Michael, for the first time, deliberately smeared an easel and the wall; participated in some of the block throwing; and shouted in excitement when stimulated by the wilder play of Wayne and Frank.

Norman was ever watchful, excited, and fearful yet thrilled vicariously by the excited antics he observed. With Wayne present he was less capable of doing things on his own, as he had in the prior session. Yet, it was obvious to the worker that Norman almost studied Wayne's ways of acting out, as if he had to know the pattern exactly.

The worker sustained herself well during this hyperactivity. She was almost always able to limit excesses, and the possibility of manic behavior by individuals or the group as a whole, by using indirect methods of intervention. When Frank was throwing his ball against paintings on the wall, the worker carefully made repairs to one of them, an act sufficient to inhibit further throwing by Frank, at least for the moment. Toward the end of the session, when Wayne and Frank pretended to "bowl" using blocks, she retrieved some of the blocks to restore a semblance of order, an action that was also sufficient to limit the wild play and that was accomplished without censure or prohibition.

Also shown in this session are rapid alterations in behavior, from a nodal state (intensified) to an anti-nodal (quiescent) one, the latter occurring for some minutes during refreshments. The group had taken a respite when assembled for refreshments. Interestingly, Wayne commented about things being "too quiet."

Activated behavior continued to mount for many months. Wayne became more and more aggressive, at times almost defiant, and more abusive of the other boys, now including Frank. In numerous ways Wayne continued to test the worker, by spoiling materials, interfering in the other boys' activities, grabbing food, smearing regressively, and in other ways. Yet, he also continued to make bids for special attention from the worker, occasionally giving grudging acknowledgment as she responded to his bids. Wayne still contrived to visit the worker in her office between sessions. There were times, however, when he unexpectedly came upon the worker in the hallway and did not acknowledge her, as if he was embarrassed. Wayne's ambivalent feelings about the worker were becoming more and more explicit, an indication of anxiety stemming from the growing positive transference. The relationship gratified him and threatened him at one and the same time. He had a compelling need to discharge anger and hostility. The worker maintained her accepting role in the face of the boy's alternately provocative and mildly compensatory behavior. Sometimes she had to intervene more directly with Wayne to protect the others.

Frank had also become more aggressive; often he was impulsive and negativistic, but never to the same degree as Wayne. Frank could shift more easily into acceptable behavior, limiting himself and sometimes the other boys. Norman and Michael took increasing part in games with Wayne and Frank. They required no limitations from the worker. Both of them were being influenced by the aggressive "demonstrations" of Wayne and Frank.

The reader will glean the quality of this phase in the group from the following excerpts.

Sessions Nos. 26–46, Excerpts

. . . Wayne took his ball from his pocket. Then he took the brush from Norman's easel and painted the ball orange. He bounced the ball against the wall. Much later the worker washed the wall and the floor, where the ball had left paint marks. Frank said to Wayne, "You're dirtying Mrs. K.'s wall!" Michael said to Wayne, "Why don't you make a circle on a paper, hang it on the wall, and throw the ball at it?" Wayne took a paper and did exactly as Michael had suggested.

. . . The worker was putting away the blocks that Wayne had used.

"Wait," said Frank. He knocked the buildings down by throwing blocks against them. When he finished, the worker put the blocks away. Frank helped.

. . . Wayne said to Norman, "You're beady-eye, like a dog. Get down!" Norman got down on all fours and Wayne led him by the hand like a dog.

. . . The worker was still inflating the Palooka when the boys arrived. (The inflatable bop-bag was introduced for the first time to redirect physical aggression.) Frank: "Can I blow it?" The worker allowed him to. He gave up after a while. Wayne said, "I've got one at home. I'll do it." He did. Michael: "We'll take turns" (in striking the Palooka after it was blown up). He continued, "Wayne, *you* tell us when to go." Wayne: "Get outa here!" Norman, meanwhile, boxed at the air and danced in a circle as he did so. Wayne and Frank punched the Palooka back and forth excitedly, yelling at it, "Get up—there you go! You Palooka!" Soon the Palooka deflated; the bottom was ripped. All gathered about. (This was only the first of many Palookas that either became subject to repairs in succeeding sessions or had to be replaced altogether, so much were these toys abused by kicking, punching, and throwing.)

. . . Frank said, "Everybody's doing something but Norman. He's a big dope." Wayne added, "He doesn't do anything in class either." Wayne grabbed Norman about the neck and said, "Say 'Ouch.'" Norman struggled and looked upset. The worker walked over, saying, "It's better not to do that." Wayne released him. Frank then said, "Make me a hat, Mrs. K. A cowboy hat." Wayne: "Make me one, too." The worker did so.

All sat down for snacks. Wayne said, "I'd like to break that bell. Then we wouldn't know time's up!" Frank added, "Mrs. K. has a watch." Wayne replied, "It could stop." Michael: "Then we'd *never* leave."

. . . The play room was set for a Christmas party. Wayne noticed names on the gift packages. "Here's mine," he said, opening and finding a toy rocket. "How does it go? Mrs. K?" The worker showed how to shoot the rocket into the air. Frank picked up his gift. "Boy, Mrs. K., this must have cost thirty-five cents." Then they sat quietly, eating cookies and candy and drinking punch. Michael said, "We could eat and eat 'til we're stuffed!"

. . . Wayne spoke to Frank. "Hey, Frank, you got changed to Mrs. B's class. She's mean!" Frank replied, "No, she's not. If you're nice to her she's nice to you. Right, Mrs. K.?" looking to the worker. She nodded.

. . . It was time to leave. Wayne put a sign on his unfinished block structure: "No one touch this."

. . . Norman was throwing a male puppet against the wall, saying, "You're mean. I'll beat you! You're mean to your wife."

. . . Frank and Wayne dumped puppets in water at the sink, then threw them on the floor. "We're cleaning up," said Wayne. Then both boys danced about singing, "Handy Andy! You're Handy Andy," chasing Norman as they sang. They waved the wet puppets in his face. They backed him into a corner and pushed the table and chairs in front of him. The worker walked toward them and they stopped. Wayne then said to her, "I need twelve papers for the months. Can I take them, Mrs. K.?" (meaning construction paper for a calendar that he wanted to take when he left) The worker said that he could. Frank: "Ooh, he's taking paper." The worker said, "I know." Wayne smeared some paint on Norman's face. Norman said nothing.

Wayne and Frank were throwing balls against a painting on the wall. The worker said, "That's Michael's." Wayne said, "Can I hit your painting, Michael?" Michael replied, "It's torn already. Go ahead." "I'm not doing it," said Frank, "I'm listening to Mrs. K." The worker repaired the painting and attached it to the wall again. Again Wayne hit it with his ball. It fell down. The worker gave it to Michael. Wayne's ball then accidentally hit a jar of red paint on the easel, spilling it over. The worker mopped up the mess. Wayne then put lids on all the rest of the jars.

. . . Norman said to Wayne, "Why do you want to play me? You'll win me." Michael: "He [Norman] doesn't think he'll win. He might be surprised and win some day." Michael and Norman boxed with each other, using puppets as gloves.

Individual Interview with Norman

During a supervision session it was suggested to the worker that she see Norman alone, to determine whether she could modify his responses to the provocations of the others. His passive, masochistic manner only seemed to evoke more such harassments from Wayne and Frank.

The worker saw Norman for a brief time in her office. As an introduction she spoke of the play group, and Norman expressed positive feelings about it. Then she asked him why he did not stand up more to the others when they teased or provoked him. At first Norman replied, "I don't know." Then the worker suggested that he take cookies when offered and not wait for the other boys to give him approval to do so, particularly Wayne and Frank. Norman replied, "I'm afraid they'll beat me up." The worker assured him, "You can do it." He didn't comment further. The worker let matters stand at this, thinking she would observe whether he would assay a different behavior at the following session.

Excerpts, continued

. . . Wayne climbed to the top of one of the lockers. "Boy," he said, "I could bomb everyone from up here!" The worker walked over and merely stood quietly near the locker. Wayne climbed down, collected blocks of various sizes—naming them "bullets, rockets, bombs"—and carried them to the top of the locker. The worker stood by as Wayne raised his hand, ready to toss a block across the room. "Watch out! Get away, Mrs. K.," he said. The worker said, "I'm standing here in case you fall." Wayne tossed the block. Michael said, "You'll hit someone on the head." The worker added: "It could happen." Wayne then slowly pushed all the blocks down the side of the locker. They made much noise, but he did it carefully (so they would not hit anyone). Frank had been busy washing the sink and the mirror over it. He called to the worker, "Look, Mrs. K. New sink! New mirror!" The worker replied, "Nice and clean."

. . . Frank held up the pump used to inflate the Palooka, asking, "What's this for?" The worker explained. Wayne tried the new pump (a recent addition to the group). Michael said, "The first time we had a Palooka he got dead!" Wayne: "Yeah, we killed him!" Worker: "It's a toy. It broke. I sent it back to be fixed." Frank: "I hope they don't charge a lot."

. . . Wayne asked, "What's wrong, Mrs. K.?" The worker replied, "They are using the round table so I'm setting here." Wayne: "No, I mean no food?" The worker realized that Wayne was referring to the absence of the usually visible box of cookies and other items for the repast. She said, "Oh, today I brought a big cake. It's here in the bag." Wayne: "I'd like to crush and eat the whole cake!" The worker placed the cake on the table. All but Frank sat. He continued to draw. The worker carefully counted those present, then cut the cake into as many pieces. She served each boy in turn, finally herself. Wayne said to Norman: "Gimme that cake, Norman." The worker looked at Norman, catching his eye briefly. Norman bit into his cake. Wayne said, "I'm starved. I didn't eat breakfast. I wish we had snacks like this in class." Michael said, "Yeah, we only get pretzels." Wayne: "I'm fainting from the cake!" He leaned back, falling off the chair. Michael laughed, "It's so good. It made him faint!" When it was time to leave, Wayne said, "I'll break that bell!"

. . . Wayne went to an easel and began to smear. He took three brushes in one hand, dipped each in a different color, and painted with all three together. Then he moved to the other easel, saying, "Mrs. K., that's my painting." Worker: "I'll put your name on it." Wayne answered, "I messed this one up," referring to his second "painting." "Where shall I put it, Mrs. K.?" he went on. The worker said, "Over here. It will dry." He did as she suggested. Then he painted a design with great care. No colors were mixed haphazardly as in the past.

One of the boys found a toy paper blower, a party favor such as is common at children's parties. Norman looked at it. Wayne blew it into the faces of the boys. Norman: "Lemme see." They all assembled to watch. Frank: "Whose it is, Mrs. K.?" Worker: "Did any of you leave it last week?" Michael said, "Not me." The others also said it wasn't theirs. Wayne said,

"Someone left it here." The worker said, "Sometimes when there's a play in the auditorium a class uses this room to dress up." Wayne said, "I'll kill them!" All discussed the fact that someone had been in the play room. Wayne filled the paper blower with water. Frank pulled it from him. They tore it and threw the pieces to the floor, and the water splashed from it.

. . . Meanwhile Wayne asked the worker to make a heart for him. "Here, Mrs. K., I want a great big valentine." The worker cut it for him. She looked up at Frank, who was now hitting a ball against the entrance door. Wayne climbed on a chair next to the door, pointing to the doorjamb. "Look, Mrs. K., this is broken." The worker told him she would have it fixed. Wayne took the heart the worker had made for him. Walking by the easel, he accidentally dumped the jar containing water. "Ooh, look what he did, Mrs. K.," Norman said. The worker walked over. "It was an accident," she said. Wayne: "Somebody will clean it up."

. . . Frank turned to look at Michael's work, saying, "That's a nice valentine. I'll make mine next time when there's more red paper."

. . . Wayne took blocks at random, then raised one as if to throw it across the room. The worker said, "It's better to slide them." Wayne slid one across the floor. Then he took the broom and said, "I'm playing hockey." He pushed blocks like a hockey player. He continued to hit the blocks near the supply shelves. Michael said, "All the paper will fall down" (because the blocks were hitting the bottom of the shelves and shaking them). Wayne to the worker: "Mrs. K., the paper will fall. What should I do?" The worker replied, "Maybe you could build with the blocks." Wayne then took all the blocks and began to build with them.

. . . Norman took the mother puppet and danced it around the room. (In supervision conference, the worker described his movements as definitely effeminate. She reported this more and more often in describing the manner in which Norman cavorted about.) Wayne said to Norman, "Give me that. I'll show you what to do with it." Norman compliantly handed him the mother puppet. Wayne placed it on a large block, took another block, and hammered the puppet furiously. Norman withdrew to the other end of the room and stood in a corner while watching Wayne.

. . . Norman came into the play room smiling and said, "Wayne's absent." He put his coat away and danced around the room. He sang beautifully and danced the Charleston. When Frank entered, he went right to the Palooka. He said to Norman, "What are you so happy about? You fag!" Norman continued to dance and sing.

. . . Wayne sang. Frank occasionally strutted away from the easel and snapped his fingers in a dance as Wayne continued to sing. Frank went back to the easel. He put a dab of paint on the wall. The worker looked at him, and then he wiped the paint off. Wayne handed the worker the loom he had been using and said, "Here, Mrs. K., finish this."

. . . When snacks were served, Frank continued to paint. Wayne said, "Maybe the painter doesn't want to eat, Mrs. K." The worker smiled,

"Maybe." Later, Wayne said to the worker, "Mrs. K., you did this wrong." He took out part of the loom weaving that the worker had been doing for him.

Wayne turned to the worker while standing at the easel. "This painting is in my way," he said. The worker asked, "You want to paint?" She removed the painting and put a fresh sheet of paper on the easel. Wayne said to her, "Make me a bunny." The worker asked, "With paint?" Wayne: "No, here's a pink crayon." Later, when the worker had finished the drawing, Wayne said to her, "That's a gushy bunny you made, Mrs. K."

. . . Wayne heard the escorts at the door. He opened it and yelled, "Get out of here!" He added, "Mrs. K., they're here. They want to come in." Worker: "They can't. Not until you leave." Wayne to worker: "Take that to your office and I'll get it after lunch" (giving her the rabbit drawing she had made for him earlier). After lunch he came to the worker's office and she gave him the drawing. Wayne said, "Thank you, Mrs. K."

. . . After awhile the boys carried the Palooka across the room. Then Wayne said, "C'mere, Norman. Hit him." Norman left the easel, where he had been painting, and began to hit the Palooka as Wayne and Frank yelled. Wayne said to Frank, "Count." Frank counted to ten, aloud. Then Frank said, "Who's the winner?" Wayne answered, "Norman!" Wayne and Frank both raised Norman's hand in the air, announcing: "The winner!" Norman grinned.

(Last session in June) . . . Wayne distributed the doughnuts, giving one to each boy. He also gave the worker one and said, "Here's yours, Mrs. K." The worker was pouring soda. Norman: "Ooh, presents!" Frank opened a corner of his package to peek at its contents. "Marbles! Boy, cat's eyes!" Wayne said, "Let's have a game of marbles." Frank: "With whose?" Wayne: "With Norman's." Norman: "Oh, no!" Wayne looked toward Michael. Michael said, "Not mine."

The boys moved to the other table. Michael took his cup of potato chips and candy. Wayne said to Frank, "Is this the last time?" Frank said, "That's why the party." The worker told them, "This is the last meeting. We'll come back after summer, when school starts." Norman: "We'll come again next year?" Worker: "Yes."

Comments and Interpretations

The foregoing chronological excerpts, covering many months, provide an overview of developments in the play group. Most of the events reported require no elucidation with respect to their manifest and underlying meanings, but some episodes warrant examination.

The excerpts are replete with references to Wayne, which indicates his continuing, focal position in the play group's interactions. Notable are his growing rivalry with the others and his vacillation between generalized aggression, open anger, and muted defiance of the worker. His extraordinary ambivalence is shown by his open bids for the worker's exclusive attention alternating with negativism at times. There are revealing incidents of Wayne's inner turmoil. He referred to "killing" the Palooka, while the other boys commented less emotionally about the Palooka being broken and the need to repair it. More dramatic was the incident when Wayne seized the mother puppet from Norman, who was expressing mild, negative feelings toward it. Wayne, on the other hand, "killed" the puppet, violently smashing it between two blocks. So intense was this "homicidal" play that Norman was forced to withdraw to the farthest point of the play room; he could not tolerate the sight. One can only wonder about the severe rage that Wayne had repressed against a maternal figure that was cathartically discharged in this act, possible incorporating the worker in its symbolic displacement. In view of the rigid, punitive, and uncompromising nature of Wayne's mother, it is probable that he had had little opportunity to ventilate his feelings against her. Yet, despite Wayne's acting out, replete in the excerpts are instances of corrective, self-limiting, compensatory behavior in which Wayne unwittingly revealed his dependency needs and sought "forgiveness" and nurturance from the worker.

During the last session in June, Wayne was again frightened by the thought that the play group experience was coming to an end, although he had experienced such a vacation hiatus before. The worker had to reassure him. He was finally capable of saying "thanks" to the worker for holding the rabbit drawing, something he had not been able to do heretofore.

The worker had growing concern about Norman despite the minimal ego strengthening that was evident in him, as shown in his mild defiance of the worker through imitating some of the negativistic antics he had seen the others perform. When he was "ordered" about by Wayne and Frank, Norman's almost abject compliance debased him. This was countertherapeutic. It is fascinating how Wayne and Frank, who usually rejected or teased Norman, attempted to "model" him in aggression to "make a man" out of him by showing him how to "fight" the Palooka. The worker detected effeminate mannerisms in Norman more frequently. It is interesting that these became apparent at moments when Norman felt secure enough to reveal hidden feelings in spontaneous play: anger against his mother, anxiety about marital discord (his parents'?), and other affective responses that had not been revealed in the group before. It was more and more evident that he was extremely immature, with masochistic tendencies. It was probably a latent homosexuality in Norman that provoked Wayne and Frank to reject and plague him, thus unconsciously affirming their own masculinity. The worker's observations tended to confirm that Norman was intellectually limited, perhaps borderline in intelligence, something that had been suspected at the beginning of treatment.

While Frank joined Wayne in acting out, he demonstrated more intactness and a firmer positive transference to the worker. Several times Frank took the role of a neutralizer, helping dissolve conflict situations. While he did exhibit negative transference behavior from time to time, it was not as enduring or as abrasive as was Wayne's. An interesting sign of Frank's social growth was revealed when he spontaneously praised Michael's work, which he had not done prior to this. Also, Frank defended the image of his new teacher, correcting Wayne's derogatory description of her. Frank affirmed that she was indeed "nice" if one "is nice to her."

Michael continued to "open up" with each succeeding session. He actually smeared the setting when painting—the easel and wall—a symbolic assault on the worker; he attacked the Palooka; he was more verbal and interactive; and he expressed pleasure openly. Michael also acted the role of the group's "prophet," mindful of the changes that were already taking place. More than once he commented about things "changing" in the future. He told Frank that sharing of food would improve later; he stated that Norman was fearful of joining in aggressive action but that he would be able to do so sometime in the future. These comments reflected inner perceptions and probably his hopeful wishes for himself.

The group was jealously possessive of the play room. The open suspicion, then expressed anger, toward other children who occasionally used the room is interesting. First the boys played with the found symbol of the "stranger"—the toy blower; then they tore it to shreds. And Wayne still wished to "break" the bell that signaled termination of sessions. Michael and others jokingly spoke of being able to "stay forever" in the play room.

While the worker had to intervene to protect Norman and to modulate Wayne's and Frank's more active "play," she accomplished this judiciously, without conveying disapproval. With respect to the incident when she served an elaborate cake, this was done to help some of the boys deal with their need to grab food, a sign of excessive orality. There are several procedures available to a worker when some members of a play group have difficulty in learning to share food. A pattern of grabbing can be blocked by offering a sumptuous food item that makes it incumbent on the worker to cut and serve, thus providing equally for each child. The attractive offering captures the attention of the children and inhibits grabbing. This way a worker not only indulges them with a special "treat" but also interferes with an immature pattern of behavior. It is usually necessary to use this technique several times, as the worker did in this group. In addition, the worker models appropriate social behavior as she distributes the offering, asking a child, "Please pass this to Michael," "Which flavor would you like?" and so on.

At this point in the group's development, portions of evaluation reports are given containing information reported by teachers, parents, and others. As was noted earlier in this book, progress reports are done periodically during a group's existence. The following material was extracted at a point when the play group had met for two years.

Michael: His teacher wrote that Michael's work skills were "so good that he was awarded a certificate." He had gained a year in reading. In the playground, he now participated in class games. The teacher described him as a "normal, healthy child." He took time to think through a response before answering in class lessons. This comment supported the worker's observations that Michael, when in the play group, at times reflected carefully before volunteering comments about events taking place. While Michael was not aggressive socially according to his teacher, he did get along with all the children. He played with them if invited and joined in their conversations. This was a decided improvement over the past. In all, the teacher found Michael more relaxed.

Michael's mother described him as less irritable, less shy, and much less concerned about school attendance. He had been fearful about attending at the beginning. She said he had not had an asthma attack in a long time. (At no time did Michael reveal symptoms of asthma in the play group.)

Norman: The teacher reported that Norman used materials well. He was occasionally creative; his drawings were "interesting." His penmanship was "beautiful" at one time; now had become "sloppy." Norman's academic progress was "nil," as she put it. He still spoke timidly, in a low voice, although the same teacher indicated that at times he could be "antagonistic, passively resistive." Classmates barely recognized his presence. Interestingly enough, she saw no contact between him and Wayne, who was in the same class. (From comments made by Wayne in the play group, he gave the impression of abusing Norman in class and elsewhere. Evidently this was untrue.)

Norman's mother said that lately "there's something wrong with Norman. He's acting up." From her manner it was obvious that she still dominated Norman and the family generally. Her husband played an insignificant role in the boy's life, according to her. She asked the worker for a referral to a helping agency, which the worker did make. The mother never appeared there, however, thus betraying her real lack of motivation. She was evidently emotionally "satisfied" with the situation in her life and family. The worker attempted to loosen the destructive psychological bonds between Norman and his mother by encouraging Norman's attendance at summer camp. It was questionable whether the mother would follow through on the recommendation.

Wayne: The teacher described him as "robust, neat, and clean." Wayne was assertive; he spoke openly and well. She had a good relationship with him, but added that Wayne got into trouble with other teachers and school administrators. His classmates accepted him, even though he fought often. He had become conscious of girls and played up to them. Wayne would fight "at the drop of a hat" if someone mentioned his mother's name in a pejorative sense (a common provocative act engaged in by some children when they taunt each other). Academically he was achieving below his potential. The teacher thought he was insufficiently challenged, since he was brighter than most children in her class. Wayne was careful with work materials and he could be a "good monitor." She felt that Wayne could be managed by a "strong, firm teacher" and said she hoped that he would be placed in a more advanced class the following year.

Wayne's mother did not respond to a request for an interview, but the worker had peripheral contact with her on occasions when school administrators summoned her to school because Wayne had gotten into trouble. She remained characteristically belligerent and defensive, and she still blamed the school for her son's behavior, defending some of Wayne's actions as reasonable responses to the provocations of others. When Wayne spoke of his family in class or in the play group, it was usually in reference to his brother, who helped Wayne "beat up" someone when the occasion appeared to demand it. Little more could be gleaned from the mother about circumstances affecting Wayne or the family. She was intransigent.

Play group sessions were resumed in September. The boys immediately resumed a level of interaction that had existed in June, but some differences were noted. The boys now interacted more as a unitary group; Norman and Michael were less inhibited by the reserve and timidity that had characterized their behavior for a long time. From this point on, the group as a whole moved into a phase of accelerated corrective reexperience. This is a condition wherein more penetrating influences on personality take place and modifications in behavior occur as a consequence. There were still episodes with negative transference implications, but they were much less frequent and less intensive. A more significant reconstructive influence now predominated, flowing from the positive transference relationships with the worker, which were at a peak.

The excerpts that follow are from sessions 47 through 52. These sessions were critical ones for Wayne and Frank in particular; the excerpts also reveal in dramatic context the boys' "love" feelings for the worker.

Sessions Nos. 47–52, Excerpts

. . . When Wayne came in, he tossed his bag of lunch on the round table, where Michael was sitting. The bag slid to the floor. "Pick it up, will ya, Michael?" asked Wayne. Michael obliged. Wayne punched the Palooka like a punching bag, saying, "Take that! Take that! And that!" Norman joined him. "Go ahead, hit him," said Wayne. Norman punched the Palooka while Wayne put on puppets as boxing gloves. Then Wayne began punching the Palooka. "He's down! Count, Norman!" Norman did. Wayne raised his hand and said, "I'm the winner!"

. . . Frank joined the boys. Wayne said, "Let's play punchball." He and Norman played, hitting puppets (they had no ball). Frank played with the Palooka, punching it. Wayne announced aloud, "Eight to three, I'm home run king! I'm king! I'm king of *everything*!"

. . . The worker was cutting leaves from construction paper. "Can I make one when you're through?" asked Frank. "You can make one now if you like," said the worker, helping him to get started.

. . . Wayne turned out the lights. There were screams. Norman tossed a puppet. The lights went on. All became excited and chased around a table. Michael was part of this. The lights were being switched on and off by Wayne.

. . . Norman reached for a graham cracker. Michael: "Hey, Norman, not yet." Norman put it back. All the boys helped themselves to crackers and they drank. Frank took another; the others followed. Then there was grabbing for the remainder.

Wayne said, "Boy, it's hot here" (it was). "We ought to have a fan here," he added. Worker: "We could use one." Wayne: "I got one at home." "How big?" asked Michael. Wayne stretched his arms and said, "Like this. Too big to bring." Frank put his cup in the sink. The worker cleaned the table.

. . . Wayne and Frank whispered. Wayne then grabbed Norman. Frank grabbed Michael. Both boys forced Michael and Norman into the clothes locker.

. . . When the worker arrived she found a box of copper foil, embossing tools, and other new items. A message was brought to her from the assistant principal indicating that he had sent the materials. Wayne arrived. The worker noted that the tracing paper she had ordered had not been included. She sent Wayne to the office to obtain some. As the boys gathered around to see the new supplies, Frank said, "I helped Mr. S. give out the supplies. I told him we needed this. I didn't bring it to your room [office], Mrs. K. I thought you'd leave it there and we need it. O.K.?" "Good," replied the worker. She demonstrated for the boys how the foil could be used, and they all became engaged in this work.

. . . Wayne finished his project, then looked for the Palooka. "Norman killed Palooka," he said. The worker said, "I forgot to bring it." (She was having it repaired once more.) Wayne said, "We need wood to hammer our pictures on" (that is, to mount the copper etchings that the boys had been making for the past several weeks). Worker: "I'll bring some next week."

. . . Frank started on another copper plaque. He called out to Wayne, "Wayne, hammer mine for me." Wayne did so, first his own, then Frank's. Wayne painted borders in red and green on the wood, framing the plaques. Frank said, "I'm putting one in my room and one in my aunt's." Michael was struggling with his. Wayne showed him how to hammer the nail in. Frank was teasing Norman, and Wayne said, "Leave him alone." Frank retorted, "Make me!" He went on: "You bother him, why can't I?" Wayne walked over to Frank and shook his fist at him. Frank pushed him away, and Wayne returned to his work. Michael painted his plaque red. Then Frank did his in orange and said, "Look, Mrs. K., it's real beat!" [nifty]. The worker nodded.

. . . Wayne knocked the blocks over. Then he said, "Mrs. K., do you and those monitors put everything away when we go?" "Yes," said the worker. "Why don't they do it alone? I don't like that monitor. I hid, but she found me." Wayne then put all the blocks back on the shelves.

. . . Cookies were being distributed. Wayne gave one to the worker; it was broken. He said, "No, here's a good one, Mrs. K."

The boys were speaking of integration in the South at the time this group was conducted, 1962. Wayne: "Mrs. K., that guy got into college." Michael: "Yeah." Frank: "I wouldn't want to live in Mississippi." Wayne: "Bloodshed! I'd like that; and the guns and gas!" Michael: "They had guns with points [bayonets] on 'em!"

. . . Wayne opened the door to the auditorium and yelled. The worker said, "It's better to leave the door closed." Wayne: "Is it bad?" The worker replied, "No, but a teacher out there might come in and we don't want that." Wayne: We'd beat her!" Frank: "We'd throw her out!" Wayne continued: "Does anyone come in? I bet workmen do. There are footprints." (There were, in fact, in the plaster dust left by workmen who had been repairing the room.) The boys continued to speak of throwing intruders out of "their" room. The bell rang for lunch. Michael left, as did Frank and Norman. Wayne hung around and then he left.

. . . Frank had brought magazines to cut out and he pasted pictures in a booklet he was making. Wayne made Halloween pictures. Michael worked on copper foil. He asked the worker for more wood. She said she would order some more; they were temporarily out of wood. Norman smeared paints at the easel a while, then he worked with copper. Wayne hung around at the end of the session. He gave his picture to the worker and said, "Take this to your office. I'll come and get it."

. . . The worker had prepared a Halloween party. She served doughnuts, candy in little paper cups, and soda. Wayne and Frank had two doughnuts each. There was one left over after everyone had had some. Wayne cut the remaining one in halves, giving them to Norman and Michael.

Frank was hitting his ball against the wall and the easel. Paint got on the ball, and it accidentally hit the worker's skirt. Frank washed the ball. Later, at snacks, he said, "I'll be bad. All day."

. . . There were different escorts, and they accidentally brought another boy instead of Michael. The others gathered about. The worker said, "It's the wrong Michael." Wayne said, "He's a trespasser." Wayne escorted the boy back to class, returning with Michael.

. . . The boys played in pairs, Wayne with Michael and Frank with

Norman. They played ring toss, Candyland, and checkers. Wayne directed most of the games.

. . . Wayne helped himself to all the cookies. Then he divided them with Frank. Wayne distributed the cookies, half of one at a time to Norman and Michael and also to the worker. At the end, each person had received two cookies.

. . . Norman and Michael were playing against Frank and Wayne. Wayne taunted Norman about his poor playing ability. Frank joined in the banter. Wayne said, "I saw you on a bus, Norman." "Yeah," replied Norman, "I went shopping." Wayne: "I nearly bust a gut laughing! Your mother said, 'I'll slap you, Norman, if you don't stop that!' Right there on the bus!" Norman blushed and mumbled, "We was goin' to Jamaica Avenue."

. . . Frank played with the Nok Hockey game. Looking up, he said, "Play you, Mrs. K.?" The worker joined him in the game. When she scored, Frank called out, "Hey, Norman, even Mrs. K. is better'n you!"

. . . It was quite warm in the room. Frank: "We ought to have air conditioning." The worker was cutting out Christmas decorations. Wayne: "Got any green paint, Mrs. K.?" The worker looked and said, "No, I'll try to get some." Wayne asked, "Make me a Christmas picture?" The worker nodded and proceeded to do so. Frank won the game and then sat next to the worker and started cutting out Christmas decorations also.

. . . The worker started to set the table. Frank moved over, not knowing where to work. Worker: "You can work here." She took the things off the woodwork table and helped Frank move his materials there. Wayne said to her, "That's a nice Christmas picture." The worker had put Wayne's picture on the wall.

. . . The bell rang. Frank and Wayne ran into the clothes lockers, which still held the boys' jackets, and they banged the doors shut behind them. Michael: "Wayne, just let me get my coat." Wayne came out and said, "Could I take some paper?" The worker nodded. Frank: "Me too." Norman: "Me too." They all took paper and left. Wayne returned and said, "I'll go this way today. Goodbye, Mrs. K." Worker: "Goodbye, Wayne."

. . . Frank took his ball and began to play handball against the wall. The ball brushed the worker. Wayne saw this and demanded, "Say 'I'm sorry!'" "Sorry," said Frank. The ball then touched Wayne. Wayne again ordered: "Say 'I'm sorry!'" Frank: "What for?" Wayne: "It hit me!" Frank: "Make me!" Wayne lunged at him, grabbing Frank by the collar. The boys tussled furiously, insulting each other. Wayne yelled, "You're scared!" Frank: "I'll kill you!" Wayne taunted: "Yeah, if you had Walter and them kids! You can't beat me alone!" Frank replied, "Lay offa me, Wayne." Wayne persisted, "You say you're sorry!" Wayne took off his jacket and tie. "Step outside and fight," he said to Frank. Frank: "I like it here. It's nice and hot.'' When they left at the end of the session, Wayne said to Frank, ''Let's play in the yard.'' Frank: ''Yeah, I don't have to eat.''

. . . Wayne and Frank painted at the easels. They played handball against a wall after that, but not before carefully cleaning their ball to keep the newly painted wall clean.

. . . Frank was throwing his ball against the wall. It fell into a cup of red paint on the easel, and Frank reached for it. It was stuck in the cup. ''Look Wayne, I'm all bloody,'' he said. Wayne was intensely interested in his woodwork and didn't respond.

. . . The boys arrived except for Norman, who came in later. Wayne said, ''C'mon, I got a game for real boys! O.K. if we play cards here, Mrs. K.?'' The worker nodded. (Wayne had brought a deck of playing cards.) Norman arrived. ''Can I play?'' he inquired. Wayne: ''He doesn't even know *how* to play!'' Worker: ''You could teach him.'' Wayne: ''O.K., c'mere, Norman. Sit right next to me. I'll show you how.''

Comments and Interpretations

The above excerpts describe activities involving the group more as a whole, which is typical of a therapeutic play group during a reconstructive phase. The comments that follow, however, are focused on individual children in order to show the cumulative effects of therapy. While the dynamic evolution of a therapeutic play group and the quality of ''groupism'' that develops are important features, it is the corrective effects that these exert on individual patients which are fundamental.

Michael: In these sessions some experiences were altogether innovative for MIchael, which had the effect of joining him closer to the group. He participated in most group games, alternately on different ''sides.'' Michael seldom worked alone on his projects as he had done in the past. He was conversational, expressing himself freely. Sometimes he could be mildly argumentative. Notable is the absence of timidity, and his increased aggressivity. Frank and Wayne shut him in the clothes locker, but he was able to remonstrate with them. There were still no somatic signs of asthma.

The incident in which Michael was in the clothes locker illustrates an interesting phenomenon in group therapy with respect to children like Michael. Fearful children start in group treatment as isolates, protectively removing themselves from immediate contact with other children because of fear and anxiety. Aggressive group members tend to ''respect'' the withdrawn child's self-defensive maneuvers. This was the case for a long time with Michael and accounted for Frank and Wayne's responses to him. However, as frightened children overtly demonstrate more security and some aggression on their own part through participation, they become perceived and reacted to differently. By virtue of their newfound strengths, they become accessible to the group—"fair game" for provocation and "targets" for aggression. These are "coming out" experiences, and what would have formerly been intolerable to the frightened child now acts as a strengthening experience.

Norman: He was still subject to mixed handling by Frank and Wayne—teasing and derogation, and occasional supportive help from them. However, the comments about him made by Wayne and Frank were "diagnostically" accurate. The boys' remarks implied that Norman had not essentially changed, despite his occasional manifestations of spontaneity and mild aggression. There were no evidences to show that such qualities had become assimilated into his essential character.

Norman was attracted to the newly introduced crafts materials. Yet, he periodically reverted to messy, regressive play, usually with paints and water. This indicates an inordinate fixation on oral and anal levels. While one gains an impression of improvement in Norman from time to time, the change is superficial, lacking integration. Norman enjoyed the group experience; there was no question about that. In essence, it represented a "treat" for him, a departure from all other social experiences in his life, experiences in which he had had repetitive failures. Wayne's description of the accidental meeting on the bus conveyed the quality of Norman's immaturity and compliance in the face of enormously debilitating and overwhelming strictures from his mother.

Frank: He was happily engaged in creative activities with crafts and other materials and was obviously enjoying his accomplishments. His beaming pride when he called the worker's attention to his work—"It's beat!"—and his remarks about giving his aunt a finished plaque for her room, as well as one for his own, were evidences of improved self-image and ego strength. The worker's introduction of the crafts media fostered his interest in creative work. Such libido-binding activities are capable of tapping aggression and channeling it into sublimative outlets. They should be introduced into therapeutic play groups during the corrective phase, a phase of assimilative experience. This use of new materials further emphasizes the principles of *specificity*. This means the choice of appropriate crafts, games, and play items in accordance with definite psychological considerations and also the *timeliness* of their introduction. For example, the worker introduced the Palooka figure at a time when aggression in the play group was at a pitch where intervention had become necessary.

Frank expressed himself positively toward the worker; he showed concern for her person and was responsive to her sustaining interest in him. He sought praise and was at times in rivalry for her attention, but not excessively so. In one episode, he and Wayne drew a distinction between the accepting, helpful worker and other teachers. The boys said they would "throw out" the latter if they "dared" to enter the play room. Yet, there were moments when Frank still needed to discharge cathected inner feelings of resentment toward adults, using the worker as a displaced object. Frank harbored within himself the traumatic effects of having been "deserted" by primary libidinal objects when he was much younger, events that could not have been prevented but took their toll. The deaths of his mother, father, and maternal grandmother in a short space of time afflicted him sorely. When such events occur early in a child's development, they are conceived as purposive. We know that young children can "blame" parents for dying. The reader will remember Frank's early announcement to one of the group members: "I got no mother, no father, no grandmother. They're dead"— with occasional repetition of this theme later.

Thus, the positive transference relationship to the worker not only acted as a symbolic background for Frank's cathartic release of emotions, but it also provided a sustaining emotional nurturance that was essential for him. When Frank accidentally soiled the worker's clothing with his ball, he became instantly contrite, then angry. His comment that he was going to "be bad . . . all day" reflected ambivalent anger and compensatory feelings. It was equivalent to saying: "This is a 'bad' day for me! I accidentally did something to Mrs. K., which I did not mean to do. It bothers me. I don't know how to handle this feeling. It makes me angry. I'll be 'bad' all day as a consequence." Frank did say he was sorry, at Wayne's insistence. Frank did appear to be sorry for the accident involving the worker, but his anger brought him to defy Wayne; this reveals Frank's still aggressive capability. After defying Wayne, Frank later made up with him.

Repetitively we note how the worker fulfilled Frank's requests for special materials and how she helped him immediately upon request. She praised and acknowledged him in other ways, carefully, not fulsomely; the latter would have made him suspicious of her. Frank now involved the worker in a game for the first time. For him this represented an affectional contact.

Wayne: He continued to be focal in the group's activities. Wayne, of all the boys, showed the most change in the period of time covered by these excerpts. Gone was the negativism and defiant behavior he had formerly exhibited toward the worker.

In its place we see manifestations of concern for her and almost open warmth. The deliberate suspicious and challenging behavior that had been typical for him in the beginning had dissipated for the most part. He was now spontaneous and creative, as expressed through his work with the new crafts media and his accomplishments with tools. The others recognized this and sought his help. And Wayne responded to their requests, even volunteering to assist them. He was happy about and proud of his status in the play group, announcing braggadocio-like: "I'm the king of *everything*!" Yet, Wayne had not become compliant, a model of "goodness." He was still independent and strong, openly aggressive at times, as when he fought vigorously with Frank. Also, Wayne could still be provocative, as shown when he turned the room lights on and off. At the same time, Wayne could be a neutralizer, acting to reduce conflict situations, a role that had far from typified him earlier.

Wayne now organized group games and participated more appropriately, without always ordering the other boys about, as had been his wont. He still liked to tease Norman, as when he closed him in the locker with Michael. Also, he described what was for him a most amusing incident on the bus between Norman and his mother. Still in all, there was a quality of reasonableness now that made Wayne altogether more tolerable, to both the worker and the other boys. The worker had much less occasion to intervene to keep Wayne's behavior within bounds. He was more tractable and self-limiting.

Most striking of all is the nature of Wayne's personal relationship with the worker and the incidents in which this was displayed. He trusted her; this was a critical change from the long-standing, generalized distrust that he had exhibited toward her previously. Further, Wayne tended to solicit her attention, still seeking to remain alone with her or contriving to come to her office. This was especially apparent when he gave her his picture and told her that he "will come and get it." When the worker limited him against opening the play room door, Wayne asked questioningly: "Is it bad?" The worker assured him that it was not, and she was able to impress him with the reality situation. In these episodes, Wayne demonstrated not only an increased tolerance for frustration but a much better accommodation to reality. Wayne volunteered to find the "right" Michael; also, the worker did not hesitate to send Wayne to the office for tracing paper. In many ways he had become more responsible.

Improvements noted in the boys and in the group as a whole continued during the remainder of the school year. The group sessions were fruitful and enjoyable. Occasional abrasive interactions occurred, but these were resolved mostly by the boys without intervention from the worker. Their demonstrated capacity to deal more effectively with conflict situations was further validation of the intrinsic changes in each boy, except in Norman's case. While Norman continued to enjoy membership in the play group, even more so since he was less harried by Wayne and Frank, he nevertheless showed no fundamental independence or improvement in ego strength.

A psychological assessment was made on Norman, and a recommendation followed to place him in a special class for intellectually limited children. This was done about two months before termination of the play group. Since much personal attention was given to children in the special class, it was decided to observe Norman's adjustment without the support of the play group. During this time the worker saw him occasionally in her office individually. Norman appeared to be quite happy in the new class and not bothered by the fact that he was no longer attending the group. The reactions of the boys to Norman's absence were interesting.

Session No. 73, Excerpts

. . . The worker was pumping up the Palooka. Frank: "Got it fixed?" Worker: "It's a new one." Frank said, "I know. Wayne broke the last one." Worker: "It was an accident." (This time it had been, in fact.) Wayne entered. He said, "I can blow that up easy, Mrs. K." The worker gave him the pump. He blew it up partly, then suddenly jumped up and said, "I gotta go see the way they fixed up the auditorium." (New lights had been installed. Also, Wayne had a new responsibility in school: he was on the projection squad, hence his interest in events in the auditorium.) Frank said, "Me too," and he left with Wayne. They soon returned.

. . . Michael was playing the bingo game. Wayne said, "Hey, Norman isn't here." Frank: "Yeah, where is he?" The worker replied, "Norman isn't coming any more." Frank said, "Bet I know why. We picked on him too much." The worker said, "You helped him a lot. You tried hard. Now I'll see Norman alone, a different time. I see many children, you know, sometimes in groups like this, sometimes alone." Wayne said, "Yeah, we tried to help him, but he's still a nut!" Then he said, "Hey, Michael, I'm playing with you."

Comments and Interpretations

Of interest is the boys' continuing awareness of Norman's limitations. Wayne's pejorative comment was uttered almost sympathetically. Frank's admission that Norman's leaving was due to their teasing was well responded to by the worker, who not only reassured the boys but complimented their efforts to help Norman.

Prior to this session, the worker introduced additional crafts work opportunities: lumber for woodwork (with a workbench) and leather work. The boys were enthusiastic about these new activities and made creditable objects. Wayne and Michael saw fit to make wooden "passes" such as students carry in the corridors when leaving classrooms, which they gave to their teachers as gifts.

As noted, Wayne had been selected for the projection squad, which had responsibility for the use of all the school's audiovisual equipment machines in both assemblies and individual classrooms when requested. He was quite proud of the assignment and carried out his duties conscientiously. On the day of the eighty-second play group session, Wayne came to the worker in advance of the session to tell her that he was "assistant chief" of the squad that day and that he had to show a film at the time the play group was to meet. He obviously wished to keep this assignment. The worker told him that it was an "important" job and assured him that she would understand his not coming to the play group. This occurred again a few weeks later, when another assignment conflicted with his attending the group.

Frank also had a school assignment, as a street guard controlling children's movements at the crossing during lunch dismissal and at the end of the school day. Frank was also proud of his work and performed creditably. For both Wayne and Frank, this was a far cry from their intransigent behavior in school when referred for help.

The boys were in the first semester of the sixth grade when the decision was made to terminate the play group. At the end of the school year they would be graduated to a junior high school. It was felt that termination should be made at the half point in the school year, thus providing an opportunity to observe how they accommodated without the support of the play group. Announcement of termination was made in session 85, as noted below.

Session No. 85, Excerpt

. . . The worker mentioned during snack time that "our group has been meeting for a long time." She added that the group would discontinue after the Christmas vacation. Wayne was the first to respond to this announcement: "Everything ends," he said matter-of-factly. He added: "We've been coming since the third grade." Michael and Frank agreed with this observation. The worker assured the boys that she would still be in the school and that they could come to see her if they wanted to. There were no more comments from the boys about termination. Wayne and Michael returned to sawing.

Session No. 88 (Last Session)

The table was set with a chocolate layer cake, soda, a wrapped gift for each boy, and a large Christmas stocking filled with candy. Wayne said to Frank and Michael: "See! I *told* you there'd be a party!" To Michael: "Let's go, Michael!" They put their coats down. Frank: "Boy, I'll open it! It's a book!" Wayne: "Could be a game." Frank opened his package. "'Robin Hood,' boy! I like this kind of book. We never have this kind." Wayne said, "I'll open mine. Gee, 'Sherlock Holmes.' Great! Look, a gun! [picture]. I like this book." He went on: "Let's see yours, Michael." Michael replied, "I'm not opening mine." Wayne: "Let's peek." They tore a tiny hole in the wrapping to see. "Bet it's 'Peter Pan,'" said Wayne. "Yeah, must be 'Peter Pan,'" added Frank. Michael: "Give it back! It's double wrapped. Right, Mrs. K.?" The worker nodded. "Thanks," said Michael. "Thank you," said Frank. Wayne: "Yeah, thanks a lot!" Worker: "You're welcome." The worker served cake and soda. Frank: "Great cake!" All ate.

Wayne and Frank talked of a visit that the glee club had made to a school in another part of the borough. Wayne and Frank sang with the glee club; Michael did not. Wayne said, "It was boss, real boss! What an auditorium! Two stages! Did you see that curtain!" The last remark was directed to Frank, who replied, "It was all white—outside—and all white inside." The worker asked, "What do you mean?" Frank: "All the kids were white. Everyone was white. We were the only colored ones (the entire glee club was composed of black children). I was embarrassed." The worker asked, "Why?" Frank: "They were all so white! I was embarrassed—until we began to sing."

Wayne continued: "Wait 'til they get to *our* school!" "Yeah," said Frank. Michael said, "In a couple of years they'll make our school gorgeous. We'll get an auditorium like that too." Wayne continued to describe the seats. All listened and commented.

The worker asked, "Who wants more cake?" Michael: "I do." Wayne: "I'll take a piece, too," Frank: "I'll take a piece." Wayne: "Great cake!" The worker commented: "This is the last time we'll come here." Michael replied, "Can't we come to the end of the year?" (June). The worker said, "We met for almost three years. I don't think we need to come anymore." Michael persisted: "We can come back anytime we want to, can't we?" The worker said, "You can come anytime you need to." Wayne: "They are all slaving away in class and we're having a party! Hey, what happened to Palooka?" Worker: "The air leaked out." Wayne began to blow it up. Frank said, "Say, who's been playing with the stage?" (Frank was referring to a puppet stage that the boys had built cooperatively from lumber.) The worker replied, "Some boys." Frank looked at various toy items strewn about the puppet stage. He said, "Look, a tree, Christmas gifts, and kids. Look, it's nice." Then he asked, "Next week can I take it home?" Worker: "Yes." Frank: "I'll come and get it."

"Anyone want more cake?" asked the worker. Michael: 'I'll take a piece home." The worker cut a slice and wrapped it in a napkin for him. Wayne said, "I get hungry on my post. I'll take a piece, too." Frank: "So will I." The boys got to talking about their Christmas gifts. Wayne said, "Wish I could get a projector like the one in the auditorium." Frank: "Do you know the curtain is broke?" Wayne replied, "I know who did it." Michael: "Who?" Wayne: "I can't tell." Frank: "Bet I know." Wayne: "Well . . . It's Clyde. He climbed the ropes. He thought he's Tarzan! And it broke!" The others laughed.

The lunch bell rang. Frank said to Michael, "Michael, you ought to get a head start walking home this afternoon." The worker started to clean up. The boys were leaving. Michael said, "Thanks, Mrs. K." Frank and Wayne: "Thanks."

Comments and Interpretations

Impending termination of the play group was announced during session 85 and accomplished in session 88. Procedurally it is necessary to allow four or five sessions following an announcement of termination so that children may work through their reactions to the impending separation. Some may express dismay, followed by benign regressive behavior, as if to demonstrate their unreadiness for termination. Often children will reminisce about earlier sessions and notable events that took place in the play group. These are normal "mourning" responses, and usually transient ones. Workers assure the children that they are free to "visit" following termination. Some do, but usually this tapers off, which is evidence of security and autonomy. Other children, who may still be dependent, may require other resources that can be implemented individually. Not every child in a play group will necessarily be at the same stage of improvement at the point of termination.

Wayne, Frank, and Michael displayed unusual strength in reacting to the announcement of termination. Momentarily they became silent. Then Wayne maturely commented that it had been a "long time" in the group. The others agreed. Michael assured himself that the worker would be available if needed. Wayne and Frank had already had several months of preparatory "weaning" through the recognition they had received as a result of their respective school assignments as special monitors. The tone of the last sessions was notably warm and friendly as described by the worker. There was a measure of sadness at termination, experienced by both the boys and the worker.

Follow-up

Three days after the last group session, the worker found a personal Christmas card that had been slipped under her office door in her absence. It was signed by Wayne and Frank. Later Wayne came to inquire about whether she had received it. She thanked him.

The following day Michael stopped the worker in the corridor and presented her with a beautifully wrapped gift. It was a scarf.

Frank met the worker on his return to school after the holiday. He told her everything "was going fine." He volunteered also that he had spent part of the holiday indoors because of poor weather.

Wayne visited her the following day to tell of a trip he had made with his class to a television station.

The boys graduated six months after termination of the therapeutic play group. Michael received an award for cooperation at the graduation exercises. He was also a runner-up in the athletic awards. His teacher reported that Michael's attendance had been excellent all semester. He was present every day except for one week when he had the measles. When Michael had been referred in the third grade, his absences were frequent because of asthma and other illnesses. His parents confided to the teacher how pleasantly surprised they were because of his good health. They were amazed by his ability to attend school so regularly during the past year.

Wayne played the drums in the school orchestra at the graduation exercises. He received another reward for school service and a special commendation for his work in both the school band and the glee club.

Frank was introduced by his teacher at the graduation assembly as the choreographer of the sixth-grade dance presentation. He danced beautifully with the group and was given hearty applause by the audience. His aunt came to the worker to thank her personally for her assistance. She said, "Without your help Frank would not have gotten through school. He'll be a fine boy."

Six months after the boys were in junior high school, the worker inquired as to their adjustment. Excerpts of communications from guidance counselors follow:

Wayne: "After somewhat of an uneven start, he has settled down and seems quite happy here. I have spoken with his mother, who gave me some of the details concerning his background. . . . I think that Wayne's adjustment will continue to be satisfactory since he was able to proceed consistently in the right direction. Much of his early temper outbursts have faded, and he smiles more and seems friendlier and relaxed."

Michael: "Michael has made an excellent adjustment. I have had about six interviews with him. He seems to enjoy school and he appears to have made many friends. He is a quiet boy who is well liked by both his teacher and his peers. Michael's grades on his report card reflect his excellent adjustment. . . . His excellent work in art indicates a special interest and talent. . . . Michael was placed in grade seven in September because he is reading close to grade level. If his work continues at the same level, he will probably be promoted to grade eight. Michael is a wonderful boy and I enjoy working with him.

Frank: The junior high school attended by Frank did not send a written report in answer to the worker's request, so she had several direct phone conversations with a counselor at that school. The counselor commented that Frank did not communicate freely with her in interviews. She thought Frank's aunt was having "some trouble" with him. The group worker telephoned Frank's aunt to find out what was happening. The aunt said that she was still employed daily and that Frank was very much "on his own" now. He had not been able to attend school for several days recently because he "had no pants." The worker volunteered to find a summer camp placement for Frank. The aunt added that she had received no complaints about Frank from his present school.

Summary

Wayne and Frank, pre-delinquent children who were approximately nine years of age when referred from third grade, were treated in a therapeutic play group for a period of two and three-quarter years, during which time eighty-eight group sessions were held. The presenting behavior problems of the boys were severe acting out, truancy, and defiance of authority. Both were defensive in their relationships with adults and suspicious of efforts made to help them, qualities characteristic of acting-out children who, early in their lives, have had conflicts with authoritative adults in homes, schools, and the community.

The choice of a therapeutic play group as the helping method was predicated on the premise that both Wayne and Frank were ego-intact and capable of developing a positive transference relationship with a group worker, a factor crucial for change. Such positive transferences were successfully established with both boys after a considerable amount of time during which the worker's forbearance and acceptance of them were subjected to repeated trials. Under the necessary corrective psychological conditions, substantial improvements were effected in the boys. They developed healthier, more relaxed superegos, improved self-images, an enhanced ability to trust well-intentioned adults, and self-confidence.

_____

CHAPTER 4

Martin

MORTIMER SCHIFFER

EMOTIONAL PROBLEMS of young children are best treated as soon as detected, at a time when personality and character structure are still malleable. When psychotherapy is properly implemented, children's personalities are subject to change, whereas adolescent and adult patients can only be helped to cope better. While the foregoing is true with respect to most problems affecting children, it is particularly pertinent in cases where the basic problem is characterological. In these instances it is important that corrective procedures be instituted before elaboration and habituation of character structure take place.

One such problem in young children is deviant sexual identification, a condition in which their behavior and interests are of a nature more identifiable with members of the opposite gender. These children require extended treatment because character structure tends to crystallize rapidly in the absence of psychological intervention. Activity-group therapy has proved to be unusually effective in aiding the sexual identification problems of young children.

It is helpful to involve parents in therapy because they are significant libidinal objects during a child's early and later development. Since some parents have an unconscious "investment" in creating and perpetuating atypical identity problems in their children, it can be anticipated that at some points in treatment such an unconscious intent will make itself manifest in the form of parental resistance. This has been observed in many instances with parents who, despite the fact that they seek clinical help for their children, hinder the therapeutic program in subtle ways. When parents refuse to participate in therapy but allow their children to be involved, the helping process is usually carried on with difficulty. Nevertheless, it has been possible to work successfully in school-based treatment programs with children of such parents. Resistive parents will accept assistance for their children in schools whereas they would otherwise oppose referral to a community-based agency. In the educational setting, the helping professionals are viewed more as educator-specialists than as therapists. This dilutes the implicit threat that may be associated with the orthopsychiatric disciplines of social work, psychology, and psychiatry when encountered in agencies.

The case we will present concerns a boy with a serious problem in sexual identity. His mother did not recognize the problem as such and, for reasons to be enunciated in the record, was not motivated to expose her son to any procedure concerned with "problems." Nevertheless, it was possible to treat the boy in a theraputic play group for a long period of time.

Martin

Martin was seven years, ten months old, in second grade, when referred by his teacher to the guidance counselor. His height was average, but he was obese, with particular fleshiness on the hips and breasts. His dress was immaculate; he appeared in school daily wearing a pressed white shirt, a tie, and ivy league trousers. His neat appearance was almost incongruous in contrast to the majority of poorly dressed children in the school, who came from families with limited incomes in a highly depressed socioeconomic area of New York City.

Martin's teacher described him as immature. She said he was extraordinarily anxious about academic achievement, unable to tolerate the mildest criticism, and quick to cry if he made the slightest error. Martin was extremely voluble, sometimes compulsively so. He sought attention constantly and always wanted approval, even though his academic achievement was more than satisfactory. He read very well. The teacher suspected that Martin's struggle for success and recognition was in response to pressure from home, particularly from his mother.

Martin literally "purchased" a measure of social acceptance from classmates through giving them gifts—candy, crayons, or other items with which he always seemed well supplied. If children sought him out, it was because of these "goodies." They certainly did not find Martin's company desirable. In occasional aggressive situations with some of the "tough" boys in his class and in the neighborhood, Martin resorted to verbal maneuvers and harangues and would become helpless when such tactics failed. In the classroom he would often beseech the teacher for protection.

Martin enjoyed writing; he had an active imagination. He was also interested in music and collected records. He was altogether unskilled in active games. He lacked many qualities of other boys his age, both in physical appearance and in mannerisms. As a consequence, other boys teased him derogatively using pejorative expressions that stressed his effeminacy.

Martin's mother responded to the counselor's invitation to visit school. She was obese and suffered from high blood pressure. Her voice was surprisingly harsh; she spoke in a loud, booming fashion. She displayed only minimal interest when informed about the referring teacher's concerns; she was patently defensive. However, she offered information freely. Actually, she sought reassurance that Martin had no "real" problems and that she was an adequate mother.

The family was intact, consisting of the parents, two older children in their early twenties, a daughter of eleven, and Martin, the youngest. The father was a salesman, the mother a self-described "busy housewife." The family occupied an adequate apartment in a slum neighborhood. They probably remained in this neighborhood, as did a number of similar families, because of ethnic origin. They were Slavic, part of an enclave that resided in the area for several generations but was now vastly outnumbered by a black and Puerto Rican population.

The following developmental history was easily elicited from this garrulous mother. Martin did not speak until two years of age. He was bottle-fed until age three and at the time of referral, was *still* being fed by his mother. In explaining this, she said she was concerned because Martin was highly selective about food, and she excused her feeding him with the rationalization that "he wouldn't eat otherwise." For instance: "I have to force him to eat hot cereals." Also, she still saw fit to dress him because, "If he did it himself, he would look so sloppy!" Martin talked interminably, according to her (obviously in the same compulsive way she did). He would ask countless questions—"Even when he knows the answers. Can you believe it?" She described his intelligence, reading ability, and interest in music pridefully, as if these reflected her particular influence. According to her, Martin had many friends, but closer questioning revealed that most of his leisure time was spent with his sister and her girlfriends. They liked to "dress up" in play and Martin always participated, using his sister's clothes. (Much later it was learned that he also used his mother's garments.) When Martin did play with boys, they were considerably younger than himself. Martin did argue with his sister at times.

The mother unwittingly revealed awareness of problems with her son at moments when her garrulousness betrayed her. However, she was quick to correct herself and to deny any atypicality in the boy's behavior, even when no such meanings were alluded to by the counselor. Once she likened Martin to her husband, whom she described as a "worrier," overly concerned about the family's health. "Martin is like that, too," she said. "He'll get up during the night to make sure his briefcase is closed, or see if his homework is in order."

She portrayed herself as a warm, generous, and carefree person. Her household was described as a bustling place, always filled with visitors. She concluded the interview with a detailed account of her own school days, her academic achievement, and her later success as an office worker. Her parting remark was: "See how much I talk! I was always like that—talk, talk, talk!"

The basic problem was that of a boy with severe disabilities in personality, character, and social adjustment. He was absolutely neat, and already obsessive and compulsive with respect to possessions and some routines. He manifested anxiety under stress. He had confused sexual identity, and the possibility of latent homosexuality existed. Most of this was due to an absolutely overwhelming mother, aggressive in her "busy" mothering role, infantilizing her son and efficiently castrating him psychologically at the same time. The father, a passive man, was an "ideal" neurotic counterpart to his wife, and he buttressed the pathognomonic influence within the family. We can only surmise the unconscious factors underlying the mother's overdetermined behavior, the nature of her role as mother and wife, and, possibly, a need to deny unconsciously her rejection of an unwanted last child.

Ideally, the objective would have been to refer the parents to a community agency resource, which was available. However, despite the mother's volubility and apparent "warm" presentment of herself, she was flatly resistive to a mild suggestion that some agency resource might be found to "help" Martin and counsel the parents. Since she did agree to let Martin join a "play group" with some other boys, which was under formation, it was deemed advisable to initiate therapy in this way and to try to involve the family in the future. Our initial impression, which later proved correct, was that we would not be successful in mobilizing the parents to enter treatment. It was planned to see the mother periodically and to try to effect modifications in her handling of Martin, particularly with respect to the severe infantilization she subjected him to. Otherwise, any possibility of therapeutic success would be hindered by her countervailing influence.

During the following two and a half years, while Martin was treated in the same therapeutic play group, the worker found that it was a delicate procedure to sustain the mother while advising her with respect to Martin and managing her periods of resistance during which she tried to terminate.

The Other Group Members

Martin was placed in a play group with four other boys from first and second grades, all approximately the same age. A short synopsis of the referral information concerning the other children follows.

Paul was seven years, ten months of age, a sad, unhappy child. He had been deserted by both parents and was being raised by grandparents in a crowded household with his siblings, cousins, and other relatives. Paul did not get along with other children and sometimes was aggressive toward them. His teacher tried to defend him, and he liked her, although he resented other adults. He sometimes came to school with welts, evidently from beatings received at home.

Jesus, eight years old, was disruptive and uncooperative in class; had poor peer relationships; pushed and hit other children; was learning below capacity; liked his teacher but required much of her attention; bragged a lot and made up grandiose, fantastic stories about family experiences; and had experienced head injuries requiring hospitalization and stitches.

John, eight years old, was referred by his teacher because of passivity and daydreaming. His mother described him as nervous. He refused food, cried in his sleep, and complained of dizzy spells and stomachaches. His mother had to dress him to get him to school on time; she often hit him; and she felt he was "stupid."

Theo, seven years, eight months old, was referred as very aggressive and a poor achiever. He had to be separated often from other children because he annoyed and kicked them, was disliked by his peers, and showed an ability to respond to the teacher.

The play group remained virtually intact for two and a half years. Ninety group sessions were held, and Michael attended eighty-four; most of the six absences were due to illnesses.

Sessions Nos. 1 through 4, Excerpts

After a relatively short period of acclimatization, the play group became active. The children rapidly discovered the permissiveness of the worker. Even Martin, surprisingly, began to act freely and regressively. After the first four sessions, the worker recorded: "Martin's vocabulary is adult-like, but his explosive speech reveals anxiety. He gets excited when things don't go his way. At such times he becomes verbally assertive and he appeals to the worker in a demanding, yet dependent manner. He appears enamored of his accomplishments and feels superior to the other boys. However, in direct contacts with them he shows uncertainty and doubt. The worker's permissiveness seems to confuse him. Martin appeals to her constantly and evidently wonders about her feelings and her failure to act authoritatively. He talks incessantly, about anything and everything. At the easel he paints sloppily, splashing paint from the jar, making blobs on the paper. He works with blocks and repetitively asks the worker to look at his work, soliciting her approval. The worker acknowledges his bids for attention by looking where he directs and nods, usually without comment.''

Because he was confused by the worker's permissiveness, Martin tested her, almost deliberately. He would ''announce'' aloud that he was going to throw blocks over, and when they actually crashed he would quickly explain that the incident had been an ''accident.'' Once when he deliberately over-turned his cup of milk, he said, ''Oh, well, accidents will happen, you know!'' In admonishing other children, he sounded like a scolding adult in language and manner. Once when helping another child with blocks, he said pedantically, ''Use your head. Let's *all* use our heads. We've *got* to use our heads!'' While he enjoyed the play group, he did become anxious because of the absence of a controlling adult, which he was accustomed to. As a consequence, he attempted to establish controls by acting like an adult.

Despite his confusion and ambivalence, after a few sessions Martin be-came even more spontaneous and regressive. This was most apparent when he painted. He would stand at the easel and paint with abandon. He jumped up and down excitedly and made loud noises. At such times he was very agi-tated, perspiring a good deal. Despite this infantile messing, Martin became concerned if a drop of paint got on his clothing. Once he asked the worker, ''Do I have paint on my face? Look at my face. It is full of paint. I'll have to wash it.'' He went to the sink, washed his face, returned to the easel, and splattered once again, then announced, ''I'm splashing!'' and again rushed back to the worker and asked her if he had paint on his face. When she said, ''No,'' he replied, ''Then why do I feel splashy on my face?'' Several times he commented, ''My mother will scream,'' or ''My mother will kill me!'' After messing with paint he played with water. He surreptitiously spilled water on the floor and then announced that he had to clean it up. He took the mop and proceeded to swish the water about. He then squeezed the wa-ter back on the floor and repeated the messing and cleaning all over again.

Comments and Interpretations

The worker was impressed early on by the rapidity with which Martin's be-havior, usually controlled and obedient in his classroom, became so manic and impulsive in the play group. This drastic change indicated that his ego defenses were rather brittle, which led to rapid regression. This situation ne-cessitated close observation by her in the event that some monitoring might be necessary. She had already cautiously applied herself in this direction. When Martin painted so messily at the easel, the worker silently spread newspaper about. This silent intervention was enough to act as a brake against excessive regression. Marvin seemed to revel in the freedom of the play group, and then, alternately, he would become anxious about his behavior and become impelled to seek reassurance and comfort from the worker.

Session No. 5. Present—Martin, Theo, Paul, Jesus, John

This group session is reported in its entirety to give the reader a sense of the boy's fluctuating behavior, his interactions with the other boys and the worker, and the quality of the group's activities. By the end of the session, the respective roles and status positions of the group's members had come into sharp definition.

Paul and Jesus came in together. Both wore white shirts with short sleeves, and they looked shiny and happy. They were smiling broadly. They said, "Hello," in unison, and the worker returned their greeting. Soon Martin, Theo, and John followed, in single file. John and Theo were smiling. Martin said, "I was practicing in the auditorium." The worker looked at him and nodded. Jesus said, "I was too." Martin said, "I am in a play. I'll have to go back."

Paul took the colored plastic blocks and seated himself at the square table; John joined him. Both boys were building separately. Martin took pick-up-sticks and walked to the round table, saying, "I'll take my pick-up-sticks and play. I go first." He turned to the worker and said, "Mrs. T., will you play with me?" The worker looked at him. He drew a large chair to the table and said, "This is for Mrs. T." Jesus and Theo joined, both yelling, "I'm first!" Martin said, "No, I'm first. I said *I'm* first!" Theo said, "Mrs. T. is first. Girls go first!" Martin threw the sticks out and began to move them. Theo said, "Take the white one." Martin replied, "O.K. Pick it up." He took the white stick and began to play. Theo: "You moved." Martin: "No, I didn't. It just hit. That doesn't count." The worker silently rose from the table and went to the other side of the play room while the boys were arguing. Paul and John were talking. The worker heard Paul say something about "my brother."

At one point, the worker was standing with her back to the room when she heard a loud noise from the direction of the round table. Martin was yelling, "No, don't do that. Stop! Mrs. T., make him stop!" Jesus yelled, "I go now." Martin: "No. It's my turn!" Then: "It's Mrs. T.'s turn." He called to her, "Mrs. T., it's your turn. Come and play." The worker replied, "As soon as I finish this." She was straightening some papers. Martin walked over to her and said, "Then I'll help you. I'm going to help you." As he approached, the worker started walking toward the round table. He circled around her with his hands stretched out, almost as if he wanted to hold her, and said, "I'm going to help you." She continued to walk on, looking at him. He then turned and sat down at the square table, from which John had now risen. John said to Paul, "I'm going to help you build a house whether you like it or not." Paul replied, "Go away, I'm using these." Martin interjected, "No, I am. I need them." He grabbed a block. Paul grabbed it back. Martin became very agitated. He began to yell and jump up and down saying, "No, I want it. You give it to me. I'll hit you!" He came to the worker with tears in his eyes. "Mrs. T., I want the blocks and he won't let me play with them. Make him give it to me." Paul yelled, "I'll punch you in the nose!" Martin returned to the table, threw some blocks gently over the table to the floor, and ran to the shelves. Paul looked toward the worker with a shy smile and then said, "See, he doesn't really want them anyway."

Martin took a car-race spinning game and brought it to the worker asking, "Will you play with me, Mrs. T.?" The worker nodded. Martin looked for a place to set the game down. John had rejoined Paul at the other table. Martin said, "We'll play here," indicating with his arm the place at the table where Paul and John were occupied. Martin yelled at them, "Go away, *we* need this place!" When this maneuver failed, Martin then went to the table where Theo and Jesus were playing a game and set out the racing game. The worker played with him. He commented each time she made a move, saying the number aloud or telling her what moves to make. He made similar comments when it was his turn. The worker's car was the first to reach the goal. This ended the game, and she rose from the table. Martin said, "Oh, come on." He put the game away and said, "I'm going to paint. I'm going to paint Jesus." He started to giggle. He went to the easel and then said, "Mrs. T., will you help me? It's hard to put the paper on." The worker clipped the paper onto the easel for him. He began to jig in front of the easel, laughing and saying, "Look at Jesus, I'm painting Jesus!" Jesus said, "Oh, shut up, Martin." Martin: "Look at Jesus [the painted figure]. Look at what I'm doing to him!" He was splashing paint on the paper, smearing it. Jesus walked over to look. Jesus said, "I'll paint you!"

Both boys now were at opposite sides of the double easel. Martin had become quite wild, splashing paint with two brushes, one in each hand, and jigging up and down nervously as he did so. It looked like a dance of abandon. He splashed paint on Jesus, who called to the worker, "Look what he did!' He splashed paint on me!" The worker came to look and said, "When it dries I'll be able to take it off."

Martin ran to the sink and said, "I'm full of paint! Do you have any soap in the house?" Then: "May I use your sponge?" The worker nodded. Martin washed his arms, saying, "This is bath water." Meanwhile, Theo and John left the table and went to play with the big blocks. When Theo passed Jesus, Jesus hit him in the back playfully. Theo clinched with him for a moment, then broke away and went back to the blocks. Martin said, "How do you spell 'Jesus'?" He looked at the worker. Martin then said, "J - e." Jesus responded by spelling his name. Martin said, "Now, I'm going to paint Theo." Theo looked at him in a menacing way, then looked toward the worker. Martin said, "How do you spell 'Theo'?" Theo stood at the easel and spelled out his name.

Martin left the easel and obtained an animal lotto game. He went over to the worker and asked her, "Will you play this game with me?" The worker sat down at the round table with him. He set out the cards for both and began to pick the pictures. The worker sat but didn't participate. (Martin was making all the necessary moves.) Jesus began to play with Theo and John. They spaced themselves in a triangle and began to use big pieces of clay as a ball. The worker left the table where she had been seated and said to them, "These pieces are too big. You can get hurt." She returned to the round table where Martin sat and said, "It's time to set the table." Paul and John began to bring chairs to the table, then they sat. Theo joined them. Martin jumped on Jesus from the back, giggled, and said, "I'll make a milk shake." Jesus fell to the floor. Martin shook him, yelling, "A milk shake! Shake him up! A milk shake!" He continued to repeat this refrain. Then he yelled, "I'm serving! I'll pour the milk." The boys had already begun to pour milk, and Martin randomly filled cups. Jesus remained seated on the floor. Paul said to him, "Come and drink your milk. Jesus replied, "I don't have to drink milk."

John grabbed most of the cookies and began to eat them. Paul said, "Stop grabbing. You boys are like pigs. Put them back!" Jesus, who had gotten some cookies, threw them back on the serving plate. Theo and John grabbed once more. Paul became agitated and grabbed the rest, protesting all the time that they were behaving like pigs. Martin made several attempts to fill the worker's cup, but each time he tried this, she picked it up to drink. He then picked up his own cup and held it out toward John, saying, "I'm going to spill this in your face." Theo said, "Go ahead, I'd like to see you. You wouldn't dare." Martin replied, "Oh, no? I would so," and flung out his hand with the cup at eye level. John got up. The milk did not spill.

Jesus had left the table and was shooting guns with John. Martin joined them, took the gun from John, and then put it down. Martin returned to the table and said, "Jesus is a bad boy. Look what he is doing." Jesus taunted, "Martin is a baby." Martin repeated, "Baby, baby, stick your head in gravy." Jesus came toward Martin, who cried out, "Mrs. T., he is hurting me. He has a big lump of clay." Jesus looked at the worker and laughed. Then he asked if he could go to the bathroom. Martin asked if he could leave the room to see what time it was. Paul said to Jesus, "You want to go to the bathroom so you can beat up that kid." Martin came back into the play room, saying, "It's eleven o'clock. I have to go back to the auditorium."

Jesus began to wrestle with Theo and John. Jesus complained to the worker, "They don't let me go to the bathroom." He walked to the door and then came back to wrestle some more, saying again, "Mrs. T., they don't let me go." John picked up a stick from the floor and gave it to the worker. Paul, who was seated at a table, pointed to something under it. While the worker looked, Paul crawled way under the table and came out with a small block, holding it up for the worker to see and smiling. He continued to play with blocks. Martin began to play with the big blocks, saying to the worker, who stood nearby, "Look out, Mrs. T., I'm building a house."

The escorts knocked at the door. One of the boys said, "It's time to go." Martin asked, "Is it time to go, Mrs. T.?" The worker replied in the affirmative. Martin ran to the door, saying, "I can find my way back alone." The escort stopped him in the hallway and said, "You have to wait for me and the other boys." The children left quietly. Paul was the last one out of the room, having lingered at the blocks, looking at the worker and smiling at her.

Addendum: When Theo first came into the play room, he very carefully removed a pencil case from his neck, where it had hung from a string, and tacked it to one of the display boards. A few minutes after the session ended, he returned to say he had forgotten it. The worker nodded, pointing to where it hung. She smiled at him.

Comments and Interpretations

Martin involved the worker in a game at the beginning of the session and repeatedly sought her attention or assistance when he got into trouble with the others. Despite the aggressive capacities of most of the other boys, Martin did not hesitate to provoke them, as witness the altercation with Paul, who threatened to "punch him in the nose." Later, Martin mockingly made a picture of Jesus and also of Theo, who was the toughest boy in the group. While the boys retaliated in response to Martin's teasing, they surprisingly did so with restraint. The worker had the impression that they recognized in Martin a quality of immaturity that set him apart in some special way. So far there had been no scapegoating of Martin.

Martin became slightly manic following his regressive smearing with paints as noted in his jerking body motions, squeals, and remarks. Even as he cleaned himself at the sink, ostensibly fearful of his mother's reactions, the cleaning process degenerated into infantile messing. This pattern continued during the refreshment period, when Martin defiantly took over the control of the pitcher of milk to pour for "everyone," quite messily. He also included the worker, teasingly trying to fill and refill her cup, despite the fact that she had just filled it. The worker offset this by holding onto the cup and sipping from it, without saying anything. And, after indulging himself in this infantile way, Martin babyishly criticized Jesus, who had been joining the others in competing for the cookies. "Jesus is a bad boy!" Martin said. One wonders whether this remark was rhetorical in a sense, reflecting Martin's excited estimation of his own behavior.

Almost at the end of the session, Martin said that he had to return to the auditorium, where his class had been rehearsing a play, but he did not do so—this after he had announced at the start of the session that he "had to go back." It is evident that the play group experience was more important to him, as much as he liked to be part of dramatic productions with his class. When he finally did leave the play room, he wanted to go back to his class unescorted: "I can find my way back alone."

The play group as a whole was acting out without any seeming concern for the worker's reactions, apart from an occasional glance in her direction by some of the group members. There were manifestations of positive transference to the worker, with a moderate degree of rivalry. Paul and Theo competed for her attention. Noteworthy is Theo's "forgetting" to take his pencil case and having to return to the play room after all the others had departed. He used this same ploy in subsequent sessions.

The worker permitted the group much latitude without interfering in the give and take between the boys. This included the incidents when paint was splattered and grabbing for cookies occurred. So far the children had demonstrated an ability to stabilize and regain composure after tilting with one another. Despite the propensity of some for anger and fighting—Theo, Jesus, and Paul—the boys had not as yet shown this to excess. Rather, their altercations were moderate, within tolerable limits, not necessitating intervention by the worker. As already noted, even Martin's provocations did not evoke from the boys the kind of punishment that they were capable of inflicting.

It has been noted before that children who are capable of much anger and impulsivity seldom demonstrate such behavior to the same degree in the therapeutic play group. In their homes, neighborhoods, and classrooms, such children freely act out against what they perceive as a hurtful, rejecting world; in contrast, in a play group, the positive transference and the children's wishes to perpetuate it (despite occasional episodes of negative transference) serve to modulate their behavior. Because they are exposed to the worker's unconditional acceptance of them as they are, they become able to respond in compensatory ways to the guilt feelings engendered by acting-out behavior. At no time does "bad" behavior evoke from the worker negation, denials, rejection, or any alteration of her therapeutic image. This solidifies the positive transference.

As time passed, the worker noted that the boys were becoming less tolerant of Martin's immature provocations and his general manner of conducting himself. They showed this by teasing him more and more and also by chasing him away from participating in their activities, sometimes hitting him. There were instances when the worker had to use indirect interventions to deflect the boys' aggressions against Martin when he could not sustain himself. The boys verbalized a good deal about Martin. In the tenth session, John said, "You are a butchhead and fatty." At another time he derided Martin: "You are a girl!" It was apparent that one of the reasons accounting for Martin's persistent provocations was his desire to ensure that they knew of his presence. Martin insisted on recognition, regardless of the punishment to which he would be subjected for such negative attention. Another factor accounting for the teasing was a feeling of uneasiness that is often generated in latency-age boys by a peer with effeminate ways, perhaps latent homosexual tendencies. Rejecting Martin was equivalent to dissociating themselves from an unconsciously perceived threat to masculine identity.

As mentioned earlier, Martin was placed off balance by the permissive adult. Every time he got into a hassle with another boy, for any reason, he would literally scream to the worker for help: "He took my blocks!" or, "Look what he's doing!" Another common refrain was, "He won't let me play!" When the worker failed to respond to these complaints, Martin became insistent: "*Make* him stop!" "*Tell* him to give it to me." "*Make* him go away!" "*Tell* them not to make so much noise." Martin's comments showed his confusion in comprehending the worker's tolerant role, the difference between her and other adults he was familiar with. Once he said to the worker, "How come you are not talking this time? I mean, do you have laryngitis?" When the worker replied in the negative, he continued: "Well, why *don't* you talk? You have so much to talk about. Look at what they're doing! You *have* to talk to them!" At the beginning of the following session he said, "I hope you don't have laryngitis today!"

The worker, of course, did not adopt the authoritative position that Martin appeared to want her to. She also sensed that he really did not want her to, despite his verbalized complaints. His vocalizations soliciting stronger adult control were ambivalently accompanied by an equally driving wish to act out in ways that he had already amply demonstrated. It was only when he became momentarily overanxious about the worker's not controlling the group (including himself) that he sought "outside" authority. He said to the boys, "I'll tell your teachers," and, "I'll go to the principal." This had no effect on the others, who were more certain of the worker's acceptance and comfortable in the fundamental security of the play group setting.

It was necessary that Martin find the strength and courage to release his anger against the adult person more directly, instead of denying or compromising it by perpetuating a dependency relationship. Only then would he become capable of discharging spontaneously the strong feelings he had repressed. Such catharsis was essential if there was to be any penetrating effect of therapy. We had not long to wait.

The following series of excerpts are from sessions near the close of the school year. They illustrate the quality of Martin's behavior, some of the new directions it was taking, and the significance to him of the play group.

Session No. 7, Excerpt

. . . Paul was the first to finish his refreshments and leave the table. Martin drank, talking at the same time. "You want to hear a joke?" he said to John, and continued: "What's your name? What's your name?" Theo said teasingly, "His name is 'Buddy'!" Martin: "This joke is between 'Buddy' and Theo." John said, "My name is John, not 'Buddy'!" Theo teased, "You *are* 'Buddy.' That's your name!" Martin went on, "This joke is between John and Theo." Theo said to John, "Why do you have two pretzels?" John replied, "Because I'm a pig!" The boys laughed. Martin went on: "You want to hear another joke? Theo asks Jesus, 'Why do you drink all that soda?' And Jesus said, 'Because you are the *fat lady*'."

Comments and Interpretations

Martin's mother was very obese; the worker was also a large woman. Martin was actually making oblique disparagement of his mother through displacement. His "jokes" had a free association quality, despite their apparent silliness. This was one of the beginning evidences of Martin's growing negative transference toward the worker. Martin was almost obsessively preoccupied with matters concerning identity. Witness his repeated remarks when he was at the easel, announcing that he was "making Jesus" and also Theo, designating them in his blurred, smeared paintings as "baby" and using other derogatory terms. In this behavior, Martin projected unconsciously his own concerns about himself.

Session No. 7, Excerpt, Continued

. . . Paul went to the easel. He got the blue smock he had worn the preceding week, slipped it on, and stood in front of the worker. She buttoned it up the back for him, which is what he had wanted her to do. Martin said, "I'm going to wear this one." He took a white smock and brought it to the worker. She buttoned it. While the worker was doing this, Martin volunteered, *"As long as you don't make me wear barrettes."*

Comments and Interpretations

Two factors are significant. Martin was in rivalry; he wanted to be treated as Paul was. Secondly, and of greater import, was the implication of his next comment, which was again a free association because it had no manifest bearing on the episode: "As long as you don't make me wear barrettes." To the best of our knowledge, Martin's mother did not force transvestite play upon him, although her pathognomonic influence was indeed responsible for his dressing in girls' clothing. In his remark, Martin unconsciously fused two libidinal objects—mother and worker. Yet, at the same time he was capable of acting differently in the separate presences of each, in his home and in the play group.

Session No. 7, Excerpt, Continued

. . . Jesus arrived in the play room first. He semi-fell over the threshold, smiled, and said, "Hello." Paul entered, also smiling. Both went to the supply shelves. Martin came in. He went to the easel, put on a smock, and while buttoning it came up to the worker and said, "I like this room. I come here every Tuesday."

Comments and Interpretations

Martin's unsolicited, spontaneous remark points up his positive reactions to the play group experience. Somewhat later in the same session he said, "Look, Mrs. T., how am I doing?" When the worker looked at his painting, Martin continued to chatter: "I'm making Cream of Wheat®. How do you like my Cream of Wheat?" Once again Martin was displacing from his mother to the worker. His mother still supervised his eating, feeding much cereal to him and insisting that he eat it. In his play in the group, Martin derided the Cream of Wheat—thus deriding his mother via displacement.

Session No. 9, Excerpts

. . . Martin brought a box of plastic blocks to the session. He said, "I brought these from home. My mother said, 'Now you can play quietly.' " John and Theo came over to look at the blocks. Martin said, "Go away, these are mine. Mrs. T., why do you have to have troublemakers in here?"

Martin picked up a wheel and a stick attached to it and went over to Theo, saying, "I'm going to give you an injection." Theo began to hit him. Martin got quite angry and frightened at the same time. He started laughing but soon began to call the worker desperately, on the verge of tears. Theo was angry with him for real, and was punching Martin. Martin bravely tried to grab Theo's arm and kicked him. Theo continued to hit Martin, dancing back out of his reach after each blow. Martin withdrew to the blocks.

Comments and Interpretations

Martin's mother was evidently aware of the nature of the boys' obstreperous behavior in the play group. We have no way of knowing whether Martin pointedly kept her aware of this for his own purposes, or whether she queried him about the group's activities. In either case, she was obviously disturbed by the boys' behavior, particularly Martin's participation in it. *In absentia*, therefore, she attempted to make him the "good" boy who played "quietly." Martin did paraphrase his mother's message: "Why do you have to have troublemakers here?" However, Martin was being affected too significantly by the therapeutic experience to have his mother's admonitions take effect. He continued to act out in the very same session. The "hypodermic" episode had unconscious, sexual meaning; witness Theo's angry reaction to Martin's attempt to "inject" him. One cannot but admire Martin's attempts to retaliate against Theo, the most aggressive boy in the group.

Session No. 11, Excerpts

The following excerpts are taken from the last group session prior to the summer vacation.

. . . When the table was set, the boys brought the chairs to sit down. Everybody sat except Paul, who continued his game at the other table. As the worker began to open the soda bottles, Paul came to sit at her left. Martin said, "No ice cream for me. I hate ice cream. Does this soda have vitamin C? It *has* vitamin C, Mrs. T., doesn't it?" He turned to Theo and began touching him, saying, "Cottage cheese." Jesus said, "Martin is a baby. Martin is a gibberish mouth." As the worker sliced the ice cream, Martin repeated, "None for me. None for me! Remember, I don't like ice cream." Theo said. "Me, too." Martin: "None for me. Don't give me any." Paul: "That's the *fourth* time you said it."

The worker said, "This party is our last time until we come back. This afternoon children aren't coming to school because the teachers work on record cards. That's why I had our meeting now." Then she inquired: "How do you like coming here?" John replied, "I love it." Theo said, "I liked playing and doing things." Paul: "I want to come every day!" Martin: "I love it." The worker said, "I have a present for each of you," and proceeded to distribute them, each one wrapped in gift paper with the boy's name on it. Each gift package was the same—a rubber ball. There was much excitement when the boys discovered that the balls were "high bouncers." Theo inquired: "How much did they cost?" The worker told him. Paul looked at his ball and said, "When I play with it and it gets dirty, I'm going to wash it. Every time it gets dirty I'm going to wash it, and when I go down to play with it everybody will say, 'Oh look! A new Spaulding!'"

Toward the end of the session, Martin was sitting alone at the round table. He had a scissors and was holding the edge of an oilcloth covering that the worker had put out before serving refreshments. He snipped a cut several inches long, saying, "I'm going to cut this." Then he addressed the worker directly: "Look, it's cut. I don't know how it happened."

Comments and Interpretations

Typically, the last session of the play group before vacation is a party, with special refreshments and a gift. While most of the boys simply expressed delight, Martin was still responsive to more symbolic meanings related to food and its donor. He questioned the food's vitamin content—a remark that alluded to his mother's constant reminders of the need to eat properly. Martin then called Theo "cottage cheese," an apparent *non sequitur* but, in fact, a remark meaningfully associated with food and his mother's obsessive preoccupation with it. Finally, in repetitive injunctions to the worker instructing her not to serve him ice cream, Martin again unconsciously used her for symbolic resistance against his mother's plying him with food. Jesus was prompted by Martin's remarks anent the ice cream to say that Martin talked "gibberish." It could not, of course, be expected that Jesus would know the unconscious motivation for Martin's remarks. However, the latent meanings underlying Martin's comments give logical meaning to the "gibberish."

Martin symbolically assaulted the worker (mother) by cutting the oilcloth table covering. This was dramatic. He *deliberately* called her attention to the act, then professed not to know how it had happened. Witnessed here is an important denouement in therapy: a first expression of Martin's direct, undisguised hostility. After the act, his anxiety was reflected in his comment that he didn't know how it had happened—an impulsive remark calculated to disown what was perhaps a homicidal wish.

Since the beginning of the play group, Martin had barely partaken of the refreshments. He usually refused to eat, tended to waste the food, and used it regressively, spilling and spoiling. In these ways he defied the worker (mother), an aggressive retaliation.

Before the end of the school year, the worker was able to interview Martin's mother again, having accidentally met her one day when she appeared in school. She had come to help Martin's teacher with costumes that the children were to wear in a circus presentation in the assembly. The mother started the interview by commenting on the children in the presentation: "How wonderful they are! And their costumes! Weren't they terrific?" Further: "I made about thirty-two telephone calls before I found a place to rent Martin's costume." Martin had a leading role in the play, as ringleader of the circus. He wore satin breeches, a red riding jacket, and a black top hat. When the worker inquired about the need to rent a costume for Martin, since all the other children were dressed in costumes they had made from crepe paper and other decorative materials, the mother replied, "How could I make a ringmaster's costume? I *had* to rent it."

The mother then leaned back and queried the worker, "So, tell me, how is Martin?" Instead of replying directly, the worker asked her what she thought about Martin. The mother said he was improved; he now played with another boy in the same building. "Mind you," she added, "his mother will only let *Martin* in to play with her son. What do you think of that? She won't let other boys in because they are too rough, but she wants Martin. You know why? Because he is so nice and he plays quiet." Then she went on to describe Martin's eccentricities once more, as she had done at the time of the first interview. She again said that Martin was "just like my husband." She still stood over Martin when he ate and fed him frequently. "After all, when I cook a pot of farina in the morning he *has* to eat. So I get eight or nine spoons into him." (Note the relationship of this to Martin's comments about Cream of Wheat in the group)

When the worker inquired about Martin's play with his sister and her friends, the mother answered that the children still played "dressing up" but that now Martin was dressed as the father. She added that he also used to don his mother's clothes during dress play. She described Martin as very affectionate, saying that he kissed his mother and sister before going to bed. One night his mother had asked why he did not kiss his father also. Martin replied, "When boys reach a certain age they don't kiss their fathers; they just say 'goodnight'!"

Just as in the first interview, much of the information that the mother offered volubly was in defense of Martin's behavior, as though she had need to pile up evidence to refute allegations about Martin that she anticipated would be made. Throughout the interview she kept asking what the worker thought of Martin and why she was concerned about him. Then she offered as "proof" of Martin's improvement an episode in which she saw him fighting a boy in the street. (More of this later.) Also, Martin now went to school unescorted. She expected some "trouble" to arise over this.

Despite the mother's defensiveness in speaking of Martin's improvement, intended to convince the interviewer that he need no longer remain in the play group, it was evident that some definite changes had indeed taken place in the boy. The worker focused on these and supported them further by pointing out how much more competent Martin was in socializing with his peers and in work achievements in the group, adding that the play group

would continue in the fall and that Martin would certainly continue to benefit from attending should he wish to do so.

Martin's teacher also reported changes. Martin appeared more relaxed
and accepted suggestions from her without the same anxiety that had been
characteristic of him before. He was still overconcerned with achievement
and getting good grades. It was learned that some children accompanied
Martin to his home daily after school, and his mother gave them cookies
and candy. This appears to be a tactic she used to ensure Martin's continued
relationships with peers.

From the worker's summary: "Martin's behavior in the play group has
been toward abandon and relinquishing of self-control. If, following this
breakdown of his defenses, he can develop enough ego strength to separate
from his mother, he will be freed to grow and develop. However, if these
strengths are not forthcoming, the play group experience could prove harmful to him." The worker felt that she would have to continue talking with
the mother during the following school year in an effort to help her relinquish tight control over her son.

The teacher gave the worker a copy of a short composition done by
Martin. The class had written on the subject "One Wish." Martin had writ-
ten: "If I had one wish in the whole world. I wish I was Superman, because
I would never hurt [be hurt]. I could fly. Nothing would stop me except
Kryptonite. I'd have X-ray vision and I'd have super strength. But there is
no such thing as Superman, but just the same I wish I was Superman."

The composition reflects excellent command of language, spelling, and
organization of thoughts for such a young child. Poignantly, it also reveals
Martin's awareness of the futility of fantasy. Yet, it embodies his wish—
which was now coming into being—to become stronger.

After the summer hiatus, group sessions were resumed. Martin's behavior and interactions with the others began to change at a more rapid
pace. He was less ambivalent whenever he acted regressively and aggressively. He now had to withstand a good deal of physical abuse, particularly
from Theo. The worker was not intervening because Martin was sustaining
himself despite his complaints and pleas for help from her. Since he was
more resilient and stronger, the worker thought it would further his growth
to let him manage himself as much as possible. The group as a whole was in
a more nodal, activated state, with frequent aggressive episodes in which the
boys acted-out against the setting and wasted materials. There were also
more frequent expressions of negative transference toward the worker.

Sessions Nos. 12–16, excerpts

. . . Martin left his seat, went toward John and Theo, and said, "I'm glad
I'm back." The others spoke similarly.

. . . Martin was seated at the round table, alone, playing with plastic blocks. He said, "Hey, Johnny, isn't this nice?" John made no response. Martin called to Paul, "Look what I made. I made a man. Isn't it nice?"

. . . Theo, who actually had a great many cookies, said, "I've got only two. What will Mrs. T. have to eat?" Martin poured milk for the worker and said, "Here's some gasoline, Mrs. T." He also poured for John, who protested strongly. Martin then lifted the bowl that had contained the cookies (it now held only crumbs). He held it above his head, looked at John, and said, "I'm going to throw this at you." He did so. The crumbs fell on John's head and into his milk, also on the table and floor. John whined and left the table. Martin laughed and said, "I threw crumbs on the crumb."

. . . Martin finished a drawing he had been making and began to put it on the wall board. He said, "Oh, I have no thumbtacks." The worker rose from the table to get some. He found them on his own, saying to the worker, "Don't help me. Let me do this myself." The worker returned to a game she was playing with Jesus, without a comment.

. . . Martin came up to the worker and asked, "Where is the milk?" She replied, "It isn't time yet." (It was early in the session.) Martin took the cups from the shelf and said, "I'll just set the table." He walked past the table and said to Theo, "Hey, it isn't time for milk yet, but I'm putting the cups out and setting the table. Hey, boys, I'm just setting the table." He set out each cup and bowl, saying, "This is for Paul, and one for John, and one for Jesus."

. . . Martin announced, "I'm going to paint." He walked to the easel and put on a smock very deliberately, with great show. He then turned to the worker and asked, "Are these paints good?" She nodded. Martin said, "Then I'll mix them together," and proceeded to do just that, pouring jars of paint into one another. He then began to paint. He dug his brush into the paper, making blobs that looked like the splashes he had made on other occasions. Then he began to smear the blobs. Theo asked the worker to play dominoes with him. They sat at the round table. Martin left the easel and said, "I'm playing too." He played a minute, then left. He picked up a gun and went about pretending to shoot the boys in their backs, saying, "You're dead!"

. . . John arrived at the play room first. He entered quietly, hands in pockets, with an expectant smile on his face. The worker was in the corner, at the sink. He smiled at her. Martin came in right after him, and said, "Hello, Johnny." Then: "Hey, Johnny, let's hide the ball before Theo gets here, because if he has the ball he will bop bop me on the head. Come on, hide it, or else I'm a dead duck! Hurry up, here, throw it under the table." The worker had forgotten to draw the window shades, and Martin walked to the window and began pulling the shades down. At other times in the sessions, Martin deliberately raised the shades, saying, "Let's have a little more light in here."

. . . Martin said, "Gee whiz. Some day I'm going to jump into a washing machine." The worker said, "Why?" Martin mumbled something indistinguishable under his breath. John sat down on the wooden truck. He said, "Push." Martin replied, "Butch, O.K. Butch." The he said he was going to paint. He picked up a brush and said, "Wow, I spilled some paint." He looked at his heel, came over to the worker, and said, "Oh, I got red paint on my heel, Mrs. T." The worker looked at his heel without comment. Martin said, "I better wash it." He took the sponge and began to wash his shoe. He said, "It's all wet now. Wait 'til Ma sees it. She'll kill me!" (The worker reported later that she had not seen the paint spill, and she wondered whether Martin had brushed paint on his heel deliberately.)

Comments and Interpretations

Martin was very happy that group sessions had resumed. In the episodes described, one notes Martin's more direct approaches to and confrontations with the boys. Also, his work was now more goal oriented, as shown when he directed the attention of several boys to the object he had created from plastic blocks. His aggression was quite open, as when he dumped cookie crumbs and, more significantly, when he rejected the worker's suggestion that it wasn't time for refreshments and set the table nevertheless, which act he repeated in the next two sessions. The worker's remark that it wasn't time for refreshments was inappropriate; children who want to eat earlier than usual should be directed to ask the group for a decision. By using this technique a worker not only demonstrates a willingness to accommodate the children's desires for food but, at the same time, invokes the group's potential for resolving problems. In supervision conference the worker confessed that recently she had sometimes resented Martin's attempts to "take her role," as she put it. She freely acknowledged this as an inhibiting personal reaction, essentially a negative counter-transference feeling. This was the first time she had felt that way, undoubtedly in response to the more definitive trend of negative transference behavior by Martin. A dramatic instance of such behavior was Martin's "playfully" pouring "gasoline" into the worker's cup. Further, he manipulated the window shades, a task always before performed by the worker. Yet, the actuality of positive transference to the worker was also shown: Martin vied with others for her attention, as when he quickly left off painting to join her and Theo in the game of dominoes.

The episode of paint on Martin's shoe is unclear in its meaning. If he did in fact deliberately do it, it can be understood as a defiant, hostile act against his mother (displacement), despite the remark that his mother would "kill" him (uttered calmly, without his usual display of anxiety). Perhaps the incident is related to his earlier remark about "falling into a washing machine," a comment seemingly unrelated to immediate events. It may be that the remark is associated meaningfully with his regressive messing and the references to his mother's anticipated reiterations about cleanliness.

Martin was increasingly beginning to act out against the worker. She was focal in the boy's therapy, even more so than his relationships and interactions with the other group members, which were themselves far from incidental. The significance of Martin's manipulations of the window shades has already been mentioned. The worker's practice was to keep the shades drawn to keep outsiders from looking into the play room. Also, it was commonly known throughout the school that children were not allowed to adjust window shades. He had stopped seeking the worker's approval, as he had been accustomed to do earlier, but he still competed for attention from her, especially after another child had solicited it.

Martin was less provocative of other group members now. He tried to join in their games as an equal. Sometimes he volunteered to help them with their projects. Also, he displayed more capacity for withstanding their aggression. This was demonstrated by events associated with the large, soft, rubber gymnasium ball that the worker had added to the group's supplies in response to a special request from one of the boys. Possession of this ball had become symbolic of status. Theo, the most aggressive, insisted that others release it to him whenever he wanted it. Martin contrived to come to the play room early in order to gain control of the ball. At first he relinquished it later upon demand from Theo, but more recently he had been resisting doing so.

Martin's growing strength, including some awareness of change within himself (termed derivative insight in children), was shown verbally. Once, when standing on tiptoe to reach a light switch located a good distance above the floor, Martin said, "I'm not big enough yet. *But I'll grow. I've grown a lot since Easter.*" Another time, when the worker tried to assist him in a task that he had heretofore usually requested help with, Martin, blocked her, saying, "No, don't help me. I want to do this myself." Observations such as these led the worker to act even more circumspectly with respect to volunteering help (it had always been her practice to avoid sustaining his dependency bids).

Session No. 33, Excerpt

In the midst of the group's discussion during snack time, Martin suddenly said, "There's a little boy in my building who beats me up! He's only seven." Theo replied to this, "Man! Only seven! Well, he's stronger than you. You're weak. You aren't even a boy!" Martin shouted, "I *am* so!" Then he laughed, adding, "I can splash milk in your face!" He puckered his lips and squirted milk at Theo from across the table.

Comments and Interpretations

Martin's comment about the "little boy," which placed him in a position of lesser strength and thus subject to derogation from the boys, should be viewed in the context of his current preoccupation with his self-image and his struggle to improve: "to be a boy."

Session No. 42, Excerpts

The worker took the boys out of the playroom for the first time to play ball in the schoolyard. Later they returned to the play room for their usual snack. The technique of taking a play group outside its familiar setting is used when there has been sufficient growth in individual children and in the group's social controls. It serves several purposes: to broaden experiential horizons; to observe how the boys adjust in the "outer world"—a designed form of reality testing; and to begin to modify the psychological meaning of the therapeutic setting, thus bringing it more into semblance with reality.[1]

Martin was enthusiastic about this innovation, as were the other boys. He began to boast to the worker about his athletic prowess. He carried the gymnasium ball while on the way to the schoolyard, refusing to let others touch it. However, when the play group reached the yard, Martin's inability to play as well as the others became painfully obvious. He made pitiful attempts to copy what others did, but it was apparent he was inept in this game. Several times the worker tried to improve his performance without at the same time making her attempts too obvious. Martin was discouraged. When the group got back to the play room, Martin sat at a table, disconsolate. Finally he got up, handed the ball to Theo, and said, sighing, "Here, here is the ball. Take it." He walked to the easel, sighed again, and said, "I'll paint." He drew a house, was dissatisfied with it, and said, "It's spoiled."

Comments and Interpretations

Despite this setback, the fundamental improvements that had accrued in Martin were not to be offset by his failure in the schoolyard. In supervision conference, the worker described her own sense of unhappiness at seeing Martin so defeated and frustrated in his brave attempt to be as good as the other boys in an activity that had obviously assumed critical meaning for him. However, in the next session, the forty-third, all was reclaimed. Sev-

[1]M. Schiffer, "Trips as a Treatment Tool in Activity Group Therapy." *International Journal of Group Psychotherapy*, 2: 1952.

eral incidents took place that completely restored Martin, proving that he had indeed incorporated much strength.

Session No. 43, Excerpts—All Present

Several days before the regular meeting, Jesus came to the worker's office to inquire about whether the group could visit the playground again. The worker said it would be all right if the boys agreed to it. On the day of the session, an hour before it was to begin, John visited the worker and asked whether they would meet. The worker assured him they would.

Martin and John arrived with their escorts. John was smiling, hopping up and down. Martin's face was badly bruised. As the worker was about to inquire about it, he volunteered, "On Thursday I fell into a car. It was awful! I went bowling on Saturday. Bowling is good. Big fat Jackie pushed me into a car. When I woke up, my nose was bleeding." He then set out the wooden wedge figures on the floor, in an arrangement like nine pins, and began to knock them over with the gymnasium ball. John tried to take the ball. Martin said, "No, I'm bowling. You want to play?" John sat on the wood truck and pushed himself along the floor. Martin bowled over the figures, then set them up again, saying, "I knocked them all down except the kids" (boy and girl wedge figures). John said, "I'll play." Martin: "I'll set them up for you. Wait, not yet." He set them up. John knocked over eight of them. Martin called out the score. There was a noise at the door, and Martin went over to see who it was. "Is that you, Paul?" he asked. Paul entered, followed by Theo. The escorts were leaving. The worker inquired as to Jesus's whereabouts. She looked to the left and saw him in the corridor, hugging the wall. Jesus said, "I'm not coming in"; he apparently was resistant because the worker had not promised that the group could go outside. The worker said, "I'll miss you. I'd like you to come in." She turned and reentered the play room to find Theo hassling Martin over possession of the ball. Martin held the ball and all the wooden figures in his arms, protectively.

. . . Jesus said, "Can't we go outside?" The worker replied, "It's up to the group." John: "Hey, let's all go." Martin: "Sure. Let's go out and play ball." It was cloudy and cool out, and the worker mentioned that they did not have jackets with them. Jesus said, "I came to school like this." Paul added, "We can go back to get our jackets." The worker said, "All right." Jesus then said, "My teacher has a big ball" (basketball). The worker gave Jesus a note asking his teacher to borrow the ball.

. . . While they were assembling to go to the schoolyard, John's teacher happened to come along the corridor and Martin told her, "We're going to the Tenth Street yard to play ball." The teacher noticed his battered face and asked, "What happened to you?" Martin replied, "I fell into a car and got all banged up!'' The teacher said, ''Just like a boy.'' Martin laughed, strutted, and said, ''All banged up like a good boy should.'' Another teacher happened to walk by, and Martin again volunteered, ''We're going to the Tenth Street yard to play ball.'' Paul and John had run on ahead and were hiding. The worker and the others looked for them.

. . . In the yard, Martin took the smaller rubber ball and began to play with it. The others ran about kicking the basketball. Martin pointed out, ''There are two new baskets. A boy in my class got the ball in five times. I got it in twice.'' The worker said, ''Good for you!'' Martin shot for the basket with the small, rubber ball, then ran after the other boys, saying, ''Hey, give me a chance; it's my turn now. Let me do it. Can't I play?'' Theo threw the basketball to him and Martin kicked it, his shoe falling off when he did so. The worker said, ''It's a very heavy ball,'' thinking to mollify Martin. He, nonplussed, replied, ''It's a light shoe!'' The worker organized a game of shooting for the basket, to focus the uncoordinated running about. She suggested that each boy take two turns and demonstrate how to shoot for the basket. Martin then tried. Theo kept grabbing the basketball and shooting out of turn. The group yelled at him to stop. Later, he and John kept the ball to themselves. Martin complained to the worker that it was not fair. Meanwhile, he held onto the rubber ball during play with the basketball.

Once again the worker organized a game, this time in a circle. She began to throw to each boy in turn. Theo again grabbed it when Martin's turn came. The worker said to Theo, ''Theo, you stand here.'' Meanwhile, having obtained the ball, she threw it to Martin, who caught it successfully. This was difficult for him to do, because he still had the smaller ball under one arm. He finally tossed the smaller ball aside and continued to play catch.

The boys inquired about the time, and the worker said it was time to go back to the play room for a snack. Some of them ran ahead eagerly as they passed through the corridors and up the staircase.

. . . Martin said, ''I'll bring it to the table,'' (the refreshments). The worker poured while Theo, Jesus, and Paul grabbed for pieces of cake. Paul said, ''Oh, oh, here is some for you, Mrs. T.'' Theo said, ''She doesn't want any.'' Jesus: ''Of *course* she does.'' Paul put back a piece, and the others grabbed up the remainder. Martin did not touch the food. Instead he went to the other table to work on a calendar.

. . . When the boys left with their escorts, Theo contrived to remain with the worker. He asked her to play a game of dominoes with him. (Note: Ordinarily no child had been staying in the play room for a significant length of time when the sessions ended. Occasionally this ''rule'' was broken because of unusual circumstances affecting individual children. In this instance, the worker did so because recently Theo had been acting even more aggressively, not only with Martin but with the other boys, some of whom had been complaining about this. The worker had had to intervene several times to keep Theo from actually hurting others.) The worker was aware of Theo's great affect hunger, as demonstrated in other sessions when he lagged behind after the group left. The worker took advantage of this opportunity to chat with Theo about recent events in the group. She introduced the subject of his fighting, suggesting to him that some of the other boys weren't "as strong" as he, and that it might be a good idea not to "play so rough." This carefully delivered suggestion seemed to be accepted by Theo without his feeling censured.

Comments and Interpretations

Martin was indeed badly bruised and scratched, yet he was extremely proud of his "wounds," which to him meant that he was "one of the boys." He also, when describing his "accident," spoke of other, seemingly unrelated events that had taken place over the weekend. There actually was relatedness between the two: bowling represented another "first" experience for Martin, an activity associated with his growing interest and participation in active sports. As for the "accident" that had brought him into contact with an automobile, details were provided later by his mother, who had witnessed it from her apartment window. Martin's twice-volunteered recounting of the incident to the two teachers was evidence of his excited valuation of the event. Before the play group left for the schoolyard, Martin engaged John in a "bowling" game, one that was goal-oriented, quite unlike games he had initiated in earlier sessions.

We note how the worker directed Jesus's request to go out to the play yard to the group for decision. Even though Jesus had requested this several days prior to the session, and petulantly remained in the corridor when the escorts brought him because he thought the group should go outside immediately, the worker correctly invoked the group's authority for decision-making. This technique enhanced the group's perception of itself as a social force. Also, it demonstrated again the worker's continued trust in the boys. Increasingly over time, a therapy group becomes a regulating, disciplining force. Whereas in the beginning such a social influence is notably absent because of the narcissistic needs of individual children and their preoccupation with self, as each child matures there is a welding of individual strengths into a larger, compelling social *gestalt*. In activity-type, noninterpretive group therapy, the primary corrective influence stems from therapy *by* the group, supplemented by the supportive positive transferences of children toward the worker. On the other hand, in the analytical forms of group therapy—Play Group Therapy and Activity-Interview Group Psychotherapy,[2] as in analytical groups with adolescents and adults, the dynamic process is therapy of individuals *in* a group.

---

[2]Play Group Therapy and Activity-Interview Group Psychotherapy are the titles of the standard methods of analytical group treatment that were devised by S. R. Slavson following Ac-

We note again Martin's stubborn resistance against Theo, even during a period when Theo's heightened aggression had become a problem for the entire group. Despite Theo's interference with the game, the worker managed to organize it for a time and in so doing assured Martin greater success in his athletic endeavors.

On the way to and from the playground, some of the boys violated school rules, by running away from the group and hiding and by behaving boisterously in the corridors. This is not unanticipated when a play group begins to spend some of its meeting time elsewhere in the larger school setting, in an outdoor play yard or an inner gymnasium. In this instance the worker chose not to intervene because the behavior was not extreme. Should it become so, a worker can arrange in advance that a school administrator confront the group. Such a person acts as an outside authority, increasing the children's awareness of the distinction to be made between the unusual permissiveness of the group experience and the more restrictive reality of the school. Such awareness must necessarily evolve during a play group's terminal phase of treatment—a reestablishment of improved reality functioning that is necessary if the children are to solidify the gains acquired in treatment. When a therapeutic play group is at an advanced stage, the worker begins to introduce more and more situations that call for decision-making by the group as a whole and require that choices be made among activities. Through this strategy, the children are confronted with reasonable frustrations so as to build up their tolerances. The almost absolute permissiveness and unconditional acceptance that characterized the worker's attitude at the beginning of treatment must be modified at the proper time, with the worker using sensitive techniques to assist the children toward more effective coping. Because the children have been "loved'," they become more capable of loving, which makes them receptive to reconstructive, educational interventions from therapists, without acting out or regression. Most children are receptive to new learning when guided by adults whom they love and respect.

During the next session, the forty-fourth, Martin made references to his desire to become a "big boy," as he put it, when telling the worker that in upper-grade classes "only the big boys" are allowed to open windows for teachers, and that he "will have to wait, but soon will be big enough!" Later in the same session, he volunteered, as he built a structure with blocks, "I'm going to build a house [group?] *everybody* can live in." Martin's remarks at this and other times, were unusually dramatic and meaningful. Both the worker and the author were inordinately impressed with such

---

tivity-Group Therapy. Play Group Therapy is employed with children of pre-school age, whereas Activity-Interview Group Psychotherapy is used with older latency, prepubertal children.

spontaneous verbalizations by Martin, which were so keyed to his nuclear problem and to his conscious feelings of change within himself. Probably the pointedness of his remarks was partly attributable to his good intelligence, his excellent command of language, and a tendency to verbalize readily. Nevertheless, it is noteworthy that at this stage in treatment, when his successes were being crystallized into fundamental changes in his character, his former garrulousness changed into insightful comments, an example of derivative insight.

The close of the second school year occurred with the fiftieth group session. Martin's mother was again invited to school as part of the regular evaluation process. She leaned back in the chair and, almost exactly as in the previous interview, inquired: "So, tell me about Martin." The worker made a few comments and then redirected the mother to describe how she saw matters. As usual, she needed little urging. She started by saying, "He's a changed child!" When specifics were asked for, she continued, "Well, he's a regular little man. He's a *real boy*! He has become so independent. He goes out to play by himself. Imagine! Sometimes two hours pass without my looking for him or even knowing where he is! Two hours! When did such a thing ever happen before?" She offered further examples to show how Martin had changed, in her eyes. "He dressed himself. Once he came up from the street all muddy and dirty. He said, 'Oh, it's all right. I'll wash.' He want to the sink and washed himself. He has lots of friends. He plays with boys on the block. He loves to play ball. He's a Dodger fan. And another thing I noticed. He's not such a sore loser anymore. He never cries. If he gets into a fight with his sister, he lets her have it! He used to come and cry to me, but no more."

She then referred to the incident reported in session 43. Her version differed from Martin's. From her window she had seen him playing with boys on the street. One boy pushed him out of the game. Martin had provoked the episode, according to her. The other boy said Martin was "out" (a term meaning he had been "tagged"). Martin did not agree, and he pushed the boy first. This boy, who was bigger than Martin, got the best in the fight. Although the mother saw the scrape on Martin's nose, she did not interfere.

More information poured from her. She reported that when Martin made errors in his homework, he was no longer concerned over it. He would shrug and say, "Well, I did something wrong; so I got an example wrong. That's nothing." Once he came home from school and announced: "Well, I *finally* did it!" He then explained, "I got 50 [a failing mark] on a test!" The mother exclaimed, "Can you imagine that? The *way* he said, 'I *finally* did it!'"

The mother described that her husband found Martin changed. He said, "Now it will be a pleasure to take Martin swimming."

She added, "My husband took him last week, and he dressed himself. He put on his trunks and dried himself." She volunteered further: "I don't have to feed him now. When he's in a hurry he eats and runs out. If he lingers with his food or carries it around the house, I take it from him and down the street he goes!''

Toward the end of the interview she said, ''I'll tell you the truth. I'm too sick to bother with him much. I have very high blood pressure; so that helped him a lot, too.''

Comments and Interpretations

Most of the mother's remarks require no elaboration; the reader can appreciate their significance with respect to Martin and their confirmation of changes observed in the play group. One additional factor, however, merits attention: the mother's reference to her own state of health. In constellatory problems of the type found in this family, it is not unusual for a mother to develop somatic complaints when a child who is focal to the neurotic interactions and psychomalignant homeostasis begins to improve. It is this factor which necessitates the treatment of parents coincidentally with their children. But such an approach could not be effected with this family.

The next contact with the mother occurred in September, when school resumed. She telephoned the worker. The gist of the conversation follows: ''Martin isn't going to be in your group this year, is he?'' When asked why she had raised the question, she said, jocularly, ''Well, he's a regular little hoodlum now. He certainly doesn't need it [the play group] anymore. He is so fresh, oh my! I hardly saw him all summer. He was always in the park, running around with his friends. He goes to the movies, and bowling, far away from home. He only *plays* in your room. And he doesn't need it anymore. When he was in second grade, he needed to learn to play with other children and not be a baby—right? But now he does beautifully. He doesn't get into trouble, but if another kid starts up, he hits back.'' Once again she questioned the need to continue Martin in the play group. The worker thought it best to see her in person and arranged an appointment.

A week later in the interview with the worker, she spoke again of Martin's changed behavior. She then expressed concern lest the school ''think'' that Martin was really emotionally disturbed, assuring the worker that he was a ''wonderful boy.'' She was concerned about possible entries being made on school record cards indicating emotional instability. She was given assurances that this would not be done. (Note: the play group records, interview material, and so forth were never permitted to be viewed by anyone other than the play group worker and the author. Notations were never made on record cards.)

The mother then went into a lengthy description of her husband's problems. The worker again ventured the suggestion that it might be helpful to discuss these matters on a regular basis with someone in a community agency. As in the past, however, the mother resisted the idea. The worker easily convinced her to let Martin continue in the play group.

At the first session in the fall, the worker introduced new, advanced crafts activities. They were of a level that the boys could master. This procedure is done to keep abreast of children's advancing abilities and to provide higher levels of achievement in projects that are notably ego-strengthening. Woodwork was one of the new activities, and all the boys took to it eagerly. Martin was thrilled with woodwork and applied himself to it almost to the exclusion of all other materials. He quickly gained enough skill to fabricate simple projects, and his reactions to these were expressed in vocal superlatives. He was seldom seen without a hammer in his hand. Often he exclaimed that he would become a carpenter. This successful involvement with resistive materials had great meaning for him in further reinforcing his sense of masculinity.

The play group was continued until the boys had completed fifth grade, by which time a total of ninety sessions had taken place. Martin's attendance was practically perfect; the average attendance for the group as a whole was more than 95 percent. This was unusual considering the frequency of illnesses of young children, particularly in ghetto neighborhoods. The children were observed in follow-up during the final year, prior to transfer to junior high schools.

About half a year prior to termination of the play group, Theo's family moved away from the neighborhood. Because the worker considered Theo's continuation in the play group critical, by a special administrative arrangement he was not transferred to another school but allowed to remain. However, after a while Theo's mother objected to this arrangement, preferring to have him closer to home. Theo was transferred to a school in his new district area. His transfer was consummated following an individual interview with the worker to soften his disappointment. Another boy was added to the group to replace him. Martin continued to show progress. He was able to tolerate termination without undue anxiety. Each boy was seen individually at the time the group ended and assured that the worker was available to them should they care to visit her.

Summary

Martin's problem at referral, two and a half years earlier, was that of a boy with confused sexual identity, manifest feminine characteristics and behavior, severely repressed anger, and compulsive, obsessive symptoms. The permissive play group had a shock effect upon him initially, throwing many of his characteristic ways of behaving into disarray. Placed in jeopardy because his habituated modes of behavior were ineffective in modifying his anxiety, Martin tried to change the permissive attitude of the worker, without success. Failing in this, he became manic and extremely provocative of others. He tested the worker frequently, attempting to manipulate and control her, while he still acted dependently with her. He inevitably drew upon himself retaliatory actions from the other boys, who teased and punished him in various ways. Because the worker's therapeutic role was maintained despite Martin's efforts to bring her into harmony with his perceptions of adults (women in particular) as authoritative, he became further confused. Regression followed: smearing with paints; soiling the floor; vocalizing in an infantile way, with babbling at times; pursuing the worker about in a demanding way. The worker permitted this, intervening only when Martin became excessively frustrated or overly frightened by the group. She always *listened* to his many complaints, but she did not intervene against the other boys as he demanded. She provided Martin with sufficient surveillance and support to enable him to withstand the consequences of his behavior when it brought reactions from others.

In essence, Martin was experiencing in transference with the worker stages of psychological development which, earlier in his life, had proved debilitating. Psychologically, the therapist's role with him was oppositional in its effect to the infantilizing, castrating influence of his basically rejecting but overcompensating mother. When Martin's behavior in the play group threatened to become extreme, it was blocked by social forces—namely, the ridicule and other strictures imposed by the group. He had made the boys overanxious and sometimes overstimulated by his excessive, infantile behavior. Their episodic limitations upon him were necessary to maintain their own defenses against regression. Also, the factor of latent homosexuality in Martin had to be reacted to defensively by them because, at their latency age, it threatened their still formative identities. At the same time, however, the group—in demonstrating its own masculine qualities, aspirations, and appropriate gender behavior—provided a subtle but definitive template for Martin to pattern himself against. In the presence of such countervailing forces against characterological weaknesses, Martin's motivation to change—to be like others—gained strength and momentum. But first he had to have cathartic release for much that was already assimilated developmentally. This process of "undoing," or corrective reexperience, required much time and much repetition of reconstructive experiences.

Assured of the worker's continuing permissive role and neutrality, Martin, despite his initially regressive and negativistic behavior, was eventually able to acquire new ways of adapting. Also, he developed entirely new skills in crafts work and athletics, which helped him to sublimate. This eventuated in greater acceptance of him in the group, where he gained social status on a healthier basis.

In working through inner conflicts in the play group, Martin had two alternatives: either to leave the play group, if his anxiety became too much to bear; or to remain because his positive feelings and compensatory gains were strong enough to offset frustration and pain. He experienced some relief from the cathartic discharge of hitherto blocked feelings, which could take place only after a weakening of his defenses. Later, he was enabled to relinquish infantile behavior because of the ego-strengthening that followed, brought about by his success with crafts work—especially woodwork—and other growth experiences. The corrective, therapeutic effects operated on two levels. First in importance was the positive transference with a surrogate parent, the worker, a relationship that was without neurotic quality and was the antithesis of the pathological relationship to the mother. The transference experience, for Martin, represented acknowledgment of his individuality and autonomy. Fundamentally, it was in this sustaining relationship that Martin discovered that masculinity need not be threatening. Secondly, the other boys provided opportunities for successful peer relationships and recognition, and they acted as identification models.

Several incidents pointedly revealed these influences and their effects on Martin:

While building with blocks, Martin stated, "I'll build a house *everyone* [even I] can live in."

Martin said that "only the big boys" could open windows and that he wasn't big enough yet to reach them. "I'll have to wait, but soon will be big enough!" These remarks reveal his growing pains and aspirations.

Martin's teacher had observed: "You know, he *looks* more like a real boy now."

The therapeutic play group experience not only interrupted the further development of character distortion but actually reversed the process, solidifying proper gender identity. Martin continued to improve because now he *needed* to: he had become more aware of the changes in himself. As a consequence, he became better equipped to oppose the overwhelmingly influential pathognomonic influence within his family. He practically defied his parents, refused to be babied further. He also separated himself from the confines of the home, spending much time in the playground and elsewhere in his neighborhood.

A question of some interest is the reactions of Martin's parents to the changes in their son. Since these changes were psychologically opposed to the basic neurotic constellation, with Martin in a pivotal role, it could be anticipated that with changes in the boy there would be an increase in the tension of the parents and, consequently, a growing resistance. This was, in fact, what happened. As was noted, the worker's repeated attempts to involve the family with an agency failed. With respect to the parents, the pathological problem within the family remained essentially as it was, and perhaps was heightened. It was expected that the neurotic nature of the parents' behavior might become even more exacerbated as a result of changes in Martin. In the mother, an increase in somatization occurred. The probability was that the rigid, obsessive-compulsive defenses of the father would remain in place to support him.

Martin's mother, his teachers, and the worker all described substantive changes in the boy's demeanor, his behavior, and his relationships with peers. The degree to which such pronounced changes in ego function and self-image become assimilated psychically can only be determined over time. As was noted earlier, successful therapy with young children can produce substantive mutations in personality and character structure. When changes in individuals are fundamental, it should be possible to detect them in different settings and under varying conditions. This proved so with Martin in his home, his school, and his neighborhood. Follow-up observations, which were made for approximately one year while Martin was in sixth grade, revealed that he maintained the improvement and continued to adjust well. At the end of the year he made an easy, successful transition to a junior high school.

Part II

Activity-Interview Group Psychotherapy

NORMAL ego defense mechanisms proliferate and begin to crystallize during latency development, when children ordinarily acquire broader compensatory and socially adaptive behavior. However, neurotic children are usually not psychologically equipped to manage the anxiety associated with developmental problems. They require analytical treatment that can bring intrapsychic conflicts to the surface. Once they become more aware of the libidinal, hostile, and other feelings that have been subject to repression, while involved in a safe, supportive transference relationship with a therapist, children readily become capable of relieving these emotions cathartically. This process is abetted by the presence of peers who are similarly afflicted.

During the early experimental years in group treatment, it was soon discovered that some children did not respond as anticipated to activity-group therapy when it was used as an exclusive form of treatment. It was determined that they had pervasive feelings of guilt, anxiety, and other emotional disabilities. Activity-group therapy was able to ameliorate these conditions, but it could not eliminate them. Another method of group treatment was devised—*Activity-Interview Group Psychotherapy,*[1] which included discussions of problems in addition to arts and crafts activities.

---

[1]The reader will note the varying uses of the terms "therapy" and "psychotherapy" in Parts I and II in this book. The reason for this is mostly historical, having to do with the introduction

Problems presented by neurotic children can be addressed through individual analytical play therapy. However, many children are resistive to individual treatment when it is attempted; they are more easily involved in activity-interview groups. This is due to the factor of universalization. While universalization is a phenomenon common in all activity and analytical groups and with patients of all ages, it has a more immediate, penetrating effect with young children, who, at the start of treatment, conceive themselves to be the only ones subject to frightening, forbidden thoughts, wishes, and fantasies. When they discover in groups that other children have similar feelings, they feel almost immediate relief.

The freedom to verbalize about hidden emotions, usually for the first time, becomes a potent, corrective influence. In a setting similar to that of activity-group therapy, but with fewer play and crafts materials and with the addition of libido-activating play objects such as dolls and house furniture, the treatment allows a therapist to explore with the children their inner psychic problems in addition to their overt behavior.

Libido-activating objects are of a nature to elicit through play children's thoughts and feelings on conscious and unconscious levels, especially as they relate to anal, oral, and sexual preoccupations and fantasies. Libido-binding activities, on the other hand, such as woodwork and weaving, tend to engage children's interests in arts and crafts without stimulating unconscious, repressed emotions. Materials for arts and crafts are more elaborately supplied in purely activity groups, which have a different patient population.

Some play, crafts, and game activities are also necessary in activity-interview group psychotherapy, for several reasons: to provide children with avenues of retreat should the exploratory procedures of analytical therapy become momentarily burdensome or frightening; to foster interactions between group members and thus increase opportunities for resolution of intragroup conflicts, especially when abrasive situations arise over possession of various items; to help children play out family situations and their feelings about them, using dolls, doll furniture, puppets, and similar libido-ac-

---

of the group treatment modality in the early 1930s. However, because there are some clinical considerations with respect to these terms, some background information may prove helpful. When activity-group therapy was first introduced, it was anticipated that this essentially noninterpretive treatment, which entirely eschewed the use of analytical techniques that were basic in the prevailing therapies, would be looked on askance, particularly by psychiatrists. Rather than intensify the anticipated resistance, which did occur, it was decided to use a diluted term, "therapy," instead of "psychotherapy." After a few years passed, and it was discovered that some child-patients required a group treatment that would include exploration and interpretations in addition to activities, the term "psychotherapy" was used in the treatment of prepubertal children in analytical groups. By that time, children's group treatment had begun to establish itself as a fundamental modality for a significantly large number of problems. Actually, "psychotherapy" is a more correct term for all healing procedures applied in the treatment of emotional problems. See also M. Schiffer, *History of Children's Group Therapy*, American Group Psychotherapy Association, New York, 1980.

tivating items; and finally, to gratify children's creative needs, which do not always find expressive opportunities in homes or even in schools.

Unlike in activity-group therapy, where the therapist is peripheral in the group's activities until children request assistance and where discussions are avoided, in activity-interview groups the therapist assumes a more active role, engaging in discussions with one child, several, or the group as a whole at psychologically opportune times. The gist of discussions (which are equivalent to interviews in dyadic treatment), anent feelings, fantasies, and ambivalences stems from children's individual play and also from the interactions between group members. Children's expressed feelings and their associative ideation usually relate to circumstances in their families that become displaced to the therapy group. The therapist sensitively "sets a stage" for talking and eases troubled children into personal disclosures. Mindful of their limitations, the therapist governs the pace, depth, and timing of psychological "learnings" so that children are not overly threatened.

At appropriate times, the therapist provides explanations and offers suggestions to ameliorate conditions reported by the children, or the therapist sometimes merely reflects their statements empathically. Such interventions are made circumspectly, geared to children's tolerances for emotionally troubling situations in their daily lives and their ability to cope with them. From time to time, the therapist volunteers general information concerning motivations of behavior, and also concerning human biology. Broadening children's knowledge on the latter subject is an educational aspect of their treatment. Children possess limited knowledge, and often misinformation, with respect to body structure and physiology, especially anal, urethral, and genital functions, about which they are curious.

Activity-interview group psychotherapy differs from purely activity-group therapy not only in the choice of clients for whom each method is indicated and in the nature of the treatment, but with respect to the composition of the groups. Activity groups are usually gender-homogeneous, including the therapist, in order to foster the process of identity formation of latency-age children.[2] An exception to the "rule" of gender homogeneity may be made in activity groups with children approximately five to eight years of age. Such groups function quite well with a therapist of either gender. Male and female co-therapists can be particularly efficacious in activity groups of boys and girls who have experienced traumatic separations from one or both parents (see Chapter 2). Since many of the children's emotional conflicts and ambivalences have a sexual base, the presence of both boys and girls readily ensures that there will be interactive episodes related to the children's feelings and ideas about sexuality. Moreover, the process of iden-

---

[2] On the basis of experiences with many such groups, the author has found that female therapists tend to have a functional advantage. The probable reason for this is the propensity of young children to form dependent, nurturance-seeking relationships with the therapist.

tity formation of young children, which is strongly predicated on contrast factors between the sexes, among other things, becomes more easily substantiated by the presence of members of the opposite gender.

In activity-interview groups with older children, nine years to pre-puberty, gender-homogeneous grouping with a therapist of the same gender is usually advisable in order to crystallize identity formation, a pressing developmental need for children of this age. In the relatively advanced stage of identity formation of older children, they are more inclined to seek mutual support for their personal and social needs in the company of peers of the same gender. Moreover, they are preoccupied with burgeoning feelings related to sexuality: a beginning interest in members of the opposite sex, increased sensitivity about physiology and incipient physical growth changes, and a heightened responsiveness to social mores as reflected in their perception of adult roles. For these reasons, in analytical forms of group psychotherapy, older children are more comfortable and feel freer to talk about sex-related themes and problems in gender-homogeneous groups, with therapists of the same gender.

In Chapter 5, the reader is privileged to share a therapist's demanding, sensitive, and successful experience with a group of highly troubled, older-latency-age girls. Noteworthy are her gentle introduction of the girls to the analytical intent of the group and her forbearance and wisdom in selecting situations that encouraged conversation and evoked suppressed and repressed feelings. While Katie, a neurotic and depressed child, is the focus of this report, a broad panorama is given of the group as a whole and the typical interactions occurring in activity-interview groups. Occasionally the therapist makes use of paradigmatic techniques that have value, *when carefully employed*, in evoking negative transference expressions. Katie and the other girls are actively involved in a corrective experience with the therapist (psychological parent) and with one another (psychological siblings). Didactic-type, informative statements by the therapist are entirely lacking. Instead, she carefully contrives to maximize the children's influence upon one another as a therapeutic force.

CHAPTER 5

Activity-Interview Group Psychotherapy of Latency-Age Girls

Fanny Milstein

Since the introduction of activity-group therapy for children by Slavson in 1934, there has been considerable emphasis on the values and importance of group treatment. Slavson emphasized the social hunger of children, especially those who feel alienated. He saw early that one of the values of a group was to accelerate "the initial steps in treatment,[so] that transference to the therapist was facilitated and that inter-member transferences are established. Group members act as emotional catalyzers and activate one another to discussion of their difficulties."[1]

Another value of groups mentioned by Slavson in early communications is that of peer interpretations. The verbal comments and observations that group members make about one another's behaviors frequently prepare the way for subsequent interpretations of the behaviors by the therapist or by other members. Of course, the problem with peer interpretations is that they can be inexact or premature, so the therapist has to exercise caution to protect weaker egos. Intrepretations are viable primarily if the atmosphere in which they are given is benevolent and empathic. Creating such an atmosphere is the responsibility of the group therapist. The value of peer in-

---

[1]S. R. Slavson, "Differential Methods of Group Therapy in Relation to Age Levels," *Nervous Child*, 4: 3; 1944–1945.

terpretations is also well described in the work of Rosenthal in 1968 in his chapter on interpretation in group therapy. He shows clearly how the "unique characteristic of interpretation in group therapy resides in the number of potential interpreters and how these group members participate in being objects for transference, identification, and dispensers of interpretations."[2]

In this paper, emphasis is placed on the first phases of treatment in activity-interview group psychotherapy, during which the earliest forms of resistance must be located, analyzed, and dealt with if the group is to continue. The report concerns an activity-interview group of five latency-age girls, eight to ten years old, at the Madeline Borg Child Guidance Institute in New York City. Group meetings began in October 1973, and this report is based on thirty-two sessions that were held once a week until the end of June in 1974.

The children for this group were all chosen on the basis of their behavior and, additionally, their intrapsychic problems. A few details on each of the girls in the group will illustrate the basis for their selection.

Ginette, nine and a half years old, the smallest member in size, was referred with complaints of temper outbursts at home, severe learning problems in school, and a history of constant intestinal disorders, bad dreams, and fear of sounds. She was the youngest of two children (both girls), whose parents had themselves been grossly deprived in childhood. Outstanding in Ginette's history is the loss of her chief nurturant source, a maternal grandmother, when Ginette was in second grade.

The second child, Wendy, an obese girl eight and a half years old, was referred to the clinic because she wouldn't listen to her mother or behave ever since her parents had separated the previous year, one of many separations that had taken place. She sat without moving when her mother beat her and stole money from both parents to buy sweets. Also, she feared her mother would starve her, was obviously depressed, kept her eyes down, and responded minimally to contacts. She was the oldest of three children.

The third member was Sally, an attractive girl nine years of age, the older of two siblings. She was brought by her mother with complaints that she had temper tantrums, kept things to herself, and tyrannized her mother. She also had fears of the dark and stomach pains, with no physical cause established. Sally's parents had been separated since she was five years of age, when her father walked out. Sally's problems, however, began with the birth of her brother when she was two years old.

The next member, Patricia, was a plump, pretty, and sophisticated nine-year-old. She was the middle of three children and was referred to the

[2]Leslie Rosenthal, "Some Aspects of Interpretation in Group Therapy," in *Use of Interpretation in Treatment*, Grune & Stratton, New York, 1968.

clinic because she lied, stole things from her mother to give to neighbors, used cosmetics, and ignored her mother's instructions. Patricia asked for help in making friends. She and her siblings lived with their mother, an obese, psychotic woman who was not married to the children's father. The father did try to maintain his relationship with the family, although the family was supported primarily by public funds.

The fifth and last member of the group is the one on whom we focus, ten-year-old Katie, a tall, slender, dark-haired girl with an alert, perky manner. She was referred to the clinic by her parents because she talked continuously in school, was a poor reader, daydreamed a great deal, and was in conflict with her sisters and parents. She also sat and worried about things like fires, her memory, and getting older. She didn't get along with other children, being either manipulative or hostile toward them. She was the oldest of three children, all girls.

Katie's parents were married in their teens. The father's parents were alcoholics. He was cared for by others outside of the family. He avoided alcohol and worked for periods of time, but even while employed, he sometimes stayed home and moped. Katie's mother, who felt she had received little affection from her own parents, was extremely shy and unable to face people. She complained that Katie annoyed and angered her by looking "crooked." Katie was born in the first year of their marriage, unplanned. Both parents felt that they had had children too early. The pregnancy was normal, but labor was difficult. Katie weighed seven pounds, fourteen ounces at birth, fed well, and was reported to have been a happy baby. She talked at a year and walked at fourteen months. Until three years of age (and the birth of a sibling), Katie was friendly and outgoing. From the age of five months to two and a half years, Katie was boarded out for four hours each day at the home of her mother's sister, while the mother worked. When the mother took Katie back full time, she was already pregnant with her next child. She complained that her sister had been too permissive with Katie.

It is thus apparent that Katie received insufficient nurturance from her parents, who themselves were emotionally needy. She was happy in her early years in the care of an aunt. Once home, she developed behavior disorders, daydreaming, and neurotic fears and conflicts centered around the oedipal situation, which was exaggerated by the parents' pathological overinvolvement with each other, excessive sexual stimulation to which Katie had been exposed, and the mother's pregnancy when Katie was three years old.

In 1970, Katie was given parts of the WISC test, Picture Drawings, and Bender Gestalt. The findings indicated that Katie's early childhood experiences had resulted in her having unique feelings about herself and being uncertain of what was expected of her. It appeared that many of her early emotional experiences had been confusing and overly stimulating, which resulted in much frustration. She had difficulty in adequately identifying with the female role. The findings of psychological tests administered in 1973 (Wechsler, Bender Gestalt, Figure Drawings) emphasized that Katie's learning retardation was primarily psychogenic—a neurotic inhibition due to conflict over growth. Thus, we can see that at the time of referral Katie was still fixated at a pre-latency emotional level and blocked in academic learning.

Katie was first seen by the group therapist alone. She spoke freely, was full of compaints, and was obviously terrified of her parents and siblings, and was distressed by her way of life. She was worried about forgetting things and so scared of cockroaches that she couldn't go to sleep and then was afraid of her parents' anger because she kept them up. Her father woke up every night, while her mother was a sound sleeper. At this point in the interview, Katie showed even more fear when she spoke of her feeling that when her father was tired he would "feel like killing" them. Katie felt herself caught in the middle, between her parents, and she was full of neurotic conflicts because of excessive stimulation of both her sexual and her aggressive drives. She expressed interest in a "club" in which girls helped each other, when it was suggested by the therapist, although here, too, she was ambivalent. Ambivalence was also revealed as she told of problems with her sister.

In the first group session, all of the girls came together from the waiting room. The therapist was seated at a table large enough for all, in a small room equipped with a dollhouse, play materials, table games, paints, crayon, paper, and Play-doh®. Candy, pretzels, and soda were placed unobtrusively on a smaller table nearby. It was planned to use two rooms—the small one just described and a larger one with the same equipment but, in addition, a Nok Hockey® table, a few tools, wood, nails, and three work tables.

Katie, the tallest girl, led the way to the food. She took generous helpings, sat down at the head seat nearest the food, and began to eat. Wendy, the obese girl, sat next to the therapist at Katie's left. She too helped herself to a lot of food. Ginette seemed little interested in the food but eagerly sat down on Katie's right and tried to involve Katie in conversation. Sally sat next to Ginette, opposite the therapist. Sally piled up food in front of her and looked at the other girls and at the therapist from time to time as she ate. Wendy was obviously absorbed in her food.

Katie exclaimed happily over the food and announced that she was hungry. She went on to say that her mother had brought two sandwiches to school, one for Katie and one for herself, but then the mother had eaten both. *(She thus let the therapist know at once that she had a bad mother.)*[3]

---

[3]Italicized interpretations in this chapter are by F.M.

Katie then complained about the food: "We should leave out pretzels, keep potato chips, and get a larger-size bottle of soda." *(She thus informed the therapist that the latter was also a "bad" mother—had supplied the wrong food and not enough of the right food.)* The others joined Katie in giving the group therapist directions for changes. *(Katie was a catalyzer in the group, in this instance invoking feelings against the symbolic inadequate, unfeeling mother.)*

Ginette offered a plan of her own "to divide up in twos, play Nok Hockey, get all excited, be friends, and have fun." Katie wasn't ready to join in forming subgroups, but when Ginette suggested a "Halloween party" for next week, with costumes, Katie agreed. Katie wanted to come as an angel but said that that would be difficult. "How can I come as an angel, with wings, and wear my coat?" When Ginette refused to get involved in such details, Katie became angry and said sarcastically that Ginette sure was shy. She explained to the group that she didn't mean that Ginette really was shy but that Ginette had so informed Katie. "Now," said Katie, "how could Ginette be shy when she babbles away?"

At this point the therapist thought it opportune to intervene, since there seemed to be unmet needs for understanding in both girls. The therapist said, "Maybe we could now talk about why we are here," thus setting the stage for talking about problems and feelings as one of the main purposes of the group.[4] Katie seemed grateful and then said that she "hated to tell" the group, but she had been left back in school. Ginette joined in, "Me, too," and then, pointing at Katie, Ginette, added, "She is everything like me. [implying both girls—M.S.]" When one of the others suggested that Ginette might have been left back because of her size, Ginette rejected this idea. She stood up and said that she now wanted to go to the playroom (the larger room). Katie wasn't ready. She told Ginette so, saying that she was "so starved." Ginette kept trying to divide up the group by standing up to write the word "love" on a blackboard. Katie told her to sit down. Ginette insisted that "love" was a "nice word." Katie agreed but said that Ginette should give love by being a friend. When soda was accidentally spilled, all the girls helped to clean up. While everybody was moving about doing this, Ginette suggested again that they change rooms. All agreed. Ginette burst out that she liked the therapist—and Katie.

When the group entered the large room, Sally asked Wendy to play a table game. They sat on the radiator near a window. Katie asked the therapist's permission to use the saw. *(This indicated Katie's conflict over her aggressive feelings.)* Ginette joined Katie in sawing at a large work table. Ginette decided to use only a little saw, saying that she would get hurt with the big one. Katie complained that it was hard to keep the wood in one

---

[4]Here the therapist deliberately structured the nature of the group, an important technical intervention that should be made in the first session of an activity-interview group.—M. S.

place. Wendy helped her, showing her how to use a vise. Sally took Wendy away by suggesting that they do some carving with the saw; Wendy agreed. Now Sally tried to get the others to help her, saying she had a problem: She did cutting with one hand and wrote with the other. Which hand should she use with the saw? No one answered. Sally decided to use both, saying she would use one hand "until it gets tired." Ginette tried to get Katie to help her with the sawing. Katie refused to "baby" Ginette; instead, she encouraged Ginette and said that she had to do it by herself.

The therapist was sitting at a table somewhat removed from the activities, and Katie said she was worried that the therapist "might get bored just sitting there." *(The therapist, sensing Katie's fear of abandonment and need for reassurance, said that she wanted to stay.)* Katie and Ginette were now working at a large work table. Sally was busy hammering at a nearby small work table and on the floor. Wendy was at a work table across the room by herself. She seemed able to use tools more efficiently than any of the others. Sally called out happily that everybody was doing the same thing (sawing) and added that it worked better to saw with her left hand. Ginette, however, complained that everybody was doing a better job than she was. Sally asked if they could all take turns using the vise, which Ginette had at the moment. No one answered, so Sally asked Ginette if she could use the vise; Ginette allowed her to. All the girls admired Wendy's work, which led Ginette again to ask for help with her sawing.

Ginette continued to be the advocate for gratification, leading the others back for more food. When Ginette complained of a splinter in her finger, Katie told Ginette that her father knew how to take out splinters. Sally mentioned scornfully that she had gotten splinters many times in camp, indicating that she thought the matter was minor. *(The girls were definitely not ready to "baby" Ginette.)* Katie wanted to know which camp Sally was referring to, and Sally mentioned a Jewish camp. Katie expressed surprise. Ginette wanted to know whether Katie was a Catholic, and Katie replied that she was Protestant. Ginette announced sadly that she and Katie were different because Ginette was Jewish.

Katie said, "I worry, worry, worry if I lose my money. I always have to call my mother." She asked the therapist to have a sixty-four-ounce bottle of soda next time. *(It was apparent that Ginette's emphasis on Katie's religious difference had provoked anxiety in Katie and hostility toward the therapist, as indicated by Katie's implicit accusation that the therapist had not provided sufficient nurturance [soda].)*

Ginette then asked if the group could go back to the other (small) room for more soda and pretzels. When all agreed, they did so, occupying the same seats as earlier. Ginette asked if they could stay in the smaller room and play. The therapist agreed. Soon the therapist mentioned that time was up. Ginette wanted a bag to carry her candy. Wendy joined her in clamoring for one. Sally complained that the therapist had not provided a large enough bag. Katie just pushed things into her doily and called the therapist's attention to the fact that they had finished a second bottle of soda and really needed the sixty-four-ounce size. Katie and Ginette ran out together; Sally and Wendy departed more slowly, with Wendy last.

At the beginning of the second session, Wendy, Ginette, and Patricia (a new member) were the first to arrive from the waiting room. The therapist introduced Patricia to the others. Ginette showed Patricia where they had all sat last week. Once again the group assembled first in the small room. Ginette and Wendy were in costume. Patricia was dressed as a gypsy. (The therapist had notified her about the "party" by telephone.) Patricia said she had chosen a gypsy outfit because she could always make her own costume by putting on rings and "makeup." She went on to say that she had once bought a Cinderella costume but it had kept ripping so she couldn't use it the next year.

Patricia sat down at the end of the table, opposite where Katie had been in the previous session. Ginette went for food, and Wendy followed. Patricia remained seated and began to talk. She said that she had problems getting friends. She had only one friend, who had told her that nobody liked Patricia. Patricia said that whenever she told a joke, other children turned their backs on her. Ginette asked Patricia to tell them one. Patricia said she would tell one that Jerry Lewis had told about drinking water. "If you drink water, you'll have false teeth, next time use Crest." Patricia laughed. No one seemed to be listening. Patricia then asked what the group had done last week. Wendy told her about the other room. Ginette recalled how everybody had spilled soda, and she asked the group to join her in drinking. Wendy was clumsy. Ginette began singing, "Clumsy, clumsy," but she herself asked for help with pouring, and Patricia assisted her. Patricia then asked whether anyone "goes to a Catholic school" and added that she was Italian and Spanish. Ginette told Patricia that she looked Italian but not Spanish. Ginette added cryptically that she was scared because so much was happening. She seemed to be referring to violent episodes in her neighborhood.

Patricia agreed with Ginette's comment and told the group that she had heard on the news about a ghost injuring a lady. She said the ghost had set fire to a cellar or attic and the lady who lived there had died on the stairs, eight years ago.

Ginette interrupted to tell the others that they weren't allowed to eat so much because some food had to be saved for the other group members. Patricia asked if they knew how to spell her name. She wanted to know from Wendy how many letters there were in her name, and whether Wendy knew the multiplication table and how to do division.

Sally then came over and sat where Patricia had been sitting. Ginette asked Sally if she was hungry. Sally said she was and helped herself to some food. Patricia then asked Sally if she was Catholic. Sally replied in the negative. Ginette asked the group if anyone wanted to play a game with her. Patricia agreed, and they played darts while Wendy kept score and Sally ate.

Katie entered late, wearing an angel costume. She informed the group that she was going to the girls' room to "fix it up." When she returned, she seemed restless. Patricia, the new member, was telling the others about trips to Europe and mentioned places where her brother had been taken by her father, but not she. Sally, Ginette, and Wendy supported her, agreeing about how much more their siblings got than they did. Following this, the girls began to comment admiringly about one another's costumes.

At this point Katie asked if the group could go to the other (large) room and saw wood. All but Patricia agreed. Patricia complained that she needed to eat. The others told her that they could get food later. They all then agreed and left. When they reached the large room, Katie ran to the big work table and began to saw, with more assurance than last week. Wendy, Sally, and Ginette also sawed. Wendy and Sally were again at a small table by themselves, while Ginette worked near Katie. Patricia played by herself at Nok Hockey. Sally announced to the group that she had gotten further with sawing this time than last week. The therapist remained seated at a table, alone. Katie stopped sawing and asked Ginette to play Nok Hockey with her; Ginette did so. Patricia joined Sally in sawing.

Sally reminded the group that they could go back to the small room to eat. All agreed. Sally again seated herself with food opposite the therapist. Katie sat at one end of the table, with Patricia at the other end and Wendy next to the therapist. All but Ginette ate continuously. Katie initiated conversation by asking Sally why she hadn't dressed in costume like Katie and the others. Sally replied that her mother wouldn't let her. The others suggested a possible reason for her mother's refusal: that Sally lived in a bad neighborhood and her mother might be afraid that Sally would get "poison" from some people who gave out Halloween treats. Sally agreed that this was what bothered her mother.

Patricia kept talking about Sally's mother—how she was "right and wrong" about Halloween. Patricia said that kids should have fun on Halloween and holidays, yet one could find a razor in an apple. Katie decided that this was enough. She couldn't tolerate Patricia's fears and changed the subject by asking the group, "How do mothers pay for stuff under the tree?" Patricia and Ginette talked about Santa Claus. Katie acted the skeptic, wanting to know if Santa Claus had ever existed. "Mothers," she added, "are around all the time." Patricia persisted in her beliefs, saying, "Many years ago Santa Claus was real, but now he is dead." *(This was probably an unconscious reference to her father, who was out of the home and didn't support the family.)* Patricia added that parents still wanted their children to think there was a Santa Claus. Katie now agreed with Patricia: "Santa Claus did die, and mothers don't want children to know so mothers took over." Katie now wanted to know where Santa Claus got all the money that he must need to buy gifts. She then made fun of Santa Claus's appearance, commenting about his being fat and old. *(Katie's conflict about growing up and her use of humor as a defense are shown here.)*

Now everybody began to talk at once. Katie told the group that only one person should talk at a time. Patricia began to talk about witches, about how they had their own way of curing people. *(Recall that Patricia had a psychotic mother.)* Katie told Patricia that there were no doctors around at that time. *(She may have been implying that conditions are safer nowadays.)* Katie was bothered by the content of Patricia's remarks. With increased and mounting anxiety, she burst out, "Everybody is a blabbermouth this week!"

Katie began to use a stick like a wand, saying she was turning people into "shiny princesses, frogs, and gypsies." She announced that she was Tinker Bell. When Ginette mentioned that her birthday was on Thanksgiving, Katie said hers was earlier, November 8. Ginette said she was going to have a birhday party. Katie told Ginette it was too bad that she, Katie, lived so far away. *(Katie was apparently defending herself against the possibility of not being invited.)* Katie continued to play Tinker Bell, saying that she had told her mother she had a lot of fun here and couldn't wait until Thursday—"club day." Katie now began to play with the dollhouse, putting bunk beds one on top of the other, five beds high. (Katie's family consisted of three children and the parents.) She announced that she would prefer to sleep on the bottom. Patricia called out that she always liked to sleep in the middle.

Ginette complained that she had broken a crayon. Katie comforted her, telling her, "It is O.K.," and talked about her own fear of "falling and dying," in comfortable tones. *(Katie was able to speak in comfortable tones because she had recognized Ginette's anxiety, equated it with her own, and gained comfort from sharing a common feeling of distress.)*

Patricia couldn't tolerate this talk and asked Katie, "How can you talk if you're dead?" Katie replied that "her ghost" was talking. Patricia pretended to telephone for a doctor, to tell him that Katie was sick. Sally joined Patricia in phoning the doctor. Ginette, however, informed them that the doctor "wasn't in." Ginette could tolerate the conversation about ghosts better than Patricia or Sally. *(It is of interest that Patricia and her older sister had tried to get help for their mother's recognized psychotic condition, whereas in Ginette's family most pathology was denied.)*

When Katie saw Sally getting ready to go home, she rushed to draw what she called "a pretty girl picture." It had no eyes, nose, or mouth. Patricia drew in the missing features. *(Patricia was the new member of this session. Katie had tried to reject her, demonstrating, through displacement, feelings of hostility and fear of rejection by a psychological sibling. It should be recalled that Katie was returned full-time to her parents when her mother was pregnant, thus losing at the same time her loving "aunt-*

mother" and, because of their involvement with the new sibling, whatever nurturance her parents were capable of.)

In the third session, everyone was present except Patricia. There was some conflict over seats. Ginette suggested that the group should eat and talk about Lincoln Center, a cultural center for the performing arts. Because the atmosphere was apparently full of tension, the therapist asked if there was something the group wanted to talk about.[5] Katie then told of her mother's going to stay with her aunt, who was sick. She went on to say that her family was made up of three girls. She said it would have been better if they had a brother, so her father could show him all the cars and trucks. Katie suddenly burst out that she "hates boys." Ginette joined in saying that she herself had been left with her grandmother, and that was worse. [than not having a brother.—M.S.] The therapist commented that they were talking about feeling left out and might be wondering also about why Patricia was absent. Katie said she wasn't sure, but it did make her angry that Patricia wasn't here. She wanted to talk to her "face to face." The girls told the therapist to phone Patricia and expressed anger with the therapist when she informed them that Patricia had no telephone. The therapist accepted their anger and said "I should have reminded Patricia more to come today." (*At the beginning of this third session it is evident that there was discontent in the group. The therapist spoke openly to the group about their discontent—"being left out"—to encourage negative transference reactions, claiming it was "her fault" and offering herself as a "bad object."*) The group members responded to this and joined in verbalizing anger against the therapist.

At this point Katie asked to go to the playroom (large room), which the group did. Using a hammer, Katie made what she called a dollhouse and was happy with the results. Ginette told her, "You have to get real angry to hammer." Kate kept repeating, incredulously, that she was good at hammering. Ginette said enviously, "Katie can do anything."

In the fourth session, Ginette asked the group to have a birthday party for her. Katie replied to Ginette's request, "If we have a party for Ginette, then the food has to be only cake and ice cream or everybody would get sick." (*Katie apparently felt a repetition of her early traumas* [in that she was forced to separate from her family while her mother worked. Then, when she returned, her mother was pregnant. Katie was jealous.—M.S.].)

The therapist intervened, asking why the girls were so angry. Katie said she didn't feel like sawing today because her dollhouse had fallen apart. She also commented that her father didn't think she was any good. The therapist said "It looks as though I am not any good. I haven't been much help to Katie, and I had better work harder." Ginette wanted to talk about mak-

---

[5]The therapist intervened to stimulate conversation on central issues. In the first group session she briefly described one of the purposes of the group—to discuss problems. This "message" is reiterated on occasion tactfully when conditions lend themselves to it.—M.S.

ing something for her birthday party, which the group had agreed to have. Katie wouldn't allow this, asking instead how many of the girls lived far away from the guidance institute. (*This seems to show some resistance to coming to group sessions.*) Ginette handled this change of subject by ignoring Katie and suggested that the group go to the other room. This was done, and Katie complained that the play room was freezing. Now the therapist said, "Why is Katie so angry?" Ginette agreed that Katie seemed angry. Ginette added that Katie didn't any longer come early to the "club," as she had used to. Katie said that the bus trip took so long and added that she thought Ginette was being "creepy" today.

Katie, Ginette, and Sally were hammering at the large table. Wendy, for the first time, left her sawing and joined them.[6] Sally showed the therapist that one nail wasn't enough and so she put in two. Ginette consulted Sally about the paddle she was making and Sally confidently told her how to fix it. Ginette responded, "O.K., mummy." Sally told her, "I'm not your 'mummy.'" Sally wanted the others to go back with her to the small room to get more food. They refused. Sally asked if nails got "headaches" from being banged on the head.

Ginette asked the therapist to play with her at the table, but before they started, Wendy came over and Ginette asked Wendy to play. Sally again wanted everybody to go back to the small room for food. The others suggested that she go by herself. She did so. When Sally returned, she sat at the table with the therapist. Ginette and Wendy ate and watched the other two at play.

Ginette told the group about how her father had thrown out something she had made in the group. Katie burst out at the therapist with obvious frustration, saying, "You should have gotten smaller nails." Katie complained further, speaking directly to the therapist, that she didn't provide enough soda and that the others in the group didn't help her.[7] Katie returned to working with wood. She worked better, made a small table, and asked the group to go back to the small room. All agreed and did so. Katie wanted to eat on the table she had made, and Ginette joined her. Katie boasted that the table was holding up well. Ginette admired it. Katie carried her table proudly over her head when the group left.

In the next session, the fifth, all but Patricia arrived in the small room. Ginette asked the therapist if they could help set up the cake and ice cream. The others joined in putting down plates and forks. As the girls began to eat, Katie said happily, "Today we have everything." Ginette told the group, "You see, here you have to ask for what you want." After this, Katie asked the group, "How about hammering?" Everybody cheered

---

[6]This is an example of the purpose of an "isolate table," which allows for a child's self-protective withdrawal from interaction until she is prepared for it.—M.S.

[7]These episodes reveal how the therapist's self-criticism concerning her ineffectiveness (paradigmatic) successfully induced negative transference feelings.—M.S.

"hurrah," clapped hands, and went to the large room, where Katie at once examined the wood and nails and complained that there were no very small nails. (The therapist had been bringing smaller nails each time they were requested, but evidently this did not satisfy Katie.) Sally began a conversation about an accident she had seen in which twins had been hurt by a car. She had been hammering and announced to the group that she had forgotten which hand to hammer with. Wendy told her to use her right hand. Sally insisted that she would use her left hand. Ginette now asked the therapist, "Do you tell our parents what we do? Don't tell them anything."[8] The therapist agreed. Katie again finished a table for herself and helped Sally finish hers. She also made a chair, which she announced to the group was for her one-year-old sister. Katie held it up, wanting everybody to look at it, and said, "My father can stand on *this* one!"

Katie didn't attend the sixth session, which was to be the birthday party for Ginette. She telephoned to explain that there was no one to pick her up in the evening. (*The real reason for her absence was probably that she could not yet accept sharing a [psychological] sibling's birthday party.*) Ginette was angry with the therapist about Katie's absence, becoming even angrier when it was learned that Katie could not be reached on the telephone.

When Katie returned for the seventh session, she was full of anger, said "Boo" to Ginette and Sally. Also, Katie wanted to know *how they could help each other* if they didn't like each other. Sally explained that they could help each other even if they didn't like each other in the same way that someone with problems who says she has no problem could be helped. Katie then told Ginette that Ginette had a problem because she couldn't come to group by herself (Ginette was brought by her father). Ginette then reminded Katie that Katie had a problem too: "to find out her problem."[9]

This interchange led Katie to say she was "depressed." She remarked that her mother had thrown out all her "stuff" when she cleaned. Ginette tried to comfort Katie by suggesting that they would make something for the "club." (*Thus Ginette offered the group as a second "family."*) Katie agreed to Ginette's suggestion. At this point Ginette wanted to know how many "clubs" the therapist had in a day. The therapist asked, "How many should I have?" Katie said, "Just us."

In the eighth session, Katie continued to show hostility and rivalry. When Patricia again seemed to get attention, Katie wanted to change rooms. (*It is apparent that she was struggling with hate for this newest "sibling."*)

By the tenth session, Katie seemed to have come to identify somewhat with her group peers, as she agreed with them that girls got blamed for trou-

---

[8]This is an example—common in analytical group treatment—of children's awareness of the investigatory nature of the analytical procedure, and also a manifestation of the positive transference (trust in the therapist).—M.S.

[9]This exchange indicates the extent to which the girls now saw fit to interpret motivations of behavior, in a sense acting as co-therapists.—M.S.

ble rather than boys. In this session, Katie said she was making a birdhouse and recalled how she used to have birds and lost one that died. Wendy didn't want to talk about this at all, but Ginette wanted to talk "baby talk" with Katie, who joined her. Ginette let Katie know that she herself was more mature, but told Katie she was still her friend.

Katie's feeling of identification with the group members continued to grow, as shown in the eleventh session. The other girls said they wanted to bring friends to the group, but Katie told them emphatically that she liked the group better without friends. When the others wanted to talk further about bringing friends, they called attention to Katie's efforts to change the subject. Katie then said that if friends came, the girls would want them to keep coming. Patricia joined Katie, saying that the friends might get attached to the girls presently in the group. Katie was adamant about friends not coming to the "club." She said she didn't want to come if Ginette brought a friend. Now Ginette grasped her meaning and said maybe Katie was talking this way because she liked her (Ginette). Katie whispered to Ginette that she was worried people might laugh at her (for liking Ginette so much). Ginette said that people wouldn't find this funny. Patricia joined in and agreed that in serious matters people don't laugh.

Katie then asked everyone to look at her new outfit and said that her mother "wanted her to look nice for the 'club'" and made her change clothes before she attended. (*Katie thus informed the group of how much it meant to her.*) Katie again insisted that she wanted no new girls; she wanted to "stick to" the five.

In the thirteenth session, Katie reported that she was going to stay at her grandmother's because she liked it there. "Grandma," she said, "will go out and buy me a radio. Isn't that nice?" She went on to say how nice the members of the "club" were too. Wendy loaned her a bus card. However, Katie still complained about Ginette because, she said, "Ginette doesn't think I am pretty." Katie wanted to know who Ginette thought was pretty—it certainly isn't Ginette."

Ginette retorted that her *mother* was pretty. (*It was apparent here that Katie was struggling with guilt feelings in her transference reaction to Ginette, who represented the rejecting mother; the group as a group had become "nice."*) To protect Ginette from the intensity of Katie's hostility, the therapist said that it was she, the therapist, who wasn't pretty—that she was an "ugly old lady."[10]

Ginette added that her own mother said Ginette was "pretty ugly" even though the mother looked exactly like Ginette. (*Here Ginette implied that sometimes we reject in others what we reject in ourselves.*) Katie

---

[10]This rather blatant, paradigmatic statement has questionable merit. Had the children's remarks about their mothers' appearances been uttered to the therapist *directly*, in engaged conversation with her, the therapist's rejoinder would have had more logical connection. As it was, the girls were well on their way to expressing their own understandings of their feelings.— M.S.

seemed to understand part of this [projective identification, M.S.] and said that Ginette's mother was calling herself "ugly" whereas mothers didn't usually say that. Ginette agreed and said her mother was "crazy." (*Here we see that the therapist's use of herself as a "bad object" freed the group members to see and talk about the "bad" in their mothers [in the therapist] and, as we will see later, the "bad" in themselves.*) Katie went on to say that mothers are "weird." She remarked, "You say, 'Why can't I do this?' and they say, 'You just can't.' "

In the fourteenth session, Katie complained further about her mother, who made Katie cry by cutting her hair. Katie then complained that the therapist should buy different foods. (*She was displacing her negative feelings toward her mother on to the therapist.*) However, for the first time, Katie asked the therapist for help with her woodwork.

In this same session, Katie let everyone know that she "had a problem and didn't want to remember it." She reported that one Sunday she hadn't cleaned the dishes right, and her father had punished her by saying she couldn't play with friends for a day. One of the family's original complaints was that Katie had no friends!

In the eighteenth session, Katie finally reported a school problem: her class had been changed and she was angry because she had gotten switched around. Ginette wanted to know who kept changing her to another class, and Katie said her father. Ginette told Katie that she should just tell her father that she wanted to stay in the same class. Katie, obviously distressed, reported that her father didn't want anyone to know why the change had been made; she said it was because she had ticks in her hair so the teachers kept sending her home. During this session Katie kept calling on others to help her with her work. They kept telling her that everybody had to do the work alone. Katie finally decided she would tear cloth material rather than cut it.

In the nineteenth session, Katie informed the group that she agreed with Sally that "it's no problem to hate boys," but added that she had a boyfriend. She said she now liked some boys, but very few. She later told the group she had gotten sick—water had come out of her anus. She said she thought that soda gave her gas. The therapist asked, "Maybe I made you sick, because I bring soda?" Katie said she got sick from soda at home too. She added that her mother loved soda and always bought it, and Katie sneaked it from the refrigerator.

Later, when the others complained about how hard sewing was (they were making rag doll cats), Katie joined in and said to the therapist that the group didn't have good needles or good wool. The therapist agreed and added that maybe she (the therapist) should have brought in the rag doll cats all finished. Katie talked about sleeping on her cat doll. She put it in a bag, hugged it, and called it her "baby."

In the twentieth session, Katie told about how her father used to be able to take her work apart so easily. "He won't be able to do it with *this* table!'' She was asked by the therapist why her father took her work apart. Katie said that he had needed a piece of wood. She said she had gotten very mad and hollered at him. Her father had put on his glasses and said, "You wouldn't hit a man with glasses on, would you?"

In the twenty-first session, when Ginette returned after an absence and asked if she had been missed, Katie showed her anger at the "desertion" by saying "no one missed" her but added that Ginette was Katie's "first friend." Katie opposed the addition of a new group member, which she had also opposed previously, saying she was sure the new girl would be "snotty." (This group was originally planned as an *open group* in that the membership was not to be fixed. It was assumed that there might be movement of members in or out of group.[11])

In the twenty-fourth session, Katie brought a friend. The friend, Katie said, had a problem of fighting with her sister. Katie said that her friend couldn't confide in her mother, just like Katie, because her mother didn't believe what she said. Katie added, "This is the problem with mothers. They never believe you." Katie then let the group know that she had problems with other girls, saying that she played with only one friend. Katie said she had figured out why: because her friend was jealous and didn't want Katie to have other friends. While all the girls were busy painting, Wendy said, "This is a fun day." Katie told her, "You can say that again." (*Here we can see the enhancing of Katie's self-image within the supportive, accepting climate of the group.*)

At the following session, Katie brought a different friend, saying she wanted to show the girl the nice things she made. Katie added that her friend was shy and said she had brought her to the group to help her talk. In this session, the twenty-fifth, the therapist said that the group had been requested to use only one room and asked the girls to decide which one to use. All asked for the large one.

The therapist asked, as was her practice from time to time, if there were any problems to talk about. Katie said she had had a nice week. She had gone swimming and played with her dog. Katie said her boyfriend had seen Katie in her bathing suit and she had screamed. She explained that she had felt shy. Sally didn't see any problem in this shyness. Wendy disagreed, insisting that screaming because one was shy was a problem. Katie decided she didn't want to talk about it. Ginette told her, "That's what we're supposed to do." (This is an example of Slavson's "primary group code," where all groups reach a point of understanding their reasons for being and demonstrate a commitment to group aims and to the methods necessary to achieve those aims.[12])

---

[11]To the extent possible, all children's therapy groups are best maintained as *closed groups*, especially in the beginning and middle phases of treatment.—M.S.

[12]S.R. Slavson and M. Schiffer, *Group Psychotherapies for Children: A Textbook*, International Universities Press, New York, 1975, pp. 67, 251, Glossary.

Now Katie told the group that her father had said she was not going to come any more. When the others wanted to know how Katie felt about this, she said she didn't want to come; she preferred to play with her friends. Ginette told Katie that she should come until she "lost" her problems. Katie responded that she used to be afraid of cockroaches but wasn't anymore, and that the group had helped her with regard to boys. Ginette wanted to know what would happen if Katie didn't come back and became afraid of cockroaches again. Katie said she was sure she'd be all right. At this point the therapist intervened, saying to Katie, "How about your helping the others in the group?" Katie agreed that she wanted to help them. She added that everyone was making her feel that she didn't want to leave. All the other girls said they wanted her to stay. Katie told them that she would think it over and make her own decision. The therapist said, "I guess I am not a good leader." Katie denied this, saying that her reason for possibly leaving was that she had friends at home who felt bad. Ginette told Katie that the group members were her "real friends." Katie replied that she saw them only once a week and her other friends every day. The therapist said, "Maybe we should meet every day." Katie went on to say that she and her friends "kiss goodbye." The therapist asked if the group members should also kiss, so that Katie could feel they cared. Katie liked this idea.

The therapist now asked if perhaps she should be the one to kiss Katie, because Katie might not think the therapist cared about her.[13] Katie denied this, saying she knew the therapist cared. When the therapist asked how she knew, Katie said she just did. The therapist wanted to know why Katie felt the group members might not care for her unless they kissed her. Katie said kids are different. The therapist then proposed the idea of a "club" of just Katie and therapist. Katie rejected this idea. (*The therapist was exploring Katie's wish for an exclusive relationship with her mother, as shown in this transferential reaction. The therapist was able to do this in an individual interview exchange because the other girls were busy doing other things at the moment.*)

During the twenty-eighth session, Katie wanted to know how long the "club" would continue to meet. Then she focused on the therapist, and asked how old she was. The other girls told her the therapist was "a million years old" but it would be better if she were ten years old! Katie told the therapist that she wouldn't talk until the therapist told her age. When Patricia said she didn't care about age, Katie dropped the subject.

Ginette suggested that the group have its snack. Children of this age continue to need to express themselves through play and motor activities. The snack helps set a stage for the "talking" part of group sessions. *It*

---

[13]This conversation also took place between the therapist and Katie out of hearing by the group. In analytical group psychotherapy, a therapist may avail herself of opportunities for individual interviews in addition to group interviews when conditions indicate a need for the former.—M.S.

might be added that the use of two rooms was an experiment to encourage talking. It did to some extent. However, it was apparent that the movement from one room to the other interfered with the fuller development of transference reactions to the therapist and between group members. The procedure of using two rooms was therefore abandoned.[14]

In the twenty-eighth session, the girls seemed happy, perhaps because of their aroused interest in the therapist, and angry because of anticipated changes [in pattern of use of rooms.—M.S.] (They retaliated with a request for different foods; and with much more talking.) Patricia got the others to say "thank you" to the therapist, in unison. Katie called out, "Look what we have—a feast." She added, "I don't know how to thank you." Ginette told her, "Just eat; don't talk!"

In the twenty-ninth session, the girls continued their interest in marital situations, about which they had had a discussion before. They talked again about "fat ladies," with Katie saying, "Boys don't like fat girls." The therapist asked if sometimes boys might have something to do with girls being fat. The girls all began at once to talk about babies, and Katie told of a "fat lady friend" and her children. Now Katie wanted to draw a girl. She asked for drawing materials, especially a brush for painting, and continued this activity into the next session. Katie now became interested in Wendy and her mother, particularly wanting to know whether Wendy's mother was home when Wendy arrived. Katie let Wendy know that she wouldn't like Wendy's circumstances: coming home and finding her mother out. When Wendy said that she had a brother and sister, Katie replied that she herself had two sisters, but added that since she was the oldest she wouldn't feel safe if she came home and her mother wasn't there. She reported that she never stayed alone. Ginette told Katie that she was big and could stay alone. In the next session, Katie made a crib instead of a table.

Prior to the last session before vacation, the thirty-second, all the girls asked that the therapist bring presents and that both presents and a snack be given out at the beginning of the session. For their presents, all the girls except Katie chose "squirmles," which were caterpillars on a string. Katie asked for a diamond ring—"not real, of course."

When the ring was given to her, Katie said, "Oh, my God," and asked for help to put it on. Ginette commented that she might not come back to the group. "After all," she said, "I come for fun. I have no problems." Katie told her she *did* have problems: "You have only boys on your mind."

---

[14]The use of two rooms proved fruitless, if not a handicap to treatment, as the therapist discovered. Meaningful communication between group members and with the therapist flows opportunely from interpersonal interactions at any point in a group session, from rancorous episodes between children engaged in crafts activities, for example. While it is true that the coming together for a common repast does tend to induce communication of a significant personal nature, it does not necessarily preclude this occuring at other times. The use of two rooms was a technical error, an artificial inducement which inhibited the intended outcome.—M.S.

Katie went on to say that she herself would have to come back. The therapist said, "I need you all." Katie responded that the therapist "wouldn't die" without them. The therapist interpreted this to the girls as hostility toward the therapist for planning a vacation and said further that maybe it would be a good idea if she "died" because perhaps then they wouldn't have to come back.[15] Then the girls began to talk about school ending. Katie burst out, "I'll miss everybody in the 'club.' Everybody should kiss goodbye." Sally reminded Katie that she hated kissing. Katie said she hated kissing boys.

In summary: We have described how an analytic form of treatment—activity-interview group psychotherapy—was used in helping a severely disturbed ten-year-old girl. Katie was referred because she talked continuously in school, was a poor reader, daydreamed, worried, and was unable to get along with her parents, her sisters, or other children. When she started in activity-interview group psychotherapy, Katie was in the fourth grade, and reading at second-grade level; was worried about fires, her memory and getting older; and was conflicted in all her relationships with people. She was the oldest of three children, whose parents had felt themselves unready to have children. Katie was with an aunt, part-time, until the age of two and a half, from which time on she remained at home full-time with her parents. When she returned home, her mother was pregnant. It was then that Katie changed from a happy, friendly, outgoing child to a daydreaming, depressed, fearful, and, conflicted one.

Her initial adjustment in the group was primarily on an object level, as she sought oral gratification in the form of food. Katie formed a supportive ego relationship with one girl, who found a reflection of herself in Katie. Katie displayed hostility toward the others but also showed some ambivalence. The group's acceptance of Katie's initial manifestations of anger and hostility gradually enabled her to tolerate these feelings without anxiety. She then began to manifest an improved self-image and positive transference reactions to others. Gradually her deeper, more neurotic distress became revealed, as well as her forbidden wishes.

As Katie's transference relationships grew stronger, she became freer and sought more than just emotional or verbal support. Through negative transference, she became able to ventilate cathartically her feelings toward her parents, displacing them to the therapist, who had sensitively prompted the expression of the child's repressed hostility. It is interesting how Katie, and the group, became psychologically sophisticated to the point where they could interpret displaced feelings.

[15]Paradigmatic stimulation by a therapist, which is intended to loosen or dissolve a patient's resistance and evoke a repressed or suppressed emotion or wish—in this case the girls' underlying hostility toward their mothers—is not always successful. This is usually so when the repressed content is too dangerous to be acknowledged, even by displacement to the therapist.—M.S.

Katie insisted on physical contact, for her a form of nurturance. Through her behavior with group members, she also showed early levels of sibling identification. She became able to verbalize the ways in which she was being helped to overcome her fears, to acquire friends, and to make advances in learning. This is an example of derivative insight, which is typical of children.

The improvements in Katie were confirmed by her parents. For Katie, the therapy group represented a healing second family.

Part III

Combined Treatment

CASES in which purely activity group therapy and activity-interview group psychotherapy were used as exclusive treatments were described in previous chapters. While many children can be treated through group therapy alone, there are some whose problems are such as to require both individual and group therapy. There are a variety of possible permutations in the use of group and individual therapy with children. The treatments may be carried on concurrently, or one method may follow the other. Depending on changing circumstances, treatment may be individual to start with, then in a group, finally combined. Or, a child may be returned to individual treatment from a group. Moreover, there are instances in which children who have successfully completed a course in dyadic therapy require a tapering-off social experience in a conditioned setting in order to solidify their improvements. Contrariwise, a child whose problem indicates the need for analytical play therapy, but who resists it, may be eased into it later by participating in an activity group.

The initial choice of treatment depends on a careful assessment of the presenting problem to elucidate its primary elements. In the cases of young children, however, well-defined diagnoses at the onset of treatment are the exception rather than the rule. This is because personality and character structure are still formative and subject to changes. Where pathology is blatant, it is possible to make more definitive diagnoses, and the treatment can be more specifically determined. Yet, even if diagnoses are accurate and the best attempts are made by therapists to implement treatment, it still does not follow that in all instances children will be amenable to the indicated therapy. This brings up an intrinsic advantage of a group treatment approach: It virtually eliminates children's resistivity to the idea of therapy. A group also provides an excellent perspective from which to observe a child's adjustment. Much valuable information can be obtained about idiosyncratic behavior, coping ability, and other capacities and incapacities in a differential diagnosis. The value of this input is to refine diagnoses, while at the same time the group provides a corrective experience. Should it be necessary to modify the treatment program later, to include individual therapy or to use it exclusively, a child usually becomes more tractable because of the group experience.

In activity therapy, it is also possible to assess a child's dependency needs through determining the nature and depth of transference to the therapist, with its negative and positive manifestations. In cases where the transference is focal and intense, it indicates the strong probability of a neurotic problem. This differs from the situation with children who have primary behavior disorders and some character problems, in which the transference relationship is much less intense. For such children, it is the group that exerts the primary, corrective influence; therapy is accomplished mostly *by* the group, whereas in analytical groups, treatment is essentially of the individual *in* a group.

In Chapter 6, the case of Henry, the transference relationship to the group therapist proved to be strong and remained so, despite the boy's interactions with the other children. Henry showed much ambivalence toward the therapist, soliciting his exclusive attention at times and acting provocatively toward him at other times. This pattern continued even after Henry began to show improvements in his social adjustments. The group became increasingly meaningful to him as time passed, but the experience did not seem to affect his more deeply entrenched pathology.

Henry was in activity group therapy for one year, following which a psychiatric evaluation led to a revised diagnosis of schizoid behavior, and individual treatment was recommended. However, Henry refused to continue individual treatment after fifteen sessions, despite his apparent need for intensive dyadic therapy. This is not atypical with many highly disturbed latency-age children, who can be notably resistive to analytical procedures.

This case reveals how markedly different can be the behavior of a child in the permissive environment of an activity group as compared to his behavior in other settings—home and school. In school, Henry's behavior and achievement improved, as did his relationships with peers. Yet, at the same time, in the therapy group he began to regress after initial improvements. Such a pronounced discordance in behavior in different settings is an indication of a neurotic or more serious problem. After four years of therapy with Henry, mostly in the activity group, another psychiatric evaluation resulted in diagnosis of a character disorder with underlying schizophrenic functioning. There was a pathological residue that was not responding to activity-group therapy, despite some visible improvement—primarily a strengthened ego and more masculine identity. Henry was terminated in group therapy and referred for individual treatment, which he was now able to tolerate. One principle in children's group therapy is well defined by Henry's case: the need to have available both individual and group methods of therapy in family and child guidance agencies.

When a child is in combined treatment, it is advisable that different therapists be used. The question as to whether they should be of different genders is best determined empirically, except that in activity group therapy with older latency children, the therapist should be of the same gender as the children. Theoretically, the use of both male and female therapists in combined treatment has a psychological advantage because it enables a child to work through problems associated with both parents in the displaced transferences with the therapists. However, as seen in Henry's case, this theoretical advantage is not always achievable.

In the case of Ellen, Chapter 7, there are parallels to the way in which individual and group treatment were employed with Henry, despite the differences in the children's presenting problems. Ellen's treatment also shows the need to alter the method used in compliance with changing circumstances at different points in therapy. In Ellen's case, individual play therapy began when she was five and a half years old because of her intense anxiety, dependency, and phobic reactions to school. Treatment was terminated after two years, at which time she had improved, but it was reinstituted a year later because of poor school achievement and a lack of friends. After some time in individual therapy, Ellen was placed in combined treatment for a year. She then continued in activity group therapy exclusively and remained in the group for three years. Many of her rigid, compulsive habits and signs of sibling rivalry were eliminated, and she was able to form satisfactory relationships with peers.

CHAPTER 6

Limitations of Activity Group Therapy: A Case Presentation

LESLIE ROSENTHAL / LEO NAGELBERG

ACTIVITY GROUP THERAPY is a specific form of group treatment which utilizes a permissive environment to provide a healing, corrective, maturing and emotionally re-educative experience for specially selected children in latency.[1] The permissive atmosphere, established by the neutrality and passivity of the therapist, facilitates the expression of repressed hostilities and instinctual drives whose enactment outside the group is not socially sanctioned. The setting enables children to regress and thereby release tensions associated with earlier levels of development. Acting out of hostile and destructive impulses is met with neither criticism nor approval; rather it is accepted as indicative of the child's contemporary personality needs.

Activity group therapy is nonverbal in that no discussion is initiated by the therapist and interpretation is given under only very rare circumstances. Emotional re-education derives from the social interaction of the children with each other in actual living situations within the setting of the group "family."

This form of treatment has not been found suitable for the severely neurotic child who generally needs interpretative therapy. The permissive

[1] Slavson, S. R.: "Criteria for Selection and Rejection of Patients for Various Types of Group Psychotherapy." *International Journal of Group Psychotherapy*, 5:3-30, 1955.

atmosphere cannot assimilate the unrestrained aggression of the psycho-path, the psychotic or the brain-damaged. Activity group therapy can address itself most effectively to the mildly neurotic, the behavior disorders and certain character disorders. For treatability in group therapy, there must be certain minimal ego strengths and inner controls as well as the desire to be with and to be accepted by one's peers—a phenomenon which Slavson has termed "social hunger."

Within the broad framework of categories acceptable for activity group therapy, there may be individual children who have a need to behave in such a way that the effectiveness of the group is limited. They may do this by openly or subtly courting expulsion from the group. In addition to this desire to reject the group, we may find a concurrent need to merge with the group and find in it a haven of refuge. Such a constellation may originate in the child-mother relationship where the need to merge with and separate from the mother has remained unsolved. Although this unsolved primary relation places limits on the effectiveness of activity group therapy, sympathetic understanding of the origin of this behavior may help significantly in enabling the child to remain in the group and to make personality gains. We feel that in a time of wide expansion of activity group therapy as a treatment medium, it is helpful to clarify its therapeutic scope, mark its borders and recognize its limitations. For this purpose we are presenting the case of Henry in whom activity group therapy effected definite gains. Yet, because of the personality structure and dynamics involved in the case, treatment in the group setting could achieve only partial results and supplementary individual treatment was required.

Case History

Henry was referred to the Child Guidance Institute at age eight and a half for excessive shyness, social isolation and academic difficulties at school where he was described as "a very slow learner." He was unwilling to leave the house to go out to play, was unable to separate from his mother and would not greet relatives, claiming he had forgotten their names. At school he displayed little interest and was failing in most of his subjects. At camp during the summer, just prior to referral, Henry had been described as extremely infantile, provocative, enuretic and withdrawn. After three weeks at camp he had not learned the names of any of his bunkmates nor the counselor's name. He sought the counselor's attention by throwing pebbles at him. Henry was unable to participate in competitive situations and preferred girls younger than himself as playmates.

The salient feature in the developmental history was Henry's premature birth in the sixth month of pregnancy, a birth he barely survived. He was incubated for two months and was fed by eye dropper every half hour for the first ten weeks. There were indications that the mother had been extremely overprotective of Henry throughout his life.

Complete physical and neurological examination of Henry at a medical center a year prior to referral revealed no abnormalities. Psychometric tests found Henry to be functioning on a dull-normal intelligence level despite average intellectual potential. Some unevenness in intellectual functioning was noted.

At the time of referral and for quite some time after both Henry and the mother had commenced treatment, little was known in the areas of parental background and familial interaction. The mother, a tall, masculine-looking person, was reluctant to give more than the bare details of her background and scrupulously avoided expressing any negative feelings of any kind. At the start of treatment the only information available was that the mother was the next to the youngest in a family of seven children. She described her own family as having always functioned on a constantly harmonious level, avoided any reference to her own mother and referred to her father in almost reverential tones as a brilliant man who had been a community leader. In the early individual interviews with the mother, she was markedly ingratiating, underplayed Henry's social difficulties and concentrated on his school problems, politely implying that teachers were to blame.

Henry's father, a waiter who had been working nights for many years, seemed to play a distinctly subordinate role in the family. In an early contact with the agency he negated his paternal role on the basis of his working hours. He told of having unsuccessfully attempted to interest Henry in athletics and commented, "Henry would make a very nice little girl."

Henry had one sibling, a brother ten years older. The mother described an ideal relationship between them. The brother, a college student at the time of referral, was planning to become a social worker and had been an influential factor in the mother's decision to seek help for Henry.

Henry was referred to activity group therapy since it was felt that this treatment milieu would offer a growth-producing atmosphere to this infantile and withdrawn child and provide needed opportunities for masculine identification. Close observation of him was recommended since the possibility of deeper pathology was suggested by the general picture of withdrawal.

The first Progress Report based on Henry's first thirteen sessions in group therapy described him as "extremely shy and withdrawn." In the first several sessions he wandered tensely and aimlessly around the room and was frightened by the small electric saw. His first steps toward interaction with fellow members were taken when he participated with other boys in ridiculing Alex, a severely regressed youngster. This was followed by a period of imitation of Alex in such activities as mixing paints and glue and smearing these on the furniture as well as on himself. At times Henry left sessions virtually dripping with paint. Henry's relations with other members were then marked by provocativeness with accompanying inability to defend himself against the attacks elicited by his behavior. Concurrently, Henry expressed intense liking for the group to his mother, looked forward all week to receiving weekly reminders of his "club" meetings from the group therapist and marked the meeting time on his calendar for the entire year.

At the close of his first season of treatment in group therapy, Henry showed continued infantile behavior. He did not work constructively, would start projects in imitation of other group members, but invariably would drift away and resume smearing paints. Provocativeness and fearfulness in relation to the other boys continued. Henry displayed a pattern of walking close to the walls and cautiously avoiding the middle of the room as if in expectation of attack. He showed complete inability to defend himself until the last session of the first year. On this occasion he had smeared a stronger boy with paint and when the latter attacked him, Henry fought back briefly and said aloud to himself: "Come on, fight back!" At the same time the mother reported that Henry had become somewhat negativistic toward her and had told her that he disliked her because she was always "bossing" him. There was some activation in the social area with Henry having made one friend and having expressed strong interest in attending a camp reunion.

Thus, in his beginning adjustment to the group, Henry cautiously probed the new environment. As he witnessed the therapist's permissiveness toward Alex's regressive activities, he was then able to act upon his own impulses to mess, smear and express his hostile and destructive wishes. This opportunity for free acting out of feeling was therapeutically crucial for Henry since in his familial relations, the expression of resentments and negative feelings had been dammed up. Fearful of human contact and markedly unsure of his capacity to achieve on any level, Henry perceived that in his new "club" there was no pressure to participate or compete and no demands for achievement but rather an acceptance of each member as he was. As Henry in his play with "anal" materials released tensions adhering to earlier levels of development, the energies liberated were then available for use in his current adjustment. The unconditional acceptance [by] the therapist, the satisfaction of his deep social hunger for contact with his peers, the opportunity to express dammed-up feeling—all contributed to the reinforcement of Henry's weakened ego structure. These newly acquired strengths were reflected in his ability to begin to assert himself against his mother's pervasive domination and to take the first significant steps toward socialization and sharing his life with others.

At a psychiatric conference held after completion of this first year of treatment, Henry was seen as a considerably disturbed child who, in addition to behavior disorders, was exhibiting schizoid behavior. Individual treatment, [combined] with group therapy, was recommended.

After four months of individual treatment with a woman worker he was described as "resistive, ambivalent, generally nonverbal, and frequently commented in a whining tone that he did not care to come." After fifteen interviews he stopped coming for individual treatment. At this time an initial diagnostic formulation had been made of "primary behavior disorder, preoedipal type" with the main pathology seen in the formation of an "orally passive character development."

During this period of individual therapy the case worker had arranged for psychological testing. Henry was ten years old at this time. He was found to have average intelligence, but his infantile drawings indicated that he preferred to act on a level almost four years below his chronological age. Outstanding characteristics on the projective material were his guardedness, fear of contact and fear of coping with new situations: he showed long response time to Rorschach cards and a tendency to preface a response with the remark, "I don't know." He was seen as a youngster whose feelings were not released in personal relations but were rather excessively expressed in fantasy life, increasing his introversion and impeding active social contact. The evidence in the projective picture pointed toward a defensive and withdrawn personality structure and tendencies to remain content with a peripheral, watching attitude toward life as reflected in his Rorschach responses "people looking at each other" (M:C-5:0).

A somewhat peculiar response was given to Card I where he saw "Two people standing on their heads and holding one person." This response seemed to bespeak an overly literal approach to things heard or seen and, more significantly, his own confused approach in even simple matters of human contact. On the basis of this response the psychologist felt that the possibility of a schizoid or schizoid-like adjustment could not be excluded. Yet, positives were seen in his respect for reality (5 popular responses) and his awareness of correct procedure. Possibilities for more direct emotional release were seen in the response to the last card where he saw "fireworks" and the response given twice "Two people dancing" suggested that he could conceive social interaction.[2]

It was after the first year of treatment of mother and child that the decision was reached to combine the therapeutic responsibility for each in the person of one therapist. It was felt that the case should not be separated since separation had become a constant battleground of tension and ambivalence between Henry and the mother with the unsatisfying separation at birth serving as the prototype. Thus, there were daily arguments between

---

[2]It should be noted that in the middle of Henry's second year of treatment, the group therapy program was interrupted by the loss of the group therapy meeting room for six months.

Henry and the mother around her wish to have him go outside to play and his equally strong desire to remain in the house. Therapeutic approaches were also evolved to deal with the mother's pervasive defensiveness and enable her to express her strongly destructive impulses toward the boy. The mother was told that she had been terribly deprived by Henry's premature birth in not having had the opportunity to warm and nurture him in her body for the full nine months; that instead of having a red-cheeked, healthy and energetic baby of whom she could have been proud, she had gotten a puny, shriveled-up creature who barely survived. The mother responded eagerly to this approach and several weeks later was able to go off on a vacation with the father for the first time in her married life.

In accordance with the treatment plan, the mother's individual therapist also became Henry's group therapist, a move which was received with obvious approval by both Henry and his mother.

In his second year of treatment, Henry made considerable gains. Initially he ignored the therapist. He would not greet him and during sessions would turn his back to the adult. As this behavior was accepted, it was followed by progressively greater contact with the therapist and open expression of ambivalent feelings. Henry began to seek help from the therapist with arts and crafts projects and at the same time began to test him severely. While engaging in such destructive acts as cutting at the observation screen or making gaping holes in the walls, he ostentatiously sought to draw the therapist's attention to his behavior. For four consecutive sessions, when the therapist was clearing up, Henry stepped into the sweepings and scattered them about. The adult's calm and permissive reaction to these provocations seemed to have critical significance for Henry. His testing in these extreme forms steadily abated, and strong feelings of positive transference emerged along with indications of identification with the therapist. It appeared that the therapist had passed the test. The following gives a picture of Henry's ambivalence and testing in the period described above.

Henry arrived early, entered silently and avoided looking at the therapist (unsure of the adult, testing him by ignoring him; the therapist's silent acceptance of this behavior shows that he has no need to be liked and also conveys respect for Henry's feelings). From time to time Henry shot quizzical, sizing-up glances at the therapist (becoming interested in him). When Maurice (a new member) arrived, Henry kept his back turned and made no response to the therapist's introduction of the new boy (resentment of the new sibling in the "group family" and continued testing of the therapist by ignoring him and exhibiting antisocial behavior).

Later, Maurice approached Henry, watched him making a shelf, offered suggestions and soon the two were working jointly on Henry's project (this acceptance of Maurice indicated that Henry's prior rejection of the newcomer had been aimed primarily at the therapist). Maurice then decided to make his own shelf and announced that he would work at another table where a second vise was available. Henry, in a pleased manner, supported Maurice in this decision and offered hammer and nails to enable Maurice to work independently (Henry's fear of intimacy). When Maurice invited Henry to play ping-pong, Henry indicated that he would play after completing his shelf. Later he said that he had decided not to play after all (continuing rejection of the new sibling and indirectly of the therapist, also fear of competition and intimacy).

Later Henry asked the therapist where the garbage can was and whether there were other boys in the club (seeking contact). He then joined Stanley in throwing the ping-pong ball at the walls, glancing intermittently at the therapist (testing becoming more overt).

Six [sessions] later Henry arrived early and quickly began work on a shelf. When Maurice came, he approached Henry and asked if he would like a candy. Henry seemed very hesitant and cautious before answering affirmatively (Henry's social and oral needs overcame his basic suspiciousness of others). Maurice gave him a candy and remarked that he was not wearing his glasses, although he was supposed to wear them all the time. In a friendly tone, Henry explained that he also was supposed to wear his at all times but did not (Henry established human contact on the basis of shared rebellion against adult authority).

Henry took one of the plane models which the therapist had brought for the group, sought the therapist's help in assembling it and worked on it very briefly. He then *broke it up into little pieces* and tossed these into the air just as the therapist was passing by him (rejection of the therapist's gifts; anger at his own inability to assemble the plane and fear of failure; provoking and testing the therapist). He then took a second model from the closet and loudly asked Maurice if he wanted to see how easily the model could be sawed in half. Henry proceeded to do this and then dropped the two pieces onto the floor with a triumphant flourish (encouraged by the absence of retaliation from the therapist, Henry goes on to test him more severely and is pleased at his own audacity).

After a while Henry explained to the therapist that he wanted to make a shoe-box, added that it was for his father and asked the adult to get it started. The therapist did the initial sawing and Henry then took over the rest of the job (acceptance of therapist by requesting help and using him as support in a masculine activity).

Henry then accepted Maurice's invitation to play King of the Hill atop the wood-box, each attempting with considerable pushing and shoving to stand exclusively on the box (therapist's acceptance of Henry despite his hostile acts strengthens his feelings of self-worth and gives him the security to compete with Maurice and to experiment with his emerging masculine aggressiveness).

At the close of the session when Andy, a new member, addressed the therapist as "Counselor," Henry corrected him and advised him that the therapist was the "leader of the club" (growing trust in and acceptance of the therapist).

Henry requested the therapist to send him cards announcing each meeting, compared him favorably with his brother who was also a "club leader" and asked for a wallet exactly like the therapist's.

Within the group as a whole Henry continued in a peripheral role. Anxiety and fearfulness in the face of any conflict persevered. However, on several occasions he was able to participate, if only briefly, in aggressive, masculine, competitive activities such as batting a ping-pong at another member or engaging him in the game of King of the Hill. Messing and smearing with paints had ceased completely, although Henry at times encouraged other members to spill paint on the floor. A mid-year Progress Report stated: "Henry is beginning to test his aggressiveness, first against the therapist, then briefly against fellow members. He appears to be becoming bolder as his experimentations are permitted. Although still generally withdrawn, there are definite changes, especially as compared with the grossly infantile child described in the first year of treatment."

In the last several sessions of the year Henry began to ask the therapist to play quiet games with him and when the therapist after a while allowed another child to play in his place, Henry accepted this and seemed to derive as much pleasure as he had when alone with the therapist. When the group went on an outing, Henry participated in baseball and later proudly told the therapist that this was the first time he had ever hit a baseball. He also began to accept invitations from other members to play ping-pong in contrast to his previous pattern of anxious and resentful rejection of these overtures.

At four consecutive sessions Henry displayed the following interesting behavior: He walked about the room and carefully examined the walls, at times tapping lightly on them with a hammer. Wherever he found a hole or weak spot, he repaired it, crudely but carefully. Perhaps, in the deepest levels of his unconscious, Henry perceived the group as a womb and was seeking to ensure that he would not again be prematurely expelled.

The mother reported at this time that Henry for the first time had gone down to the playground by himself. Further evidence that gains achieved in the group were being carried over in Henry's over-all life adjustment was reflected in his subsequent camp experience. When the mother visited, Henry took her by the hand and proudly introduced her to his bunkmates by name. He also had begun to greet and kiss his relatives upon meeting them.

Henry began his season of treatment by coming by himself to the group for the first time when the mother was unable to bring him. Though initially anxious about this venture, he later expressed pride in the achievement. In this period Henry seemed to solidify and integrate the advances toward maturity which had begun to emerge in the previous years. He looked happier and more relaxed. A subtle differentiation occurred in Henry's relationship with the therapist. Although he continued at intervals to turn to the adult for complete security and acceptance, there was a gradual, yet discernible transfer of libido from therapist to group. There was greater readiness to participate with fellow members in all areas and an increased willingness to experiment with masculine activities as illustrated by the following excerpt from one of Henry's third year group sessions:

From the beginning of the session Henry aggressively tested Harold, the new member whom he had accepted quite warmly at the latter's first session the previous week. When Harold inquired about refreshments, Henry warned him belligerently: "I'm cutting the cake. If you touch it, I'll kill you!" For a while the two boys sat side by side making earrings and both then showed their completed work to the therapist. When Maurice arrived he harried Henry by throwing aluminum discs at him and then ordered Henry to pick these up. Henry stubbornly and despite his fear of Maurice refused to comply.

During the refreshment period both Henry and Maurice pleasurably recalled instances when each had been alone with the therapist and had had a great deal of refreshments. When Harold, in a move to ingratiate himself with the therapist, washed the dishes, Henry remarked disparagingly, "Look, we have a new woman" (anxious that therapist might prefer Harold; development of concrete ideas about masculine and feminine roles as separate and distinct). After refreshments the members paired off for a clay fight. Henry had a look of exhilaration on his face as he charged, shouted and threw his clay pellets with abandon.

Later when the therapist played ping-pong with Maurice, Henry displayed interest in the game by standing nearby and intermittently asking the score. After a while the therapist handed his racquet to Henry who then proceeded to play with Maurice. Henry's playing showed considerable improvement and at one point when he was ahead in the game, he was unrestrainedly joyous. At the close of the session, Henry asked the therapist for a dime and left, saying, "So long, Les. I'll see you next week."

To be noted in the session just quoted is the relative ease with which Henry related to the therapist and fellow members in a variety of situations. It should also be noted that Henry was still unable to defend himself physically although he had become more assertive on a verbal level. Infantile components continued to be present. Henry derived considerable satisfaction from stacking up wood and then toppling it over with a resounding crash. When frustrated, threatened or made anxious, i.e., when fights developed in the group, Henry expressed his feelings upon inanimate objects in the room such as striking briefly but savagely at walls, tables and doors with hammers and saws.

During this period his mother gave the information that Henry had on his own joined a neighborhood center which he attended two days a week.

Henry's group therapist had continued as the mother's individual caseworker. His discussing of her resentment around the circumstances of Henry's birth seemed to have had a guilt-relieving effect and she was then freed to give cathartic expression to this trauma. There were indications that on a phallic level, this birth had the significance of something having been torn from her body. It was revealed that Henry had been conceived immediately after her father's death. The mother was helped to express her pervasive disappointment at having such a pitifully inadequate replacement for her gifted father. Following this she recognized that in demanding emulation of her father from Henry, she had set standards of achievement which he could not possibly attain. There was more open discussion of her background which brought out her identification with her father, her competitiveness with her brothers and her rejection of her feminine role.

As Henry's work at school became more satisfactory and his mother was no longer called to school to be confronted with Henry's failing performance there, she was able to shift the focus in interviews from Henry to her own life patterns and interpersonal difficulties. She expressed the understanding that in the past she had constantly sought to organize and dominate others and recognized that this pattern had had negative effects upon her family and social relations. The marital situation was discussed with the mother recalling her complete lack of preparation for the sexual aspect of marriage and examining her need to marry a weak, inadequate person whom she, in her own words, had "adopted." In interviews she placed a greatly increased emphasis upon Henry's brother who apparently represented a phallic extension of herself. His entry into the army aroused great anxiety in her since she unconsciously perceived his departure from the home as a castration of herself.

She now dressed in a more feminine fashion, presented a more womanly appearance and expressed progressively stronger feelings of adequacy as a woman and mother. In one of her last interviews she verbalized that she no longer had to be "manager and director" of other people's lives. Her case was then closed.

In his fourth season of treatment at age thirteen, Henry seemed to have reached a plateau. The process of ongoing improvement which had brought him from a position on infantile and fearful isolation to one of participation and acceptance within the group seemed to halt there. While retaining the gains achieved in the first three seasons of treatment, Henry still showed certain persevering negative behavior patterns. These patterns are illustrated in an excerpt from a report of a group session which can be considered as typical for this period: "Henry wandered about the room from one brief destructive interval to another. With a hammer he squashed shells used in making jewelry; played briefly with the bowling game and then threw the balls around the room, poked at the observation screen with a broom; played with milk spilt on the refreshment table, then put the empty milk container into a bag and threw this around; took the box of nails and threw handfuls of these backwards over his shoulder; tore paper into little pieces and strewed these on the floor close to the therapist. At the close of the session he asked the therapist for a nickel."

Thus, Henry's activity continued to be marked by a distinct aimlessness and a succession of small annoying if not destructive acts. Although he was an accepted member of the group, a detached quality and an underlying lack of substance characterized his relationships. While experimentation with verbal self-assertion continued, i.e., his emphatic insistence on giving out refreshments, Henry was still unable to back this up with a physical effort when necessary. When faced with direct attack he withdrew or attempted to deflect the aggression elsewhere. There was continuing need to provoke and test the therapist by confronting him with the annoying acts described above and by requesting money at the close of each session.

A follow-up interview was held with the mother in mid-year. She presented a favorable picture of Henry's over-all adjustment. He had two friends and had greatly surprised the mother by participating enthusiastically in a football game for the first time. At school Henry was passing his major subjects with marks of 65 to 70 and doing better in such areas as shop and music. The mother happily compared these marks to the 20's and 30's Henry used to receive. She felt he was showing sensitivity in his familial relations and gave the following illustration. Henry's young sister-in-law had sent tickets to a dance recital in which she was to appear. Henry's first reaction was a disdainful one to the effect that he did not care for dancing and would not care to attend. However, a little later he stated that perhaps he should go since his sister-in-law would feel badly if he did not accept the invitation.

Three months before the close of this fourth treatment season, Henry was retested psychologically. This retest emphasized the continued presence of his introversion, preference for watching rather than doing things, and his fear of intimacy. Out of eleven responses there were four percepts of people or animals "looking at each other" (M:C.-5:0, W:M-6:5). His drawings of people were naked and indistinguishable as to sexual characteristics, reflecting his infantile outlook as well as his undeveloped capacity to see himself as a separate person.

His Rorschach responses—"a witch coming toward you, mouth is open, like grabbing me," "people looking, staring at each other," "sea horses looking at each other talking"—indicated not only that he was clinging to a magical, make-believe world but also that he was unable to tolerate the threatening aspects of his instinctual impulses; these he projected onto the outside world, leading him to react in a suspicious and paranoid or paranoid-like context. It may well be possible to speak of pseudo-identification. Having hardly any personal identity of his own, he takes on too fluidly whatever role seems to be demanded of him. Hence his identifications were considered as fragile and unsubstantial.

Although the retest presented a somewhat more serious picture, in view of the paranoid-like context of his fears, there nevertheless were a number of positive changes which seemed to have occurred in the years between tests. He did not seem to be so overtly dependent on external support as he was before, seemed able to mobilize his energies much more quickly (average response time was 17 seconds as against 35 seconds on the first test) and above all he seemed far more ready and able to accept routine behavior and the common forms of social adaptation. Furthermore, although he remained afraid of seeing or feeling the aggression of others, he seemed more able accept the aggressive aspect of one's functioning. For instance, instead of seeing "Two people dancing," as he did on the first test, he saw "Two people trying to grab something." Similarly, where he had seen "Two pigs" on the first test, he formed the concept of a more aggressive animal, namely, "Two wolves."

The diagnostic impression was that this was either "a character disorder, schizoid type in a passive personality," or "a character disorder with borderline-schizophrenic functioning." The fact that Henry had maintained his intellectual standing was seen as a therapeutic gain. It was felt that his increase in ego assertiveness—although evidently a gain—had also increased his overt fearfulness of attack from the environment.

Discussion

After three years of treatment in exclusive group therapy (with the exception of the brief interval of individual treatment in his first year), it was felt that a considerable therapeutic gain had been achieved in this case. From fear of his fellow beings, which had resulted in isolation and unrelatedness, Henry had advanced to the point where he could share his life with others in playing, struggling and competing. He had been able to relinquish his addiction to obviously infantile forms of messing play in favor of participation with peers in appropriate masculine-aggressive activities. He had mobilized himself to use his average intellectual potential to achieve a much more adequate adjustment at school so that this no longer constituted a site of continuing ego defeat for him. His conception of adults as agents of domination, exploitation and prohibition had undergone considerable change through his relationship with the group therapist, thus paving the way toward improved relations with teachers, counselors and relatives.

Perhaps the most significant changes had occurred in Henry's conception of himself is that his self-image no longer reflected a picture of a helpless, castrated, fear-ridden and infantile child. However, certain continuing patterns and fears reflected in his group adjustment, and noted on the psychological tests, seemed to represent a pathological residue which could not be reached in activity group therapy. The persistence of Henry's provocative behavior in the group seemed to be an expression of an unconscious desire within him to be expelled from and rejected by the group, a need perhaps originating in his initial expulsion from his mother's womb.

It was the understanding of Henry's need to experience repetitively rejection which enabled the group therapist, and through him the group, to assimilate Henry's behavior. As a therapeutic countermeasure, the therapist used constant acceptance, above and beyond that implied in his role. The understanding of the motives underlying Henry's action helped to control countertransference feelings in the therapist which might have led to major errors in his relationship to the boy and possible loss of the case, before Henry benefited to the extent to which he did.

Yet, the inability of activity group therapy ultimately to reach Henry's need to limit the group's effectiveness (by constantly courting expulsion) constituted the limitation of this treatment method in this case. His powerful regressive drives (the need to receive the *total* nutrient care interrupted by birth and not received in later upbringing) could not be fully resolved in the non-interpretative setting of activity group therapy. This constellation needed working through in the individual therapeutic area. Thus, the decision was made to close Henry in group therapy and to refer him for individual treatment.

CHAPTER 7

Individual and Group Therapy of a Latency-Age Child

JOHN C. COOLIDGE / MARGARET G. FRANK

DURING THE PAST GENERATION the traditional treatment in child guidance clinics for children of latency age has been individual, usually once a week, psychotherapy. We know that the child of this age group normally invests much of his energy in peer relationships, finding therein an opportunity to strengthen and broaden his own identity, both through group identification and by comparing the similarities between himself and others of his own age. This maturational process necessarily involves a partial exclusion of the adult world.

Certain children utilize psychotherapy to focus on selected areas of their difficulties which are manifestly represented in their peer relatedness. But often they insist that such difficulties do not exist. The limited effectiveness of psychotherapy with such children is related to their need not only to deny the specific doubts, fears, and tensions which arise when with other children but also to prove to themselves that they have achieved the norms of peer trust as a bastion against infantile dependence upon the adult world. To admit frailty in this area is mistakenly perceived as surrendering to their original infantile status.

Activity group therapy is often able to prove effective with such children because its setting and techniques are compatible with the developmental phase of the latency child. Within the group, penetrating observations made by his peers are often more meaningful to the child than those offered as "interpretations" in individual psychotherapy. The immediate reward for giving up outmoded ways of adaptation is a closer bonding to the group. In the laboratory of the group there is no punishment for regression and there is mutual tolerance for trial and error attempts to master new social skills.

In clinics which offer three types of treatment—individual psychotherapy, group psychotherapy, and combined (group and individual) psychotherapy—there is an increasing need to clarify the specific therapeutic contributions which each type of treatment can best make. It is evident that with such knowledge therapists are in a better position to plan in advance for the treatment of each latency child and to be more flexible as treatment proceeds of adjusting therapeutic techniques to the specific characteristics of the patient.

The following case illustrates the considered use of all three modes of therapy.

Individual Psychotherapy

Ellen C. was brought to the clinic at age five and a half, with the classical school phobia symptoms of morning agitation, nausea, vomiting, and tearful clinging to her mother. The problem about school was so acute that there was little parental concern about Ellen's almost complete inability to establish and maintain meaningful friendships with other children. Ellen and her mother were accepted for individual treatment. Our study of the situation revealed that there had been many disturbances in the family. Both parents had emigrated from Europe following war experiences. Neither was a content or secure person. Both had had unhappy relationships with their own parents. While pregnant with Ellen, Mrs. C. had developed severe toxemia, and a hemorrhage at seven months had necessitated an emergency caesarean section. This had been a highly traumatic event for Mrs. C., and there were many references in her contacts with her caseworker which indicated that she felt a deep resentment toward Ellen for somehow damaging her. Ellen weighed three pounds at birth and remained at the hospital for seven weeks. She suffered from a profound anemia during the first six months of her life which required several hospitalizations for study and treatment. Feeding difficulties emerged immediately. There were hour-long feedings during which she laboriously consumed only one or two ounces of milk. Eating has continued to be a source of concern and mutual tension between mother and daughter, as have sleep disturbances, manifested by Ellen crying and demanding to sleep with her parents. In general, Ellen was a dissatisfied baby whose physical care took an enormous amount of time.

Nursery school was considered when Ellen was three, but the idea was abandoned. Mrs. C.'s need to isolate Ellen was augmented by pressure from the grandparents to keep Ellen away from crowds because of their fear of germs. By the age of four, Ellen had not been permitted or stimulated to play with other children.

Ellen's only sibling, Jonathan, was born when she was four. She reacted to this event with considerable regression, glued herself to her mother wherever she went, and simply would not leave her side. An effort to enter Ellen in kindergarten a month later ended in total failure. At five, a second attempt at kindergarten was made possible by the presence of a very motherly school principal to whom Ellen transferred all her clinging impulses. However, the adjustment was most precarious. She constantly hovered close to an adult and refused to mingle or play with the other children. It was at this juncture that treatment started.

Ellen's mother was seen in casework treatment during all the five years that Ellen came to the clinic. Mrs. C. was always immaculately dressed, with literally never one hair out of place, and she stressed being "unemotional and reasonable." She was, at first, intensely ambivalent about coming to the clinic, but only later revealed that she had developed symptoms of nausea, stomach-ache, and vomiting during the first month of casework, the very same symptoms Ellen manifested on school mornings. Her unresolved hostile dependency toward her own mother soon came to light and she recalled her old feelings of being constantly disapproved of and ridiculed. She began to see that behind her confusion and anxiety about dealing with Ellen and her fear of "frustrating" her lay the same resentments her mother had felt toward her. As she recalled her own fearfulness and rebelliousness as a child, she reacted with increasing anger to Ellen's provocation and demandingness. Growingly she could see the intensity of the mutual anger between Ellen and herself, and finally was able to admit that she felt she hated Ellen when she did poorly; at such times her attempts to help Ellen with her homework became horrible wrangles. She became aware of Ellen's retaliatory wishes, understanding why she often looked dead to Ellen when the latter awoke early in the morning and observed her mother sleeping.

Mrs. C. also revealed her own childhood deficit in social areas. As a young girl in Europe she was highly restricted in her activities by the rigid, disapproving, and dictatorial policies of both her parents. She was expected to behave like a proper lady at all times and all spontaneous behavior, including her tomboyishness, was severely frowned upon. On the other hand, she was never really given a helping hand in developing social graces or in finding a feminine role. She was frequently told to protect herself, but neither parent would explain against what or why, consequently leaving the question shrouded in mystery and fear. It was no wonder than that Mrs. C. was quite unaware of both the depth of her own need to hold Ellen close to herself and of the severity of Ellen's real inability to relate with peers. One of the most important aspects of work with the mother was helping her to relinquish this hold and to allow her daughter social freedom. As a consequence of this increasing permission to move out of the home, Ellen became progressively often confronted with her peer problems.

Ellen's father, a dozen years her mother's senior, appeared to be disinterested in the children. He was a rigid, inflexible man who was easily perturbed by even the ordinary noise and activity of children. He withdrew from their care as much as he could. He was undemonstrative, took his wife's love for granted, and wanted to be waited upon. He was so intensely bound to his own mother that Mrs. C. once wistfully stated she had "married a mother-in-law rather than a husband." Her own fear of abandonment compelled her to repress her frustration and to cater to his idiosyncracies rather than to protest. He resisted the clinic's attempts to involve him in the treatment program, but brought Ellen to the clinic several times when Mrs. C. was not able to. He revealed his concern for Ellen's unhappiness and raised the question of the possible use of tranquilizers, stating that he himself took Equinal at times of stress. He saw himself as an introvert who suffered silently along with Ellen. He explained his fear of emotional pain and told of his avoidance of serious theatre, stating that life was serious enough. He finally told Mrs. C. that he thought Ellen got her trouble from him, that he too had a "heaviness of heart" when he had to leave the house for work. Mrs. C. was amazed to learn that he could feel so intensely.

The first year of treatment revealed with clarity the nature of Ellen's human transactions. Her pinched pale face with dark shadows under the eyes displayed the effects of her ravaging anxiety. Her mannerisms and motions showed a mixture of intense restriction alternating with abrupt impulsive movements which gave to her demeanor an erupting, bursting quality. She was dressed immaculately, like a doll, and in many ways in her behavior seemed to alternate between being a doll to please her mother and showing violently that she was not a doll but a viable child.

In the first interviews, Ellen would not budge from her mother's side except to make short sorties to experiment with paints, crayons, or toys. Her mother whispered that she had never before used a brush. Anxiety and irritability arose quickly on each of these ventures, and after a span of several minutes she quickly retreated to her mother.

In the third interview, Ellen selected finger paints which at first she used most gingerly with one finger. Her control over her intense wish to mess broke down quickly and within several minutes both hands, the table top, and her own clothing were covered. She gesticulated with black dripping hands toward her mother. Then, out of anxiety, she asked her mother to wash her. Her mother angrily complied, scrubbing her arms forcefully in cold water inspite of Ellen's whimpering complaints. The next interview was cancelled, as were alternate interviews for the first three months. The ambivalence toward treatment was equally acute in both mother and child.

Gradually, Ellen's enormous preoccupation with her two-and-a-half-year-old brother, Jonathan, came into view. Behind this lay her confusion about sexual identity and a prodigious envy of Jonathan's masculinity. Total preoccupation with such problems completely consumed the therapy hours. In this respect, Ellen resembled a child of two and a half to four.

The controlled permissiveness of the therapeutic relationship provided Ellen with a badly needed opportunity to explore through direct action some degree of emotional expression. As already described, at first there was only precarious control over the original unmodified forces. Ellen, however, gradually found strength through the mechanism of identification with the aggressor, which she used increasingly as her chief mode of both expression and defense. For months she re-enacted the role of the fuming, exasperated teacher who bullied the student (therapist) for "unspeakable," yet unlabeled crimes. Her vindictive orders were issued from an angry distorted face while pounding on the table. Occasionally she erupted into a physical attack on the therapist, indicating the intensity of her bottled-up feelings. Her behavior revealed, with poignancy, the deep fear of annihilation in this little girl who had almost lost her life after birth. Attempts to clarify verbally the mechanisms or content only paralyzed her with fear and aggravated her behavior.

The first indication of concern about peer difficulties took place in the fourteenth month of treatment and heralded her first real recognition of the peer world around her. Until this time Ellen simply had not been developmentally ready to have friends. She initiated a game about school buses, and during this her therapist suggested she might have some concerns about fellow schoolmates. She replied quickly that the boys were fresh, said "ain't" and "shut-up" and other "unspeakable" terms, and half admitted that the actions of these boys caused her concern. She added that she herself never used such words but gave evidence that she might like to sometimes. She then promptly changed the subject. The rest of the hour was spent in tidying up the office as if to emphasize control. Her reaction to these boys, in effect, was an extension of her sibling difficulties. This became apparent in the next several sessions in which her envy of her brother reached new heights. She smashed an ashtray, threw things around, reported that she had told her brother he could not expect to have her mother all to himself, and gave other indications of tormenting him. No more references to peer difficulties were made nor could they be solicited during the remainder of that year.

Ellen's school attendance improved considerably and treatment was discontinued with both mother and child at the end of the second year.

One year later, Ellen's mother returned asking for a consultation because of her daughter's increasing worry about her schoolwork. Ellen and her mother were reinstated in treatment. Ellen, now eight, looked and behaved as she had previously. She was listless and bored and complained about her schoolwork and teachers. She was asked if she had any friends and immediately she said she had none. In this consultation, her tenseness, irritability, and inhibition suggested that her extreme ambivalence was still holding her immobile.

However, that summer the first of a series of more relaxed family vacations at the shore seemed to help. The following fall Ellen showed for the first time a pleasant and friendly streak which heralded at long last some separation from her pre-genital past. In treatment there were indications that Ellen had an increasing desire for friends. Once she admitted she thought she was too bossy, and once she stated she wished she could have more friends, but in general Ellen could not deal therapeutically with the underlying difficulties.

There was still so little distance from oedipal and earlier developmental tasks that the intrusion of pre-genital impulses into her peer relationships was difficult for her to control. To prevent such regression and to keep her limited capacity for peer relatedness intact, Ellen held herself aloof when troubled by such events as the rambunctiousness of the boys in the bus. She was also reluctant to become too peer-oriented because of the threat this imposed to the mutual but neurotic closeness needed by both her and her mother. Perhaps most important of all was Ellen's wish to avoid the unbearable self-image of a lonely little girl who was deeply frightened of other children. Ellen was only too willing to let this sleeping dog slumber. Her reluctance to work on these problems was motivated by the unconscious fear of the regression which would necessarily have taken place in treatment if the conflicts underlying her peer difficulties were exposed. Thus, Ellen's defenses converged to block off communication, both in dramatic play and verbalization; the very tools through which individual psychotherapy is effective.

Combined Therapy

When Ellen was ten, it was decided to recommend activity group therapy in addition to individual psychotherapy. The expectation was that group interaction would mobilize conflictual material which Ellen could bring back to her individual psychotherapy. It was further expected that the group process itself would hasten a realignment of internal forces and defenses and consequently lead to more appropriate adaptation.

True to the nature of Ellen's defenses she could not bring to her psychiatrist thoughts and feelings about the group. However, she quickly began to change. She developed more of an ordinary girl's demeanor and became more casual. She began to mention names of neighborhood friends and within several months received invitations to other girls' homes. Her mother reported strides in her social progress as indicated by a marked increase in the number of phone calls.

It was realized after a year of combined treatment that anxieties mobilized in the group would not be brought to her psychiatrist and that Ellen continued to view individual treatment only as an opportunity for companionship. On the other hand, strides being made in the activity group indicated that, given Ellen's patterns of defenses, this was currently the treatment of choice and could better provide for Ellen the tools for latency living. Consequently, individual psychotherapy was discontinued.

During Ellen's five years of individual treatment, some gains had been made. Her need for perfection, her exaggerated fear of attempting anything creative, and her marked fear of disapproval had been touched upon. The sibling rivalry continued to be a central focus and finally some of her seductive feelings toward her family members emerged. The earlier crude control over impulses and later identification with the aggressor were now largely replaced by a constrictive social conformity and reaction formation, which at least gave her a formula for behavior although at too great a cost. It was recognized that Ellen still was anxious, restricted, and impoverished in her personality, and it was hoped that in the future she might be more accessible to individual psychotherapy and eventually be able to work through verbally her basic anxieties.

Group Therapy

The pre-school child acquires a first identity from his parents, and with this as a foundation he is ready to begin the quest for an independent existence. He moves out from his family to join the society of children, and the peer group becomes the proving ground where the child learns to live with people outside the family.

Ellen was not able to take this important step forward because of fears that she would have to relinquish all claims on earlier satisfactions. Her problems were hard to reach, at this point, in individual therapy. This was in part due to her need to keep a tight lid on her conflicts and in part related to her developmental stage. The latency child is apt to shut adults out of much of his world.

When Ellen arrived at her first "club" meeting at the Judge Baker Guidance Center, she appeared as an attractive, well built, ten year old. She greeted the new situation with a pinched, tight expression, which was to tell of her tension in group situations for many months to come. She entered the large meeting room and was greeted by her group leader[1] who introduced herself to Ellen. In turn, Ellen learned the names of the five other girls who had also just been invited. It was many weeks before Ellen could tell some of these children apart, and indeed it was months before she got all their names straight. To her, at first, these five girls of her own age were an indistinguishable and frightening mass. She did not realize that they had been se-

[1]Actually the therapist's role is not that of a "leader," which term more accurately describes an adult's functioning in group activities with normal children. The reader will note the term "worker" in some other chapters—M.S.

lected to attend this group with as much careful thought as was involved in the decision for her membership. While the six girls shared the same hunger for closeness to the adult and for friends, their strengths and problems were reviewed and weighed so that no personality problems would interfere unduly with the group's potential for promoting healthy functioning. What might be a problem in one child was selected to counterbalance a problem in another child. Thus, Ellen's overly rigid defense patterns were chosen to set off the impulsivity of another girl. The ease that another child had in expression of conflicts was chosen to stimulate the more reticent.

As is the procedure with each new child, Ellen was invited to look around her "club room." The walls were lined with cabinets which contained arts and crafts material: woodworking tools, clay, paint, leather and jewelry kits, etc. There were work tables, a toilet connected to the club room, and a kitchen area with shelves for food and cooking utensils, a stove, and a dining table. At this point, this rather casual setting filled Ellen with anxiety. She undoubtedly wondered if she would be accepted by the girls and if, in turn, she would like them. Further, she probably questioned who the adult was and what her expectations would be. Finally, she was concerned with the materials and whether she had the ability to use them well.

For the first time in her life Ellen entered a social situation which at least guaranteed the physical proximity of five other girls, although the guarantee obviously could go no further than the fact that most of these girls would be present week by week; companionship and emotional proximity would have to be achieved by Ellen herself. Still, this was an immediate improvement in her life situation, for at this time her behavior toward peers could not have attracted five constant playmates who would not walk away from her in response to her provocations. Secondly, although it would take Ellen and the others quite some time to discover this, she had close at hand an adult who was ready to protect, help, and feed. Unlike the adults known to these children at home, in school, or in neighborhood clubs, there would be no demands for behavior above the level of their emotional abilities and no retaliation for regressive expression. Finally, the total atmosphere was one in which Ellen could approach the children and the adult in her own fashion and at her own pace.

Ellen entered the group bringing with her the defensive and relationship patterns observed in her individual treatment and in her life at home. In the first session, she responded to her own anxiety by turning to the adult to structure the situation, asking what she should do. She received the reply that she could do anything she liked. True to form, Ellen responded by removing herself from the children and the adult to work with paper and crayons. Her drawing, clearly a self-portrait, was of a flower, petals tightly held at the side of the stem, placed precisely in the center of the page and carefully bound with a heavy border. Although her back was turned and her head bent, she was ever watchful of the other children and of the adult.

About forty-five minutes before the end of this first meeting, Ellen sat down to the first of many group meals. The combination of her family's request that she maintain the dietary laws of her religion plus her own neurotic food habits increased her tension greatly. She carefully attended the leader's response to be active testing of a less inhibited girl who declared her dislike of one of the food items. The leader answered, "You don't have to eat anything you don't want," but, it was weeks before either she or the other children truly believed that the adult meant this.

In many ways Ellen's behavior during this first session typified her first weeks of reaction to the group experience. She remained on the sidelines with her back turned and yet was watchful. She discovered that the materials contained elements of safety, permitting her essentially to be present and busy and yet not have to interact directly. Even the range of materials available permitted her safety since she did not have to use the messiest, i.e., the clay and paint, or those which involved force and activity. She was free to maintain her rigid defenses against her impulses. Her drawing of the framed flower was repeated with little variation for quite some time.

Despite what appeared to be a picture of relative inactivity, a great deal was going on within the group and Ellen. While Ellen was watching, the other girls, according to their own problems, were more actively making their feelings and wants known. Ellen's eyes and ears were always focused on the hammer-banging activities, the arguments which erupted in jump-rope tournaments, and the smearing of paints and clay which were part of the more active testing and more open expression of conflict of the other children. At mealtime she viewed lapses in table manners with an increase in her own anxiety, and she scanned the leader's face for some trace of the responses she expected from an adult. One might say that while the other children were actively testing the leader, Ellen's quest went on vicariously through the actions of others.

But five girls will not let a sixth sit out for very long, and soon Ellen slipped into group interaction, letting herself be drawn by the others. While she was not yet able to take responsibility for her own actions and wishes, she would let herself be drawn into things by the other children. We might ask why it was that five girls would not allow another child to remain isolated from the group. There were undoubtedly many factors involved. Perhaps the children sensed Ellen's anxiety about them, anxieties which they shared but handled differently. Perhaps they saw her as too good and controlled, and their own increased regression could not tolerate her sharply contrasting behavior. Perhaps they feared that she would receive more from the adult in her side-line position and thus pulled her into their activities. Whatever the reason, we count on this characteristic in placing children like Ellen in groups.

By the middle of her first year in activity group therapy, Ellen was participating in tag, jump rope, conversation at the dinner table, and joint work with the materials, although she tended to seek out the more retiring girls like herself for partners. While her interactions increased, she was quick to retreat whenever any situation threatened to stimulate the expression of her own anger. Thus, she would return to solitary work with materials if any game disintegrated into an argument or if competition was part of the interactions. During this time Ellen turned more to the leader for protection and giving. She had learned that the adult could be approached for help at any time no matter how unrelated the requests were to the child's own actual abilities. In this vein Ellen came to the leader constantly to have directions read that she was able to read, to help her start on one project or another, to ask the leader's opinion of what colors to use.

As time went on, Ellen became freer to express her own true feelings. Her sense of safety was due to the direct feeding of the adult's support and her observation that the leader did not punish the other children when they exposed their conflicts in behavioral terms. With the release of her feelings, her group interactions lasted for a longer time. She no longer retreated from arguments but angrily stamped her feet and insisted that the girls conform to the rules and regulations. If retreating was necessary because of the potency of her feelings, her face wore the expression of her mood. Her activity of retreating was no longer drawing the flower but hammering out metal ashtrays. She was at least somewhat aware of the hostile expression that the activity involved for once she was heard to call out while pounding, "Does anyone have a headache?"

During this time, no matter what activity she engaged in, she brought with her her battery of rules, exhibiting no flexibility. This rigid defense acted upon and was at the same time affected by those children whose concept of right and wrong was less intense than hers. Toward the end of her first year in group therapy one could hear Ellen declaring loudly that another child was a "cheat," which the latter admitted while at the same time accusing Ellen of being a "goody-goody." Ellen's expressions of hostility and her regressive swings were never as full as those of the other children, nor did they seem to tap fully the well of feelings within her; yet at the same time the tightness of this child's exchanges began to diminish.

As Ellen's exchanges with the children became freer the height of her conflict could be observed in her use of and approach to the leader. In every way short of the physical clinging of a toddler she clung to the leader. Her fear of loss of the adult was expressed in her attempts to capture the leader's attention and being for herself even as she involved herself in interactions with the other children. A barrage of anxious questions about her work were fired at the leader constantly: "Peggy, do you think that I'll get this done today?" "Peggy, do you think my mother would like this kind of earring?"

In the second year of activity group therapy, Ellen was displaying her dilemma dramatically. In the language of behavior she was asking: Will I lose my mother if I venture to grow? a question fraught with fear, longing, hostility, and healthy striving. The leader responded to each and every request but never lost sight of reality. Even if her questions had to be answered with an, "I don't know, Ellen," they were answered. And often the reply was given to Ellen that as soon as the leader did such and such for Ginny, she would work on Ellen's request. That Ellen became aware of some of the nature of her demands became obvious when, after a period of time, the requests came with a self-conscious smile and the anxiety in her voice decreased. Before she cut down on the requests, she went through a period in which the questions and demands had little or no force behind them; they were an empty ritual, once loaded with meaning but soon to be abandoned.

The most dramatic shifts in Ellen's behavior were seen at the dinner table. This was partially due to the fact that many of her greatest fears of regression and exposure of her oral-sadistic and dependent needs were stimulated around food. In addition the mealtime was intentionally structured both to feed and stimulate the working of sibling rivalry. A basic portion of food was served to all the children and then the extras were placed in the center of the table. Neither Ellen nor the other children realized that, by plan, there were never enough seconds to go around. In the first meetings of this group, the extras went unnoticed. Finally, a child freer in expressing her wants turned to the leader to request another helping and received the reply she was to hear for many sessions to come, "The extras belong to all the girls and it's up to you all as to what to do with them." This reply at first left the group silent and Ellen watchful. Some weeks later, a stronger though no more hungry child initiated the question to each girl in turn: "Is it okay with you if I have another?" To her distress and Ellen's, who quickly declined, she found that two girls wanted more food, though there were only two pieces. As is common in early stages of these groups, the children move into a kind of law of the jungle when they realize that the adult is not going to impose order. Battles rage, with primitive solutions like: "first come, first served" or "whoever gets their fork in first." True to form, Ellen remained apart from these wrangles, except that the fighting of the others made her sufficiently anxious so that she was prompted to offer sensible advice. Her ideas were usually rebuffed and it was pointed out that she had no say in the matter since she had said she did not want any more. It should be noted that Ellen's dietary customs were taken into account by the leader; whenever meat was served, there were items that she could eat that also became extras, so that she would not be excluded from this area by the food itself. Perhaps it was the provocation of the girls who pointed out to her that she had no say unless she claimed an extra, perhaps it was her greater freedom to assert herself that led Ellen soon to be counted in on desiring an extra.

In the middle of the second year, Ellen and the girls reached a peak of conflict over two extra pieces of French toast. If they divided them in half, all would have their extras, pointed out Ellen, rightfully. But one child insisted on having a whole piece and this was too much for the rest. Ellen grabbed her half, screeching her reasonable idea over and over again and said, "You are all pigs and I can't stand the way you yell and argue." Ginny replied, "We are pigs, we're hungry and arguing never killed anyone." Ellen seemed stunned by this remark. Its impact could be observed in the weeks that followed as she permitted herself to assert and argue. In time, the girls worked out reasonable ways of managing the food.

The group was terminated after three years. By this time many changes could be observed in Ellen. Essentially, she was (and undoubtedly always will be) a person who relies on rules and regulations to structure her life, but she had attained a degree of flexibility and humor about herself so that she was no longer excluded from groups; indeed, she was able to make an important contribution in both her therapy group and elsewhere. In her overall functioning there was a freer use of the energy and ability which had previously been so tightly bound.

Her mother's social worker observed that Mrs. C. watched intently the changes taking place in Ellen as she interacted with the group and vicariously received permission to act similarly. She consequently found greater rewards in her own increased social activities. It seemed as if the mother, at long last, had a chance to learn some of the basic ingredients of peer relatedness which she had never been allowed to acquire in her own youth.

Conclusions

The presentation of the work with Ellen reviews our attempt, following recognition of the relative failure of individual treatment, to find a therapeutic regimen which could circumvent Ellen's known defensive framework and offer more effective help. To some degree, this was achieved. Ellen belongs to the host of children who have been severely traumatized before the development of verbal communication. Such children suffer lifelong amorphous anxiety underlying the later more specific symptomatology, and they learn only with great difficulty to communicate such affect through the use of speech. Many such children showing similar signs of severe anxiety, irritability, hostility, and guilt swell clinic treatment lists, are treated for greater or lesser number of years, and finally terminate with minimal or no basic improvement. It is our belief that child guidance clinics need to increase their range of treatment techniques to suit the varying needs of these children. We view activity group treatment as an important tool in the clinical armentarium. Since its mode of operation is essentially noninterpretive, it can often help these latency children whose emotional defect is primarily preverbal in origin and who are so often inaccessible to individual psychotherapy.

Part IV

Cooperative Therapy

In cooperative therapy a child and his parent, or parents, are simultaneously involved in psychotherapy, usually with different therapists. The treatment of all participants is carefully monitored and integrated by the several therapists to ensure that the fundamental family and individual problems are dealt with. The methods used may be individual or group therapy for one or several persons or a combination of both, depending on diagnoses and changing circumstances.

In family and child guidance agencies, it is general practice to engage parents in treatment or counseling even when, initially, the child is designated as the primary patient. Most problems of children are consequences of discordances in the complex psychodynamics within families, which accounts for agency policy that at least one parent must participate on a consistent basis. In a significant number of cases, parents who do not ordinarily seek clinical assistance for marital and other problems affecting families are helped to address these situations once a child has been accepted for therapy.

Children are sensitive barometers of the emotional climate in families. Even before serious psychological conditions in families become overt, their effects on children are discernible. The interrelationships and the interactions between family members constitute a psychodynamic *gestalt* that tends to maintain itself. It has a homeostatic quality in that any significant alteration in the accustomed behavior pattern of one person, either child or parent, becomes reflected responsively in the behavior of the others. At times such reactions are induced by extrafamilial influences of a nature imposing extraordinary stress, such as unexpected loss of a family member through death or another circumstance, or severe economic conditions such as loss of a parent's employment and forced removal to a different geographic location. Such trials can exacerbate and bring to the surface incipient family problems. The strains of severe economic conditions in recent years have been detected in a marked national increase in the number of marital conflicts, desertions, instances of wife and child batterings, and other traumas.

In community agencies, mothers are usually more active participants in treatment along with their children. There are several reasons to account for this. In most families, fathers are the primary breadwinners and are not as available to attend clinics during the day. Although agencies have attempted to cope with this by scheduling evening hours, such efforts have not proved as successful as intended. Also, some fathers use the excuse of daily employment as resistance against becoming involved.

Another factor that accounts for mothers' engagements in psychotherapy is that they are the primary nurturing persons when children are young and generally considered more accountable for children's physical and emotional welfare, including the task of finding and participating in clinical programs. In recent years the traditional role of mothers has been subject to question and challenge due to the influence of various movements in which women have sought—and partially obtained—emancipation from this role. One effect of this trend has been to increase fathers' awareness of their psychological influence in the family, particularly their effects on children's growth and development. This has made them somewhat more responsive to clinical agencies.

Another recent development, one that has had the effect of bringing fathers into treatment, is the advent of "family therapy,"[1] a treatment approach in which all members of a family, except for the very young, are brought together in common interviews with a therapist. Thus, fathers become meaningful participants in a process wherein the family is helped to examine and comprehend its conflict situations and learn how to manage them in healthier ways. Such a group procedure has value also in diluting the focus on individuals, thus reducing resistance, individual accountability, and guilt. Children, in particular, may respond favorably in family interviews because they no longer have to feel that they are responsible for family discord, as they are wont to do.

In families that are socially and economically disadvantaged, there is still another factor that influences the degree to which parents participate in

[1]There are some clinicians who consider this to be a special form of counseling, not psychotherapy. Nevertheless, they do acknowledge its merit in dealing with some intrafamilial problems.

treatment along with their children. Economic survival often mandates that both parents must work, making it unusually difficult for either one to co-operate with treatment programs. The day-to-day problems affecting survival are inordinately difficult, and it becomes economically costly when parents have to take time off from work to keep appointments at community agencies. Schools, notoriously, have much difficulty in getting parents to visit when special situations affecting their children arise. Only the direst emergencies will mobilize parents to a point where they will appear when summoned, or to follow up when referred to agencies. They will do so more often for physical illness of children, less so for emotional and behavioral problems, unless these become so severe as to mandate their cooperation. For these and other reasons, in disadvantaged communities, when situations arise that affect the emotional health of a family, it is not uncommon for the parents to judge their child to be solely responsible for his exceptional behavior—the target patient—and thus he becomes the focal participant in treatment.

Agencies that maintain a rigid policy of not accepting children for treatment unless one parent participates automatically exclude many children in dire need of corrective psychological services. This was the prevailing circumstance with some of the children who were described in Chapters 1–4, who were maintained in group treatment for extended periods of time without a parent becoming significantly involved. In some cases children who live under the most debilitating emotional conditions have been in school-based treatment programs without their parents being willing even to attend an initial interview. The parents have given willing—sometimes grudging—consent to their children's involvement merely in order to terminate the school's "bothering" them. A common underlying feeling on their part is that if they can tolerate a young child's physical incontinence, or timidity, or aggressiveness—why can't the school?

It is important to bear in mind that resistance is inherent in all parents, not just low-income families whose attitudes about clinical services are shaped by their socioeconomic circumstances. Further, even though "family therapy" and other innovative procedures have been developed, emotionally troubled children and adolescents do not lend themselves easily to treatment. Children and adolescents are prone to feel, and act, in such ways as psychonoxious experiences in their families force them to accommodate to exceptional circumstances. Because of their intrinsic narcissism, a quality of the immature psyche, they are less conscious of and unresponsive to the judgments of parents and other adults with whom they have regular contacts. This is especially so in families where there exists a basic neurotic constellation between parents and children. Such a situation was illustrated in the case of Martin, in Chapter 4. As Martin made palpable improvements as a result of therapy, his mother began to decompensate.

In the case in Chapter 8, concerning Leon and his mother, there exists a symbiotic bond between an emotionally troubled, marginally retarded boy and his severely disturbed mother, a condition that is further exacerbated by the behavior of a passive, dependent father. The parents' neurotic interactions with each other and with Leon had etiological roots in the pathological relationships the parents had in their own respective families. Thus, the treatment had to impede and alter pathological phenomena that spanned three generations. It is questionable whether treating Leon alone could have effected more than superficial change in him. Moreover, as the record will indicate, it is unlikely that the mother would have countenanced treatment of the boy alone. Even with the employment of comprehensive clinical services—psychiatric, psychological, and social work—it was difficult at times to keep therapy on an even keel because of the florid emotionality of the mother and her impulsively expressed resistances.

As for Leon, his presenting difficulties indicated the need for individual, analytical therapy, which he resisted at first. The treatment plan was modified: for Leon, *combined* therapy—individual and group; for the family, *cooperative* therapy, with the mother as the focal parent and the father to be involved as much as circumstances permitted.

This case presentation is a thoroughly documented history of orthopsychiatric practice utilizing the services of the primary clinical disciplines. With Leon, both male and female therapists were used concurrently during combined treatment in order to foster masculine identity in a character-deficient boy. Also illustrated is the manner in which a child's participation in a therapy group generates fruitful topics for exploration in dyadic treatment.

Another facet of the family treatment program involving Leon is how the homeostatic, neurotic interactions became subject to further strain under the episodic influence of changed behavior in one member. This case history is a vivid description of the complex psychodynamics within families. It reveals not only how psychomalignant conditions affect children's development, but also how the conditions resist the interventions of psychotherapy. The case is also an example of *transference in reverse*. As noted earlier, this is a phenomenon in which a child's transference to a therapist begins to affect his perceptions of his parents and his emotional ties to them. Further, the child's improvements as a result of treatment alter for the better the parents' perceptions of the child. Some of the pathological elements of the child's transferences to both parents become mutated as successful treatment occurs. This takes place in a child unconsciously through a partial fusion of his libidinal relationship to the therapist with that to the parents. The child is enabled to form more efficient compensatory defenses against emotional threats within the family. Meanwhile, parents, despite the occasional imbalances created in the nuclear neurotic condition as a result of treatment, begin to respond with more wholesome adaptations to their child. This often spares them from constant preoccupation with the child and they begin to treat him in better ways. Leon became better able to cope with his parents despite the continuing strains put upon him by their severe pathology.

CHAPTER 8

Cooperative Therapy of Mother and Child—Leon

S.R. SLAVSON

THE CASE OF LEON is presented *in extenso*. Particular attention is drawn to this case for several reasons. Leon was in treatment at a family agency for a considerable length of time, as was his mother. The boy presented a difficult personality problem, compounded by below-normal intelligence. He was in combined treatment, individual play therapy and activity group therapy; his mother was seen on a regular basis by a psychiatric social worker. Much integrative work was necessary in coordinating the treatment of the boy and his mother. After termination of treatment, follow-up contacts were maintained for more than one year with both patients to determine their adjustments. Of interest is the fact that, despite the boy's low intelligence, he was doing acceptably in high school.

The case records show the involvement of orthopsychiatric clinical procedures in a community agency. The material is presented historically, documented from the records of the psychiatric caseworker, group therapists, two psychological assessments, and psychiatric conferences, including periodic evaluation conferences and a terminal report. Complete group protocols are not included, but synoptic reports from the group therapists comprise a major part of the documentation, which provides a progressive

Note: I am indebted to the late S. R. Slavson, who consented to the inclusion of this case study in edited form. It is taken from his unpublished manuscript entitled "Activity Group Therapy: Five Case Histories"—*M.S.*

picture of the boy's treatment. While Leon was seen by two social workers in turn during the period of treatment, he tended to resist their analytical efforts. He would speak mainly of single, overt episodes that had occurred in his activity therapy group and of superficial concerns in his daily life. He constantly defended against examining the underlying motives of his behavior. However, individual treatment was supportive in that both social workers were able to protect him from the seductive, demanding manipulations of his mother. The changes that took place in Leon's character structure and in his adjustment can be traced to a strengthened ego and improved self-image, which resulted from intensive treatment in activity group therapy, supported by interventions through individual treatment.

Referral Summary for Group Therapy

PROBLEM AND PERSONALITY

Leon was an only child, age ten, who was referred to the agency by his mother because of negativism toward her. He was unruly, stole from his mother, and took pleasure in pitting the parents against each other. He did not get along with other children, partly because his mother limited his contacts out of overprotectiveness. He showed excessive concern with cleanliness and social punctiliousness and was anxious about dirtying himself or destroying objects. He was fearful of the dark, of being alone, and of dying through illness or drowning. Leon had been dominated and infantilized by his mother, who still bathed and dressed him, over his objections. He had always shared the parental bedroom, on occasion sleeping with his mother. Leon suffered from bronchial asthma from the age of six months to five years, during which time he received much attention. He had not had attacks in recent years.

PHYSICAL DESCRIPTION

Leon was a short, plump boy with a round face and high-pitched voice; he lisped slightly. His speech and manner had an air of effeminacy. There was a feminine distribution of fat on his buttocks, chest, and arms. He tended to overeat, showing tremendous interest in sweets, and had some food aversions—especially dislike of vegetables—in which he had been indulged by his mother. Leon conformed to his mother's demands for cleanliness and neatness. There were indications that when Leon was away from home he was sometimes less careful about his personal care, partly because his mother was not present to assist him and partly out of rebellion against her.

FAMILY BACKGROUND

This boy was part of a neurotic family constellation. He was the only child of a couple married late in life. Mrs. S. was a stout woman with no life outside of her son and household. On the surface she was aggressive and demanding, and, despite a rather limited intelligence, she had considerable ambition. She had attempted to fulfill her interest in schooling and her desire for social conformance through Leon. Her handling of the boy was inconsistent, almost seductive. She fondled him at times and was also punitive with him, at times, threatening to place him out of the home. She spoke of her own nervousness, and she was now at a point where she saw herself as being in rivalry with Leon for both material comforts and the relationship with the social worker.

Leon's father was a passive man, employed as a taxicab driver for over twenty years at a limited salary. He indulged Leon's desire to be left in peace. Leon acknowledged that his father was his favorite parent. The parents constantly quarreled about methods of handling Leon, and the boy provoked these arguments out of a need for attention, even if only in a destructive way. There existed much financial strain, with Mrs. S. feeling keenly the responsibility of managing on a marginal income.

SCHOOL ADJUSTMENT

Leon was in the fifth grade. Mrs. S. had always emphasized school achievement and had been dissatisfied with Leon's progress from the beginning. Although Leon conformed in behavior at school, he was beginning to show inattention and spoke openly about disliking school. Recently he had been switched to a special class for "slow learners." It was unclear at this time whether his retardation in learning was due to limited intelligence alone, or whether it was another aspect of rebellion against his mother.

ADJUSTMENT TO OTHER CHILDREN

Until the past summer, Leon had had no real friends and preferred playing with girls. Other children called him "sissy" and "Mary." Although this effeminate trend in relating to other children was still evident at the time of referral, Leon was beginning to play with other boys and was engaging in some superficial aggressive activities. When he was with other children, Leon tried to dominate them and provoked fights. Actually, he preferred to play with dolls and with other objects that helped him to vent aggression. He was careful to conceal such feelings from observers.

ADJUSTMENT TO ADULTS AND AUTHORITY

Leon was ingratiating, polite, and overanxious in trying to please adults. His underlying fear of adults was evident from this behavior. In his relationship with the caseworker, he had several times given evidence of a "peeping" tendency. He listened once at the partially opened door of her office to a conversation between her and another client. He was very protective and defensive of himself and projected blame on others for the problems that beset him.

ADJUSTMENT TO CAMP

The coming summer was scheduled to be Leon's first trip away from home for a lengthy period of time. He had considerable ambivalence and fear about the coming separation experience. Only after some pressure from his mother did he agree to attend camp for one month. It was expected that he would probably suffer from homesickness.

REASON FOR THE REFERRAL FOR ACTIVITY GROUP THERAPY

This boy had been subject to maternal protection and domination for too long. In casework treatment, he had recently given some evidence of rebelliousness and of dissatisfaction with his submissive relationship to his mother. The mother, also, had recently indicated a desire for a change in her relationship with her son. It was felt that a stay in summer camp might give both Leon and his mother an opportunity to concretize their present attitudes and, especially, would provide Leon with an opportunity to share the freer social atmosphere with peers. After a camp experience, it was considered that participation in activity group therapy would further capitalize on the boy's basic need for autonomous growth, would help him strengthen his ego capacities, and would foster a better self-concept. This might lead to a healthier sexual identity and to behavioral patterns capable of ensuring continuing social status. Finally, it was felt that a substantive relationship with a "model" male figure, in the person of a group therapist, would also assist Leon in forming a healthier identity.

Progress Report, Activity Group Therapy, January 19, 1965

Background. See referral summary.
Attendance. Leon attended the first session of the group on October 19 and had not missed a session since then. He was always half an hour late because of his attendance at Hebrew school.

Physical description. See referral summary.

Personal Appearance. The boy was generally neat and clean in appearance. He showed anxiety when some other group members spilled paint on his cap, saying that his mother would "kill him." Except during the first session, Leon did not as a rule wash his hands before the refreshments. He had recently been observed playing with paint, which is of interest in view of his excessive concern for cleanliness. Leon's physical movements had a feminine quality. It was learned that during his stay in summer camp, some of the campers used to call him "Mama S."

Food. Leon showed no special anxiety with respect to food. He was always interested in knowing what had been purchased for the refreshment period. His eating habits were acceptable as compared to those of some of the other boys. He always helped in preparing the table and liked to serve the other boys.

Cooperation. Leon voluntarily helped the worker in cleaning up the room and preparing for refreshments. He did this more often than the other boys. Leon was also very willing to help others, and he was the first to respond when a boy suggested playing a game. He participated in group discussions, abiding readily with the decision of the majority. At times his suggestions were accepted by the group.

Attitude toward materials. Leon had so far shown no interest in any activity except painting. While at first he was dependent on the worker, Leon had become able to work by himself. He spent a lot of time walking around the room, searching through the supply cabinet, and preparing refreshments. He was definitely not handy with materials and tools and showed little imagination.

Attitude toward new group members. Leon was friendly and talkative with new members. He did not participate when some of the boys attacked new members who were added shortly after the group was initiated.

Attitude toward fellow members. Upon arriving at his first meeting, Leon asked the worker whether David D. was a member of the "club."[1] He complained that David had annoyed him in camp during the past summer. Despite this beginning, Leon subsequently showed real fondness for David. When Charles, the strongest boy in the group, attacked David, Leon took the latter's part, threatening that he would not come to meetings if Charles continued to fight with David. David, on the other hand, delighted in teasing Leon by calling him "Mama S.," which Leon took good-naturedly.

Leon was in the habit of working alone most of the time. He had, however, talked to most of the boys in the group. Whenever there was the slightest sign of a fight among the boys, he withdrew. During the third meeting,

---

[1]In activity group therapy, the group is introduced to beginning participants and new additions as a "club," the purpose being to avoid a clinical connotation. The aim is to relax the children, which would not occur if the therapeutic intent of the method were to be emphasized. This practice, which is necessary with purely activity methods of treatment, is not used in the analytical group procedures. —*M.S.*

Leon offered to trade card pictures with each of the others, apparently trying to ingratiate himself with them. While at first he was submissive with the other boys, Leon began to stand up for his rights during the past several meetings. When David took a piece of carbon paper away from Leon, the latter went over and pulled it out of his hand. In general, when attacked by another boy, Leon made an attempt to fight back but, when not successful, he whined to the worker for help. During a trip to the movies, Leon hit David and Herbert with an umbrella when they made noise. In the course of a tussle, Leon once threw Harold, the weakest group member, on the floor, but he felt apologetic about it later. Leon was accepted by most of the boys despite the fact that they called him "Mama S.," in a good-natured way.

Attitude toward the group worker. When Leon came to the first meeting, he greeted the worker warmly. He knew the worker from camp. Leon said that when he received the invitation letter to the "club," he never dreamed that the worker would be "the leader" of the "club." Leon was clearly attached to the worker. He was very anxious for approval, and he showed the worker every little thing he did. He once broke the electric jigsaw in attempting to use it experimentally and seemed afraid, apparently expecting to be yelled at. Leon repeatedly tried to sit next to the worker during refreshments. He also made sure to walk next to the worker on the street when the group went outside. He was in rivalry with Charles in this respect. Beginning with the third meeting, Leon took various materials home. Most times he said he "needed it for school." More recently he was in the habit of taking colored paper sheets without asking the worker's permission to do so. When the others left after refreshments, Leon invariably stayed behind waiting for the worker to leave. He asked the worker the same questions over and over. When some of the others remarked about his constantly "bothering" the worker with questions, Leon told them, "It's none of your business!"

Attitude toward school. During the seventh meeting, Leon showed off his report card from Hebrew school to some of the boys and to the worker. He had only one "C"—for conduct. He also mentioned that his public school teacher had told him that she wanted to "kiss" him for all the gifts he had brought to school that he had made in the group.

Attitude toward family and home. Leon was accompanied to the first group meeting by his mother, who asked him anxiously if he would know how to get home by himself. Leon seemed resentful and annoyed and acted as if he wanted his mother to leave the room as soon as possible. Before leaving, she reminded him to be "a good boy."[2]

---

[2]It is to avoid just such embarrassing incidents for group members that the usual practice in activity group therapy is for the worker to prevent parents from entering treatment rooms. As sensitively as possible, parents need to be constrained from doing so. If persistent in their attempts, they should be given a few moments with the worker *outside* the entrance door. Another reason for this practice is to avoid the children's associating the permissive worker with their parents. —*M.S.*

Language and speech. As noted earlier, Leon had a high-pitched voice and spoke with a slight lisp. He whined and complained frequently, especially when he was attacked by a group member.

Special abilities and disabilities. It is of interest to note that on a trip to the movies Leon seemed frightened during exciting episodes. He covered his eyes with his hands when someone was being shot. He also showed discomfort whenever there was much noise in the meeting room due to hammering. Recently Leon had shown much interest in fire play.

Evaluation. Leon was an infantile, fearful, overprotected boy. He related to the worker on a childish, dependency level. There were already signs of increasing assertiveness in the boy, in his relations to both the worker and the other boys. His practice of taking materials home without asking consent might be one way he was testing his strength in defying adults. Leon's recent assertiveness was an indication of growth, since at first he tended to be submissive and overly dependent on the worker. His extraordinary interest in fire play was probably associated with a conflict in relation to some aspect of sexuality. It needed to be watched in the future.

Integration Conference,[3] March 1, 1965

The caseworker, group worker, and director of group therapy were present. For description of the presenting problem, see referral summary.

The caseworker had been treating Mrs. S. intensively. She also was seeing Leon on a regular basis.[4] Mrs. S. had made an excellent transference. (This had been her first experience in treatment.) She informed the caseworker that she envied Leon's being in a group and would like to join one herself. The caseworker reported that Leon was very fearful, and she just played games with him without attempting to involve him analytically. At one time during November, Leon said that he did not want to come every week. The caseworker noted at that time that Leon was getting much satisfaction from his participation in group therapy. He spoke to her about what was happening in the group and also mentioned David, whom he was fond of. He described the general pattern of group activities and at one time complained about the fighting that was going on.

Leon told the caseworker that he had a book in which he kept a record of the marks of every child in his class. Once when he walked into her of-

---

[3]Integration conferences are conducted at regular intervals for the following purposes: to evaluate the current treatment situation in relation to the presenting problems and the initial diagnoses and treatment plans; to further illuminate the meanings of clients' behavior; to integrate information obtained from several sources—in this case, from the psychiatric caseworker who was treating the mother and boy separately, and from the group worker; and to decide, on the basis of the information submitted, the future course of treatment. —*M.S.*

[4]A pertinent question is whether it was advisable to have had both patients in individual treatment with the same therapist rather than with different ones. —*M.S.*

fice, he brought a window pole in with him, which was ordinarily kept in the hall corridor—this without asking. At one session he had a piece of tape that he kept snapping directly toward the caseworker. Also, he skipped all around in her office. Leon always carried a packet of matches. He liked to control the interviews and enjoyed winning competitive games with the caseworker.

The group worker reported that Leon had attended sixteen out of nineteen group sessions. Leon was frightened, infantile, and effeminate when he started. The time the boys spilled paint on him he became very anxious, but now he spent a good deal of time painting. He used brown, red and a little bit of black paint. Presently he displayed no anxiety about dirtying himself. Earlier the boys had called him "Mama S.," but now they no longer did so. Leon still had a habit of taking materials home. Once he took a packet of materials with him without asking the worker for permission. He brought it to his teacher in school in order to ingratiate himself. At one time Leon used to isolate himself in a corner of the room, but he now participated and ran after the other boys. He "invented" smoking, making cigarettes out of the basket-weaving material. He took pride in this even though he acted as if the "smoke" tasted awful. Sometimes he walked about the room carrying a lighted candle. When Leon first came to the therapy group, he limited his activity to tracing pictures. Now he spent much time playing with fire and painting.[5]

RECOMMENDATIONS

1. Leon needs as many interactions with males as possible, particularly those of a nonthreatening nature. Fire play should be tolerated to help him work through unconscious feelings associated with it.
2. Continue him in activity group therapy.
3. Encourage and support all his masculine endeavors.
4. Encourage particularly his attempts to work independently, without appealing to the worker.
5. The composition of the therapy group should be monitored to ensure that the other boys are not overly threatening to Leon.

Progress Report, Activity Group Therapy, May 4, 1965

Out of the twenty group sessions covered in this report, Leon attended seventeen; two of the absences were caused by illnesses. At first, he used to

[5]Almost inevitably, emotionally disturbed children reveal ambivalent emotions with respect to fire. In activity group therapy, provision is made for them to experience fire play safely. A large board made of fire-resistant asbestos is available, in addition to a coil heating hot plate.

come late because of his attendance at Hebrew school, but recently he had arrived at the meeting room before the regular meeting time. Although he was still neat and clean in his personal appearance, Leon was not as anxious as he used to be when he got paint on his clothing. He showed no special concern for personal cleanliness in the group. There was a change in regard to Leon's effeminate mannerisms. The boys apparently sensed this change in him and no longer called him "Mama S.," as they used to do both at camp and during the early group meetings.

Leon continued to show an interest in food and, in line with his generally increased assertiveness, had on a number of occasions taken the initiative by asking the worker to buy frankfurters. His interest in cooking the food for the other boys continued. Recently he had begun to prepare cocoa on the electric hot plate for himself when the other boys indicated that they preferred milk. He was frequently instrumental in restraining the others from grabbing food in a disorderly way.

Although he still remained behind with the worker after the others had departed, Leon no longer helped to clean up the meeting room or the table. He continued to help other boys with their projects upon request. He was at the same time adamant in his refusal to do so when there was something else he wanted to do by himself. From being a follower, Leon had assumed a leadership quality in relation to the other boys. He showed lively interest in the group discussions, trying to persuade the other boys to accept his suggestions. He was often successful.

Leon's proficiency with crafts materials had also undergone marked change. While he used to do nothing except draw, he had now begun to paint wood objects that he had crafted. He still spent much time in fire play. He also drilled holes in wood with a brace and bit. He imitated some others in making a "policeman's club," for which he needed some help from the worker. Very recently, he used the jigsaw (which he had once broken because of ineptitude) and a hand saw in fabricating a wooden gun. For this latter project, he did not require any assistance from the worker. This is of particular significance, since during his earlier meetings he seemed to be fearful of using tools and especially the jigsaw because of its noise.

Leon quite openly showed resentment of guests brought to group meetings by other boys. At one time he went so far as to say to one guest, "You don't belong here." However, when Norman, a new group member, attended his first meeting, Leon was very friendly. Norman loaned Leon a pair of binoculars that he had brought with him. Leon was no longer isolated from the other boys. Quite to the contrary, he mingled freely, and he

---

These items are there for the worker and children to prepare cooked food for refreshments, but children also soon learn to use them in making fires. Anxiety, fear, hostility, and other feelings become decathected when there is freedom to experience fire play in the permissive climate of a therapy group. See also the film *Activity Group Therapy*, distributed by Film Library, New York University, Washington Square, New York, New York. —*M.S.*

was quite assertive with them, especially when they provoked him in any way. When the boys tried to stop him from playing with fire or from taking things home, Leon told them to "mind their own business." On occasion, Leon even assumed the role of instigator, encouraging the boys to engage in horseplay or inciting them to play tricks on a particular boy. Although he was still fearful of actual fighting, he no longer withdrew at any sign of aggressiveness by others. Leon's attachment to David, which was probably related to a secret admiration of the latter's masculine qualities, continued. At the same time, however, Leon had revealed some feelings of hostility in regard to David. He once joined another boy against him, and also went so far as to actually throw a heavy candle and paint at David when the latter provoked him.

As mentioned previously, the boys had recognized marked changes in Leon. They now respected him as a group member and, at times, even as a leader of the group. This change of attitude was clearly expressed on one occasion, when David kiddingly called Leon "Mama S." but at the latter's resentment with this remark, changed it to "Papa S."

Leon's ambivalent reactions to the presence of occasional guest visitors is an indication of continuing "sibling" rivalry, even though he was showing increased independence in his relationship with the worker.[6]

Leon was still attached to the worker, but not as much as heretofore. He admired the worker. At the same time, however, there were numerous occasions wherein Leon directly expressed a desire to prove more powerful than the worker. The worker permitted this, without retaliation. Leon was obviously pleased at such times. As mentioned previously, Leon no longer continued the habitual pattern of helping the worker to clean the room. Formerly this was due to his need to ingratiate himself. When he learned that this was not necessary to maintain the worker's attention, he was able to relinquish much of the pattern. Leon was still in the habit of remaining behind after the other boys had left. He also offered to carry packages for

[6]Guests are permitted at group sessions. While this is allowed, it is necessary to study its implications, particularly as they affect the interactions between regular group members. Group members invite friends to attend with them for various reasons: sometimes it is because a child feels threatened in the group, and he gains security in the company of an "outside" friend; in other cases, the motivation is to demonstrate to a friend the social status he has achieved in a "club," and thus hopes to reinforce his image in the eyes of the friend. In every instance, the worker has to determine the reasons for invitations to friends. The presence of a guest is bound to trigger some rivalry in the group members, and an "epidemic" of guest visitors may follow as the members rival with one another for the right to bring friends. If it appears that the group is unable to resolve this competitive interplay, and it threatens to continue, possibly interfering with the group's dynamics, the worker intervenes. He arranges for a letter to be delivered while a group is in session. This letter is from the agency's office, requesting the worker to read it to his or her group. It calls the group's attention to the fact that the presence of friends is getting too costly and the group is "exceeding its budget" for supplies, food, and excursions. This form of outside intervention takes the onus of prohibition from the worker. More importantly, it always serves to terminate a situation that the group has been unable to manage by itself, a situation that it no longer finds acceptable. —M.S.

the worker; open doors for him, and so on. He was rivalrous with the other boys on occasion, but this is not atypical in such a group. Before the beginning of each session, Leon asked the worker to hold his carfare. He continued to take colored paper home and also asked for such things as airplane pictures and small pieces of other items. On one occasion he borrowed a coping saw and a small game to take home, but he returned these items at the subsequent meeting.

Since about the tenth group session Leon had shown an intense interest in fire. He began by lighting a candle that he had brought with him, carrying it about the room wherever he worked. Subsequently, he initiated smoking of reed, which the others joined him in doing. Following this, he began burning pieces of paper and wood on the large asbestos board. At times he would carry a burning piece of wood aloft, saying, "I am the Statue of Liberty." Once he held two hollow amber rods at the faucet and let water pour through them, which strongly suggested the act of urination. The time he spent in fire play gradually diminished and, during the last two meetings, he did not play with fire at all, spending most of the time working with tools and lumber.

Leon continued the remarkable growth already indicated in the earlier progress reports. From being originally an infantile, fearful, and castrated youngster, he was assuming more and more a masculine identity. He had become assertive, in relationship to both the worker and the other boys. Through expressing repressed aggression and through repeated tests of his newly discovered strength in the group, he had gained feelings of increased security and potency.

Integration Conference, June 28, 1965

The caseworker and group worker were present. For a statement of the boy's problem, see the referral summary and the report on the last integration conference.

The caseworker reported that Mr. S. took over the mother's role in this family. He apparently did all the house cleaning and washing. According to Leon, the mother spent most of her time talking to the neighbors. She was an aggressive, castrating person. The caseworker expressed the feeling that the group worker, besides being a masculine symbol, also represented maternal aspects for Leon, because his own father served as a mother figure.[7] When Leon spoke of the group, he mentioned how much he enjoyed the food. He also talked about the worker, mentioning to the caseworker that he was planning to get a gift for him. (It is of interest that while Leon spoke

---

[7]This is a questionable interpretation. The group worker in no manner replicated the ambivalent behavior of the father, rather, the worker tended to *reinforce* masculine identity.

to his caseworker of wanting to get silk stockings for the group worker, he actually brought him a summer tie.) In line with the boy's thinking about adult roles, the female caseworker unconsciously assumed masculine imagery for Leon. At times he called her "brother."

Leon kept his appointments with the caseworker. While he was still guarded, he now asserted himself more and behaved more freely in the casework therapy. In sum, he was demonstrating with the caseworker some of the changes reported in the therapy group. There seemed to be homosexual features present in the boy. He was still confused as to where he stood in regard to the sexes. He complained to the caseworker about his mother. From Leon's remarks, it appeared that the father was compulsive and rigid.

Mrs. S. had also been keeping her appointments and had made progress. Despite her limited intelligence, she related easily to the caseworker, in a passive way. She had a weak and inadequate father. As a result of treatment, she had recently become more interested in her personal appearance. She manicured her nails and arranged for a permanent wave. Recently she spoke of trying to lose weight. Mr. S. had been very much attached to his own mother, who had died recently. Mrs. S. felt that she was instrumental in breaking this bond and in taking him away from his (her?) mother. She told the caseworker that prior to her mother-in-law's death, her husband used to visit her "like clockwork."

Mrs. S. seemed to be completely identified with Leon, with whom she was also in a sibling-rivalry situation. On the one hand, she felt compelled to give him things; on the other, she felt sorry that she had to give in to him, because she was jealous of him. She also was envious of Leon's attendance in a group. However, her attitude had changed somewhat and she was giving the boy more freedom. She reported that he was now beginning to bathe himself, showed more freedom in his relationships with other children, and played, as well as fought, with boys his own age. He played ball on the street and came home "filthy like a pig." She did not get upset over this anymore. However, when during the recent physical examination of Leon for camp, the doctor discovered athlete's foot, she felt guilty once again and depressed, and she regressed in her handling of Leon. She began to bathe him again. However, once more she stopped this, following a discussion with the caseworker.

It was felt that the most important gain Leon had obtained from the group was his identification with the worker as a masculine father figure, as opposed to his own father, who played the role of a mother in the home. Leon had been helped to express his repressed feelings of aggression, and the free atmosphere in the group had enabled him to relax his excessive concern for cleanliness. The boy's behavior was becoming more typical of that of youngsters his age, and he had been able to give up his need to ingratiate himself with adults.

RÉCOMMENDATIONS

It was recommended that

1. Leon continue in activity group therapy.
2. A treatment conference was planned to discuss the advisability of having separate caseworkers for Leon and his mother.
3. The caseworker was planning to refer Mrs. S. to a mothers' group.

Memorandum, June 11, 1965

The caseworker phoned the group worker to say that Mrs. S. had not been in to see her for a few weeks because of illness. She was suffering from hypertension; she felt that she had a heart disease and was afraid she would die. Leon had mentioned recently to the caseworker that he might not continue coming to the "club" and seeing the caseworker. The reasons for this remark were not clear. There was a possibility that it had something to do with Leon's strong fear that his mother might die, particularly since the maternal grandmother was very close to death following a heart attack.

Leon had been behaving in group treatment much the way he did at the end of last season. The only difficulty was that he now came more than an hour late to meetings because he attended Hebrew school in the afternoons.

It was planned to maintain close touch on these matters while the caseworker would try to work through with Leon any fears he had with respect to his mother's illness.

Memorandum, November 26, 1965

The caseworker phoned that she finally was able to make a home visit to see Mrs. S., who had been ill. She reported that a great deal of pressure was being placed on Leon to continue attending Hebrew school, which interfered with his attending the group. He was being placed in a position of either having to absent himself from Hebrew school or not come to the therapy group. He found it more difficult to make a choice now because of his guilt feelings about his mother's illness and his fear that she might die. The caseworker raised the question with Leon's father, and the latter promised to take up with his wife the matter of excusing Leon from Hebrew school one day a week.

Memorandum, December 20, 1965

The group's meeting time was changed to Fridays, so that Leon was no longer involved in conflict with attending Hebrew school. The caseworker reported that Leon had expressed delight with the change. Mrs. S. tried to prevent Leon from attending the group at its new meeting place because it was farther away from their home. But Leon put up a strong fight with her, forcing the mother to let him attend. This is of particular significance because Leon had never been able to stand up against his mother so forcibly in the past. Leon also mentioned to the caseworker that he was happy about the new meeting place because he would now have a chance to travel on the subway with the worker. He knew that the worker usually traveled downtown by subway.

Progress Report, Activity Group Therapy, January 21, 1966

Leon attended ten group meetings out of the last twelve. The absences were due to illnesses, Leon's and his mother's. As noted earlier, until the group moved to its new meeting room, Leon came late because of the conflict with Hebrew school. Once the meeting day was changed to Friday, Leon was always on time. He came to each meeting neat and clean. However, now he did not give any indication of worrying about cleanliness and neatness, as in the past. Quite to the contrary, he did not wash his hands before refreshments when other boys did so.

There was further change in Leon's effeminate mannerisms. His interests had become more typically boyish and he acted more like a boy, assertive and at times even aggressive. He also seemed to be less motivated to prepare food for the group, although he still occasionally did so. He brought a pen knife to one meeting and played with it, throwing it on the floor. Though in the past Leon had shown obvious fear in reaction to openly displayed aggressiveness by the other boys, he now watched a fight with Charles and his friend with obvious enjoyment and without anxiety. Leon played an aggressive game of "hockey" with Charles, using a wooden bowl as a puck. At one meeting Leon got into a "fencing fight" with sticks as swords. Once Bernard threw Leon's cap on the floor, which threw Leon into a rage. He began to hit Bernard, who became frightened and gave in to Leon. Since that time Bernard had been avoiding Leon, or giving in to him. This was the first time the worker had observed Leon engaged in an actual fight with anyone. While a bit anxious about fighting, Leon seemed on the whole very pleased and reassured by the result.

Leon had established a rather close relationship with Ivor, a new member, who was also a fairly frightened boy. Leon's earlier attachment to Charles, the strongest member of the group, continued, and when Charles failed to attend sessions at the group's new meeting room, Leon repeatedly asked the worker about him. Leon continued to be outspoken and assertive in the group. He occasionally assumed a leadership role and was one of the more influential members when discussions about trips and refreshments took place. Only recently, some of the boys asked Leon to show them how to make a lanyard; it seems he was expert in this fabrication, having learned how to do it at camp. When the boys began pleading with Leon to make lanyards for them, his attitude was very independent, and he played "hard to get." In contrast to his earlier tendency to draw or paint, he now worked a lot with wood and leather. Leon also liked to play games and had been recently observed initiating much horseplay and hilarity, especially when playing "cops and robbers." Obviously the boys had detected changes in Leon and now respected him. Some of the weaker ones were actually afraid of Leon.

In general, Leon's relationship to the worker continued along the lines described in the previous progress report and in the integration conference. Although he remained physically close to the worker during meetings, there was a definite lessening of dependence on the worker, and Leon was able indirectly to express hostility toward him. Leon continued to take materials home, but not as often as heretofore. Leon now took the initiative in requesting that the group go on excursions and also asked for special foods for refreshments.

Leon's interest in fire had lessened, although he still indulged in fire play occasionally. On a trip to the movies, the worker observed Leon covering his eyes during a cruel scene in which a man was thrown to wild animals. This was similar to the incident that had occurred when the group went to a movie another time. Leon appeared to be afraid to walk by himself in the neighborhood where the new meeting room was located. On one occasion Leon intimidated several other group members, making them promise to walk him to the bus. The boys did not seem to comprehend the real reason for this, namely Leon's anxiety about walking alone in the dark.

Leon continued to derive a great deal from the group therapy experience. In particular, his ego strength had grown, and he was able to express hostility freely without fear of retaliation from others. His identifications with the worker and the boys had reinforced masculine traits in him. The group was extremely meaningful to this youngster.

Integration Conference, March 20, 1966

The caseworker and group worker were present. For a statement of Leon's problem, see the referral summary and earlier integration conference reports.

At the last psychiatric conference and evaluation, Dr. H. diagnosed Leon's problem as a psychoneurosis. He felt that the behavior disorders had lessened as a result of casework and group treatment. The aggressiveness shown by Leon in the group could be considered a defense against his passive, homosexual wishes toward the group worker.

The caseworker reported that both Leon and his mother had been seen regularly since the summer, until the month of February. Leon was beginning to talk more about his feelings and, at one point, his attitude toward sex differences was taken up. He seemed very anxious during this discussion. Subsequent to this, Leon's mother and grandmother became ill, and for a while the boy did not attend group meetings because of anxiety over his mother's illness and a fear that she would die. In addition, the parents were keeping him from going to the group because of Hebrew school. (For details, see the memoranda of November 26 and December 20.) After his mother had become ill, Leon talked more freely to the caseworker. He expressed desires for independence from his mother and wanted to be free to do things for himself, such as combing his hair and washing himself. He would also write compulsively during some of his interview sessions, which the caseworker felt was an identification with his mother, who put a great deal of emphasis on her handwriting ability. When the mother went to the hospital for two weeks, Leon and his father remained in the home most of the time. On New Year's eve, the mother went to a party with several women while the father remained at home. Mr. S. once threatened Leon that he would report him to the caseworker if he was "bad."

In February, Leon broke several appointments with the caseworker. When he returned, the matter of resistance was taken up with him, but he nevertheless failed to keep several appointment after that. The mother was not seen by the caseworker during this period of time. The caseworker felt that the mother's failure to keep appointments was related to her last home visit, when Mr. S. had followed the caseworker out of the apartment to talk to her alone. This may have made Mrs. S. angry and suspicious.

Earlier in treatment, Mrs. S. spoke of her own fears in relation to her mother's illness. When she complained to the caseworker of various aches, the latter suggested that a medical examination was in order. Mrs. S. actually became sick soon after a medical examination, and she blamed the caseworker for this. Her accusations had a distinct paranoid quality.

The caseworker was about to leave the agency and planned to transfer the case to another caseworker. Neither Leon nor his mother knew of this at the moment.

The group worker reported marked improvement in all areas. Leon had become assertive and often even aggressive, both verbally and physically. On one occasion Leon had a fight with Bernard, with Leon winning. (For details, see the progress report dated January 21.)

RECOMMENDATIONS

It was recommended that

1. Leon continue in activity group therapy.
2. The caseworker planned to schedule another psychiatric conference

to determine further treatment plans and discuss the transfer of Leon and his mother to another caseworker.

Psychiatric Conference, April 5, 1966

This psychiatric conference was called to determine future treatment plans, in view of the need to transfer the clients to another person. The psychiatrist, caseworker, casework supervisor, new caseworker, and group worker were present.

Dr. H. stated that Leon seemed to have developed resistance to individual treatment after the subject of his confused sexual identifications was brought up in one of the interviews. At that time, the youngster also talked about his fear of death, which seemed tied up with his mother's current illness. As noted earlier, he missed several sessions with the caseworker following this but subsequently returned.

The caseworker gave details of Mrs. S.'s illness. She seemed unable to walk, and the hospital was not able to establish the cause for this, stating only that it was probably due to "nervous factors." Dr. H. thought that the diagnosis might be Astasia-abasia, adding that a more detailed report should be obtained from the hospital. It was thought that in her illness Mrs. S. was unconsciously identifying with her own mother, who had been very ill recently. The mother also got satisfaction from her husband's having to wait on her while she was ill. Dr. H. stated that she seemed to be more disturbed than was originally thought. In addition to depression, there may have been phobic mechanisms present due to a basic fear of death. Leon's psychoneurosis appeared to be of the same nature, reflecting the boy's unconscious identification with his mother. In view of the mother's illness, it was thought that the agency might have to refer her to the hospital's psychiatric services should it be necessary for her to remain hospitalized for a considerable time. Even though this might transpire, it was considered essential that Leon's present treatment program—both individual and group therapy—be maintained.

In October, Leon had told the caseworker about wanting his own room at home, but his mother still had not arranged it. Dr. H. felt that this request was related to a reactivation of Leon's sexual conflicts due to pre-pubertal factors. The problems related to sexuality seemed to have become more upsetting recently. Leon was conflicted about sexual identity and unsure about his masculine role. His group experience had been of great importance in that it had given him a sense of the advantages of acting like a boy. Nevertheless, his anxieties were still strong because of his identification with the mother. Because of the partially homosexual relationship with the father, Leon unconsciously sought to be taken care of by him. Dr. H. felt that Leon's identifications with his parents were too fluid. One interpretation of the effect upon Leon of the caseworker's visit to the mother during her illness was that the caseworker was behaving the same way toward Leon's mother that his father did—"waiting on" her. This created anxiety in Leon because of his unconscious fear that the caseworker might also "wait on" him. This dynamic could have accounted for the boy's recent resistance.

In general, the mother was a castrating person, while the father was effeminate and passive. On the one hand, Leon had been identifying with his effeminate father. Opposed to this, in group treatment, there was an increasing tendency for the boy to also identify with the masculine "father" substitute, which had resulted in considerable strengthening of the boy's masculinity. It was felt that Leon's increasing anxiety due to the onset of puberty would have to be dealt with in individual therapy. Dr. H. indicated that in the two years of contacts with the agency this was the first time that Leon's neurotic symptoms had become so exposed. He felt that the manner in which Leon behaved and related to his caseworker and the group worker was of much interest and an example of how the *two forms of treatment could be integrated in helping a neurotic child.* Leon talked frequently in his group about the caseworker, having recently mentioned in an upset manner that "he was getting a new social worker."

When the therapy group began to meet on Friday afternoons, which was also the time for Leon's casework interviews, Leon refused to change his appointment with the caseworker to another day. Consequently, he came directly to the group meeting after seeing his caseworker. Dr. H. commented that at this time, when Leon was being transferred to a new caseworker, his membership in the therapy group and the support he received there would assist him in accepting the transfer. Moreover, the group continually reassured Leon about his sexual identity.

Progress Report, Activity Group Therapy, May 27, 1966

This report covers the period of from January 21, the date of the last progress report, until the end of May. During this time Leon attended eleven meetings out of sixteen. Five absences occurred starting in April. They seemed to coincide with the time when Leon announced that he became a member of the Police Athletic League. When Leon was asked by a group member about one of his absences, he explained that he had gone bike riding that day and had not had any carfare left to come to the group.

Leon's lack of concern for order and cleanliness, indicated in the last report, continued. Even when some of the other boys urged him to go to the bathroom and wash his hands prior to refreshments, he refused unless his hands were very dirty. Leon's relationships in the group were characterized by spontaneity, freedom, and assertiveness. Not only was he able to stand up for his rights, but he also had repeatedly been an instigator, and he tried to dominate some of the weaker boys. While Leon had in the past spent most of his time working with various crafts materials or playing games, he now concentrated on his relationships with the others. He was liked and accepted by all. He appeared to have lost all his former effeminate mannerisms. After he showed his new PAL membership button to the group, Bernard and Herbert also joined the PAL, displaying their buttons at a subsequent meeting.

Although Leon continued to like Charles, he had recently developed a closer relationship with Irving, a relatively new group member, than with Charles. This may have been because Charles had not attended group meetings for about three months. During the last group trip, which Charles did attend, Leon suggested to him that they go to a museum some day, perhaps on a Sunday. Charles agreed to this and wrote down Leon's home address. Leon's friendship with Irving had helped relax the latter boy, making it easier for him to become accepted in the group. Leon and Irving usually talked about summer camp or school.

Leon was frequently responsible for initiating games such as checkers and puzzle games. Occasionally he urged others to accompany him elsewhere in the settlement house where the therapy group has its meeting room to watch a girls' dancing class in the auditorium. While Leon spent most of his time in the group playing games with others or talking to them, he also fabricated projects with various materials. He no longer spent time painting or drawing, as had been the case when he started. He had recently made lanyards, amber rings, and objects from lumber. He got much recognition from the group because of his proficiency in crafts work.

In keeping with the increased freedom that Leon displayed in relationships with the other boys, his dependence on the worker had decreased significantly. While he still showed his attachment to the worker, he did not spend much time with him. He no longer sought to ingratiate himself with the worker as in the past. Moreover, he had no need to do group chores, which is something that had typified his behavior in early meetings. Occasionally he gave evidences of vying with the worker to prove his superiority. This was particularly clear during a checkers game. Leon was very careful and anxious with every move he made, lest he lose the game. He seemed relieved and satisfied when he won.[8]

Leon's intense interest in food had subsided. He no longer asked for second helpings of cake, although the other boys still did so. As mentioned

---

[8]This is an example of the need for a worker to be sensitive to a child's motivation—and basic needs—in a game situation. In this instance, the worker ensured Leon's winning by careful manipulations. The worker was well aware of the important meanings associated with Leon's being able to challenge the psychologically formidable masculine object that the worker represented. Leon's anxiety during the checkers game was a reflection of his fear of the potent, masculine adult—the object that symbolized his inner conflict over sexuality and identity. For Leon this checkers game represented a *critical event* in treatment. —*M.S.*

in the last progress report, Leon spoke occasionally about his caseworker to the group worker. When the caseworker left the agency, Leon informed the group worker. At about that time, there was one meeting when Leon appeared more subdued and quieter than usual, and the worker felt that this was related to the change of caseworkers. This change in Leon did not last, however, since he came and announced with equanimity that he had a new social worker, someone who had the same surname as he.

There was still some evidence in the group of Leon's preoccupation with sex. In addition to using a brace and bit to make holes in wood, Leon had also recently used a heated nail to burn initials in the plastic rings he made. His interest in fire play was not so strong as it had been in the past, and less than that of the other group members at present. During a recent trip made by the group, Leon rode a bicycle quite well and derived much pleasure from the fact that some of the aggressive boys were unable to ride.

In general, Leon's progress continued along the same lines mentioned in the last progress report. He had gained enough security to begin to associate with boys outside his therapy group. His membership in PAL is of particular significance in this respect.

RECOMMENDATIONS

It was recommended that Leon continue treatment in activity group therapy to help him consolidate the gains he had already made and to further deepen his identification with a strong "father" figure.

Integration Conference (Excerpts), June 13, 1966

Since the last psychiatric conference on Leon, the mother had been assigned to her own caseworker. Mrs. S. was now physically able to move and to go visiting. However, she still spent a great deal of time in bed. She had consulted a private physician, who had sent her to a neurologist. The latter recommended a period of hospitalization for the purpose of tests and observation. A report was sent to our agency following this, diagnosing the mother's condition as anxiety hysteria. Because of his wife's illness, the father was now entirely responsible for taking care of the home. He himself was emotionally disturbed and suffered from ulcers. He had to keep busy all the time to master his anxiety. Leon was reported originally as sleeping in the parental bedroom. It was later noted that for a time he was placed in a different room to sleep, but apparently he insisted upon being returned to his original bed. While his mother was ill, Leon helped her, even to the extent of helping her to dress.

. . . Leon was seen only four times by the new caseworker. He talked of marriage. His concept was that a married couple shopped together and fed their children. He thought that the mother usually became ill because she was the weaker of the pair.

. . . Leon's fear of the dark was still evident. He told his caseworker that when he was alone at home in the dark, he thought he heard voices. He had become very guilty over his mother's illness.

. . . Leon talked a great deal about his therapy group to the caseworker, and he seemed to feel secure in the group. He also spoke to her about his liking to write. He told her that in camp he had written letters for other boys. He also wrote while in the group.

. . . The group worker reported further improvement in Leon's adjustment. He had lost his effeminate mannerisms, and he behaved very much like a boy of his age. As described in earlier reports, he was now accepted by the others, who no longer teased him and called him names.

RECOMMENDATIONS

1. Continue in activity group therapy.
2. Schedule an integration conference in November to reexamine the treatment situation.

Memorandum, October 28, 1966

Leon told the group worker that he would not be able to come to meetings any longer because of Hebrew school and his need to study for his coming Bar Mitzvah. The caseworker spoke with his mother by phone. Mrs. S. insisted that she was paying for Hebrew school and would no longer permit Leon to come to the group meetings. Leon had not been using his individual interviews constructively, and the caseworker felt that if he could not attend the group in addition, it might be necessary to close the case in the agency. It was agreed, however, that in view of the great need for Leon to attend the group, it was necessary to employ all means to enable him to continue. In order to discuss this problem and the possibility of transferring the case to exclusive group therapy it was agreed to hold an integration conference.

Integration Conference, November 12, 1966

This integration conference was convened for the purpose of discussing Leon's recent resistance to casework treatment and the fact that he had been unable to attend the meetings of his group regularly because of a conflict with attendance at Hebrew school. The caseworker, group worker (a recent replacement for the original group worker[9]), director of group therapy were present.

The caseworker reported that Leon had taken a great deal of responsibility in the home during his mother's recent illness. His mother had been operated on for a small tumor on the spine. Partially as a result of the mother's illness, the caseworker believed that Leon had regressed somewhat in the home, becoming more submissive to his mother, in contrast to his earlier improvement wherein he opposed her domination. On the other hand, the camp report this year had stressed that Leon was more outgoing in his relationships with his peers and had made an even better adjustment than during the prior camp season.

Leon had been attending Hebrew school every day now, and he had not seen his caseworker for over a month. When he did come to an interview, he talked very little, stating that everything was "fine" at home and on the outside, and his only reason for coming to the agency was that he wanted to be able to return to camp. When the caseworker phoned Mrs. S. to see whether Leon could be excused from Hebrew school to attend the group meetings, the mother insisted that Hebrew school was more important and that she would not arrange for Leon to be excused.

During the most recent interview, Leon had told his caseworker that he missed his "club" (therapy group) but, not only would he not be able to come to the meetings because of Hebrew school, he would also not be able to keep his appointments with her. Toward the end of the interview Leon said that he would at least try to talk to his mother about the possibility of being excused from Hebrew school to attend the group.

The group worker reported that Leon had finally come to the most recent meeting of the group, after missing three. Apparently the boy had again stood up against his mother's wishes and had insisted on coming to the group meetings, which meant so much to him.

In discussing the boy's resistance in individual therapy, it was thought that this hinged mostly on transference to the previous caseworker, to whom he had been much attached.

The group worker reported that when Leon came to the first meeting following the summer hiatus, he seemed to have changed somewhat in behavior. He did not finish any of the projects he began. It was felt that this temporary regression was due to the loss of the former caseworker and the transfer to a new one. The worker noted that in the group, recently, Leon

[9]It is a standard practice in activity group therapy to replace the original group worker when the group has reached an advanced stage and the clients have demonstrated improvements. This is done to foster the clients' abilities to accommodate to reality changes and to strengthen their tolerances in several areas. Changes are also effected in the composition of activity therapy groups to accomplish the same ends. —M.S.

would stand up firmly for his "rights." In contrast to his earlier behavior, the boy did not seem to show any fear of his aggressive actions.

Despite the temporary resistance in individual therapy, it was felt inadvisable at this time to accept Leon for exclusive group treatment, in view of the fact that he still needed individual help. It was considered that the mother's refusal to participate in treatment and her use of her physical disability were the complicating factors.

RECOMMENDATIONS

1. Leon should continue in activity group therapy.
2. Attempts should be made to continue him in individual therapy.
3. If it should prove impossible to work through the boy's present resistance, the Group Therapy Department would accept the case temporarily for exclusive treatment.

Progress Report, January 23, 1967

The report covered the period from October 1, 1966, to date.

Of a total of sixteen group meetings, Leon attended five. The absences were still due to his Hebrew school attendance. After coming to three meetings, Leon stopped for a month, then came back saying that in the future he would be taking off one hour from Hebrew school to come to the group. He then attended two meetings in sequence, the last one on December 9. After that, his mother insisted that he continue in Hebrew school full time until his Bar Mitzvah in April.

When he did attend, Leon came early. Upon arrival he was neat and clean. However, in work and play he was unconcerned about keeping clean. Occasionally he expressed his intention of washing his hands before eating, but he did not do so. He still had no effeminate mannerisms. Only on two occasions did he show an interest in cooking, when heating pots of water. He made no fires and showed no overt concern for food, but he did volunteer once to go for refreshments.[10]

Leon's activities in the group were generally spontaneous, with occasional overt aggression. While in previous years he had spent much time

---

[10]In advanced activity therapy groups, the children assume the maintenance chores that the worker formerly carried on. This includes not only preparation and serving of the repast, but also leaving the meeting room to purchase refreshments. At a time in a therapy group's development when the worker feels that the children are ready for such responsibilities, he suggests to the group that they work out for themselves a procedure for sharing such chores. Of course, in many groups the worker's intercession is unnecessary because the group members themselves suggest taking over the duties. The introduction of procedures to have a group assume maintenance chores is one of several innovations in treatment that foster social responsibilities, including the democratic experience of group discussions and decision-making. —*M.S.*

working alone with materials, he was now active with the other boys. He instigated dueling games and climbing over a wooden partition near the entrance door. He took a leading role in this and scolded those who did not play earnestly or who showed fear. Although he did not actually initiate fights, he stood up to others who became aggressive toward him. This season there were no incidents of his being teased for effeminacy. Leon was argumentative and led discussions at the refreshment table. He seemed to know what he was talking about and what he wanted. He spoke of school, camp, and other experiences he had had.

There was a change in the group's composition this year, so that Leon found himself with only two other boys from the original therapy group. He related well to the new group members, accepted them, showed them the materials and other group activities, and tried to make them feel comfortable. He befriended Richard, a withdrawn boy. He had a number of arguments with Jack, one of the new members. Only on one occasion did Leon bring a friend to a group meeting. Leon did not try to dominate him. Rather, he seemed secure in his relationship to his friend.

There was a change in group therapists this season. During the first several meetings after the introduction of the new worker, Leon showed some feelings about the loss of the former worker. He revealed this in a tracing he made that depicted a child writing and mailing a letter. He did not complete the tracing, nor did he take it home with him. He always was friendly toward the new worker. While he talked with him and sought approval, he revealed no unusual dependence on the worker. Leon asked the worker for the keys to open and lock the meeting room door at the beginnings and ends of meetings. This was probably an assertive attempt to replace the worker. He now would ask the worker's permission to take home colored paper. He lingered behind to make sure he was the last to leave. He still desired to walk with someone on the street, an indication of continuing concern about the neighborhood. In general, Leon's progress continued unabated, with no regression toward femininity and dependence. To the contrary, despite the minor bids for the new worker's acceptance, he demonstrated much ego strength and confidence. He acted like a normal boy, with masculine interests and outgoingness, and even though he only attended a few meetings this season, he showed a consolidation of his former gains.

Memorandum, January 29, 1967

Leon did not attend the past seven meetings. The caseworker reported that he was actively in the process of preparing for his Bar Mitzvah. In view of this, he would not be able to attend the group or come to see the caseworker.

Integration Conference, February 13, 1967

The caseworker, group worker, and director of group therapy were present.

The caseworker reported that she had not had many contacts with Leon since the last integration conference, because his mother had been pressuring him very much about Hebrew lessons. During the few interviews that Leon attended, he would run to the blackboard and write. He explained that he loved to do this. He also played word games with the caseworker. He did not talk about his family or his feelings. He still slept in the room with his parents.

Mrs. S.'s treatment was terminated earlier in the year. She seemed to be better physically. Since she had not been seen recently, information was lacking about Leon's behavior at home. According to Leon, he had no problems or difficulties. The question was raised of the desirability of maintaining contact with Mrs. S., if only occasionally. This was of particular importance because the boy was still being kept in the parental bedroom even though he was entering adolescence. Otherwise, if contact with the family ended entirely, not much more could be accomplished.

Leon had not been attending the most of the recent group meetings because of his preparation for the Bar Mitzvah. Out of a total of nineteen meetings, he attended six. For some time, Leon rebelled against his mother and came to the earlier meetings, despite her refusal to give him permission. Subsequently, he stopped attending, but he did come to the most recent meeting, which had been an excursion on a Sunday; he did not attend Hebrew school on that day. It was felt that the group still meant a lot to Leon. When he went on the recent group trip, he had already figured out when he would be able to resume regular attendance after his Bar Mitzvah.

The caseworker raised the question of a possible transfer of Leon for exclusive group treatment, in view of the fact that he would not start attending the group again until April. It was deemed advisable to schedule a psychological examination and a psychiatric conference prior to arranging for his transfer to exclusive group therapy.

RECOMMENDATIONS

1. Leon should continue in activity group therapy.
2. The mother should be seen through a home visit in order to obtain information about Leon's current adjustment at home and in the community.
3. The caseworker would arrange for a psychological examination and a psychiatric conference to determine future treatment.

Psychological Examination, March 20, 1967

PROBLEM

Question of the boy's intelligence level; his borderline schoolwork; his family's concern about his slowness and possible mental retardation; his inarticulateness and apparent lack of awareness of his problems in individual treatment.

BEHAVIOR

Leon did not appear for the first examination that was scheduled, so a new appointment was made, which he kept. Leon was described as rather small for his age, sluggish, with closely bitten nails and a very hoarse voice. He was compliant from the beginning, but clearly frightened about the whole examination. When faced with a new task, his hands would often shake; whenever he failed he would look sad. But, however discouraged, he continued to work in a dogged fashion. While his concern about his intellectual capacity was never fully dispelled, he did find some tasks which he enjoyed and from which he could gain a degree of satisfaction. Gradually during the examination he became much friendlier with the examiner, responded to jokes and encouragement, and was often willing to talk about himself. He impressed one as being a sweet, gentle kind of person, with a lack of defensiveness and a willingness for self-exposure that one seldom finds except with dull youngsters. At the end of the test, he apologized for not having come for the first appointment. When asked about this, he replied, "I was kind of scared." He agreed with the examiner that the test hadn't been so bad after all. He spoke of enjoying camp, and proudly showed a ring that he had made in the "club." Spelling and arithmetic were his best subjects in school, according to him. He was very frank about how seldom he read. He said he looked at all the "funny" books and *Popular Mechanics* pictures, but he never read them unless he "had to." Lately he had been studying for his Bar Mitzvah, which took up most of his time, and he looked forward to the time when he no longer had to do so. One form of satisfaction he had was helping the Hebrew teacher with the younger children; he also added that in public school the teacher sometimes gave him papers to correct. When asked about his ambition for when he grew up, he said he would like to be a teacher. How much of a reality this was based on is questionable. Leon said he thought he would like to teach in public school—grammar, spelling, and arithmetic, but not reading. When the examiner suggested that in order to become a teacher he would have to go to college, Leon said he had thought about that and did not think it would be too hard for him.

EXAMINATION RESULTS

Leon was twelve years old at the time of testing. Wechsler-Bellevue: Full Scale, I.Q. 77; Verbal Scale, I.Q. 73; Performance Scale, I.Q. 84. Casuist Form Board: approximately eight-year-old level. Healy Picture Completion I: approximately eleven-year-old level. Goodenough Drawing a Man: refused.

INTERPRETATIONS

At the present time, Leon's test results placed him in a borderline group in general intelligence. Since his cooperation was good, the results seemed to offer a representative measure of his performance. There was little indication that he might have higher abilities. He was somewhat higher in the performance scale than in the verbal, but on no item was he beyond the dull-normal group.

Leon possessed a high rote memory and was also relatively good in general information and in social comprehension when the latter was presented pictorially. However, when social problems were presented verbally, he responded with an overly literal approach, with the simple cause-and-effect reasoning of a much younger child. For example: what one does when one discovers a fire in a theater: "Go back and get a hose, or open the doors to the exits." His literalmindedness and lack of ability in abstractions was even more evident with questions pertaining to similarities. At first he did not understand the nature of the task, but when the examiner demonstrated, he was able to get the point. However, after giving three likenesses, he changed again to differences, and was quite rigid and unable, even with demonstrations, to again change to an abstract, generalizing approach. The same inability to generalize was evident in his poor performance on the block design and object assembly tasks. In the former, he was able to select blocks of the correct color, but could not make the necessary manipulations in spite of a very methodical approach. In the latter task, he was able to recognize the object—on the hands, he knew he was dealing with fingers—but put the finger below the wrist. On the profile he would not remove the wrong pieces, so was unable to finish. Typical of his slow, uncertain way of reaching generalizations: for an apple—"round shape, stem, peel it; you eat it."

The two other tests confirmed the picture of dullness and confusion, but probably showed nothing pathogenic. On the Healy, he worked slowly, making many inferior placements but correcting them himself. On the Form Board, in contrast, which meant dealing entirely with shapes—visual problems without any ideational content to carry it along—Leon gave much more inferior performance. There was no planning in his work, and he saw each block as a separate piece, rather than seeing the similarity between one piece and another, so that he did the whole task at the same rate with no gaining of speed by learning. Even at the end, when he had just two pieces left that were identical with the two he had just used, he had to use the same trial-and-error method until he got them in.

Leon's refusal to do the drawing of a man is in itself very significant, because many children, while disliking this assignment, will, if they are generally as obedient and docile as Leon, nevertheless go ahead and do it. He did make an effort, drawing for a long time very faintly, and seemed to have completed the head, but then he meticulously erased everything he had done and apologized for being unable to do it. We were unable to discover whether his sense of inability was specifically related to his feelings about drawing or whether there was some block against drawing a human figure.

RECOMMENDATIONS

Leon was a boy of low intelligence but with enough conceptual ability and sensitivity to realize his inadequacy. He was often unhappy about this, but gradually, despite his sense of unworthiness, he was able to function freely with what ability he had. His rigidity, which gave him some degree of emotional security, stood in the way of better intellectual achievement. It is surprising that even with his hard work he had gotten to the eighth grade. Going to an academic high school was certainly counterindicated. Eventually Leon would have to recognize that he could not carry through his ambition to be a teacher. From one contact, the examiner got the impression that his desire to be a teacher, outside of its prestige and power values, might be tied in with a desire to take care of people weaker than himself. If this feeling continued, perhaps he could be helped to make vocational plans for such work, perhaps as a custodian, where his limited intelligence would not be too great a handicap and where his gentleness would be an asset in getting along with others. Leon also spoke with great enthusiasm about animals, so farm work was a possibility. It was hoped that when he finished his Bar Mitzvah he could discontinue Hebrew lessons, because the double academic burden was more than he should have to bear. If Leon continued in treatment, retesting a year from now was suggested, for there was a possibility that he might decline rather than improve scholastically.

Integration Conference, June 5, 1967

The caseworker, group worker, and director of group therapy were present.
According to the caseworker, Leon never talked much in individual treatment. He was interested in writing on the blackboard. Leon had not

kept appointments for the past four weeks. It was felt that his mother kept him from the interviews. The boy still slept in the same room with his parents, and this had been discussed with them to no avail. However, the mother had recently promised to move Leon to a room of his own after the Bar Mitzvah.

As noted, a recent psychological battery gave an I.Q. of 77. The psychologist felt that this was a valid score. Leon seemed to realize his intellectual inadequacy.

It was thought that the most outstanding factor in Leon's development at present was a passive, homosexual tendency, which warranted further observation. According to the caseworker, Leon continued to be a member of PAL.

The group worker reported that Leon had not come to the meetings until the end of April because of his Bar Mitzvah lessons. However, when a trip was called on another day, he came and enjoyed himself. He seemed to be less preoccupied with sex and had seldom played with fire. During a recent meeting, there was one upsetting experience when the other boys called him a "fairy" and locked him in the bathroom. It was possible that the incident occurred because Leon unconsciously activated latent homesexuality in the other boys. The question was raised of whether Leon's effeminate features had become more pronounced lately. It was planned that the first group therapist, who would be working in Leon's camp this summer, would observe Leon in this respect, since he had known the boy for a long time after his initial start in group therapy.

Leon told his caseworker that he liked the old meeting room better than the new one. He said also that the boys were fresh to him, but he stated that he intended to return to the group meetings.

RECOMMENDATIONS

1. Observe Leon's adjustment in camp this summer.
2. In the fall, transfer the case for exclusive group therapy for a period of one year.
3. Arrange for another psychological evaluation in a year. Also schedule an endocrinological examination.
4. If possible, assign Mrs. S. to a caseworker for intensive treatment.

Memorandum, August 19, 1967

In line with the decisions made in the last integration conference, the first group worker spoke with Leon during his visit to camp. At this point, he had known the boy for two years. He found him physically improved and taller. Leon's voice had become more manly; his effeminate mannerisms had definitely diminished, although they had not entirely disappeared. Leon was still a chubby boy.

It was planned to continue Leon in exclusive group therapy for one year.

Progress Report, February 10, 1968

This report covered the period from October 1967 to date. Leon had attended eight of seventeen meetings. The reasons for many of the absences were not known. Some were probably due to his preparations for graduation from public school. Leon began high school in September. He came to meetings early. There was essentially no change in his physical appearance: he was always neat and clean when he arrived and in the group showed no particular concern with his appearance. His effeminate mannerisms were not in evidence. On one occasion, he addressed the other boys as "dearie," and another time he started to cook a concoction in which he mixed soap and all the types of food he could find. It was a mischievous prank, and he tried to have some of the other boys drink the mess. His general activity continued to be assertive and spontaneous, but there were no expressions of overt aggressiveness as had been indicated in the last report. He worked with materials and also participated in Ping-Pong games, discussions, and other group activities.

When Leon came to the first of the season's meetings, he recalled aloud the incident of being locked in the toilet by the other boys and being called a "fairy." He seemed afraid of Jack and wondered whether the latter still attended the "club." But he was quite friendly with the other boys. He and Norman made a date to meet outside and go to a radio program. Leon was very interested in radio programs and occasionally invited others to go to them with him. He also talked about going to the programs with other friends, boys as well as girls. He related well in the group and was liked by the other boys. In contrast to past years, he made no fires. He no longer asked for the worker's keys to open the entrance and cabinet doors.

Leon's relationship with the worker continued to be friendly. He talked freely to him but didn't seek to win his approval. He no longer waited at the ends of the meetings to walk with the worker but left with the others. Although this was the beginning of the second year that the present worker had been with the therapy group, Leon still addressed him occasionally by the former worker's name.

In summary, Leon's behavior and expressed attitudes in the group indicated that he had matured further. It is possible that his periodic absences, which were rather irregular, were due to a growing away from the therapy group, because he had many friends outside. It was felt that he might soon be ready for a group in a recreation center.

School Visit, February 19, 1968

The caseworker[11] visited with Miss G., grade adviser of the high school, to discuss plans for Leon. It was learned that Leon had not been placed in a special class. At present he was taking a commercial course that involved classes in commercial arithmetic, science, and civics and three classes in English. The high school offered a specialized course in merchandising and bookkeeping. If Leon did not qualify for this, there was a possibility of his being transferred to a vocational school after his first year.

It was considered advisable that, for the time being, Leon should remain in his regular class so that his adjustment could be observed. If he did not do well, he would be put in a modified course offered by the school. It was planned that in February 1969 the school would reevaluate with us the desirability of having Leon transferred to a vocational high school.

Interviews with Mrs. S., February–May, 1968

Mrs. S. was interviewed on February 5, March 3, May 11, and May 18.

Mrs. S. came to see the caseworker in February, greatly upset because she had received a letter from Leon's high school informing her that Leon was to be placed in a slower group on the basis of his test results. She clearly found it very difficult to accept the fact that Leon was intellectually limited and was at present working up to his capacity. She repeatedly brought up the idea that perhaps if he worked harder he could get through high school. . . .

Mrs. S. complained about Leon's disobedience and negativism, stating that she found it extremely difficult to get him to go to bed on time. Once when she hit him, he raised his hand against her. It was learned that most of the conflict between them arose over the subject of schoolwork, since she applied much pressure in attempts to get him to do more work. It became increasingly apparent as she continued talking that she was completely incapable of dealing with Leon, and she could not handle him in a consistent fashion. Leon, in line with adolescent development and his stronger ego, was fighting the mother to oppose her attempts at domination. . . .

It was learned that Leon had finally been given a separate room to sleep in, a daybed in the living room. According to the mother's descriptions of Leon, the neurotic symptoms that had been present when he was first referred seemed to have disappeared. The boy was definitely not so concerned with cleanliness (note his previous compulsiveness in this respect), and he asserted himself strongly in the home. . . .

[11]When casework services were discontinued and Leon was placed in exclusive group therapy, the caseworker assigned to that department—in this instance, Leon's first group therapist—acted as liaison.

The father did not consider the boy a problem. Repeatedly he asked his wife to leave Leon alone and not to nag him.

The neighbors had emphasized to the mother again and again how nice and cooperative Leon was, and they disagreed with her when she said Leon was a problem. Leon now played with other boys on the street, although he was still not interested in sports. However, the mother was pleased that he was more manly and assertive—as she put it, "less of a sissy."

Mrs. S. was in the habit of punishing Leon by preventing him from attending the therapy group. This was discussed with her in detail, and she promised not to continue. Leon was very eager to return to camp, which always had much meaning for him, and it was agreed that she and the caseworker would discuss this again near the end of May.

The caseworker, having made a visit to Leon's school, was able to reassure Mrs. S. that Leon was doing as well as could be expected. Nevertheless, she continued to pressure him to study harder. Once again the caseworker explored Mrs. S.'s feelings in this respect. She cried when it was pointed out that Leon was not as intelligent as she really wanted him to be. Mrs. S. was thankful about the caseworker's visit to the school on Leon's behalf, stating that she somehow felt reassured when she got objective facts. She also felt reassured that at least she knew that the school was offering the boy the kinds of courses that would prepare him for a trade. She reported that Leon's relationships with friends and neighbors were still good.

Mrs. S. was seen in the middle of May after she had become very upset because Leon apparently had failed in two subjects. She went to the school, although the caseworker had earlier asked her not to do so and suggested that Mrs. S. discuss any school matters directly with Leon. In her anger, Mrs. S. wanted to send Leon to a work camp for the summer. She said she did not want him to go to a camp where "he would have fun." The caseworker discussed this with her in terms of the fact that she was actually defeating her own purpose with such an attitude.

During the same interview, the caseworker learned that Leon not only was spending time with boys but was beginning to show interest in girls. According to his mother, his adjustment on the outside seemed satisfactory and he had many friends. The boy, however, did not engage in many masculine activities, such as sports, although he did go on short trips to the park with his male friends.

Progress Report, Excerpts, June 4, 1968

Since the last progress report on February 19, Leon had attended sixteen out of nineteen group meetings, a decided improvement in his attendance. The absences were due to illnesses. There was no change in Leon's general appearance—he still was always neat and clean—and he arrived at the meetings early. During this period of time his effeminate mannerisms had become even less evident. At no point did the worker hear him address the other boys as "dearie" as he had once done earlier. . . .

Leon now spent much time experimenting with heating copper. He made ashtrays in a crude manner from this material and then heated them on the hot plate. He also made many lanyards and seemed to derive a great deal of satisfaction from this activity because he was the only one in the group who could do it well. . . .He often took the initiative to go out to buy the refreshments and selected Herbert to go with him. He acted verbally aggressive toward Bernard, who bragged about his skill in Ping-Pong. When the two played the game, there were many arguments over scoring. During the meeting on May 28, the boys almost came to blows, and Bernard withdrew and was apologetic to Leon. In general, Leon was liked by the other boys, and none of them made derogatory remarks to him about effeminism. Leon's relationship with the worker continued on friendly terms. When a new member, Eugene, an older boy, was introduced to the group, Leon accepted him quickly and helped him acclimatize himself.

Although Leon had made friends outside the therapy group and often talked about them, the group was still very meaningful to him, and it was felt that he should continue in the group the following year. He was going to camp again this season and was very pleased about it. To summarize: Leon's behavior showed greater maturity, positiveness of attitudes toward others, and self-esteem. He manifested greater ego strength and less anxiety. . . .

Treatment Conference, Group Therapy Department, June 15, 1968

The group worker and director of group therapy were present.

According to the latest reports from the group worker, Leon was more assertive and outgoing, and his earlier interest in playing with fire had taken the sublimated form of experimenting with metals and heat.

Contacts with Mrs. S. were reviewed, and it was felt that despite her verbalizations about wanting to place Leon out of the home, she never could go through with such a step. She was an extremely anxious, rather dull woman who was inadequate in her handling of Leon. The father was a weak man who had hardly any say in the family. (See follow-up interviews for details.)

Since the therapy group had such great meaning for Leon, it was felt that he should continue for an additional year. At the same time, it was decided to make a special effort to interest Leon in group activities on the outside during the course of the year. If necessary, the group worker would take the boy in person to a settlement house.

Recommendations

1. Continue Leon in activity group therapy for another year.
2. Prepare Leon for transfer to a settlement house.

Memorandum, June 22, 1968

It was originally planned for Leon to attend camp for one month in the summer, as in the past. However, when the caseworker learned that there were vacancies in another month also, it was arranged for Leon to remain in camp for two months. This was considered desirable in view of the increased tension between Leon and his mother, who had been completely unable to handle him.

Follow-up Interviews with Leon, June 10, 1968

The liaison caseworker of the Group Therapy Department arranged an interview with Leon because his mother had complained about his behavior and it was considered advisable to get Leon's side of the story and his general feelings. It is of interest to note that, on the same day that Leon was to have his interview, the mother again telephoned stating that she had been called to school and was extremely upset because apparently Leon had drawn some sexy pictures in his book and also written salacious words. Furthermore, Leon and another boy had been caught smoking in school. The caseworker reassured the mother that this was a rather common occurrence among adolescents. . . .

Leon was pleased to see the caseworker, who had been the group worker a few years before. Leon related to him with ease throughout the interview. He seemed grown up and sensitive. His voice, which had been screechy two years before, had changed into a deeper, masculine one. Leon spoke of camp and his plans. The caseworker commented at one point that he understood from Leon's mother that "things weren't going so well." Leon admitted that he was having some difficulty with her because she insisted that he come home early every evening. He felt that this was unjust and that she "treated me as though I'm a baby." Leon spoke at length about the many friends he had, both boys and girls. He admitted, however, that he was not good in ball games and was not really interested in them. When asked whether he was interested in going on dates with girls, Leon denied having any real girlfriends. He only walked with them when he was in a group. When he was asked about girlfriends, he smiled and said, "Oh, I'm not interested in that."

Although he had failed two subjects, Leon thought that everything at school was all right. The two subjects were science and civics. He was asked how he could be an accountant or bookkeeper, in line with his commercial course, if he failed these subjects. Leon answered that he liked to read only comics and mysteries and that kids had to read "something" for school which they didn't like, but he didn't feel he could read more science and civics. He thought it was enough to do his homework. . . .

In general, it seemed that Leon was getting along reasonably well, showing no unusual fears or anxiety. He also seemed to be much less effeminate than originally. In line with an adolescent stubbornness and a stronger ego, he was able to hit back against his extremely domineering and nagging mother.

Follow-up Interview with Mrs. S., June 25, 1968

Leon's mother was seen when she came to the agency to pay the fee for camp. She complained about the fact that Leon had gone downtown last week without telling her about it and said she was extremely worried about him. She also spoke of him as being disobedient. The caseworker took this opportunity to discuss with her the meaning of the changes in Leon's behavior—his tendency to sometimes go off on his own without telling her, and also his stubbornness. The caseworker explained these changes in terms of adolescent development, and Mrs. S. agreed that perhaps it was too difficult for her to accept the fact that Leon had grown up and was no longer her baby.

Follow-up Interview with Mrs. S., December 29, 1968

This was the first interview of Mrs. S. by a new liaison worker of the group therapy department.

Mrs. S. was on time for the appointment despite extremely bad weather. She was a stout woman with a dull expression. Upon introducing myself to her, I told her that I was replacing the former supervisor. She said she had heard about his leaving. She went on to talk about all the difficulties that Leon was presenting at this time. She spoke in a cold, rejecting manner and at no point in the conversation did she mention anything that was in any way complimentary to Leon. She showed no warmth at all about her son.

She started out by saying that Leon and her husband had quarreled and had not spoken to each other for two months, until just yesterday, when they had had company at home and the guests had gotten the two of them to "make up." Mrs. S. indicated that this was all Leon's fault and that he would never give in, and said that it was just typical of the way he was all the time. . . .

It seems that at Open School Week, early in November, Mrs. S. could not attend and suggested that Leon have his father go instead. Leon said that he didn't want his father to go, that he was "ashamed" of him. Mrs. S. became very indignant when Leon said this and went on to justify the father to Leon, explaining that he was a hard-working man on his job and at home. Mrs. S. later repeated Leon's remark to her husband, and it hurt him greatly.

Mrs. S. repeated that Leon was a problem and said she didn't know what to do about him. She wanted to send him "somewhere," where he could learn to get along and also where he would have some schooling. I asked her whether she meant a "home" of some kind, and she replied in the affirmative: "Yes, if it would do him some good, I would be willing to send him away." She went on to say that his being home was very hard on her, and also too much for her husband. Furthermore, she added, being at home didn't seem to be doing Leon any good. "It's just constant aggravation." I informed her that the agency sometimes did help with problems like this because it had its own facilities. Immediately she backtracked a bit, saying, "Well, I'm going to wait and see how things are this summer."

We discussed Leon's therapy group. Mrs. S. stated that Leon didn't seem to be too interested in going. She said Leon had informed her that he didn't like the present worker as much as he had the two prior ones, although he could give no reason for this. This was explored further, and Mrs. S. said that when the former worker and his replacement in the group were in charge of the "club" they seemed to give "everything" to Leon, always responding to his requests. She guessed that the present worker "doesn't do the same thing" and suggested that this was why Leon didn't like him as much. Mrs. S. said that she very much favored having Leon attend the "club" because she wanted him "to be with boys." She wished there were other clubs he could join in addition. I inquired as to whether there were such opportunities in her neighborhood for Leon, and she replied that she did not know of any. I then suggested to Mrs. S. that Leon come in to see me to talk about his "club" and also the possibility of joining a community YMHA that I was acquainted with. I told her that I knew several persons at this YMHA and perhaps could, with their interest, involve Leon in the activities. Mrs. S. thought this a wonderful idea. It was decided that Leon would come in within a week or two. . . .

Follow-up Interview with Leon, January 4, 1969

This appointment was arranged to discuss referral to a settlement house club.

Leon was on time for his appointment and was neatly dressed. As he entered the room, he smiled and offered his hand, saying, "Hi." He seemed genuinely glad to see me, mentioning that it had been a "long time since camp." (I had also been at his camp the preceding summer.) We spoke generally about camp for a few moments and also my becoming the "leader" in the "club." Leon knew that next summer he would not return to camp, and he was not interested in going to another camp for older boys. He thought he might be able to get a job in the summer as a busboy in a hotel owned by a relative, though he was not positive. His mother wanted him to work during the summer. He thought he would like the job. He said he knew that he could earn a "lot of money," though he realized that the work would be quite hard.

In talking of the "club," Leon indicated that he was not as interested in it this year as he had been in previous years. When I asked the reason for this, he replied that he wasn't the only one who felt that way. He said the other boys in the "club" also felt that somehow the "club" was different this year. There didn't seem as much to do as in the past. When I asked if there weren't sufficient materials and games there, he replied that there were, but that he and some of the other boys just weren't as interested in the activities as they used to be. . . .

Leon said the "fellows" in the "club" were pretty nice. He wondered, though, what had happened to Herbert, who had been a member for many years. Leon had heard from the other boys that Herbert and Mel had gotten into a fight, and he thought maybe that was why Herbert had not returned. Leon went on to tell me that Mel didn't believe that Leon was going to see me, and Mel was going to call me up at the office to check. Leon's remarks evidently indicated some feeling of rivalry, because he knew that I had seen Mel individually until he was transferred to exclusive group treatment.

Leon said he was in the second term in high school and that he had been put in a "modified" class, as he called it. He said he was doing much better this term, though he still was having trouble in some subjects. I asked how he felt about such a class, and he replied that it was a good idea because they went slower and this gave him a chance to catch up in his work and to understand some of the basics. (In view of Leon's reported I.Q. of 77, it was surprising that he was doing as well as he was.)

Leon indicated that he had a number of friends, some new ones in school and a few friends on his block. He was a little vague about what he and his friends did to pass the time, though he did state that they went on walks together, talked, and went to the movies. He added that he had a new hobby, autograph collection.

Leon reported that he had joined the Junior Masons. This organization had just started, and he was a charter member of his branch. The group met every week and was presently planning a play and perhaps a dance. So far Leon liked the organization very much, and he felt that it could be built up to something good.

I took the opportunity at this point to raise the question of his joining a community YMHA. I asked Leon whether he had heard of the one in his neighborhood, and he said he had not. I told him that a friend of mine was

the assistant director and that one of the reasons I had wanted to see him today was that I might be able to arrange for him to join. Leon said that he
wasn't interested; he wouldn't have the time. I commented that it sometimes was a little hard to join a new place, where you didn't know any of the
others. Leon said that he wasn't afraid of "such things," and that he usually had no trouble meeting people or making friends; there were these
"other things" that were keeping him from joining new clubs. I accepted
this and said that if he ever changed his mind, he should let me know and I
would try to work something out for him.

Leon felt that everything else was going along all right. When I asked
about home, he hesitated for a moment and then said things were all right
there too. I said that I knew there were sometimes difficulties at home, especially when a boy was about his age and wanted to decide things for himself
whereas the parents had their own ideas. Leon smiled and said he guessed
that was true in his home as well. . . . I asked Leon whether he now had his
own room. He said that he slept in the living room, but that no matter how
low he kept his radio, his mother always complained that she could hear it.
Leon said she really doesn't hear it but just felt uncomfortable going to
sleep with him still awake. This caused many arguments and nothing had
been settled. Other arguments arose because Mrs. S. wanted Leon to go to
bed early. Sometimes he gave in to her; other times she let him stay up but
would frequently call out to him asking when he was going to go to bed.
This annoyed Leon because he felt he should be able to stay up later and
shouldn't be treated like a baby in this respect. I got the impression that
Leon was much more assertive at home than he used to be. . . .

When the interview was over, Leon seemed reluctant to leave and continued to talk about the "club." When he finally left, he shook hands and
said he hoped to see me again soon. I told him that we would be getting together from time to time and that I was happy he had been able to visit
today.

Second Psychological Examination, February 18, 1969

PROBLEM

Previous test score of I.Q. 77. He did poorly last term in high school and
was placed in a "slow class." Purpose of retest was to clarify his ability and
the psychological picture generally.

BEHAVIOR

Leon was described as a well-developed adolescent, extremely clean in personal appearance. He wore a large ring with his insignia and three school
buttons of various sizes, ostentatiously pinned on his jacket. At first glance

he made a creditable impression: his cheeks looked rosy and healthy, and he seemed to talk and carry himself with a high degree of self-sufficiency. On closer examination, during the course of the testing, his cheeks became flushed when he worked under strain; his manner became fearful and perplexed; his body and facial expressions lacked assurance. He had little ability to initiate a task or to do his own thinking. His mental range was constricted. . . .

Leon's fearfulness was evident in the way he became agitated when called upon to finish a task. He was defensive and could not conceal a feeling of inadequacy for any length of time. He constantly strained in the direction of good performance and conformed in a compulsive manner. He talked a great deal about how much time he spent on homework. His promptness and extreme application to all the tests reflected a need to be conciliatory and to be in the good graces of adults. Failure at a task made him sad. With strained attention and bated breath, he waited for test questions, determined to do well at any cost. He was remarkably naive for a boy his age. Though he clearly was striving for superior performance, he lacked subtlety and fine discrimination. This was evidenced by the manner in which he had pinned three school buttons on his garment.

EXAMINATION RESULTS

Wechsler-Bellevue Intelligence Scale and Goodenough (unscored). Leon's intelligence scores were: Full Scale, I.Q. 87; Verbal Scale, I.Q. 91; Performance Scale, I.Q. 85.

Whereas in the intelligence test given almost two years ago, Leon ranged in the borderline intelligence group, he now functioned within the normal intelligence range. He had improved his score by ten points. His progress was most marked in the verbal sphere. Here he made a gain of eighteen points, an indication of much greater verbal freedom.

Leon now had a fairly adequate fund of information, showed a good rote memory, and did fairly well in arithmetic, though with much strain. He had apparently thrown everything into the battle for scholastic success. His extreme conformity and doggedness had helped him to extend his limited endowment to its furthest limits. This he was able to do in areas where effort was rewarded, but he was still weak in all areas where quick comprehension and conceptual thinking were called for. He found it difficult to understand an abstract problem or achieve a generalizing approach. The literalmindedness noted on the intelligence test two years ago still persisted to a large extent, though Leon was far more capable of reaching generalizations than before. Asked to find similarities between air and water, he said, "Water, you can drink. If you want cold water in the summertime, you have it right away." He could not dissociate a trend of thought from another or discern discrete entities.

Leon was visibly nervous. He was often blocked by doubt, showing much hesitation, and talked to himself while he did things on the performance test. He aspired to be a "good boy," a "teacher's pet," whose ambition is to live up to all precepts. Asked to give similarities between wood and alcohol, he said, "You should not take too much alcohol; it causes drunkenness. I learned this at school."

When asked to draw a man, he initially refused.[12] Leon immediately apologized for the refusal by saying, "We don't have drawing lessons." However, he was afraid of displeasing the examiner and immediately offered to draw letters, which were like those he had done in a stenciling class in school. Then he offered to write and said that his handwriting was like his mother's. He finally drew the head of a man but did not go beyond the trunk, which he started to draw but then crossed out. His need to avoid any awareness of bodily functions was apparent. This is further confirmed by the reinforcement of the nose in his initial attempt at drawing the face, an indication of considerable preoccupation with male genitalia.

Bender Motor Gestalt Test. On this test Leon did a lot of erasing and correcting (he carried a huge eraser with him). He was never satisfied with his results—he would go over and over his productions in correcting them, and remained doubtful about the final product. Compulsive traits were in evidence in his handling of the Bender designs.

Rorschach. The Rorschach results confirmed the impression of Leon's feelings of weakness and insecurity and of his need to be "good" at all costs. He was quick to apologize for his responses and sometimes asked, "Do you want me to see more?" Asked in the inquiry which animal he saw, he answered, "We are not studying animals in school." He was confused about his abilities; he would venture a response, then have doubts about it and say, "It's wrong." Doubt about his potency was a constant feature of his neurosis. Leon was a sensitive adolescent with a strong desire to participate and to relate to other people, but he was fearful in doing so. He had effectively repressed all impulsive and aggressive drives. The results suggested that emotional entanglements were extremely disturbing to him and that he tended to withdraw from them immediately.

Leon saw a "mask" repeatedly. This was an indication of his feeling of isolation, his fear of exposing himself to others and his need to keep himself hidden behind the "mask." He wanted to keep himself at a distance, as shown by his repeatedly holding the Rorschach cards at a distance from himself when he studied them. . . .

Leon avoided carefully all areas on the cards having sexual implications. On Card I, he saw men who "grab" a girl and "take her away." Was he the "girl" who was afraid and unconsciously desired to be grabbed by men? He blushed a great deal while giving such responses. Erythrophobic

---

[12]Note that he had made a similar response when asked to do this task on the first psychological battery. —*M.S.*

traits with exhibitionistic and voyeuristic tendencies seemed to be quite marked. Leon gave the typical response of the erythrophobic by saying, "People looking at each other and going into different directions."

Compulsive elements were also in evidence. Leon repeatedly showed a need for extreme accuracy, and he was quite sensitive to the symmetrical features of the cards.

Thematic Apperception Test. The stories revolved a great deal around the son-mother relationship. The son wants to break away. The moment he makes a decision to leave, the mother regularly faints, and he cannot leave because the mother is "very sick." Leon's description of the mother's fainting probably symbolized an unconscious wish for her death, for which he probably felt he would be responsible. In one story, he brought out the feeling that the father looked upon him as a rival. The father asks the son to do things for him; the son refuses; the father is suspicious that the son is really going out to see a girl.

Leon's unconscious identification with the female sex was strong. He described a girl in terms that a girl would use to describe herself. While writing out the stories, Leon again commented that his handwriting looked like his mother's. The stories showed little assertiveness or identification with boys' activities appropriate to his age group. The style, content, and writing of the stories had a strong feminine characteristic.

DISCUSSION

Leon had extended his intellectual powers and functions, making many efforts to expand his intellectual aspirations, and was now in the dull-normal intelligence range. He had apparently developed a compulsive character structure, which enabled him to maintain his performance for a protracted time. By isolating himself from potentially dangerous impulses, he managed to perform conscientiously. His compulsive tendencies helped him to function with a minimum of friction, at the cost of a repression of all disturbing problems of an instinctual nature. It was felt that his feelings of inadequacy would always be strong, but should he continue to stabilize on a compulsive level, he might be able to function fairly adequately both intellectually and vocationally. His need for cleanliness, accuracy, and a sense of order, should help him to function well in a commercial endeavor where he can employ these features, such as clerical office work.

Treatment Conference, Group Therapy Department, May 26, 1969

The group worker, supervisor of group therapy, and director of group therapy were present. For background, see the initial referral summary and the integration conference reports.

Leon had shown improvement in both home and school. He was concentrating on his work in school and had been able to get himself out of the "slow" class into a regular class. He talked of his friends and now belonged to the Junior Masons, where he was active in committee work. Leon had not attended meetings in group therapy this year because of conflict with his schoolwork. Leon felt that he no longer needed contact with our agency and was able to go out on his own.

It was agreed that Leon had made a good deal of improvement and was now ready for closing in the agency.

Follow-up Interview with Leon, May 27, 1969

The purpose of this interview was to prepare Leon for closing.

Leon was on time for his appointment and, as usual, was neatly dressed. He continued to relate to the worker in a warm manner and spontaneously talked about his achievements in school. He was then about to go into the third term. Leon was planning to do bookkeeping or some other kind of clerical work. It is interesting that the psychological examination also suggested this as a possibility.

In talking about his therapy group, Leon mentioned that he didn't feel that he needed the "club" any more. He now had friends of his own and also belonged to the youth branch of the Masons, where he was quite active on the entertainment and social committees. Spontaneously, he said that he still had some difficulty at home, but he didn't imagine that that would ever be straightened out completely and said that it was something he would have to get used to.

As to his summer plans, Leon had already been looking for part-time employment and had two possible jobs as a delivery boy lined up, one in a neighborhood vegetable store and the other in a tailor shop. Leon thought he would enjoy working, but he later admitted that it wasn't his idea but his mother's, who wanted him to work.

I discussed with Leon the results of the psychological examination to the extent of informing him that they revealed how he had made marked progress since he had first come to the agency. I added that I, too, felt confident that he could go along "on his own." Leon smiled and said that he also thought so. It was agreed that Leon could reapply for help should the occasion arise, but in the meantime we would consider his case closed. Leon shook hands with me and said it was going to be a "little strange" not having the agency "around." He thought, however, that he could get used to the idea of being on his own.

Closing Statement, July 5, 1969

Leon was referred to the agency in August 1964. At that time he was ten years old. His mother referred him because he was stubborn and negative toward her. He was unruly, stole from his mother, and took pleasure in pitting his parents against each other. He was not able to get along well with other children, partly because his mother limited his contacts overprotectively. He showed excessive concern with cleanliness and social punctiliousness, and he became distinctly anxious when there was a threat that he might dirty himself or destroy something. He was afraid of the dark, of being alone, of dying from illness or drowning. Leon had been dominated and infantilized by his mother, who, at the time of referral, still bathed him and dressed him over his objections. He had always slept in the parental bedroom, occasionally sharing a bed with his mother.

The boy came from a neurotic background and family structure. He was the only child of a couple married relatively late in life. Mrs. S. was a stout woman with no social life outside the household and was preoccupied with Leon. On the surface she was aggressive and demanding, and, despite a rather limited intelligence, she had considerable ambition. She was attempting to fulfill her interests in schooling and social standing through her son. Her handling of Leon was inconsistent—seductively fondling him at one moment, being punitive and threatening him at another.

Leon's father was a passive man, employed as a taxicab driver for over twenty years at a limited salary. He was indulgent toward Leon, largely from a desire to be left in peace. The parents constantly quarreled about methods of handling Leon, and the boy provoked these arguments in order to get some attention, even if only in a destructive way.

Leon had no friends and preferred playing with girls. Other children called him "sissy" and "Mary." He also played with dolls rather than with aggressive materials. With adults, Leon was ingratiating and polite and he displayed anxiety about pleasing them.

Leon was started in individual treatment, but he was soon referred for activity group therapy as well, primarily because he was not very productive in individual therapy. Also, it was deemed necessary for him to identify with masculine activities and to be able to relate to a masculine symbol to help further appropriate sexual identity.

Both individual treatment and activity group therapy were continued until August 1967, at which time it was felt that Leon could be transferred to exclusive group therapy. At the time of transfer, the caseworker stated at an integration conference on June 5, 1967, that Leon never spoke much in individual sessions. He exhibited an interesting tendency to write on a blackboard in the caseworker's room. The main treatment in casework had been on a supportive basis. In his relationship with the caseworker, Leon had an opportunity to experience a different kind of "mother" person. Activity group therapy had been helpful to Leon in strengthening his ego and in providing experiences that enabled him to bring out his latent hostility and aggression. The therapy group also served to fortify Leon's masculine identity.

In February 1969, Leon was retested and scored an I.Q. of 87. While two years before he had ranged in the borderline group of intelligence, he now functioned within the normal range. He had improved his score by ten points. His progress was most marked in the verbal sphere. Here he made a gain of eighteen points, an indication of much greater verbal freedom. The Rorschach results showed that compulsive elements were present. Leon had a need for extreme accuracy.

At the end of the report on the second examination, the psychologist stated that Leon had extended his intellectual powers and that compulsive patterns helped him to function with a minimum of friction by enabling him to repress disturbing problems. It was expected that his feelings of inadequacy would remain, but should he continue to stabilize on a compulsive level, he could function adequately both intellectually and vocationally.

The case was closed in the agency and in group therapy because of the improvements in Leon.

Part V

Group Treatment of Children with Severe Ego Impairment

Young children who are variously described as "ego-weak," "ego-deficient," or "ego-impaired," are being referred to community agencies in increasing numbers. Such children are angry, asocial, antisocial, destructive, often delinquent, and markedly suspicious of the intentions of others toward them, including parents, teachers, and peers. Seemingly they lack concern for the consequences of their behavior and manifest little guilt, which implies an absence of, or minimal, superego constraint. While these characteristics and behavior patterns are reminiscent of those commonly identified with psychopathic character structure in older children, ego-weak children possess a number of qualities that distinguish them from the latter. One notable difference is that they are not as deliberate in their actions as are psychopaths, who display an unmistakable wariness and conscious intent with respect to their antisocial actions.

Compensatory behavior, which is normally elicited as a reaction to feelings of guilt and anxiety, and which occurs with most children, is notably absent. Because of this, and because of additional idiosyncratic qualities typical of the children, the usual methods of psychotherapy prove ineffective. The presence of even one such child in the complement of a typical activity therapy group is sufficient to destroy it.

These severely impaired children are highly resistive to individual treatment when it is attempted. It makes them uncomfortable and induces much anxiety. Their potential and tolerance for libidinal binding is very weak. If standard group methods of therapy are used, either activity or analytical, their aggressive behavior becomes exacerbated. The fundamental elements of activity therapy with less disturbed children—unconditional acceptance and an extraordinary degree of permissiveness—are threatening to whatever intactness there remains in these ego-deficient children. They defend against demonstrations of kindness, particularly by adults. However, unconsciously they really need and want reasonable limits and guidance from authority figures to bring some order to their chaotic emotionality. In the absence of any therapeutic intervention, it is likely that many of these children will develop psychoses, psychopathic characters, or other serious disorders.

As early as 1959, experimental attempts were made using modified activity group methods with these impulse-ridden children. The interventions used by therapists are significantly different from those described heretofore with groups of less disturbed children. The therapist interposes himself as a mediator in situations that the children cannot manage. He may act to diminish an extraordinary threat to a child, or offer suggestions to the group about alternative ways of handling problems. The group is made more *aware* of how it can obtain gratifications through its own mediation. The therapist actively engages the children in discourse at propitious times, thereby "teaching" the advantage of language in overcoming interindividual differences and group conflicts. While using these procedures, a therapist is at no time judgmental or critical of acting-out behavior, which would entirely negate the possibility of children's responding to suggestions for modifying their ways. One basic goal is to encourage the children by demonstrating (sometimes through role-play) how they can benefit by new ways of coping. This renders them more malleable to group (social) influences. The therapist provides essential nurturance on an oral level, which is the fixated development phase characteristic of the primitive emotionality of ego-weak children. Because they have experienced early nurturant deprivation—usually of a severe nature—it is essential that the corrective group experience be *maintained for two years minimally*.

Interpretations of children's behavior are never offered. This would be fruitless since the etiology of the children's problems is rooted largely at the preverbal period of development. Thus, the use of psychodynamic interpretations is precluded. As with children with primary behavior disorders,[1] whom these ego-deficient children resemble in some ways, what one sees in their manifest behavior is basically "what they are."

Experience has shown that homogeneous grouping is most effective in modified activity therapy. Were less troubled children to be included in a group of impulsive children, they would find it very difficult to sustain themselves against the provocative onslaughts of the latter. To compose a

[1] See pp. 3–4

group solely of ego-deficient children need not be a difficult problem because even among them there is sufficient diversity to provide a workable, interactive group complement, albeit one that requires special alertness on the part of the therapist.

While the children's presenting behavior has a pronounced antisocial quality, the treatment group as a whole can acquire a behavior-modifying influence on its component members. To start with, these severely troubled children, who are capable of defying social conventions, have responsive resonance to each other's atypical social behavior. They are familiar with each other's ways. When social growth takes place as a result of treatment, the group acquires considerable therapeutic leverage in controlling the behavior of its individual members. This constitutes therapy by a group, a principle that applies in all forms of activity therapy.

This innovative, modified activity group method is experimental, but it has already demonstrated its success. With many children there is a diminution of antisocial behavior. One implication which can be drawn from this is that some degree of psychological *reconditioning* has taken place, perhaps an elaboration of what was a minimal superego influence. Also, the children may have incorporated some of the benignant, tolerant, helpful qualities of the therapist. It remains to be determined to what extent the manifest changes become assimilated and will continue to influence behavior once treatment has been terminated. Follow-up studies of the children in Chapter 10 revealed that a majority of them maintained their improvements.

It is conceivable that, in cases where there is appreciable ego-strengthening and acquired trust in a relationship with the therapist, more tolerance has developed for a transference relationship. It would be worthwhile to attempt individual therapy following such changes. This might be tried after a course in modified activity group therapy, or some children might be placed in *combined* treatment.

Chapters 9 and 10 describe applications of modified activity therapy groups with latency children. These children had been subjected to extraordinary degrees of nurturance deprivation, separation, anxiety, and severe punitive handling by parents and/or their surrogates. The consequences of such traumatization during early development are typical of children with pronounced ego-impairments.

The reader will appreciate the inordinate demands placed on therapists who work with these special groups: the need to comprehend the etiology of the children's problems; to anticipate their impulsive behavior; to become hypersensitive to their own countertransference reactions to the unusually provocative behavior of the children; and to use interventions that are markedly different from those ordinarily employed in activity group therapy.

CHAPTER 9

Treatment of Ego-Impoverished Latency Children Through Modified Activity Group Therapy

MARGARET G. FRANK

THE PURPOSE OF THIS CHAPTER is to describe some modifications in the standard method of activity group therapy designed for the treatment of children with marked disruptions in ego development. Using the activity method in its traditional form would be counterproductive for these children. While this adaptation has proved helpful with children who are not able to contain their impulses, a word of caution is in order before examining its psychological rationale and the special therapeutic interventions employed with a highly disturbed patient population.

In recent years the field of mental health has become inordinately "technique-hungry," particularly in attempting to cope with the pressing problems represented by an increasing number of children with rather primitive pathology, problems that have seemingly defied the ministrations of the conventional therapies, both individual and group. As a consequence, therapists have become frustrated to a point where they reach for almost any innovative procedures that seem promising. The author shares this frustration but recognizes a need to examine carefully new group methods to ensure that they are based in reasonable theoretical formulations and practical methodology. Deviations from proven methods of group therapy with children become valid only when they can demonstrate their efficiency, no mean task with latency-age children whose ego deficits offer a challenge to the most seasoned child therapists.

There is much clinical evidence to support the use of a group modality in treating children in latency. Experience has shown that the group approach tends to complement the usual developmental tasks associated with latency, in addition to providing therapeutic influences to correct emotional problems. These findings apply also to the exceptional children we are presently concerned with, children whose difficulties in growing stem from damaged ego capacities resulting in severe malformations of personality and character.

Activity Group Therapy: Standard and Modified

It will be helpful to draw a picture of the classical activity group therapy method, which can serve as background for the modified group procedures. The principles and method of activity group therapy, as devised by S. R. Slavson in 1934, are appropriate for emotionally troubled latency children who have relatively well-developed egos. In its fundamental application, the method employed by Slavson in inapplicable with the special children described here. Were it to be employed with such ego-deficient children, it would further challenge their limited coping adaptability and wreak havoc with the group itself.[1]

The psychological premises underlying the use of a noninterpretive activity group method and how it affects children's feelings and behavior also apply to the modified procedure with our exceptional children. The difference is in the nature of the therapist's role and functions, which are significantly altered. The most important difference in the modified group procedure is a departure from a therapeutic climate of almost unconditional acceptance of the children and their behavior, a climate that typifies standard activity group therapy. In the special activity group, the therapist assumes an active, *participatory* role whenever situations in the group necessitate it. This is mandated by the severe inability of these children to order their experiences, the major function of the ego. They are unable to tolerate frustration or to handle their impulses and affects. Thus, we see a population weak in adaptive resources.

In describing the theoretical elements and practical therapeutic interventions that are used in modified activity therapy, information has been assembled from several sources: Slavson's standard activity group method; ego psychology; observations of emotionally healthy children in group activities; and, last but not least, observations of gifted nursery school teachers whose educational efforts foster healthy maturation and development.

---

[1]For a more definitive exposition of the indications and counterindications for activity group therapy, the reader may consult S. R. Slavson, *An Introduction to Group Therapy*, Commonwealth Fund, New York, 1945.

Basic Therapeutic Requirements

The following conditions are necessary in treatment groups with children with marked ego deficits. The conditions are presented separately for the sake of emphasis but, in fact, they are interdependent: 1. A physical and emotional setting is required in which children may express their needs, impulses, and conflicts—as deviant as these may be—in safety and relative comfort. The reference is to both physical and *ego* safety and comfort.

2. This requires a nurturing atmosphere—a basic condition for corrective therapy—which is brought into being by an accepting, uncritical therapist.

3. The children must receive assistance from the therapist at indicated times while they are acquiring better social ways through active engagements with each other and with the therapist. A readiness for new "ego learnings" develops.

4. New coping skills—personal and social—have to be pragmatically experienced by the children. This mandates that the therapist often must assume a paraclinical, didactic role, typified by an understanding of the unusual needs of these children, much tolerance with their impulsive nature, and an ability to communicate with the children in a mild, reasonable way even in the midst of abrasive angry exchanges between group members.

Nature of the Children

Who are these children? They are individuals prone to handle their frustrations and problems through impulsive, unthinking action. They are "rejects" from classical activity therapy groups, and also failures in individual therapy when it is attempted. They are essentially unfamiliar with sublimation. While their vocabularies are replete with four-letter words, language itself has not become a meaningful, useful tool for socially appropriate interaction and, more importantly, it has not aided the ego in organizing and handling feelings. Despite these children's attitudes of not caring and their apparent self-assuredness, their real self-perceptions are highly negative. They conceive the world "out there" as menacing. In their perceptions of interpersonal relationships with adults and with peers, they seemingly lack awareness of cause and effect. They do not see themselves as having instrumental roles in how the world responds to them. The reactions that their behavior elicits from others confirm for them their distorted expectations.

The foregoing characterization of ego-impoverished children eschews the use of diagnostic "labels"; emphasis is placed on the stunted and limited nature of the children's ego capacities. Generally, they are children with severe pathology in personality and character.

The Value of a Group with Latency Children

As noted briefly above, a group constitutes an important mode of treatment for these children. Most young people in the latency period, no matter how disabled they may be emotionally, yearn for peer relationships, a manifestation of *social hunger* (Slavson). Children who lack this need, who are rare indeed, cannot be treated in activity groups. They will probably require residential treatment. For many children, a group as a therapeutic instrument provides an important ingredient that is lacking in dyadic treatment—safety, in the sense of emotional distance from the therapist. These children, because of deficits in early caretaking, yearn for closeness and "defend" against their wishes through the need for distance. On the other hand, a therapy group replicates the family psychologically, and it serves as an expressive vehicle for self-revelation.

Composition of Groups

The usual principles for the composition of activity therapy groups, with respect to psychological balance, do not apply in the special group. Ordinarily, in the standard activity method, children are selected with a view to how they exert self-correcting influences upon each other, one result of which is to prevent excessive acting-out behavior. The composition of the special group is homogeneous. Ego-weak children become anxious if placed with more intact children. Whatever ego integrity they may possess becomes threatened by the examples set by less disturbed children.

Yet, there are detectable differences in these children despite the common problems of immaturity, impulsiveness, and weak ego structure. For instance, a child who becomes fearful under the threat of more aggressive children, and who then clings to the therapist for protection, reveals to the group that it is possible to be close to an adult. This perception is particularly important for children who are characteristically distrustful of and well defended against adults. There is always a variety of differing emotional problems and coping behaviors that influence the nature of events in the group and are utilizable by the therapist in helping the corrective process. The most important difference in the modified activity method is the active participation by the therapist in catalyzing the limited potential ego resources the children are capable of using.

It has been ascertained from experience with such groups that even negative traits in children lend themselves to reconstructive experiences, if they are carefully monitored by a therapist. Some of these children possess a sense of humor, albeit sadistic or self-derogatory, which can be turned to social advantage in the group by stimulating verbal exchanges and encouraging a group to think about motivation. This leads to what is a relatively new experience for the children, a rudimentary exposure to self-observation. It is a good idea to include in a group at least one child who, to start with, uses language in a manner indicating some ability to think causally; also, a child who is capable of expressing sadness and disappointment, who can penetrate the character armor of self-protection and toughness that typifies these children. These qualities in the children, supported in treatment, serve as "learning models" for others.

The Meeting Room

Children who cannot discuss feelings and conflicts need enough physical space for action and separation from others until they acquire the tool of effective language in interpersonal interactions, for these children are unable to handle overstimulation and are subject to even greater regression. The materials—arts, crafts, games—meet their needs to "hide," to make things, and to communicate nonverbally. The kinds of materials and the quantities provided are selected with care, because of these children's susceptibility to stimulation and regression, which can be induced by such items as finger paints. Unlike in the treatment of more ego-intact children, where benign regression occurs as part of the therapy, the therapist blocks experiences that tend to foster regression.

In one girls' group, the persistent regressive behavior was threatening to destroy the climate of safety. In an attempt to uncover the reasons for the regressive behavior, the setting was discovered to be at fault. The agency, which had little experience in group treatment of ego-deficient children, had unwisely used a nursery room setting for the activity group. Many of the materials used by the much younger children could not be hidden from the therapy group, and these items were responsible for the extraordinarily regressive play of the nine- and ten-year-old girls.

An overview of a well-designed treatment setting reveals a group of six or seven children, homogeneous as to gender, preferably with a therapist of the same gender, in a room equipped with simple furnishings and with work and play materials of a nature to attract the children's interests and promote interactions between them.[2]

Emotional Setting: The Therapist and His "Equipment"

The most important element of the treatment setting is represented by the attitude and behavior of the therapist. Through his actions, reactions, and

[2]For more details regarding treatment settings and equipment, see S. R. Slavson and M. Schiffer, *Group Psychotherapies for Children: A Textbook*, International Universities Press, New York, 1975, Appendix.

interactions are projected the emotional tones that act therapeutically and influence the children's behavior. It is the therapist who provides the psychological nurturance and acceptance that eventually affect these guarded, wary children. It is the therapist's ministrations that establish the basic feeling of safety. It would be well to examine closely these qualities and the nature of the therapist's interventions.

Most people drawn to the field of psychotherapy, particularly those who treat children, tend to view themselves as nurturing, accepting, "safe" people, as far as children are concerned. A question arises: What aspects of the clinical role exemplify these qualities?

This and related questions were addressed by the author to trainees in group therapy who were being prepared to work with groups of children such as we are presently concerned with. The trainees were asked to list five examples of a therapist's behavior and attitudes that fulfill the requisites they deemed important.

The trainees defined "nurturance" in terms of interest, availability, "doing for the children," and caring for them. "Acceptance" was generally viewed as a willingness to tolerate children's emotional expressions and behavior whether they were liked or disliked by a therapist. "Safety" was described as a feeling in children engendered by the therapist's nonretaliation in the face of the children's acting out.

One cannot argue with these definitions, as far as they go. But they do not go far enough. The author is reminded of a group that she led some time ago. It was composed of pregnant young women who were expecting their first babies. They were not clinic patients. They were assembled from the community at large, each eager and anxious to "do a good job" as mothers. They saw themselves as loving and giving. And they were. But the notion that their role as a parent might necessitate their behaving in ways which their children would experience as painful, or that they themselves would have moments of panic, hatred, and disgust with their children and parenting, was totally alien to the picture they had drawn for themselves. Their images of what they *ought* to be as parents placed an added burden on an already challenging new experience. They were doomed to fail because of their own preconceived ideas about good parenting. The aim of this group process was to expose the expectant mothers to some of the impossible requirements they had set for themselves, and to try to have them appreciate and accept what initially seemed to them to be totally unacceptable feelings.

Like these parents, therapists who work with groups of ego-deficient children need help in accepting feelings which, to start with, do not meet the attributes they consider acceptable in a therapist. They, too, need to enlarge their definitions of nurturance to include such interventions as setting limits and moving in to interrupt children's acting-out behavior, even if the children do not like such interventions.

It is essential for a therapist to establish clearly in his own mind the differences between *protection* and *punishment*, the latter being altogether inimical to the therapeutic intent. Protection refers to actions performed by a therapist when a member, or the group itself, is subjected to undue threat. This does not refer necessarily to unpleasant or even painful experiences, but rather to *threats to the ego*. Improper punishment constitutes actions taken by the therapist when his own ego is being threatened, and he sees no alternative except to intervene promptly. Because of the countertransferential response, the action taken is usually countertherapeutic in effect. It should be borne in mind that the potential for countertransference responses in all forms of activity group therapy with latency children is probably greater than in any type of treatment, with patients of all ages. This characteristic is even more prevalent in groups of children with severe ego-deficiencies, who are prone to much provocative acting out.

Clearly, then, a therapist needs to be free to understand situations "on the spot." The keys to correct assessments of what children are doing emanate from knowledge of the special nature of their problems, the therapist's self-knowledge, and, perhaps most important, acceptance of self.

In one group supervised by the author, a situation arose in which the children were taunting a child "unmercifully." The therapist disliked the scene and wanted to protect the victim and punish the taunters. She was aware of the therapeutic pitfalls of translating such feelings into action. What was lacking, however, was recognition of the fact that, at the moment, she *hated* the group. She had never dreamed that she could have anything other than loving feelings toward her patients. Once she was helped in supervision to acknowledge the existence of her strong countertransference, she became able to modify her feelings and help the group. We will return to this vignette later to view her clinical role and behavior in light of its ego-enhancing effects on the children.

Countertransference

The reader may question the degree of emphasis being placed on countertransference. All persons who have treated child patients, particularly in groups, are aware of the great potential for a therapist to encounter residues of development problems and emotional ambivalences from his own childhood. Most therapists attempt to apply themselves assiduously to the management of situations in which their countertransference feelings arise, if they are conscious of them. Too often, however, it seems that they are concerned with eliminating such reactions entirely. This is a fruitless goal. It is more realistic to distinguish between feelings and behavior. Countertransference, whether we like it or not, will be evoked during psychotherapy.

Therapists must recognize and accept the reality of their negative feelings and trace their origins before they can help patients learn how to accept their own inner feelings and free themselves to acquire new, more adaptive behavior.

The picture the author is attempting to portray of a therapist with a group of seriously disturbed, impulsive children is of someone who is prepared to *protect, nurture* and *"teach,"* concurrently. This special treatment group and the role of the therapist will become further clarified in the context of actual vignettes from activity groups.

Six girls were referred because of extremely disruptive behavior in their respective schools. They were initially delighted with the notion of joining a group. In the early sessions, they quickly displayed social hunger, including their frustrations and their propensity for anger. The first six group sessions were punctuated by arguments and actual fights over the use of materials. The therapist could barely bring enough supplies to gratify them, and she was soon torn between feeling helpless when she stayed out of the fights and acting like a "policewoman" when she interjected herself to stop them. At a moment of temporary quiet in one session, induced by her serving refreshments, she openly shared her dilemma with the children, describing the extraordinary amount of fighting that was taking place. She literally asked the girls to share the burden of her feelings. They responded by asking why it was necessary to stop fighting, since they enjoyed it. The therapist suggested that "some day they might find other ways to have fun." She added further that while she did not think fighting was the best way, she was not telling them "they *had* to stop." Also, she said that she would not interfere unless one of the girls looked "really scared," or the whole group looked as if it could not stop itself.

At this point the therapist suggested a plan: each week group members would take turns in being a "fight watcher," in this way assuming the therapist's role. The "watcher" could consult the therapist if she wanted to and could call a halt to a fight if she saw fit to do so. The therapist concluded with an added comment that if this plan was to work, the group would have to comply with the "rule": if anyone disagreed with the "watcher," the matter *could be discussed*.

The girls were eager to be "watchers." Many disagreements arose about the correctness of "watchers'" decisions. To describe such vocal exchanges as "discussions" would be misleading. They were rancorous and angry. However, at such times the therapist became active in directing the girls' attention to their facial expressions and body gestures, relating these to possible feelings. She "wondered" aloud how each girl might better control her actions while questioning the behavior of other group members.

The fighting continued for a time before it began to abate, as did the girls' interest in acting as "watchers." What did emerge, simultaneously, were such comments as: "Hey, if we keep this up we're going to be at each other!" Or, in a light tone that was new for them, "Here comes a fight!" During this phase, the therapist would occasionally intervene, suggesting "other ways" to resolve conflict situations.

A number of themes stand out in this vignette. First, the therapist was mobilized to intervene out of overriding frustration. She was aware that she, and the group, were obviously heading for an impasse that could trap her in a nontherapeutic position. It was her responsibility to find a way out. She offered the girls alternatives, bearing in mind their limited adaptive abilities. They were accustomed to "outside" controls from adults, and punitive ones at that. While they were not individually equipped to manage themselves, the suggested peer-control device offered them, including the privilege of challenging a "watcher's" decision, provided opportunities for entirely novel experiences. They were being made aware of visual cues, were seeing the possibility of other than conscious motivation for their behavior, were identifying concealed feelings, and were using language as a tool in problem-solving.

The question arises as to why the children responded favorably to the therapist's initial suggestion. It may be that they sensed the possible loss of the nurturant person and the desired group (social) experience if matters continued as they were. Also, the girls may have wished to please the therapist. The power she offered them as "watchers" was attractive to them. The therapist, in attempting to help the children master obstreperous behavior, may have touched upon elements of ego-intactness that reflected the children's secret desire for greater harmony in their lives. None of these possibilities is exclusive of the others. The global "message" conveyed by the therapist's intervention is that she encouraged the children toward self-management. This was done by conveying continuing acceptance of the children as they were and trust in their being able to surmount problems.

At no time did the therapist act judgmental or critical. Acutally, she informed the children that she was not proscribing fighting. It could go on "as long as no one got hurt." It can be conjectured that in due time the therapist's reasonableness helped to relax inner tensions in the children so that they could learn more efficient use of language in coping with problems.

The therapist also began to respond to the girls' great interest in movies and romance magazines. She directed their attention to facial and behavioral cues in the pictures and also made up short stories to heighten the girls' awareness of these revealing factors. If one girl commented that an actress looked "sad," "mad," or "pleased," the therapist would inquire as to what observations led to such conclusions. A game was created—a sort of "feeling" charade—in which the group had to guess the feelings that they discerned in the pictures, and explain how they had arrived at such decisions. The notion of how people tended to translate their feeling through personal mannerisms was introduced by the therapist at one point when it was her "turn" to participate. She acted her role by slumping her body in a depressed stance with an obvious forced smile as if to discredit her real emotion.

Role-Playing

In its sophisticated form, role-playing helps sensitize participants toward recognition of enacted roles, thus bringing into sharper relief the feelings and attitudes of the persons whose roles they portray. In therapy groups, [with ego-deficient children—M.S.] role-play procedures can be simplified to broaden children's comprehension, as in the charade game, that people can *feel* one way and *behave* in an entirely different manner. The "scripts" need to be taken from the children's own experiences.

In another therapy group the therapist linked role-playing to the girls' interest in boys. She would assume the role of an alter ego to express the concealed hopes of the girls, their eagerness to be noticed by boys, and their fears of rejection. At the same time, in her role enactments the therapist would attempt to conceal inner feelings by acting disinterested and even hostile toward the male object of interest. First the children became adept at exposing the real motivants underlying the therapist's role-playing. Then they became more open about exposing their own feelings, which they had been incapable of doing before.

Such role-playing games have elements of *action* and *distance*. At first the children do not view themselves in the roles they enact, verbalize about, and criticize. This distance (ego defense) provides them with a sense of safety. The therapist's part in role-playing, which involves the children in identifying less than admirable traits and emotions in "others," slowly diminishes their fears of personal disclosures. As they become sensitized to the *universality* of common emotions, they become more capable—some for the first time—of recognizing such feelings in themselves. Prior to this, most of these ego-weak children had recourse to immediate acting out as a primitive defense against threat and anxiety. Whenever they could not resort to flight in self-protection, they fought. The role-playing exercises were useful in helping them see the relationship between what was formerly almost a total lack of awareness of their feelings and the automatic, impulsive behavior that was typical of them.

A group was formed of six very infantile, acting-out girls who appeared totally lacking in frustration tolerance and who habitually discharged their florid feelings without apparent concern for the effects on others. One of them had a tendency toward clownishness, and she revealed in this role a minimal awareness of her underlying feelings. There were idiosyncratic qualities in the behavior of the other girls that served to distinguish their atypical behavior.

The therapist in this group knew from the very onset of treatment that she would have to intervene, since the girls were likely to get into situations that had potential for inflicting injury upon each other. One of the problems she anticipated was that they would run out of the treatment room and perhaps explore the building where the therapy group was being conducted. To prevent the possibility of the therapist having to assume a directly prohibitive role in stopping this, other agency personnel were stationed nearby to take the girls in tow and return them to the meeting room. It was felt that once the children had been sufficiently exposed to the group and its offerings, both socially and through crafts activities, there would be less need for them to wander out of the room.

As anticipated, the girls were very aggressive from the outset. In one early session they fought over scissors; there were not enough for all to use in cutting fabric. They kicked each other, spat, cursed, and acted in almost ungovernable fashion. The therapist intervened: "Let me tell you about what some girls would do if they all wanted to use scissors at the same time." Several possibilities were described: numbering pieces of paper, which would then be drawn to establish the order of using the scissors; working in pairs simultaneously; talking over the problem and arriving at a decision. The therapist used this approach repeatedly for many months until the girls slowly began to accept suggestions for resolving differences. At no time did the therapist comment directly about the fighting, nor did she indicate in her manner that she disliked it or wanted it stopped.

It is interesting that the children's beginning response to the therapist's suggestions was the method of deciding by mechanical selection of numbered papers. This was consonant with their immaturity—a dependence on compulsive-obsessive rituals that are more typical of early development. As the number of group sessions increased, they began to show greater tolerance for talking about their disagreements.

The therapist began to "teach" the use of role-playing in a way that offered the girls an opportunity for emotive expression and also allowed for some insulation against direct expression of inner feelings, for which the girls were still unprepared. Scenarios were solicited from them, usually episodes dealing with school and encounters with teachers. One girl would represent the teacher, the other an infuriated child. The teacher, of course, was always depicted in an unreasonable, punitive role while the child's cause was always meritorious. The therapist participated in the dialogue, somewhat in the nature of a Greek chorus, describing the feelings of the litigants, particularly the child's. In describing the child's feelings, the therapist sensitively exposed an inner fear despite the outward display of aggression against the teacher, and also conveyed a secret longing to be liked by an adult. The group denied this, some saying that they "never felt that way." In one session, the therapist constructed a scenario dealing only with the girls' denials and their inability to express real fears and needs.

At this point in the group, the records of the therapist gave an impression of a drama club rather than a carefully implemented phase in psychotherapy. But the girls were very much immersed in the role-playing. It was a vehicle that engaged them actively, which was needful. And it provided them with an emotional distance while they were learning about themselves. Significantly, the girls became able to assume the therapist's analytical role, which brought them closer to an examination of the student-role and eventually their own feelings. At that time they could more reasonably apply themselves to a broader understanding of the teacher-student episodes, with more accurate affirmations of how teachers felt.

These events occurred over a period of one and a half years. In addition, the girls continued to engage in various arts and crafts and game activities. In response to the therapist's nurturing support and her active interventions, they developed enhanced capacities of talking about feelings and behavior. They learned new ways of adapting, of supporting and encouraging each other, and of planning as a group. In many ways, they acted like a well-equipped social entity.

Parallels Between Nursery and Activity Groups

Some of the technical interventions used in activity group treatment of ego-impoverished children were "borrowed" from observations of how gifted teachers behaved in nursery classes with younger children. While these teachers were not academically conversant with ego psychology and psychotherapy, they were the embodiment of emotional nurturance. Their skillful techniques promoted ego growth and development in children. Many times the author observed the careful ways in which a teacher would intervene in aggressive situations involving two or more children. In a firm yet kind voice: "Can you tell him in a *different* way that you don't like what he did to you?" Or, when a child had struck his playmate, the teacher might say: "*Tell* him that you don't want him to grab what you are playing with." With such guidance the children are made aware that adults can accept children's angry feelings and not admonish them while at the same time the children are encouraged ("taught") to learn more useful social ways. In other settings a common adult message to angry children is usually a curt "You must not hit!" What the child assimilates from such a remark is that not only his behavior but *he* is frowned upon. Feeling and action are not differentiated.

It is quite valid psychologically that observations made in nursery school settings are applicable in activity groups with highly disturbed older children. Impulsive, aggressive acts performed by prelatency children in nursery classes are developmentally "normal" because the young children have yet to acquire a level of social maturation wherein they are capable of monitoring erupting feelings and making effective sublimations. Such mature adjustments need to be learned, hopefully through educational experiences provided by adults who understand the needs and coping abilities of prelatency children.

Similar interventions with older, ego-deficient children are equally efficacious because the children, in their regressed—probably fixated—states, are emotionally akin to nursery-age children. There is one important difference, however: the older children have become hardened in their suspiciousness and distrust of adults, which defenses have to be breached before they can become accessible to corrective therapeutic influences. Nursery children, in contrast, do not possess these paranoid-like characterological defenses against adults. they are still amenable to *educational* influences when the latter are properly administered.

"EXERCISES" IN THINKING ABOUT FEELINGS

A direct translation of another technique observed in nursery classes to activity groups is a game whose purpose is to help young children view alternative behaviors and to *think about* how their acts affect other children.

In a therapy group, girls were given scenes to enact involving feelings and alternative ways of handling them. An example: "You are angry with your friend because she stood you up and you missed the beginning of a movie."

The suggestions for handling this situation were as follows:

1. When you see her, snub her.
2. When you see her, curse her out and leave her.
3. When you see her, tell her how angry you are, but say it quietly.
4. When you see her, tell her how angry you were and ask her why she stood you up.

Both "actors" and "audience" were asked which suggestions they preferred. They usually picked alternatives 1 and 2 and the "actors" always had more difficulty portraying roles 3 and 4 than the other roles. The same performers were then asked to reverse roles and act as the "friend" who had not kept the date. Another bit was added to the scenario: the "friend's" mother had been responsible for her absence. Now the group opted for the last alternative, 4, where the expression of feeling was modified and more reasonable.

Another pertinent observation about gifted teachers in nursery school groups is that they always demonstrated in their manner of making suggestions that they trusted the children to learn better ways and that they thought the children would be pleased with their newly acquired, more mature social adaptations. Two episodes illuminate this.

A three-year-old boy had trouble settling down during rest period when stories were read to the group. The teacher remarked that "some day" he, too, would be able to have a "quiet time." Several weeks later, when this child did settle down to listen, the teacher was heard to say, with evident pleasure, "Doesn't that feel good! Look how still you are able to be!"

The second episode involved two five-year-old boys and their mothers. The boys had been fighting because one had wrecked the other's block building. The mothers rushed in to mediate the fight, urging both children to voice apologies. The teacher quietly took over, countermanding the mothers. "I don't think they have to make apologies right now. Maybe later when they feel like it they will say something. It will make them feel better inside." Not too long after this, the boys were observed playing together in evident harmony. Their "apology" was consummated in pragmatic fashion, perhaps not vocalized, but certainly it was influenced by the teacher's simple, practical message.

The trust in children's abilities to learn and to compromise, depicted in these two vignettes, was paralleled in the therapist's handling of the scapegoating incident referred to earlier. At a point when the girl who was being taunted was close to tears, the therapist startled the group by interjecting: "I hope you will find some way to end this, because I'm afraid you won't feel very good about yourselves if you keep this up." The group, including the girl who was being scapegoated, had anticipated that when the therapist started to speak, she was going to scold the taunters. They were completely taken aback by the unexpected expression of consideration for the hurt child and for the welfare of the others. They were as yet unused to such tolerant understanding from an adult. Also, they were unfamiliar with the implicit trust on the part of the therapist.

At a later time in the same group, the therapist addressed herself even more directly to situations in which the same girl managed to draw the ire of the group upon herself. The therapist's comments were designed to make the girl more cognizant of the provocative quality of her behavior.

Conclusion

The aim of this presentation has been to describe how standard activity group therapy can be modified to strengthen ego functions in children who are notably weak to start with and whose impulsive anger and limited adaptive capacities would be exacerbated if they were treated in the highly permissive, *laissez-faire* environment that exists in activity groups composed of children who possess stronger egos. The methods used in the special activity groups are geared to helping the children develop improved self-images and better interpersonal relationships with peers and adults. They are encouraged through participatory group experiences to experience what represent for them entirely novel ways of resolving conflicts. They learn to use language in more appropriate ways, to recognize their deeper feelings, and to reflect about those feelings, and to govern their tendency to react impulsively.

The fact that these modifications in group therapy have proved effective is a result not only of the specificity of the described interventions but of the broader context of the treatment. The method is based on a belief that limited ego capacities can be improved in a treatment atmosphere where there exists an acceptance of children *as they are* and trust in their potential for learning other ways of behaving. To accomplish this, therapists have to understand the unusual emotional pathology of the children, be prepared to withstand the extraordinary kind of aggressive acting out they are capable of, be alert to the countertransference feelings these children induce, and be able to provide the emotional nurturance of which the children were deprived during earlier development.

CHAPTER 10

Experiential Group Treatment of Severely Deprived Latency-Age Children

Saul Scheidlinger

There has been an increasing interest during the last two decades in the problem of children with severe ego pathology. They have variously been termed "severe non-neurotic ego disturbance," "borderline," "atypical," "pre-psychotic," "autistic," or "schizophrenic."[1] The treatment efforts described in the literature most frequently involve the provision of a therapeutic environment in an institution. There has also been some experimentation in extramural settings, in which the usual techniques of individual psychotherapy are modified to suit the special needs of these children. In line with the frequently held view of a guarded prognosis unless treatment is initiated prior to age six,[2] much of this work has been carried on at the preschool age level.

This chapter deals with an experimental use of activity group therapy for latency-age[3] children (aged 8–13) who have experienced marked deprivation in their lives and consequently have developed serious disturbances in ego functioning. Carried out within the framework of a nonsectarian family

---

[1]R. Eckstein et al., "Childhood Schizophrenia and Allied Conditions," in L. Bellak, ed., *Schizophrenia: A Review of the Syndrome*, Logos Press, New York, 1958.

[2]E. Buxbaum, "Technique of Child Therapy: A Critical Evaluation," in *The Psychoanalytic Study of the Child*, Vol. 9, International Universities Press, New York, 1954.

[3]The term "latency-age" is employed loosely here and is meant to include preadolescents.

service agency, the observations and techniques to be discussed were gradually evolved in the course of our six years of work with these clients. (A few of our groups contained a majority of such cases—in most of the groups, they were in the minority. In all, such children constituted about one-third of the total number of sixty children currently in group treatment at the agency.)

Presenting Problems

What about the backgrounds of these children? About 90 percent black, with a sprinkling of whites and Puerto Ricans, these boys and girls came invariably from families with severe social and economic pathology. Marked emotional deprivation, especially in the earliest years, absence of parental figures (usually the father), and transient relationships by the mother with several men were repetitive features. Such problems as lack of mothering, frequent parental neglect with inconsistent handling, and harsh physical punishment stood out. Not infrequently the child was exposed to direct sexual seductiveness and delinquent patterns.

How, in greater detail, did some of these children appear?

Carl

Carl, age nine and a half, was extremely moody, sullen, and withdrawn. His moods seemed unrelated to external factors. He had no close relationships with anyone and gave the surface impression of passivity. Suspiciousness and shyness with adults were noted. There was a twitching of the face, and both fear of and fascination with the theme of death. At school Carl stood out as different and aloof. He worked far below his capacity and was markedly retarded in reading. Although Carl was black, he insisted he was of Indian blood.

The mother, who was psychotic, had been in and out of mental hospitals for years. During these periods the children (including an older brother and a younger sister) were neglected, often without any adult being in the picture for a number of days. Later on, a great-aunt, a sickly woman over seventy years old, would assume care of the children until her niece's return from the hospital. The parents were divorced when Carl was a baby.

Bernice

Bernice, age nine, was brought to the agency because of disobedience, poor social relationships, fighting with siblings, playing with matches, bed-wetting, and occasional thumb-sucking. She was described as an impulsive, slightly delinquent youngster who exhibited little capacity for self-control. At school she was defiant with adults. She stole money and small objects, mostly to "buy" favor with other children.

Bernice was born out of wedlock, as were her two younger siblings. Each of them had a different father, which served to enhance their confusion regarding their identity. The family unit, consisting of the mother and the three children, lived in a one-room apartment. Bernice and her sister had to share a bed with their mother.

Bernice became enuretic at the of seven after the mother had forced her to stop sucking her thumb by applying bitter fluids on the thumb, described to the child as poisons. Once the restrictions were removed, Bernice began sucking her thumb again, and the bed-wetting ceased. Shortly before the group treatment commenced, Bernice broke herself of the thumb-sucking habit by putting a piece of tape on her thumb. While successful in stopping the habit, Bernice became more withdrawn and depressed, sulking or crying frequently for no apparent reason.

Vivian

Vivian, age ten, was described by her mother and her teacher as a "nervous" child. She reacted to stress situations by becoming frightened and going to bed. Threats of whipping by the mother left Vivian shaking and trembling. She was also very fearful of insects. The mother described her as a restless sleeper who cried out in her sleep and sleepwalked on occasion. There were rivalry and aggressiveness with an older brother. Vivian was depicted by our agency's homemaker as quiet and withdrawn. She did not play like the other children and would often go off to a corner, sit in a chair, and rub her lip.

The school reported that Vivian was fidgety and talked out of turn. At camp she displayed occasional temper outbursts and rapid mood shifts. Vivian had become more "nervous" after the death of a brother several years before. Vivian and her sister had to help in caring for the youngest child.

The mother was described as a dull woman, noncommunicative, and markedly depressed. She was hospitalized for cardiac disease, and during this time a homemaker helped in caring for the children. Upon the mother's return, she became pregnant again. She did not want a fifth child—the four children were already too much for her. The father, a passive and ineffectual person, was extremely dependent on his own domineering mother.

Vivian's severe pathology emerged with particular clarity during the first few group sessions. She looked at times as though she were in a trance. She made faces, smiled, talked to herself, and even addressed inanimate objects. She was completely unable to relate to the other girls, staying close to the adult.

These case illustrations readily suggest a similarity of our children with the severe ego-disturbed cases described by Rank, Alpert, Mahler, and especially those depicted by Weil.[4] The latter discussed in considerable detail the failure in adequate ego development characterized by poor social-emotional adaptations, problems of control, and various anxiety manifestations, ranging from fears to obsessive-compulsive mechanisms. Perhaps because of the greater amount of actual deprivation and want (in addition to emotional deprivation), we were particularly impressed in our children with the degree of oral fixations—a primitive, oral greediness coupled with an impatient, hostile expectation that these needs would not be met. Hand in hand with poor reality-testing, with difficulty in distinguishing between inner and outer sources of tension, went serious distortions in the perceptions of other people, especially adults. Related to this was an underlying tone of depression with an extremely low self-concept and the problem of confused identity.

While none of these clients fitted into the concept of latency as summarized by Fries,[5] it is also noteworthy that we never worked with any in whom the ego pathology was all-embracing. Thus, along with arrested or regressed ego functions went other functions that were reasonably well developed and served as anchorage points for the therapeutic intervention.

Group Therapy Techniques

The group treatment techniques we evolved for these children constituted in effect a modification of the activity group therapy developed by S. R. Slavson in the late 1930s. Briefly, this method, devised for less severely disturbed children, stresses the acting out of conflicts and deviant behavior patterns within the framework of a permissive environment.[6] The basic therapeutic elements accrue from the interaction of the children with each

[4]B. Rank, "Treatment of Young Children with Atypical Development by Psychoanalytic Technique," in G. Bychowski, et al, eds., *Specialized Techniques in Psychotherapy*, Basic Books, New York, New York, 1952; A. Alpert, "A Special Therapeutic Technique for Certain Developmental Disorders in Prelatency Children," *American Journal of Orthopsychiatry*, 27: 256–270, 1957; M. S. Mahler, "On Child Psychosis and Schizophrenia: Autistic and Symbiotic Infantile Psychoses," in *The Psychoanalytic Study of the Child*, Vol. 7, International Universities Press, New York, 1952; A. P. Weil, "Certain Severe Disturbances of Ego Development in Childhood," in ibid., Vol. 8.

[5]M. E. Fries, "Review of the Literature on the Latency Period," *Journal of Hillside Hospitals, 7: 3–16, 1958.*

[6]S. R. Slavson, *An Introduction to Group Therapy*, International Universities Press, New York, 1954; also, "Some Elements in Activity Group Therapy," *American Journal of Orthopsychiatry*, 14: 578–588, 1944.

other and from their relationship to the therapist. An activity group consists of about eight members of the same sex and similar age, carefully selected with a view toward achieving a balance of adaptive behavior patterns ranging from aggressiveness to withdrawal. The physical setting of such a group is comprised of a large room equipped with simple furnishings, tools, crafts supplies, and games, chosen from the standpoint of their therapeutic effectiveness.[7]

The potentialities inherent in activity group therapy for helping children with severe ego pathology suggested themselves to us through coincidence. This was in connection with the use of our groups for observation of children on whom there were inadequate diagnostic data. In the course of this observation, the striking pathology of these children emerged readily enough to view. What emerged in addition was that the group experience seemed to assume a positive meaning for the children from the very beginning. Considering that most of these clients were totally inaccessible to individual casework contact without motivation for help or change, this was an important observation. We began to experiment with more and more such children, modifying our techniques along the way in line with their special needs.

The changes that we introduced experimentally differ in a number of ways from the techniques usually associated with activity group therapy. First of all, the therapist had to abandon the role of neutrality and extreme permissiveness that had worked so well with less damaged personalities. These children's ego faculties were simply not sufficiently developed for them to perceive the adult as a warm and helpful figure when he kept his verbal responses to a minimum, and particularly when he planfully failed to interfere in the face of what appeared to them as psychologically threatening group developments. As Slavson stated regarding the general kinds of activity groups, they require children with at least "minimal development of ego strength and superego organization so that impulses can be brought under control through reactions of other children and the demands of the group."[8] Thus, with the children under discussion, the therapist had to become more open and direct in his emotional reactions and verbalizations.

The therapist also had to be readier to use restraint, preferably indirectly, in the face of verbal or physical impulsive acting out. It should be noted that direct physical attacks rarely occur in our groups. First of all, there is the careful selection and "balancing" of membership. Then, there is the amazing tolerance of these groups for individuals who are "different" and particularly vulnerable. However, when restraint has to be instituted it is rarely perceived as a hostile act; quite to the contrary, we have had indica-

[7]S. R. Slavson, "Criteria for Selection and Rejection of Patients for Various Types of Group Psychotherapy," *International Journal of Group Psychotherapy, 5: 3-30, 1955.*
[8]Ibid., p. 14.

tions that, as with nursery-age children, it is viewed with relief and relaxation as the adult helps to protect the children's ego against the threat of uncontrollable impulsivity. Prior to this shift in the therapist's role, these children, when asked about the groups, would describe the leader as "not caring" or as being "afraid of the kids."

A related modification was the planned structuring of the broader group climate—even further than is usually the case—toward constancy, nurturing, and feeding. Besides the availability of plentiful supplies, especially in the early stages of the group, the traditional snack became for us a full-fledged meal carefully prepared by the therapist. While planfully providing "extras" (plus the food of absentees) for the group to deal with as it pleased, the therapist did not permit the customary free group interaction with respect to basic portions. These were assured to each child no matter how persistent the attempts to grab on the part of the more aggressive group members.[9]

We also decided that with these children's deficiencies in reality-testing, the well-known nonverbal techniques of situational interference were inadequate. The children required, in addition, frequent verbal interventions on the part of the therapist. These could be in the direction of confrontations of behavioral responses, such as "You are now quite upset," or "You are taking the wood that belongs to Fred"; more frequently, the comments were in the nature of clarifying external reality. For instance, in a boys' group some of the members giggled and playfully threatened to beat Robert up after the meeting. The therapist clarified the reality for the child by saying, "They are only teasing." Or, the adult might say, "I will not let anyone in this club beat you." In a girls' group a child said to the therapist, "Get the girls out of the bathroom or they will fall in the toilet and get swallowed up." The therapist replied, "This cannot happen."

The Treatment Process

With the above kinds of modifications, we found activity group therapy eminently suitable for helping such clients with severe disturbances in ego development. It is well known that in all children action is the natural form of communication. Also, with their more pliant personality structure, they respond more readily than adults to new perceptions inherent in current experience. Expressing problems through action rather than words is especially true of personalities with early fixation levels, for the earliest form of communication in life is nonverbal. Consequently, the actual experiencing of gratifications and the reliving of earliest traumas inherent in this ap-

---

[9]Compare this method to the freedom allowed a different type of patient population to argue and portion out food shares without intervention by the therapist. See Chapters 1–4. —*M.S.*

proach are most valuable. Insofar as the group treatment constitutes in effect a guided gratification, regression, and upbringing, current conflicts, as
well as earlier unresolved interpersonal experiences, can be relived, but with
different actors and, what is even more important, a different ending. As
one girl put it when her mother questioned her on her not overeating as
much at home as she used to: "They stuff you so much all the time in the
'club' that I don't care to eat as much now." The therapist's feeding her
once a week during the sessions had begun to carry her for the whole week!

In both of the illustrative cases presented later in this chapter the reactivation of oral conflicts in relation to the group therapist as a maternal figure is underscored. This is no coincidence, for as we have noted at another
point regarding our groups, ". . . it is around the theme of food—the buy-
ing of it, the bringing of it to the meeting room, the cooking and serving—
that the most dramatic and meaningful interactions occur. The conflicts re-
enacted here involve not only the reliving of the earliest problems in
mother-child relationships, but they are at the same time anchored in the
current reality of the children's home experiences."[10] In this context, sibling
rivalry actually became a struggle for the mother's food—for her milk in a
symbolic sense.

Bernice, the impulsive child earlier mentioned who sucked her thumb,
fought with her sister, wet her bed, and played with fire, was enraged at
other girls for bringing visitors to the group meetings. Her anger about this
kind of sharing of the food was so intense that, in retaliation, she brought
her hated younger sister to some sessions provisionally, just in case another
girl had again invited her friend to attend. Quoting from the therapist's description of a session: "Like a racing locomotive suddenly brought to a
halt, Bernice stopped short at the Ping-Pong table. Her sister Doris followed behind. Bernice did not bother to say hello or to take off her coat.
After greeting Bernice I asked her if she wanted to have her sister visit for
today. Bernice said it depended on whether or not Sally's friend was going
to stay. When Sally announced that she had brought Dora at the designa-
tion of the girls, Bernice bellowed at Doris to take off her coat."

The fact that, by bringing her sister, Bernice had further diluted the
food available for sharing, did not count. One of the prime factors was that
she had to get even. Perhaps also, on a deeper level, her sister constituted an
extension of herself, which for Bernice neutralized the food given to the
outsider, Sally's friend.

A similar self-defeating mechanism on the part of the same girl, which
ended in her destroying the food, is seen in the following incident: "Once
again Bernice claimed the food of the absent club member. She and Sally

[10]S. Scheidlinger et al., "Activity Group Therapy in a Family Service Agency," *Social Casework*, 40: 193–201, 1959.

raced for the empty seat, with Bernice pushing Sally out of the way. Sally asked Bernice if her mother did not teach her manners. Bernice warned Sally not to talk about her mother that way, but Sally provocatively repeated her question. Bernice slapped Sally, and Sally hit Bernice back. Bernice landed a hard smack on Sally's arm and the latter began to cry. After Barbara's intervention to "break it up," Sally cried a little while longer. Bernice seemed somewhat apologetic and told Sally she had warned her not to say anything about her mother. She offered Sally the contested seat, but Sally refused it. After some further interchange, Bernice poured soda all over the sandwiches. She sat at the table, pouting. Sally asked why she did that, spoiling the food for everybody, but Bernice did not reply.''

As noted earlier, such reliving of conflicts in the sphere of orality alone encompasses much of the treatment process with these severely deprived children. This should not be construed, however, as meaning that in this kind of guided regression other psychosexual levels and their related fixations, particularly preoedipal ones, do not get stimulated as well. This could occur in relation to food or any other aspect of the group interaction, such as bathroom play or use of materials or tools. To quote from another session: "As I continued to go around the table to serve the franks, Doreen said, 'It looks like we are stealing something from the boys.' Mary impatiently asked Doreen what she was talking about. After a second Sandra looked at Doreen and said, 'I get you.' Then all the girls laughed. As she bit into her frankfurter Doreen said, 'Mm, mm.' Sandra said, 'Very funny.' Nonie added sarcastically, 'Ha—ha.' Mary was the only girl who failed to perceive the phallic reference.''

Therapeutic Success and Failure

The children in our groups frequently show open awareness of the changes that occur in them and in others.[11] Take this illustration: "Jean took hold of Winnie's hand and began whirling her around. 'Last year,' she said to her, 'you used to be afraid of me. I told you that I would beat you up and you believed me. What about that now?' Winnie laughed at her in an easy way and said, 'I don't think you'd better try it now!'''

While the group treatment depicted has so far been markedly successful in modifying to a degree at least the functioning of a large majority of these severely disturbed clients, we have, of course, also had failures. These seemed to fall into two major categories. (1) the overly provocative children who, despite the therapist's repeated interventions, continued to so goad the other group members that counterattacks and scapegoating could not be prevented. Eventually these children had to be removed from the groups.

[11]This is an example of derivative insight.—*M. S.*

(2) children who improved in the group but failed to carry this over to the outside. This seemed related most often to a highly charged mutual provocativeness or sadomasochistic pattern operating at home that defied modification through casework efforts with the family.[12]

Jane exemplifies a child who behaved extremely provocatively in a group. She was referred by the school because of a violent temper and constant arguments with her peers. With adults, Jane was anxious for attention and affection. The mother openly preferred Jane's older sister and complained that Jane was willful, lied, and stole money. Jane was generally dissatisfied with what anyone tried to do for her. From the very beginning, she behaved aggressively toward all the girls in the group. Her major efforts seemed focused on hoarding supplies and food to take home with her, and on provocative teasing of the other children. The girls tried to put up with her, tolerating much of her provocativeness. Instead of calming her down, this only made things worse as she continued her sarcastic barrage directed at almost everyone. The girls soon verbalized the truth that whenever Jane came she caused trouble. The therapist's efforts to get close to Jane and to support her were of no avail, as she could not perceive the therapist as trying to help her. Her projection mechanisms and denial were so pervasive that in the face of all reality confrontations, she kept on insisting: "I never do anything to the girls. They pick on me, so I must hit back."

Bernice, who was mentioned earlier, belongs to the other category, namely children who fail to transfer the changes achieved in the group to the outside world. This severely impulsive, hostile girl with complex symptomology began to show signs of responding to the treatment after a year and a half. Besides making conscious efforts to control her intense oral-sadistic tendencies, she began to accept limitation and to cooperate with the adult and with group decisions. Her consistently warmer feelings toward the therapist were striking. On Valentine's Day she was the one who suggested that the girls make a heart for the adult. In addition, she herself made a change purse for the therapist, delaying her eating for a considerable period of time. Quite an achievement for this voracious youngster! When the gifts were presented, Bernice called out twice: "Mrs. K., we love you," to which the therapist replied gently, "Yes, Bernice."

Despite these changes in the group, Bernice continued to get herself into difficulties in the community. It was felt that this was due to the continuing pathology in the mother-daughter relationship. The mother admitted that since the birth of her latest out-of-wedlock child, the "lickings" she administered to Bernice gave her satisfaction—"relieving everything I feel in-

---

[12]In line with common practice in the family service field, a caseworker always assumes responsibility for the treatment planning for the family and for each of its members. While the children discussed in this chapter were treated in groups, individual contact with the parents was maintained. However, because of the marked pathology in these cases, such contacts are frequently sporadic and of limited effectiveness. For a discussion of the integration of casework and group work, see Scheidlinger, "Activity Group Therapy in a Family Service Agency."

side." Besides these whippings, there were frequent trips to the local police precinct coupled with threats to send Bernice away. This mutual provocativeness at home is still being studied. The caseworker has been seeing both Bernice and her mother. It is quite likely that placement of Bernice away from home will be the only solution. In this event, the group experience, which demonstrated this girl's capacity to change and grow in a supportive environment, will have served as a significant steppingstone.

The Group Treatment of Carl and Eileen

The problem of reliving earlier traumatic experiences[13] in the sphere of orality is exemplified by Carl's group treatment. This nine-and-a-half-year-old mentioned earlier had extreme mood swings, a marked distrust of adults, fear of death, no social relationships, and severe retardation in reading. His lack of "mothering" was due to the psychotic mother's frequent hospitalizations with resultant neglect of the children.

During the first session, Carl began by relating to the group with extreme caution. He was very suspicious toward the adult. Even though he spent most of his time away from the others at the "isolate" table, he was the first boy to announce during refreshments that the group should meet more often than once a week and for longer periods. Of particular significance was his voracious manner of eating, his grabbing for food and stuffing it into his mouth, using the fingers of both hands. This behavior was so much more exaggerated than that of any of the other boys, who were also deprived, that they quickly dubbed him "Greedy." This would always cause Carl to glower at them, but in no way deterred his grabbing for all "extras." The boys rather quickly accepted his tremendous needs and would usually, by tacit agreement, allow him the extra food without competition.

While there was a gradual improvement in the boy's relationship to the others by the second year, there was little change in his attitude toward food, or toward the therapist. By the third year, Carl became friendlier with the therapist, coupled with an increasing dependence on him for help with tools and materials. Concurrently, there was a dramatic change in Carl's consumption of food. At times he would pass up seconds, or would be slow enough in reaching for them so that other boys began competing more actively and directly. Carl didn't seem to be upset if they got ahead of him. His table manners had by now become quite acceptable. The mood swings were hardly in evidence. The summer camp noted for the first time a marked gain in impulse control. In contrast to the previous year, Carl could become realistically angry without "flying to pieces" or appearing to have to "sit on himself" to keep from blowing up.

---

[13]This is also referred to as corrective reexperience, as discussed elsewhere in this book. —*M. S.*

During the fourth year, the therapist noted a definite relationship between Carl's attitude toward him and Carl's food consumption. When Carl was particularly hostile to the adult, he did not even take his basic portion. During this same year, Carl brought some candy for the therapist after the latter had saved a chocolate rabbit for him from an Easter party that the boy had not been able to attend.

The case of Eileen, who was not described previously, illustrates the group treatment with an even more seriously disturbed youngster.

Eileen was referred to the agency at the age of eight and a half. She was withdrawn and fearful, and had difficulties in relating to children and adults. Her hands trembled at times and she cried easily. She had expressed concern over "sin," which seemed related to sex and to growing up generally. She had a great many fears: of noises, insects, and animals. At school she was on the fringe of the group, working far below her capacity. A camp report from a prior year stressed her bizarre behavior. She would roll her eyes, would ask seemingly irrelevant questions, and had poor reality orientation. There were also difficulties in physical coordination, some involuntary movements, and considerable overweight. Eileen, on occasion, would speak of herself as "crazy."

Eileen's mother, a primitive, self-centered woman with delinquent tendencies, had a very unhappy childhood. She had lost her mother at an early age. Following an out-of-wedlock pregnancy in her early teens, she was treated by her relatives as an outcast. Eileen was the later product of a short-lived marriage characterized by much conflict from the very beginning. Eileen was especially upset when her father deserted the family during her early childhood.

The group therapist described Eileen as pretty, somewhat overweight, with smooth brown skin and rounded, regular features. She was quiet and unobtrusive, with a facade of social ease. When ignored by the other girls, as she often was, she resorted to a mannerism in which she smiled, raised and lowered her eyes slowly, sighed, then smiled again, and turned away. Underneath, there was a mild depressive quality. When thus left out, Eileen spent much time working with materials. In this she needed considerable help from the adult. To a girl using a tool, Eileen said, "Do you want to be a boy—I mean carpenter?" thus suggesting primitive thinking and confusion regarding her identity. In the seventh session, she was greeted as "Fatso" and criticized for not talking. Her response was to smile again in the manner indicated above. Eileen announced that she was dieting because of her overweight. She never competed for extra food, quoting her mother as saying: "You eat like a bird—his beak, that is." In contrast, during one trip to a restaurant, Eileen ate with fascinated gluttony. Eileen related to the therapist dependently and with a superficial charm. The therapist also observed peculiar twitching or rotating motions of her hips when Eileen was engrossed in her work. She stopped this when another child brought it to her attention. Eileen continued to talk about her diet, but put so much mayonnaise or catsup on her sandwiches that they literally dripped. Although usually alone or withdrawn, Eileen joined promptly in games when she was invited to do so. She was compliant and passive in response to all requests made of her. She frequently did not seem to understand group decisions, being markedly preoccupied with herself. Her work with clay seemed unique and represented considerable fantasy with sexual symbolism. The same held true for her colorful, abstract paintings. Eileen preserved in the group's cabinet the head of a male, with the notion of sending it to a well-known comedian, an older man. She was unaware that the other girls viewed her repeated preoccupation with this piece of work as bizarre.

For a few months there was a difficult period during which the girls derided Eileen as "crazy." Through the intensive activity of the therapist, involving both direct support of Eileen and indirect restraint of the others, there occurred a significant shift in the group's attitudes. Most of the group, in identification with the adult, began to be supportive of the girl, including her in their games. They insisted, however, on her stopping her "crazy" acts, such as singing or talking to herself, or making the old hip movements; she complied readily. Not only did the girls accept the special closeness that Eileen required of the adult, but often even drew the therapist's attention to Eileen's needs. At the end of thirty-six sessions, Eileen had shifted from a position of scapegoat to that of being a source of group concern and support.

Eileen responded with mild, tenuous expressions of affection to the therapist's activity in her behalf. Eileen's awareness of support was evidenced by her revealing some of her concerns about the outside world, such as school or camp. Each time the therapist brought these concerns to the attention of the family caseworker who helped out with Eileen's family, there seemed to be another spurt of improvement in Eileen. She related better to the girls, and her reality perceptions seemed improved. Eileen would on occasion bring bizarre-sounding fantasy material to the adult. While not discouraging her, this was always handled through enabling Eileen to focus on the reality aspect.

The mother reported marked improvement in Eileen's functioning. The girl was cooperative and helpful around the house. She began going out to play with the children in the neighborhood. With support from the caseworker, the mother would now permit Eileen to be on her own. At camp, Eileen enjoyed herself more than during the previous year. She was less fearful and could participate in group activities much of the time. Occasionally, she still seemed confused, unable to grasp the reality expectations, being content to remain by herself. Her relationship to the counselor was one of clinging, warm dependency.

During the second year of group therapy, the girl's attendance continued to be excellent. She was noted to be taller and slimmer with marked gains in her physical coordination. The bizarre behavior patterns had disappeared. The therapist felt that there had been a definite gain in Eileen's self-concept and her mastery of environmental demands. While alone during part of each session, she was infinitely more involved with the others. She joined in when the girls initiated games. She withdrew, however, when they discussed boys and sex. While still in need of support, and functioning less adequately than any of the others, she hardly stood out as different to observers. (Our group sessions can be observed through one-way screens.) Eileen now rarely expressed fantasies to the adult or to the group and was seldom noted to be idle or self-absorbed. Her efforts to be like the others and master conventional projects occurred apparently at the cost of the more creative, fantasy-laden projects of the previous year. While still tending to need the support of the adult, Eileen paid little attention to her when really involved in activity with the group. Not only had she become a fully accepted member, but on rare occasions she even stood up to another girl.

After the family moved to larger and more attractive living quarters, there was an interesting change in Eileen's use of the special "club" cabinet. Heretofore (until the fifty-third session), it had been for her a repository for her many "treasures," including the earlier-noted head of the comedian. She had valued the cabinet so highly and constantly as to give the impression that an important part of her emotional life had been centered there. It was as though with a room of her own in the new apartment, she no longer needed this cherished, private place. Perhaps, in addition, this change connoted her broader freedom to move out of the protective setting of the group.

Following the second period of group treatment, the caseworker reported further improvement in Eileen's symptomatology and functioning. This was particularly significant inasmuch as there had been some upsetting developments in the family. Not only did the mother marry again, but she also became pregnant prior to this marriage. The mother sent her youngest child, Eileen's stepsister, out of the state to live with the child's father. This move, as well as her decision to offer the expected baby for adoption, upset Eileen considerably. On the constructive side, there was more consistency in the contacts by Eileen's father; he began visiting her once a week.

While the relationship with the mother was much better—"Eileen's no trouble," she said—the mother's primitive punitive measures continued on occasion. She described, for instance, how about once a month she would make Eileen kneel on the floor and would beat her with a strap.

Eileen's schoolwork improved to the extent that, upon her move to the new apartment, she was promoted from an "opportunity class" to a regular one. Her reading advanced noticeably, and the mother was pleased that Eileen was now eager to read the newspaper.

Despite these gratifying changes for the better in Eileen, the psychiatric consultant recommended that the long-range plan be to place all the children away from home. This was because of the mother's severe personality pathology and her complete inability to tolerate assertiveness and independence in any of the children. In agreement with this recommendation, Eileen was assigned to a separate caseworker for supportive contact three months prior to the termination of the group treatment.

Discussion and Summary

An important step in our experimental work involved, whenever possible, careful follow-up evaluations of our cases, especially during and after adolescence. The few instances in which we were able to undertake this in an organized fashion seemed promising. The follow-up suggested that the clients had generally managed to at least maintain the gains in ego functioning achieved through the group treatment.[14] On the other hand, we suspect that Weil's contention of a remaining underlying "deficient personality structure"[15] in these kinds of individuals is probably true.

In trying to assess in general the therapeutic possibilities in this group approach, the following observations emerge:

1. The children are offered a benign family-like setting where, in contrast to the situation in their homes, there is a maximum of constancy and gratification, and a minimum of frustrations. All this is enhanced by the special modifications that we introduced in the therapist's role of greater directness, protective restraint, and verbal clarification.
2. The group as an entity represents a physical and a psychological reality with which even a deficient ego can cope. It permits new perceptions, possibly ranging from the deepest unconscious levels (i.e., primitive identification with the mother-group) to the initially unsettling conscious realization of this uniquely different kind of "club."[16]
3. Within a climate of controlled gratification and regression, early conflicts are reenacted with a consistent, strong, and accepting parental figure. The stress is on the anticipation of and unconditional meeting of needs.
4. Various degrees and types of relationships are possible—none are demanded. These range from isolation, through the most tenuous

[14]C. H. King, "Activity Group Therapy with a Schizophrenic Boy: Follow-Up Two Years Later," *International Journal of Group Psychotherapy*, 9: 184–194, 1969.
[15]Weil, "Certain Severe Disturbances of Ego Development in Childhood."
[16]Slavson, "Criteria for Selection and Rejection of Patients for Various Types of Group Psychotherapy."

primitive identifications involving the borrowing of another ego's strengths, to real object ties.

5. The "dosage" of gratifications (love offerings) is determined by the child on the basis of his or her readiness to accept them, thus permitting gradual removal of defenses. At the same time, demands made upon the child are minimal.

6. The support of the other group members, the reality-geared group environment, and the nondirective role of the therapist tend to minimize and counteract the fears of overwhelming impulsivity and of domination or destruction by the adult that are so frequently inherent in these kinds of problems.[17]

7, While no attempt is made to enter a child's inner autistic world, with its primitive fantasies, the boundaries between reality and fantasy are repeatedly emphasized.

8. With the free flow of emotional gratifications, arrested ego development can be resumed, step by step. The child learns to postpone immediate satisfactions, to recognize and respond to the requirements of reality, and to find pleasure in playing games or working with tools and materials.

9. Inevitable changes in individual self-concepts are closely intertwined with healthier perceptions of the adult, of other children, and of the group as an entity, thus counteracting identity confusions.

In summary, we have depicted the usefulness of a guided gratification, regression, and upbringing through a modified form of activity group therapy for severely deprived latency-age children. Conflicts are expressed and reexperienced in this kind of setting through action, rather than words. The direct gratification of unmet oral and other pregenital needs through food, arts and crafts materials, and the like, offered by the adult, was found to be markedly effective in fostering improved ego functioning. The consistent, accepting parental figure, coupled with the benign image of a group entity, promoted changes in the clients' perceptions and expectations of the environment and of the people in it. The cumulative effects of these group experiences were an improved self-concept, better ego control over impulses, and enhanced reality-testing.

We hope that further experimentation with such groups may well show the way toward reaching children during the latency period who, if not treated, tend to succumb to active psychoses or to develop highly destructive antisocial patterns in adolescence.

---

[17]I. Kaufman et al., "Childhood Schizophrenia: Treatment of Children and Parents," *American Journal of Orthopsychiatry*, 27: 683–690, 1957.

Designs of Treatment Rooms

ALL METHODS of children's group therapy require settings with sufficient space to allow the children to engage in activities comfortably without needless frustration. One part of a meeting room should provide a large, unencumbered floor space for easy access between areas where children usually congregate to work or play, and also to accommodate the active games that a group as a whole sometimes engages in. At the same time, provision is made for timid, passive children who tend to isolate themselves during the early stages of treatment.

A meeting room that is too large diminishes opportunities for interpersonal interactions between group members. It also tends to stimulate hyperkinetic activity by children who are so inclined by either temperament or age. This is especially the case with children who are approximately five to eight years old. On the other hand, a small, constricting floor area can increase the provocations of acting-out children and frighten passive ones who cannot find a space for withdrawal.

A toilet facility is best located with immediate access from the meeting room so that children are under the therapist's surveillance at all times. When a toilet is at a distance from the meeting room, this inevitably leads to management problems. The therapist is forced either to permit a child to leave the meeting room unescorted or to take him to the toilet, the latter being highly inadvisable. When a toilet is not immediately accessible, it is imperative that an assistant remain outside the meeting room during an entire session to escort children. This spares the therapist from assuming an authoritative role with respect to limiting children's behavior outside the meeting room, which would negate the necessary accepting, permissive role.

A water supply within the meeting room serves many purposes. In its absence a large metal basin can be substituted. Water play is particularly important in the treatment of young children.

Children five to eight years of age require smaller floor areas than do older ones, regardless of the treatment method employed. With younger children a therapist has to be closer to them should they seek assistance, and in instances where prompt intervention may be necessary. Groups of young children are more easily induced into hyperkinetic (supernodal) behavior by excessively large, open spaces. Contrariwise, they become more fretful and

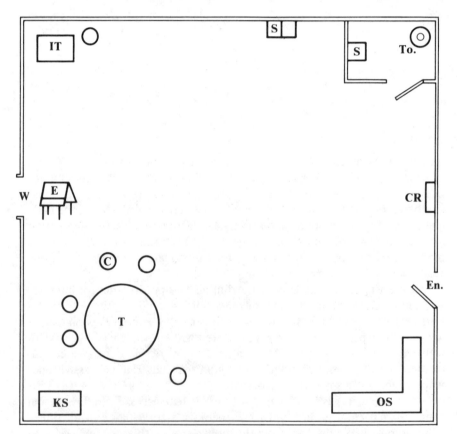

Figure 1. Design of treatment setting for children five to eight years old.
C—Chair; CR—clothes rack; E— easel; En.—entrance; IT—"isolate" table; KS—kitchen supplies; OS—open shelves; S—sink; T—table; To.—toilet; W—window.

tense in overly confining spaces. A practical formula for computing floor area for this age group is to allow 30 square feet per person, including the therapist. Thus, an average activity or activity-interview group, which contains about five children, needs about 210 square feet of floor area, roughly a room 15 feet long and 12 feet wide. With older latency children, nine years of age to pre-puberty, 50 square feet for each person is an adequate unit of measure. An average activity or activity-interview group is comfortable in a setting 20 feet by 20 feet in dimension.

In addition to the general requirements, other factors may necessitate variances in standard room size, design, furnishings, and materials. Primary among these factors are the age levels of the children and the nature of the group treatment method—activity or activity-interview group therapy, or a variant of these methods.

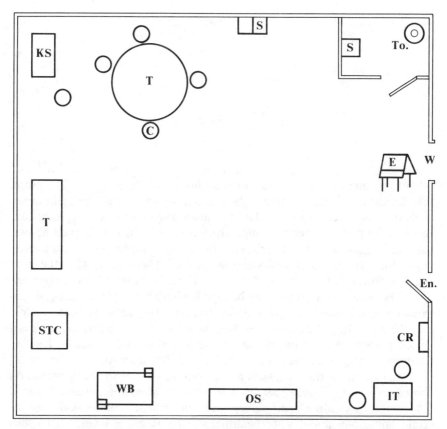

Figure 2.   Design of treatment setting for children nine years old to pre-puberty
C—chair; CR—clothes rack; E—easel; En.—entrance; IT—"isolate" table; OS—open shelves; KS—kitchen supplies; S—sink; STC—supply and tool cabinet; T—table; To.—toilet; W—window; WB—workbench. *Note:* For activity-interview groups the long table may be removed.

Furnishings, and Materials for Crafts, Play, and Games

THE FIRST IMPRESSION a child should get upon entering a meeting room should be that of a setting which invites his use of its offerings. Therefore, the furnishings—tables, chairs, shelves, and so on—should be plain in appearance, easily accessible, and utilizable without children having to be concerned about soiling and marring, which is usually the case in their homes, in schools, and in other formal environments. Unupholstered furniture is more functional, and all tables and chairs should accommodate to the average age and size of children in the group.[1] Used furniture is better than new.

The same meeting room can be used for both activity and activity-interview groups. However, this will necessitate removing some items and restoring them for the different groups. In purely activity group therapy there is a more generous supply of arts and crafts materials and games, in keeping with the therapeutic intent and procedures. This is done to maximize the interpersonal interactions between group members and with the therapist. As noted previously, activity therapy is an ego-level form of treatment designed to strengthen children's self-perceptions, foster better coping skills and social adaptations, and develop healthier superegos and more effective subli-

---

[1]Some upholstered furniture is used in special groups. See p. 78.

mations. Since active explorations of children's feelings and motivations by a therapist is entirely eschewed in activity therapy, the sought-for outcomes are dependent mostly on an essential positive transference with the therapist and meaningful social interactions within the group. The evolvement of the therapy group itself as a psychologically corrective influence upon its members is an essential element of activity therapy.

On the other hand, some work and play materials provided in an activity-interview group need to have more of a libido-activating nature in order to evoke individual and group behaviors that reflect children's emotional stresses and inner conflicts. Such materials provide opportunities for the therapist's explorations through individual and group interviews.

In analytical-type groups, an oversupply of materials tends to cause children to "escape" from meaningful contact with each other and renders it more difficult for a therapist to insinuate himself into children's play to explore it for meanings. Therefore, arts and crafts activities in such groups should be more limited yet sufficient to engage the children and to bring them into contact with each other.

In all forms of group therapy with children, their age levels should govern the types and complexities of manipulative materials and implements. Older children would react with scorn to dolls, playhouse furniture, and similar items, which they would consider "childish." Younger children can be completely frustrated in attempting to use tools and materials that are used in advanced crafts work, such as lanyard weaving and metal embossing. A simple loom, construction paper, and paste, among other items, are more fitting to these children's abilities. In accommodating to children's needs, therapists should be guided by the therapeutic group method to be used and the physical and developmental capabilities of the children. From time to time, special accommodations will have to be made in some therapy groups to meet idiosyncratic features of individual children or of the group as a whole. Also, some items such as an inflated plastic "bop" bag may be introduced or removed from time to time at the therapist's discretion, in accordance with his assessment of changing circumstances in the group's dynamics.

The items listed below are basic materials for purely activity and activity-interview group therapy. However, with the latter method, some items, as indicated earlier, are libido-activating and are therefore not suitable for activity groups.

All materials used in children's group therapy should be psychologically relevant to the nature of the therapy. Recreational items are included, but these, too, are of a nature to foster meaningful communication between group members. An overabundance of supplies tends to vitiate the therapeutic process. This applies to therapy groups of all kinds, with children of any age.

For Children Five to Eight Years of Age[2]

Wooden blocks: A full set, including several large hollow blocks and planks; also several autos, trucks, and airplanes made of hard wood, to incorporate in block play.

Dolls: One set of family dolls, including grandparents (skin color white and black—either or both depending on client population), made of rubber, six to eight inches in height; also a doctor, fireman, policeman, and various animals.

Hand puppets: Rubber, family set and grandparents (skin color as needed); also a doctor, policeman, fireman, crocodile, and blackbird.

Face masks: Two—one a menacing face, the other benign.

Large inflated plastic figure (with repair kit).

Sandbox: Clean sand, two pails, and shovels made of plastic material to avoid cuts.

Water play: A can, suction bulb, rubber tubing, several small floating toys, a sponge, large mop, and paper towels.

Play-Doh, plasticine clay, ceramic clay: Choice as needed.

For art work: Pastel chalk, crayons, poster colors, artist's brushes (various sizes), two smocks, newsprint cut in large sheets, drawing paper, colored construction paper, several inking pens and pencils, a ruler, paste, and two scissors with blunt ends.

For crafts work: Materials to be used in crafts should be uncomplicated and within children's abilities to fabricate simple projects in one session, or in not more than two. Young children's attention spans are limited, and they are encouraged and pleased by completion of projects that they can take home. Models to assemble may be used at times, but these also should be simple.

Looms: Two, for making pot holders; with cotton loops of different colors.

Leather or plastic forms: Pre-cut; also lanyard material that can be used to make simple items: purses, pencil case, and so forth.

Bead work: Beads of various colors and sizes, with string.

[2]See also M. Schiffer and S. R. Slavson, *Group Psychotherapies for Children: A Textbook,* International Universities Press, New York, 1975, Chapters 4 and 22, and pp. 436–437.

Woodwork: Squares of plywood of various small sizes (⅜ inch thick), balsa wood, two hammers, two saws, one coping saw, pair of pliers, and nails. *Note*: Tools should be of sizes and weights that are suitable for young children.

Games: A simple spin board game, such as Chick-in-the Coop®, several jig saw puzzles (wood), one soft ball.

Kitchen supplies: Cups, saucers, plates, serving plates, cutlery, napkins, soap, dish towels, and plastic tablecloth.

Maintenance items: Large pail, broom, brush and dustpan, rags, sponge, soap, and supply of old newspapers.

Note: For activity-interview groups only: a family set of dolls with sex organs and removable clothing; also a playhouse with furniture, a crib, baby carriage, one large doll, nursing bottle, and toy stethoscope.

For Children Nine Years Old to Pre-Puberty

ACTIVITY GROUP THERAPY

Woodwork: Woodwork table with two vises, two hammers, two rulers, one brace with set of wood bits, one cross-cut saw, one rip saw, two coping saws, one wood clamp, two files, one plane, one screwdriver, one pliers, sandpaper, nails, brads, screws, short lengths of soft pine (½" × 6"), squares of plywood (⅜" × 2' × 1'), and balsa wood.

Metal: Foil—copper or aluminum, 36-gauge; embossing tools; copper or aluminum disks with molds and shaping mallets for fabricating small plates; and one pair of metal snips.

Leather: Pieces of leather or synthetics, lanyard material, a hole puncher, snaps, and assembly tools.

Pyro pencil set: One, for wood-burning artwork.

Models: For assembling cars, planes, boats, and so on; for occasional use.

Artwork: Poster colors, brushes, construction paper, drawing paper, paste, sets of crayons and crayolas, pastel chalk, tracing and carbon paper, two scissors, one stapler, several pencils and ballpoint pens, plasticene and artisan's clay, and large sheets of newsprint.

Miscellaneous: Pipe cleaners, string, assorted beads, needles, thread, cloth, and two looms with cotton loops.

Games: One combination checkerboard and Chinese checkers, a Ping-Pong table and equipment, and Nok Hockey.

Kitchen supplies: Same as on page 369. Also an electric hot plate with fireproof board.

Maintenance items: Same as on page 369.

ACTIVITY-INTERVIEW GROUP PSYCHOTHERAPY

The same room can be used for both activity group and activity-interview group therapies. However, as was pointed out earlier, in the latter type of therapy fewer materials are available for children because a significantly large part of each meeting is devoted to group discussions with the therapist. It would be difficult for a therapist to implement such discussions in a room that is elaborately supplied with arts, crafts, and game materials. Several recommended media are woodwork, leather, metals, and art supplies, also several games—one table game, the other a more active one such as Nok Hockey. The amounts of materials and the tools necessary to use them should also be limited. In the analytic group procedure, less emphasis is placed on food, including preparation of snacks. There is no need for a hot plate. A simple snack served at every session is sufficient—something to drink and cookies or cake. Preferably food is served during the last half of each session, when the children are assembled at the round table for group discussion.

　　Since the children for whom activity-interview group psychotherapy is indicated, and the techniques of the therapist, are notably different than in activity group therapy, the therapist has more discretion in how the materials and their introduction may be modified depending on ongoing conditions in a group.

Glossary

Acclimatization: A beginning, temporary phase in group therapy during which time children accommodate to what represents for them an entirely novel experience with an unusually tolerant therapist in a highly permissive environment.

Activity group therapy: A treatment method used with latency-age children; the corrective process flows from interactions between children and with the therapist; verbal, exploratory techniques ordinarily used in analytic therapy are entirely eschewed.

Activity-interview group psychotherapy: An analytic method for children with neurotic problems; discussions take place in addition to a limited number of crafts and play activities.

Anti-nodal behavior: Behavior of a therapy group typified by relative quiet and equanimity; follows upon episodes of hyperactivity (see *Nodal behavior*).

Closed group: A therapy group where membership is constant; recommended for young children who are easily threatened by changes in a group's composition because of fears of separation and loss (as opposed to *open group*).

Combined therapy: Conjoint individual and group treatment, usually with different therapists.

Conditioned environment: A treatment climate that encourages children's free behavior and interaction with others.

Contagion: Emotional "infection" in a therapy group, induced by the behavior of one child (see *Group infection*).

Contrast models: In identity formation; physical differences and typical behavioral patterns of members of the opposite gender, which serve as reinforcers of a child's identity by crystallizing his own sense of gender differentiation.

Cooperative therapy: Concurrent treatment of a child and his parent(s), with different therapists.

Corrective reexperience: Experiences in therapy which counteract the pathogenic circumstances in families that caused a child's emotional problems.

Co-therapists: A male-female therapist team; used in special treatment groups (see Chapter 2).

Critical event: An episode occurring in activity group therapy wherein the newly acquired but, as yet, unexpressed ego strength of a child becomes manifest under the stimulus of special circumstances in an ongoing group interaction. One example: a formerly frightened, withdrawn child actively resists the provocation of a more aggressive group member.

Derivative insight: A child's awareness of positive growth changes in himself, due to a strengthened ego, an improved self-image, and a healthier superego.

Dynamic equilibrium: Characteristic of a therapy group that is in good psychological balance, capable of restoring itself to an anti-nodal state following periods of hyperactivity.

Escorts: In school-based group treatment programs, older children who serve as monitors to accompany children to and from their classrooms to meeting rooms.

Exclusive therapy: Treatment of a child in either individual or group therapy; in some cases the latter method is used to prepare resistive neurotic children for dyadic treatment.

Group balance: Homogeneity in the composition of a group with respect to the children's types of problems; designed to ensure a corrective psychological balance (see *Dynamic equilibrium*).

Group ego: This is a global concept of a unitary force resulting from an accretion of social growth in a group; invests it with extraordinary corrective psychological influence on its members; typical in activity groups.

Group infection: The spontaneous spread of behavior through mimicry (see *Contagion*).

Group interviews: Discussions between a therapist and an individual child, or several children in an activity-interview group; also with a group as a whole as a regular part of each meeting.

Halo effect: A child's improvement as a result of treatment invests his perception of the total school environment favorably, where it was formerly viewed as authoritative and oppressive; results from unconscious displacement of his perception of the benign environment of the group treatment setting; occurs in a therapeutic play group in an elementary school (it also occurs in all forms of group therapy with children and adolescents when conducted in schools).

Heterogeneous groups: Groups composed of children of both genders; typical of analytical groups with young children and of special activity groups (see Chapter 2).

Homogeneous groups: Groups composed of children of the same gender; typical of activity therapy groups.

Instigator: A child who stimulates interactions in a group; may be a negative or positive instigator (as opposed to *Neutralizer*).

"Isolate" table: A small table located tangentially in a group meeting room to provide a feeling of security for a timid, passive child, especially in the beginning phase of therapy.

Libido-activating materials: Play and game activities and materials that tend to evoke feelings and expressions of a personal nature on conscious and unconscious levels; characteristic of some of the materials supplied to children in activity-interview group psychotherapy.

Libido-binding materials: Arts and crafts materials that engage children in manipulative activities and projects which submerge affect.

Neuters: Weak children who follow others and are easily influenced by them.

Neutral: The typical demeanor of a therapist in activity therapy; children feel free to "use" him to meet their needs; in this sense the therapist is a *tabula rasa*.

Neutralizer: A child whose personality is such as to exert moderating influence in restoring a group to a state of equanimity from episodes of turbulent interaction (as opposed to *Instigator*).

Nodal behavior: Hyperactive behavior by a group.

Nuclear problem: The central elements of a child's presenting problem.

Primary behavior disorder: A psychological problem that is reactive to parents' authoritative and punitive treatment; probably a common emotional disorder of latency-age children; activity therapy is often indicated as the exclusive treatment.

Reactive behavior disorder: See *Primary behavior disorder.*

Resistivity: Children's initial overt defensiveness toward and resentment of psychological treatment, especially individual therapy; it is much less apparent when group therapy is used; not to be confused with *resistance*, which is mostly unconscious.

Situational restraints: Built-in features in group treatment meeting rooms; enable children to use the room and its offerings without the possibility of injuries (for example, padded support columns and radiator enclosures).

Sloughing off: The elimination of symptoms in young children through ego-strengthening, without insight formation; characteristic of group methods of therapy, particularly activity therapy.

Social hunger: A universal need for the company of others.

Substitute gratification: An intervention used mostly with young children in treatment, in which the therapist substitutes a game or other activity enjoyable to children; designed to block or dilute countertherapeutic behavior.

Supernodal behavior: Hyperactivity of a therapy group as a whole; usually a temporary phase in treatment in a well-balanced group; if persistent, the group's composition has to be reevaluated.

Supportive ego relationship: A symbiotic relationship between two children; usually involves a strong child with a weaker one, although there may be other psychological patterns.

Therapeutic play group: A substitute title for activity group therapy with young children in school settings.

Therapy by a group: A treatment mode in which a therapy group and its interpersonal interactions act as the primary therapeutic influence; without verbal, analytic procedures; as in activity therapies.

Therapy in a group: A treatment mode associated with analytic therapy; the individual is central; the group serves as a psychological vehicle for examining and discussing the behavior of individuals.

Transference in reverse: A child's changing perception of his parents in an improved light, resulting from a long-term positive transference relationship with a therapist.

Unconditional love: Total acceptance of a child by a therapist; does *not* include acceptance or sanction of acting-out behavior.

Universalization: The heartening effect experienced by a child when he observes, often for the first time, that other children in a treatment group have similar fears and problems.

Valence: The intrinsic, relative ability of materials to evoke children's feeling, both conscious and unconscious; items of high valence—dolls, finger paints, water; low valence—models to assemble, leather work.

Comprehensive Bibliography of Children's Group Therapy

This Bibliography includes most publications—articles in professional journals and books—on the subject of group treatment modalities used with children, from approximately 1934 to the present. It has been compiled from many sources, part from the extensive annual surveys on therapy groups by the *International Journal of Group Psychotherapy*, the official publication of the American Group Psychotherapy Association.

Most of the items concern applications of group methodology with troubled children, including, in addition to the subject of group therapy, descriptions of groups used in guidance, counseling, remediation, and other paraclinical procedures that are employed in the prevention and/or correction of children's disabilities. The publications are divided into sections to assist readers who have particular interest in special child populations and their unique problems.

The publications listed in the Bibliography have not been subject to evaluation for relative merit. The reader will be able to determine for himself whether or not they serve his professional interests. However, articles that provide especially useful basic information on various aspects of the standard methods of children's group therapy are indicated by asterisks.

The dates of publication should not be construed as an indicator of present applicability. The articles and books that are cited describe basic theories, principles, and practices of children's group therapy, and they should prove of practical value to persons presently engaged in group treatment of children and to others who are planning to do so.

375

While this Bibliography is probably the most extensive one extant, there are bound to be some worthwhile articles that have not been included. Such omissions are inadvertent.

Children's Group Therapy: General

ABRAMOWICH, C. V., "Effectiveness of Group Psychotherapy with Children," *Arch. Gen. Psychiat.*, 33: 320–326, 1976.

ABRAMOVICH, R., et al., "An Observational Assessment of Change in Two Groups of Behaviorally Disturbed Boys," *Jrnl. Child Psychol. Psychiat.*, 21: 133–141, 1980.

ALPERT, A., "A Special Therapeutic Technique for Certain Disorders in Prelatency Children," *Am. Jrnl. Orthopsychiat.*, 27: 256–270, 1957.

ANDERSON, N., and MORRONE, R. T., "Group Therapy for Emotionally Disturbed Children: A key to Affective Education," *Am. Jrnl. Orthopsychiat.*, 47: 1; 97–103, 1977.

AZIMA, F., "Group Psychotherapy for Latency-Age Children," *Canad. Psychiat.*, 21: 210–211, 1976.

BARCAI, A., and ROBINSON, E. H., "Conventional Group Therapy with Preadolescent Children," *Intl. Jrnl. Group Psychother.*, 19: 3; 334–345, 1969.

BARNES, M., et al., "The Collaboration of Child Psychiatry, Casework, and Group Work in Dealing with the Mechanism of Acting Out," *Am. Jrnl. Orthopsychiat.*, 27: 2; 377–386, 1957.

BARSKY, M., and MOZENTOR, G., "The Use of Creative Drama in a Children's Group." *Intl. Jrnl. Group Psychother.*, 26: 105–114, 1976.

*BECKER, M., "The Effects of Activity Group Therapy on Sibling Rivalry," *Jrnl. Social Casework,* June 1948.

BELL, J. E., "Family Group Therapy: A New Method of Treatment for Older Children, Adolescents and Their Parents," *Publ. Health Monog. No. 64.*

BELLUCCI, M. T., "Treatment of Latency-Age Adopted Children and Parents," *Jrnl. Social Casework*, 56: 297–301, 1975.

BENDER, L., and WOLTMANN, A. G., "The Use of Puppet Shows as a Psychotherapeutic Method for Behavior Problems in Children," *Am. Jrnl. Orthopsychiat.*, 6: 3; 341–354, 1936.

BETTELHEIM, B., and SYLVESTER, E., "Therapeutic Influence of the Group on the Individual," *Am. Jrnl. Orthopsychiat.*, 17:4; 8–692, 1947.

BOLLINGER, D. M., "Group Therapy at The Children's Center," *Nervous Child*, April 1945.

BOULANGER, J. B., "Group Psychotherapy of the Child and the Adolescent," *Jrnl. Canad. Psychiat. Assn.*, 13: 323–326, 1968.

BOUTTE, M. A., "Play Therapy Practices in Approved Counseling Agencies," *Jrnl. Clin. Psychol.*, 27: 150–152, 1971.

*BOWLBY, J., "The Study and Reduction of Group Tensions in the Family," *Human Relations*, 2: 123–128, 1949.

BROSS, R., "Mother and Child in Group Psychotherapy," *Intl. Jrnl. Group Psychother.*, 2:4; 358–368, 1952.

BUXBAUM, E., Technique of Child Therapy: A Critical Evaluation," in *Psychoanalytic Study of the Child*, Vol. 9, International Universities Press, New York, 1954.

_____, "Transference and Group Formation in Children and Adolescents," in *Psychoanalytic Study of the Child*, Vol. 1, International Universities Press, New York, 1945.

CARLIN, A. S., and ARMSTRONG, H. E., "Rewarding Social Responsibility in Disturbed Children: A Play Group Technique," *Psychother.: Theory, Review and Practice*, 5: 169–174, 1968.

CERMAK, S. A., et al., "Hyperactive Children and an Activity Group Therapy Model," *Am. Jrnl. Occup. Therapy*, 27: 311–315, 1973.

CHURCHILL, S. R., "Social Group Work: A Diagnostic Tool in Child Guidance," *Am. Jrnl. Orthopsychiat.*, 35:3; 581–588, 1965.

COCHE, J. A., and FREEDMAN, P., "Treatment of a Child with Psychogenic Megacolon Through Fantasy Therapy in a Group of Children," *Prax, Kinderpsychol. Kinderpsychiat.*, 24: 26–32, 1975.

*COOLIDGE, J. C., and GRUNBAUM, M. G., "Individual and Group Therapy of a Latency Age Child," *Intl. Jrnl. Group Psychother.*, 14: 1; 84–96, 1964.

CROWDES, N. E., "Group Therapy for Pre-Adolescent Boys," *Amer. Jrnl. Nursing*, 75: 92–95.

CUNNINGHAM, H. M., and MATTHEWS, K. L., "Impact of Multiple Family Therapy on a Parallel Latency-Age Parent Group," *Intl. Jrnl. Group Psychother.*, 32: 1; 91–102, 1982.

DANA, R. H., and DANA, J. M., "Systematic Observation of Children's Behavior in Group Therapy," *Psychol. Repts.*, 24: 134, 1959.

DANNEFER, E., et al., "Experience in Developing a Combined Activity and Verbal Therapy Program with Latency-Age Boys," *Intl. Jrnl. Group Psychother.*, 25: 331–337, 1975.

*DAVIDS, M., "Integration of Activity Group Therapy for a Ten Year Old Boy with Case Work Services to the Family," *Intl. Jrnl. Group Psychother.*, 5: 1; 31–44, 1955.

DURKIN, H., "Dr. John Levy's Relationship Therapy as Applied to a Play Group," *Am. Jrnl. Orthopsychiat.*, 9: 3; 583–597, 1939.

EGAN, M. H., "Dynamisms in Activity Discussion Group Therapy," *Intl. Jrnl. Group Psychother.*, 25: 199–218, 1975.

EPSTEIN, N., "Brief Group Therapy in a Child Guidance Clinic," *Social Work*, 15:3; 33–35, 1970.

FABIAN, A., "Group Treatment of Chronic Patients in a Child Guidance Clinic," *Intl. Jrnl. Group Psychother.*, 4:3; 243–252, 1954.

FLEISHER, A. M., "Diagnostic and Selection Considerations in Group Therapy with Latency Children," *Smith College Stud. in Social Work*, 48: 48–49, 1977.

FLEMING, L., and SNYDER, W., "Social and Personal Changes Following Nondirective Group Play Therapy," *Am. Journal Psychiatr.*, 17:1; 101–116, 1947.

FOULKES, S. H., and ANTHONY, E. J., *Group Therapy: The Psychoanalytic Approach*, Penguin, New York, 1965.

FRAIBERG, S., "Studies in Group Symptom Formation," *Am. Jrnl. Psychiat.*, 17:2; 273–289, 1947.

———, "A Therapeutic Approach to Reactive Ego Disturbances of Children in Placement," *Am. Jrnl. Orthopsychiat.*, 32:1; 13–31, 1962.

*FRANK, M. G., "Modifications of Activity Group Therapy: Responses of Ego-Impoverished Children," *Clin. Social Work*, 4: 102–103, 1976.

FRANK, M. G., and ZILBACH, J.,"Current Trends in Group Therapy with Children," *Intl. Jrnl. Group Psychother.* 18:4; 447–460, 1968.

*FREEMAN, H., and KING, C., "The Role of Visitors in Activity Group Therapy," *Intl. Jrnl. Group Psychother.*, 7:3; 289–301, 1957.

FRIEDLANDER, K., "Varieties of Group Therapy in a Child Guidance Service," *Intl. Jrnl. Group Psychother.*, 3:1; 59–65, 1953.

*FRIES, M., "Review of the Literature on the Latency Period," *Jrnl. Hillside Hosp.*, 7: 3–16, 1958.

*GABRIEL, B., "An Experiment in Group Treatment," *Am. Jrnl. Orthopsychiat.*, 9:1; 146–169, 1939; also in *Group Psychotherapies for Children: A Textbook*, Slavson, S. R., and Schiffer, M., International Universities Press, New York, 1975.

———, "Interview Group Therapy with a Neurotic Adolescent Girl Suffering from Chorea," in *The Practice of Group Therapy*, Slavson, S. R., ed., International Universities Press, New York, 1947.

GAGNON, J., "Experience de Therapieanalytique de Groupe Chez des Preadolescentes," *Jrnl. Commun. Mental Health*, 6: 210–214, 1970.

GANTER, G., et al., "Intermediary Group Treatment of Inaccessible Children," *Am. Jrnl. Orthopsychiat.*, 35:4; 739–746, 1965.

GATTI, F., and COLEMAN, C., "Community Network Therapy: An Approach to Aiding Families with Troubled Children," *Am. Jrnl. Orthopsychiat.*, 46: 608–617, 1976.

*GINOTT, H., "Play Group Therapy: A Theoretical Framework," *Intl. Jrnl. Group Psychother.*, 4: 410–418, 1958.

———, *Group Psychotherapy with Children*, McGraw-Hill, New York, 1961.

GOEBEL, S. R., "Infantile Play and Infantile Fantasies as Indicators of Group Dynamic Processes in a Group of Children at a Klauseurtagung (Group Dynamics Workshop)," *Dynam. Psychiat.*, 11: 52–63, 1978.

GONDER, L. H., and GONDOR, E., "Changing Times," *Amer. Jrnl. Psychother.*, 23: 67–76, 1969.

GRAZIANO, A. M., *Child Without Tomorrow*, Pergamon Press, Elmsford, New York, 1974.

GREEN, R., and FULLER, M., "Group Therapy with Feminine Boys and Their Parents," *Intl. Jrnl. Group Psychother.*, 23:1; 54–68, 1973.

GULA, M., Hoys House: The Use of a Group for Observation and Treatment," *Mental Hyg.*, July 1944.

HALLE, L., and LANDY, A., "The Integration of Group Activity and Group Therapy," *Occup. Therapy and Rehabil.*, August 1948.

*HALLOWITZ, E., "Activity Group Therapy as Preparation for Individual Treatment," *Intl. Jrnl. Group Psychother.*, 1:4; 337–347, 1951.

*HAMILTON, G., *Psychotherapy in Child Guidance*, Columbia University Press, New York, 1947.

HENDRICKS, S. J., "A Descriptive Analysis of the Process of Client-Centered Play Therapy," *Dissert. Abst. Intnl. 3689A.*

HEWITT, H., and GILDEA, C. L., "An Experiment in Group Psychotherapy, *Am. Jrnl. Orthopsychiat.*, 15:1; 112–127, 1945.

HOCK, R. A., "Model for Conjoint Group Therapy for Asthmatic Children and Their Parents," *Group Psychother. Psychodra-Socio.*, 30: 108–113, 1977.

*HOLLAND, G., et al., "Treatment of a Case of Behavior Disorder Through Activity Group Therapy," in *Practice of Group Therapy*, Slavson, S. R., ed., International Universities Press, New York, 1947.

IRWIN, E., et al., "Assessment of Dream Therapy in a Child Guidance Setting," *Group Psychother. and Psychodrama*, 25: 105–106, 1972.

ISAACS, L. D., and DASHEW, L., "Art Therapy Group for Latency Age Children," *Social Work*, 22: 57–59, 1977.

KAPLAN, S. L., "Structural Family Therapy for Children of Divorce, Case Reports," *Fam. Prac.*, 16: 75–83, 1977.

KARSON, S., "Group Psychotherapy with Latency Age Boys," *Intl. Jrnl. Group Psychother.*, 15:1; 81–89, 1965.

*KING, C., "Activity Group Therapy, in *Group Psychotherapy Today: Topical Problems of Psychotherapy*, Kadis, A., and Winick, C., eds., Vol. 5, Karger, New York, 1965.

KIRSCHENBAUM, D.S., "Questionnaire for the Process Analysis of Social Skills Oriented Group Therapy with Children," *Catalog of Selected Documents in Psychol.*, 7: 42, 1977.

KRAMER, H. C., "A Medical Approach to Group Therapy," *Nervous Child*, April 1945.

LEAL, M. R. M., "Group Analytic Play Therapy with Pre-Adolescent Girls," *Intl. Jrnl. Group Psychother.*, 16:1; 58–64, 1966.

LEVY, G., and DERRIEN, J., "Concerning A Trial of Group Therapy with Games for Children from Eight to Eleven Years of Age, Organized by Two Therapists," *Rev. Neuropsychiat.*, 23: 313–328, 1975.

LEVY, M. M., "Outdoor Group Therapy with Preadolescent Boys," *Psychiat.*, 13: 333, 1950.

*LIEBERMAN, F., "Transition from Latency to Prepuberty in Girls: An Activity Becomes an Interview Group," *Intl. Jrnl. Group Psychother.*, 13:4; 455–464, 1964.

LILLESKOV, R. K., et al., "A Therapeutic Club for Disturbed Boys," *Sandoz Psychiat. Spectator*, 5:3; 6, 1968.

LIMA, D. R., "Social Group Work with Dependent Children," *Hosp. Commun. Psychiat.*, 20: 122–123, 1969.

*LITTLE, M., and KONOPKA, G., "Group Therapy in a Child Guidance Center," *Am. Jrnl. Orthopsychiat.*, 17:2, 303–311, 1947.

LOVASDAL, S., "A Multiple Therapy Approach in Work with Children," *Intl. Jrnl. Group Psychother.*, 26: 475–486, 1976.

*LOWREY, L. G., "Trends in Therapy," *Am. Jrnl. Orthopsychiat.*, 9:4; 697–699, 1939.

LUCAS, L., "Treatment of Young Children in a Group," *News Letter of Amer. Assn. of Psychiat. Social Workers*, Winter Issue, 1943–1944.

MACLENNAN, B. W., "Modifications of Activity Group Therapy for Children," *Intl. Jrnl. Group Psychother.*, 27:1; 85–96, 1977.

MALLOY, B., and NAVAS, M., "Engagement of Preadolescent Boys in Group Therapy: Videotape as a Tool," *Intl. Jrnl. Group Psychother.*, 32: 3, 1982.

*MARGOLIS, L., "Criteria for Selection of Children for Activity Group Therapy," *Smith College Stud. on Social Work*, September 1946.

MARTIN, C. V., and PARRISH, M. J., "The Application of Closed Circuit Television Instant Replay as a Self Confrontation Method in Children's Group Therapy," *Corrective Psychiat. and Jrnl. of Social Therapy*, 19: 31–36, 1973.

MAST, G. R., "The Group Process in Therapy Groups of Socially Retarded Children," *Nederl. T. Geneesk*, 112: 727–729, 1968.

MEALS, D. W., and SUMMERSKILL, J., "A Technique for Dealing with Hostility in Activity Therapy," *Jrnl. Clin. Psychol.*, 7: 376, 1957.

MITTLEMAN, B., "Simultaneous Treatment of Both Parents and Their Child," in *Specialized Techniques in Psychotherapy*, Bychowsky, G., and Despert, J. L., eds., Basic Books, New York, 1952.

*MONTAGUE, H. C., "A Case of Regression in Activity Group Therapy," *Intl. Jrnl. Group Psychother.*, 1:3; 225–234, 1951.

*NAGELBERG, L., and ROSENTHAL, L., "Validation of Selection of Patients for Activity Group Therapy Through the Rorschach and Other Tests," *Intl. Jrnl. Group Psychother.*, 5:4; 380–391, 1955.

NOVICK, J. I., "Comparison Between Short-Term Group and Individual Psychotherapy in Effecting Change in Non-desirable Behavior in Children," *Intl. Jrnl. Group Psychother.*, 15:3; 366–373, 1965.

PASNAU, I., et al., "Coordinated Group Therapy of Children and Parents," *Intl. Jrnl. Group Psychother.*, 26: 213–224, 1976.

PATTERSON, G., et al., "The Integration of a Group and Individual Therapy," *Am. Jrnl. Orthopsychiat.*, 26:3; 618–629, 1956.

PECK, M., and STEWART, R., "Current Practices in Selection Criteria for Group Play Therapy," *Jrnl. Clin. Psychol.*, 20: 146, 1964.

PELOSI, A. A., and FRIEDMAN, H., "The Activity Period in Group Psychotherapy," *Psychiat. Quart.*, 48: 223–229, 1974.

PIUCK, C. L., "Evolution of a Treatment Method for Disadvantaged Children," *Am. Jrnl. Psychother.*, 24: 112–113, 1970.

PIXAKETTNER, U., et al., "Client-Centered Individual and Group Therapy with Mentally Disturbed Intermediate Students in Their Years Five and Six, *Z. Klin. Psychol. Fosch. Prax*, 7: 28–40, 1978.

*Redl, F., "The Concept of Ego Disturbance and Ego Support," *Am. Jrnl. Orthopsychiat.*, 21:2; 273–284, 1951.

*_____, "Diagnostic Group Work," *Am. Jrnl. Orthopsychiat.*, 14:1; 53–67, 1944.

Reisman, S. D., and Lee, M.,"Use of Material from Group Treatment of Child in Casework with Parents," *Am. Jrnl. Orthopsychiat.*, 26:3; 630–634, 1956.

*Rinn, R. "The Selection of Boys for Activity Group Therapy," *Smith College Stud. in Social Work*, 39: 82–83, 1968.

Ritter, B., "The Group Desensitization of Children's Snake Phobias Using Vicarious and Contact Desensitization Procedures, *Behavior Research and Therapy*, 6: 1–6, 1968.

Roberts, J., et al., "Prevention of Child Abuse: Group Therapy for Mothers and Children," *Practitioner*, 219: 111–115, 1977.

Rose, S. D., *Treating Children in Groups*, Josey Bass, San Francisco, 1972.

Rosenbaum, M., and Kraft, I., "Group Psychotherapy for Children," in *Group Psychotherapy and Group Formation*, Rosenbaum, M., and Berger, M. M., eds., Basic Books, New York, 1975.

*Rosenthal, L., and Nagelberg, L., "Countertransference in Activity Group Therapy," *Intl. Jrnl. Group Psychother.*, 3:4; 431–440, 1953.

*_____, "Limitations of Activity Group Therapy: Case Presentation," *Intl. Jrnl. Group Psychother.*, 6:2; 166–179, 1956; *also in this volume, Chapter 6.*

*_____, et al., "Family Relations as a Consideration in Selecting Children for Activity Group Therapy," *Intl. Jrnl. Group Psychother.*, 10:1; 78–79, 1960.

*_____, "Qualifications and Tasks of Therapists in Group Therapy with Children," *Clin. Social Work*, 5: 191–199, 1977.

Ross, H., Group Psychotherapy as Related to Group Trauma, *Am. Jrnl. Orthopsychiat.* 14:4; 609–615, 1944.

Sands, R. M., and Golub, S., "Breaking the Bonds of Tradition: A Reassessment of Group Treatment of Latency Age Children," *Am. Jrnl. Psychiat.*, 131: 662–665, 1974.

Schachter, R. S., "Kinetic Psychotherapy in the Treatment of Children," *Am. Jrnl. Psychother.*, 18: 430–437, 1974.

*Schamess, G., "Group Treatment Modalities for Latency Age Children, *Intl. Jrnl. Group Psychother.*, 26: 455–473, 1976.

*Scheidlinger, S., "Activity Group Therapy with Primary Behavior Disorders," in *The Practice of Group Therapy*, Slavson, S. R., ed., International Universities Press, New York, 1947.

*_____, "The Concept of Latency: Implications for Group Treatment," *Social Casework*, 47: 363–367, 1966.

*_____, Experiential Group Treatment of Severely Deprived Latency Age Children," *Am. Jrnl. Orthopsychiat.*,3:2; 356–368, 1960.

*_____, "Group Factors in Promoting Children's Mental Health," *Am. Jrnl. Orthopsychiat.*, 22: 394, 1952.

*_____, "Group Process in Group Psychotherapy," *Am. Jrnl. Orthopsychiat.*, 14: 104–120, 346–363, 1960.

*_____, "Group Psychotherapy," *Am. Jrnl. Orthopsychiat.*, 24: 140–145, 1954.

*_____, "Three Group Approaches with Socially Deprived Latency Children," *Intl. Jrnl. Group Psychother.*, 15:4; 434–445, 1965.

*_____, et al., "Activity Group Therapy with Children in a Family Service Program," *Social Casework*, 40: 193–201, 1959.

*_____, et al., "Group Psychotherapy Research—Open Forum, *Intl. Jrnl. Psychother.*, 27: 135–137, 1977.

SCHIFFER, A. L., "The Effectiveness of Group Play Therapy Assessed by Specific Changes in a Child's Peer Relations," *Dissert. Abst.*, 27: 972, 1966.

*SCHIFFER, M., "Activity-Interview Group Psychotherapy; Theory, Principles and Practices, *Intl. Jrnl. Group Psychother.*, 27:3; 377–388, 1977.

*_____, *Dynamics of Group Psychotherapy, Collected Papers, S. R. Slavson*, Schiffer, M., ed., Jason Aronson, New York, 1979.

*_____, "The Synergy of Children's Group Psychotherapy and Child Growth and Development, in *Group Therapy Yearbook,* Stratton Intercontinental Medical Book Corp., New York 1976.

*_____, "Trips as a Treatment Tool in Activity Group Therapy," *Intl. Jrnl. Group Psychother.*, 2:2; 139–149, 1952.

*_____, *The Therapeutic Play Group*, Grune & Stratton, New York, 1969.

*_____, "Permissiveness Versus Sanction in Activity Group Therapy," *Intl. Jrnl. Group Psychother.*, 2:3; 255–261, 1952.

*_____, with Slavson, S. R., *Group Psychotherapies for Children: A Textbook*, International Universities Press, New York, 1975.

*SCHREIBER, S. C., "Some Special Forms of Aggressiveness in Activity Group Therapy and Their Impact on the Therapist," *Smith College Stud. in Social Work*, 39: 138–146, 1969.

SEMONSKY, C., and ZICHT, G., "Activity Group Parameters," *Jrnl. Am. Acad. Child Psychiat.*, 13: 166–179, 1974.

*SIEGEL, M. G., "The Rorschach Test as an Aid in Selecting Clients for Group Therapy and Evaluating Progress," *Mental Hyg.*, July 1944.

*SLAVSON, S. R.,[1] "Authority, Restraint and Discipline in Group Therapy with Children," *Nervous Child*, 9: 1951.

*_____, *Child Centered Group Guidance of Parents*, International Universities Press, New York, 1958.

*_____, "Criteria for Selection and Rejection of Patients for Various Types of Group Psychotherapy," *Intl. Jrnl. Group Psychother.*, 5:1; 1955.

*_____, "Differential Dynamics of Activity and Interview Group Therapy, *Am. Jrnl. Orthopsychiat.*, 17:2; 293–302, 1947.

*_____, "Differential Methods of Group Therapy in Relation to Age Levels," *Nervous Child*, April 1945.

*_____, "The Group in Child Guidance," in *The Handbook of Child Guidance*, Harms, E., ed., Child Care Publications, New York, 1947.

[1]There are 192 publications by Slavson on groups and group psychotherapy, many concerning children's group treatment. (See Bibliography in *Dynamics of Group Psychotherapy, Collected Papers*, Schiffer, M., ed., Jason Aronson, New York, 1979.) Listed here are selected articles on fundamentals of children's group therapy. All are recommended readings.

*_____, "Group Therapy with Children," in *Modern Trends in Child Psychiatry*, Lewis, N. D. C., and Pacella, B. L., eds., International Universities Press, New York, 1945.

*_____, "Group Therapy at the Jewish Board of Guardians," *Mental Hyg.*, July 1944.

*_____, "Some Elements in Activity Group Therapy," Group Therapy Round Table, 1944: *Am. Jrnl. Orthopsychiat.*, 14:4; 578–588, 1944.

*_____, *An Introduction to Group Therapy*, Commonwealth Fund, New York, 1943.

*_____, *The Practice of Group Therapy*, International Universities Press, New York, 1947.

*_____, "Treatment of Aggression Through Group Therapy," *Am. Jrnl. Orthopsychiat.*, 13: 3, 1943.

*_____, "Treatment of Withdrawal Through Group Therapy," *Am. Jrnl. Orthopsychiat.*, 15:4; 681–689, 1945.

*_____, "Types of Relationships and Their Application to Psychotherapy," *Am. Jrnl. Orthopsychiat.*, 15:2; 267–277, 1945.

*_____, with Miller, C., "Integration of Individual and Group Therapy in the Treatment of a Problem Boy," *Am. Jrnl. Orthopsychiat.*, 9: 4, 1939.

*_____, with Schiffer, M., *Group Psychotherapies for Children: A Textbook*, International Universities Press, New York, 1975.

*_____, et al., "The Case of Jean Case," *Intl. Jrnl. Group Psychother.*, 1:1; 64–77, 1951; and 1:2; 154–171, 1951.

*_____, et al., "Children's Activity in Casework Therapy," *Jrnl. of Social Casework*, April 1949.

*_____, "Report to the World Federation for Mental Health," *Intl. Jrnl. Group Psychother.*, 2:1; 70–82, 1952.

Somers, R. K., et al., "The Effectiveness of Group and Individual Therapy," *Jrnl. Speech and Hearing Res.*, 9: 219–225, 1966.

*Soo, E., "The Impact of Activity Group Therapy upon a Highly Constricted Child," *Intl. Jrnl. Group Psychother.*, 24: 207–216, 1974.

Spiker, D., "Protected Groups in the Treatment of Young Children," *Am. Jrnl. Orthopsychiat.*, 13:4; 654–664, 1943.

*Spotnitz, H., et al., "Resistance In Analytic Group Therapy: A Study of the Group Therapeutic Process in Children and Mothers," *Quart. Jrnl. Child Behav.*, 2: 71, 1950.

*Sternbach, O., "The Dynamics of Therapy in the Group," *Jrnl. Child Psychiat.*, 1: 91, 1947.

Strunk, C., and Witkin, L. J., "The Transformation of a Latency-Age Girl's Group from Unstructured Play to Problem Focused Behavior, *Intl. Jrnl. Group Psychother.*, 24:4; 460–4170, 1974.

*Sugar, M., "Interpretive Group Psychotherapy with Latency Children," *Jrnl. Am. Acad. Child Psychiat.*, 13: 648–646, 1974.

*Van Ophuijsen, J. H. W., "Primary Conduct Disturbances: Their Diagnosis and

Treatment," in *Modern Trends in Child Psychiatry*, Lewis, N. D. C., and Pacella, B., eds., International Universities Press, New York, 1961.

VAN SCOY, H., "An Activity Group Approach to Seriously Disturbed Latency Boys," *Child Welfare*, 50: 413, 1971.

_____, "Activity Group Therapy: A Bridge Between Play and Work," *Child Welfare*, 51: 528–534, 1972.

VAN VLEET, P., "Rhythmic Activity: A Project in Group Therapy with Children," *Am. Jrnl. Orthopsychiat.*, 19:1; 79–86, 1949.

WATSON, K. W., and BOVERMAN, H., "Pre-Adolescent Children in Group Discussions," *Children*, 15: 65–70, 1968.

*WEIL, A. P., "Certain Severe Disturbances of Ego Development in Childhood," in *The Psychoanalytical Study of the Child*, Vol. 13, International Universities Press, New York, 1953.

WELLINGTON, J., "Group Therapy with Pre-Adolescent Girls," *Psychother.*, 2: 171, 1965.

WHITE, H., "An Adventure in Group Therapy in a Family Agency Setting," *Mental Hyg.*, July 1944.

*WINEMAN, D., "Group Therapy and Casework with Ego Disturbed Children," *Jrnl. of Social Casework*, March 1949.

*ZILBACH, J. J., and GRUNEBAUM, M. G., "Pregenital Components in Incest as Manifested in Two Girls in Activity Group Therapy," *Intl. Jrnl. Group Psychother.*, 14:2; 1964.

Groups: Nursery and Pre-School

BLOCH, J. A., "A Preschool Workshop for Emotionally Disturbed Children," *Children*, 17: 10–14, 1970.

BURLINGHAM, S., "Therapeutic Effects of a Play Group for Preschool Children," *Am. Jrnl. Orthopsychiat.*, 8:4; 627–638, 1938.

*DUBO, S., "Opportunities for Group Therapy in a Pediatric Service," *Intl. Jrnl. Group Psychother.*, 1: 235, 1951.

*FABIAN, A., and HOLDEN, M., "Parallel Group Treatment of Preschool Children and Their Mothers, *Intl. Jrnl. Group Psychother.*, 1:1; 37–54, 1951.

HAIZLIP, T., et al., "Issues in Developing Psychotherapy Groups for Pre-School Children in Outpatient Clinics," *Am. Jrnl. Psychiat.*, 132: 1061–1063, 1975.

*LULOW, V., "An Experimental Approach Toward the Prevention of Behavior Disorders in a Group of Nursery School Children," *Intl. Jrnl. Group Psychother.*, 1:2; 144–153, 1951.

*SLAVSON, S. R., "Play Group Therapy for Young Children," *Nervous Child*, 7:3; 1948.

TIPTON, G., "Mental Hygiene Principles Adapted to a War Nursery School," *Nervous Child*, April 1945.

WITENBERG, M. J., and BRUSELOFF, P., "A Therapeutic Nursery Group in a Day Care Center," *Int. Jrnl. Child Psychother.*, 1: 7–16, 1972.

Groups: Schizophrenia, Autism

*GOLDFARB, W., "Group Behavior of Schizophrenic Children," *Int. Jrnl. Social Psychiat.*, 10:199; 1964.

GRATTON, L., and RIZZO, A. E., "Group Therapy with Young Psychotic Children," *Intl. Jrnl. Group Psychother.*, 19:1; 63–71, 1969.

HARPER, J., "Embracement and Enticement: A Therapeutic Nursery Group for Autistic Children," *Slow Learning Child*, 20: 173–176, 1973.

*KING, C., "Activity Group Therapy with a Schizophrenic Boy: Follow-Up Two Years Later," *Int. Jrnl. Group Psychother.*, 9:2; 184–194, 1959.

KOEGEL, R. L., and RINCOVER, A., "Treatment of Psychotic Children in a Classroom Environment: I. Learning in a Large Group," *Jrnl. Appl. Behav. Anal.*, 7: 45–59, 1974.

LIEBERMAN, F., and TAYLOR, S. S., "Combined Group and Individual Treatment of a Schizophrenic Child," *Social Casework*, 46: 80, 1965.

*LIFTON, N., and SMOLEN, E., "Group Psychotherapy with Schizophrenic Children," *Intl. Jrnl. Group Psychother.*, 16:1; 23–41, 1966.

MASSERMAN, J., ed., "Therapies for Autistic Children," in *Psychiatric Therapies*, Grune & Stratton, New York, 1969.

*SMOLEN, E. M., and LIFTON, N., "A Special Treatment Program for Schizophrenic Children in a Child Guidance Clinic," *Am. Jrnl. Orthopsychiat.*, 36:3; 736–742, 1966.

SPEERS, R. W., and LANSING, C., *Group Therapy in Childhood Psychoses*, University of North Carolina Press, Chapel Hill, 1965.

Groups: Delinquency, Residential Settings

ABUDABBEH, N., et al., "Application of Behavior Principles to Group Therapy Techniques with Juvenile Delinquents," *Psychol. Rpts.*, 31: 375–380, 1972.

AVERILL, C., et al., "Group Psychotherapy with Young Delinquents: Report from a Residential Treatment Center," *Bull, Menninger Clinic*, 37:1; 70, 1973.

BARDILL, D. R., "Behavior Contracting and Group Therapy with Preadolescent Males in a Residential Setting," *Intl. Jrnl. Group Psychother.*, 22:3; 333–342, 1972.

BERKOWITZ, I., et al., "Psychosexual Development of Latency Age Children and Adolescents in Group Therapy in a Residential Setting," *Intl. Jrnl. Group Psychother.*, 16:3; 344–355, 1966.

CLIFFORD, M., and CROSS, T., "Group Therapy for Seriously Disturbed Boys in Residential Treatment," *Child Welfare*, 59: 560–565, 1980.

GERSTEIN, C., "Group Therapy with Institutionalized Juvenile Delinquents," *Jrnl. Genet. Psychol.*, 80: 35, 1952.

*GOLDSMITH, J., "Clinical Group Work in a Residential Treatment Center," *Am. Jrnl. Orthopsychiat.*, 26:4; 727–750, 1956.

Grossner, L. A., "Developing a Therapy Group in a Residential Treatment Center," *Jrnl. Jewish Communal Serv.*, 45: 254–256, 1969.

*Konopka, G., "The Role of the Group in Residential Treatment," *Am. Jrnl. Orthopsychiat.*, 25:4; 679–684, 1955.

Kotkov, B., "The Group as a Training Device for a Girl's Training School," *Intl. Jrnl. Group Psychother.*, 4:2; 193–198, 1954.

Oberndorf, C. P., "Psychotherapy in a Resident Children's Group," in *Searchlights on Delinquency*, Eissler, K. R., ed., International Universities Press, New York, 1949.

*Phelan, J. F., "Recent Observations in Group Psychotherapy with Adolescent Delinquent Boys in Residential Treatment," *Intl. Jrnl. Group Psychother.*, 10:2; 174–175, 176–226, 1960.

Robinson, J. F., "Therapeutic Values of Group Experiences in a Children's Institution," *Mental Hyg.*, 35: 43, 1951.

Rosenthal, P., "Group Studies of Pre-Adolescent, Delinquent Boys," *Am. Jrnl. Orthopsychiat.*, 12: 1, 1942.

*Schulman, I., "The Dynamics of Certain Reactions of Delinquents to Group Psychotherapy," *Int. Jrnl. Group Psychother.*, 2:3; 334, 1952.

*Slaiken, K. A., "Evaluation Studies on Group Treatment of Juvenile and Adult Offenders in Correctional Institutions: A Review of the Literature," *Jrnl. Couns. and Delinq.*, 10: 87–100, 1973.

*Slavson, S. R., "Group Psychotherapy in Delinquency Prevention," *Jrnl. Educ. Sociol.*, 24: 45, 1950.

*_____, "Milieu Group Treatment for Delinquents," *Proceedings of National Conference of Social Work*, 1948.

*_____, *Reclaiming the Delinquent by Para-Analytic Group Psychotherapy and the Inversion Technique*, Free Press, New York, 1965.

*_____, *Reeducating the Delinquent Through Group and Community Participation*, Harper & Bros., New York, 1954.

*_____, et al., "Activity Group Therapy with a Delinquent, Dull Boy of Eleven," *Nervous Child*, April 1945.

Sohn, L., "Group Therapy for Young Delinquents," *British Jrnl. Delinq.*, 3: 20, 1952.

*Stranahan, M., et al., "Activity Group Therapy with Emotionally Disturbed and Delinquent Adolescents," *Intl. Jrnl. Group Psychother.*, 7:4; 425–436, 1957.

Thorpe, J. J., and Smith, B., "Operational Sequence in Group Therapy with Young Offenders," *Intl. Jrnl. Group Psychother.*, 3:1; 66, 1953.

Weber, L., and Hill, T., "A Therapy Group of Juvenile Delinquent Boys," *Psychiat. Forum.* 3: 25–33, 1973.

Wollan, K. I., "The Use of Activity in Probation Work," *Yearbook, Natl. Prob. and Parole Assn.*, 1938.

*_____, and Gardner, G. E., "A Group-Clinic Approach to Delinquency," *Mental Hyg.*, October 1938.

Yonge, K., and O'Connor, N., "Measurable Effects of Group Psychotherapy with Defective Delinquents," *Jrnl. Mental Sci.*, 100: 944–950, 1954.

Groups: Mental Deficiency, Retardation, Brain-Damaged

ANDERSON, J. E., "Group Therapy with Brain Damaged Children," *Hosp. Commun. Psychiatry*, 19: 175–176, 1968.

COTZIN, M., "Group Psychotherapy with Mentally Deficient Problem Boys," *Am. Jrnl. Mental Deficiency*, October 1948.

FISHER, L. A., and WOLFSON, I. N.,"Group Therapy of Mental Defectives," *Am. Jrnl. Mental Defect.*, 57: 463, 1953.

KAZDIN, A., and FORSBERG, A., "Effects of Group Reenforcement and Punishment on Classroom Behavior," *Educ. and Training of Mentally Retarded*, 9: 50–55, 1974.

MEHLMAN, N., "Group Play Therapy with Mentally Retarded Children," *Jrnl. Abnor. Soc. Psychol.*, 48: 53, 1953.

MYERS, D. G., "A Comparison of the Effects of Group Puppet Therapy and Group Activities with Mentally Retarded Children," *Dissert. Abst. Intl.*, 31(10A) : 5234.

*SCHEIDLINGER, S., et al., "Activity Group Therapy of a Dull Boy with Severe Body Ego Problems," *Intl. Jrnl. Group Psychother.*, 12:1; 41–45, 1962.

*SCHIFFER, M., "Activity Group Therapy for the Exceptional Child," *Jrnl. for Exceptional Children*, January 1964; also see chapter in *The Practice of Group Therapy*, Slavson, S. R. ed., International Universities Presss, New York, 1947.

VAIL, D., "An Unsuccessful Experiment in Group Therapy," *Am. Jrnl. Mental Defect.* 60: 144–151, 1955.

Groups in Hospitals

ADAMS, M. A., "A Hospital Play Program: Helping Children with Serious Illness," *Am. Jrnl. Orthopsychiat.*, 46:3; 16–424, 1976.

BENDER, L., and WOLTMANN, A. G., "The Use of Plastic Material as a Psychiatric Approach to Emotional Problems in Children," *Am. Jrnl. Orthopsychiat.*, 7:3; 283–300, 1937.

FRANK, J. L., "A Weekly Group Meeting for Children on a Pediatric Ward: Therapeutic and Practical Functions," *Int. Jrnl. Psychiat. Med.*, 8: 267–284, 1978.

FREED, H., and MEALS, D. W., Group Therapy Program with Children at Philadelphia General Hospital, *General Hospital Jrnl.*, Phil. Gen. Hosp., 3:127; 1952.

HAAR, R., "Group Psychotherapy with Children and Adolescents in Hospital Treatment," *Kinderpsychol. Kinderpsychiatr. Prax.*, 29: 182–193, 1980.

HAGBERG, K. L., "Combining Social Casework and Group Work Methods in a Children's Hospital," *Children*, 16: 192–197, 1969.

SHETTEL, R., "Group Psychotherapy in the Children's Unit of the Allentown State Hospital, Penn." *Mental Health Bull.*, 30: 21, 1952.

SOBLE, D., and GELLER, J. J., "A Type of Group Psychotherapy in the Children's Unit of a Mental Hospital," *Psychiat. Quart.*, 38: 262, 1964.

STEWART, K. K., and AXELROD, P., "Group Therapy on a Children's Psychiatric Ward, *Am. Jrnl. Orthopsychiat.*, 17:2; 312–325, 1947.

SUTTON, H., "Some Nursing Aspects of a Children's Psychiatric Ward," *Am. Jrnl. Orthopsychiat.*, 17:4; 675–683, 1947.

TUBBS, A., "Nursing Interventions to Shorten Anxiety-Ridden Transition Periods," *Nursing Outlook*, 18:7; 27, 1970.

WILLIAMS, J., et al., "The Evaluation of a Psychotherapy Group in a Children's In-patient Unit," *Smith College Stud. in Social Work*, 48: 3–8, 1977.

———, "A Model for Short Term Group Therapy on a Children's Inpatient Unit," *Clin. Social Work Jrnl.*, 6: 21–32, 1978.

Groups in Social Group Work, Sensitivity Training, Counseling, Operant Conditioning, Behavior Modification

BERRY, K. K., et al., "Comparison of Group Therapy and Behavioral Modification with Children," *Psychol. Repts.*, 46: 975–978, 1980.

CLEMENT, P. W., "Operant Conditioning in Group Psychotherapy with Children," *Jrnl. School Health*, 38: 271–278, 1968.

GRAZIANO, A. M., *Group Behavior Modification for Children*. Pergamon, New York, 1972.

*GRUNWALD, H., "Group Counseling in a Family and Children's Agency," *Intl. Jrnl. Group Psychother.* 7:3; 318–326, 1957.

GUMAER, J., and MYRICK, R. D., "Behavioral Group Counseling with Disruptive Children," *School Counsel.*, 21: 313–346, 1974.

HILLMAN, B. W., et al., "Activity Group Guidance—A Developmental Approach to Counselors," *Personn. Guid. Jrnl.*, 53: 761–767, 1975.

HIRSCHBERG, J. C., "Role of Education in the Treatment of Emotionally Disturbed Children Through Planned Ego Development," *Am. Jrnl. Orthopsychiat.*, 23:3; 684–690, 1953.

HOZMAN, T. L., and FROILAND, D. J., "Families in Divorce: A Proposed Model for Counseling Children," *Fam. Coordinator*, 25: 271–277, 1976.

JEFFRIES, D., "Should We Continue to Deradicalize Children Through the Use of Counseling Groups?" *Educ. Technology*, 13: 45–48, 1973.

*KADIS, A., and LAZARSFELD, S., "The Group as a Psychotherapeutic Factor in Counseling Work," *Nervous Child*, April 1945.

*KONOPKA, G., "Group Therapy in Overcoming Racial and Cultural Tensions," *Am. Jrnl. Orthopsychiat.*, 17:4; 693–699, 1947.

LOWENSTEIN, P., and SVENDSEN, M., "Experimental Modification of a Selected Group of Shy and Withdrawn Children," *Am. Jrnl. Orthopsychiat.*, 8:4; 639–653, 1938.

MACLENNAN, B. W., and ROSEN, B., "Female Therapists in Activity Group Therapy with Boys in Latency, *Intl. Jrnl. Group Psychother.*, 13:1; 34–42, 1963.

MARHOLIN, D., and MCINNIS, E. T., "Treating Children in Group Settings: Techniques for Individualizing Behavioral Programs," in *Child Behavior Therapy*, Marholin, D., ed., Gardner Press, New York, 1978.

MAYER, G. R., et al., "Group Counseling with Children: A Cognitive-Behavioral Approach," *Child Develop. Abst. and Bibliog.*, 43: 216, 1969.

PAPANEK, E., "Treatment by Group Work," *Am. Jrnl. Orthopsychiat.*, 15:2; 223–229, 1945.

POLLACK, D., "A Sensitivity Training Approach to Group Therapy with Children," *Child Welfare*, 50:86; 89, 1971.

PRATT, S. J., et al., "Behavior Modification: Changing Hypersensitive Behavior in a Children's Group," *Perspect. Psychiat. Care*, 13: 37–42.

ROSENBAUM, A., et al., "Behavioral Intervention with Hyperactive Children: Group Consequences as a Supplement to Individual Contingencies," *Behav. Therapy*, 6: 315–323, 1975.

ROSS, A. L., "Combining Behavior Modification and Group Work Techniques in a Day Treatment Center," *Child Welfare*, 53: 435–444, 1974.

*SCHEIDLINGER, S., "The Concepts of Social Group Work and of Group Psychotherapy," *Social Casework*, 34: 292, 1953.

SCHOFIELD, L. J., et al., "Operant Approach to Group Therapy and Effects on Sociometric Status," *Psychol. Repts.*, 35: 83–90, 1974.

TARRIER, R. B., and SHAPPELL, D. C., "Groups: Guidance, Counseling, in Therapy," *Small Group Behav.*, 4: 47–54, 1973.

Groups in Schools and Learning Problems

ABRAHAM, K. A., The Effectiveness of Structured Sociodrama in Altering the Classroom Behavior of Fifth Grade Students," *Dissert. Abst. Intl.*, 3677A, 1972.

AMUNDSON, N. E., "Transactional Analysis with Elementary School Children: A Pilot Study," *Transact. Anal. Jrnl.*, 5: 247–250, 1975.

ARNOLD, T. J., et al., "The Effects of a Transactional Analysis Group on Emotionally Disturbed School-Age Boys," *Transact. Anal. Jrnl.*, 5: 230–242, 1975.

BALLERING, L. R., "The Effects of a Structured Group Approach on Anxiety in Junior High Youth: A Technique for Para-Professionals," *Dissert. Abst. Intl.*, 40:5195B, 1980.

BARABASZ, A. F., "Classroom Teachers as Paraprofessional Therapists in Group Systematic Desensitization of Test Anxiety," *Psychiat.*, 38: 388–392, 1975.

BARCAI, A., et al., "A Comparison of Three Group Approaches to Underachieving Children," *Am. Jrnl. Orthopsychiat.*, 43:1; 133–141, 1973.

BARDILL, D. R., "Group Therapy Techniques with Preadolescent Boys in a Residential Treatment Center," *Child Welfare*, 52: 533–541, 1973.

BERL, M. E., "The Relationship of Group Psychotherapy to Remedial Reading," *Group Psychol.*, 4: 60, 1951.

*BERMAN, L., "Mental Hygiene for Educators: Report on a Combined Seminar and Group Psychotherapy Approach," *Psychoanal. Rev.*, 40: 319–332, 1953.

BOYLE, D. E., "The Effects of Two Small Group Short Term Treatments on 6th Grade Social Isolates," *Dissert. Abst. Intl.*, 40: 5370A, 1980.

BUCHMUELLER, A. D., and GILDEA, M. C., "A Group Therapy Project with Parents of Behavior Problem Children in Public Schools," *Am. Jrnl. Orthopsychiat.*, 19: 106, 1949.

BURDON, A. P., et al., "Emotionally Disturbed Boys Failing in School: Treatment in an Outpatient Clinic School," *South. Med. Jrnl.*, 57: 829, 1964.

COMAN, M. D., et al., "Group Therapy for Physically Handicapped Toddlers with Delayed Speech and Language Development," *Jrnl. Am. Acad. Child Psychol.*, 15: 395–413, 1976.

CROW, M. L., "A Comparison of Three Group Counseling Techniques with Sixth Graders," *Elem. School Guid. Counsel.*, 6: 37–42, 1971.

DANIELS, E., et al., "A Group Therapy Approach to Predelinquent Boys, Their Teachers and Parents in a Junior High School," *Intl. Jrnl. Group Psychother.*, 10:3; 346–352, 1960.

DAVIS, R. G., "Group Therapy and Social Acceptance in a First-Second Grade," *Elem. School Jrnl.*, December 1948.

DEE, V. D., "Contingency Management in a Crisis Class," *Except. Child*, 38: 631–634, 1972.

DiLARA, L. E., "Listening Is a Challenge: Group Counseling in a School," *Mental Hyg.*, 53: 600–605, 1969.

EDLESON, J. L., "Group Social Skills Training for Children: An Evaluative Study," *Dissert. Abst. Intl.*, 40: 4747A, 1980.

FREY, L. A., and KOLODNEY, P. L., "Group Treatment for the Alienated Child in the School," *Intl. Jrnl. Group Psychother.*, 16:3; 321–327, 1966.

GAZDA, G. M., ed., *Theories and Methods of Group Counseling in the Schools*, Charles C. Thomas, Springfield, Ill., 1969.

GREENWOOD, C. R., et al., "Group Contingencies for Group Consequences in Classroom Management: A Further Analysis," *Jrnl. Appl. Behav. Anal.*, 7: 413–425, 1974.

GROFFMAN, L., and DODSON, A. G., "Sibling Sessions as a Means of Establishing Rapport in an Inner City Elementary School," *Elem. School Guid. Counsel.*, 6: 104–107, 1971.

GUMAER, J., "Peer-Facilitated Groups," *Elem. Sch. Guid. Counsel.*, 8: 4–11, 1973.

HANSEN, J. C., et al., "Model Reinforcement in Group Counseling with Elementary School Children," *Jrnl. Pers. and Guid.*, 47: 741–747, 1969.

HERROLD, K., "Applications of Group Principles to Education," *Intl. Jrnl. Group Psychother.*, 4:1; 177–182, 1954.

HERTZMAN, J., "Dynamic Group Experiences for Teachers and Students in the Classroom, *Intl. Jrnl. Group Psychother.*, 9:1; 99–109, 1959.

HILLMAN, B. W., et al., "Activity Group Guidance: A Development Approach for Counselors," *Pers. Guid. Jrnl.*, 53: 761–767, 1975.

HINDS, W. C., and ROEHKE, H. J., "A Learning Theory Approach to Group Counseling with Elementary School Children," *Jrnl. Counsel. Psychol.*, 17: 49–55, 1970.

HOWARD, W., and ZIMPFER, D. G., "The Findings of Research on Group Approaches in Elementary School Guidance and Counseling," *Elem. School Guid. Counsel.*, 6: 163–169, 1972.

HUBBERT, A. K., "Effect of Group Counseling and Behavior Modification on Attention Behavior of First Grade Students," *Dissert. Abst. Intl.*, 30:3737A, 1970.

HUGO, M. J., "The Effects of Group Counseling on Self-Concepts and Behavior of Elementary School Children," *Dissert. Abst. Intl.*, 30:3728A, 1970.

JACOBSON, J., "Group Psychotherapy in the Elementary School," *Psychiat. Quart.*, January 1945.

KAGGUA, G. H., "The Effects of Client Centered Group Counseling and Relaxation on the Self Concept and Negative Behavior of Junior High School Students Who Are Disciplinary Problems," *Dissert. Abst. Intl.*, 40:3782A, 1980.

KOENIG, F., "A Group Therapy Experiment in a City Elementary School," *Understanding the Child*, April 1949.

LEDEBUR, G. W., "The Elementary Learning Disability Process Group and the School Psychologist," *Psychol. in the Schools*, 14: 62–66, 1977.

LITOW, L., and PUMROY, D. K., A Brief Review of Classroom Group Oriented Contingencies," *Jrnl. Appl. Behav. Anal.*, 8: 341–347, 1975.

MASS, H. S., "Applying Group Therapy to Classroom Practice," *Mental Hyg.*, 35: 257, 1951.

MCBRIEN, R. J., and NELSON, R. J., "Experimental Group Strategies with Primary Grade Children," *Elem. School Guid. Counsel.*, 6: 170–174, 1972.

MCCOLLUM, P. S., and ANDERSON, R. P., "Group Counseling with Reading Disabled Children," *Jrnl. Counsel. Psychol.*, 21: 150–155, 1974.

MCDONOUGH, T. J., "A Comparison of Self-Instructions in Play Group Therapy in Lessening Impulsivity and Subsequent Hyperaggressivity in 4th, 5th, and 6th Grade Boys," *Dissert. Abst. Intl.*, 40:4493B, 1980.

MCLAUGHLIN, T. F., "Review of Applications of Group Contingency Procedures Used in Behavior Modification in a Regular Classroom: Some Recommendations for School Personnel," *Psychol. Repts.*, 35: 1299–1303, 1974.

MULLER, A., "Inclusion of Psychotherapeutic Methods in Group Work with School Children," *Kinderpsychol. Kinderpsychiat. Prax.*, 27: 216–220, 1978.

OXFORD, H. D., "The Effect of a Classroom Group Counseling Component on Classroom Behavior and Self-Concept of Elementary School Students," *Dissert. Abst. Intl.*, 40:5310A, 1980.

PRICE, N. I., "The Effects of Activity-Interview Group Counseling on the Self-Esteem and Classroom Behavior of Selected Middle School Students," *Dissert. Abst. Intl.*, 41:111A, 1980.

REISSMAN, E. F., and BEYER, L. M., "Group Counseling in an Elementary School Setting," *Child Welfare*, 52: 192–195, 1973.

RHODES, S. L., "Short Term Groups of Latency Age Children in a School Setting," *Intl. Jrnl. Group Psychother.*, 23:2; 204–216, 1973.

ROSEN, C. E., "The Effects of Sociodramatic Play on Problem Solving Behavior Among Culturally Disadvantaged Children," *Dissert. Abst. Intl.*, 4111A, 1972.

ROSENBAUM, M., ed., "The Leadership Laboratory: A Group Counseling Intervention Model for Schools," in *Group Psychotherapy from the Southwest*, Gordon-Branch, New York, 1975.

*SCHIFFER, M., "Helping Troubled Children in School," in *Individuality in Education*, Bank Street College of Education, New York, 1959.

*———, "The Therapeutic Play Group," in *Orthopsychiatry in the School*, Krugman, M., ed., American Orthopsychiatric Association, 1958.

*———, "The Therapeutic Play Group in the Public School Setting," *Mental Hyg.*, April 1957.

*———, "The Use of the Seminar in Training Teachers and Counselors as Leaders of Therapeutic Play Groups for Maladjusted Children," *Am. Jrnl. Orthopsychiat.*, 30:1; 154–165, 1960. `

SCHWEBLE, M., "Groups for the Educational Distraught," *Educ. Tech.*, 13: 39–44, 1973.

*SYMONDS, P. M., Education and Psychotherapy," *Jrnl. Educ. Psychol.*, 40: 1–32, 1949.

THOMBS, M. R., "Group Counseling and the Sociometric Status of Second Grade Children," *Elem. School Guid. Counsel.*, 7: 194–197, 1973.

TROESTA, J. D., and DARBY, J. A., "The Role of the Mini-Meals in Therapeutic Play Groups," *Social Casework*, 5: 97–103, 1977.

VINTER, R. J., and SARRI, R. C., "Malperformance in the Public School: A Group Work Approach," *Social Work*, 10:1; 3, 1965.

WINETT, R. A., and VACHON, E. M., "Group Feedback and Group Contingencies in Modifying Behavior of Fifth Graders," *Psychol.* Repts., 34: 1238–1292, 1974.

WODARSKI, J. S., "Group Counseling and Anti-Social Children: A Social-Learning Perspective," *Corrective Social Psychiatry and Jrnl. of Social Therpay*, 19: 6–14, 1973.

WOTRING, N. N. R., "The Effects of Small Guidance Groups on Children's Self-Concepts," *Dissert Abst. Intl.*, 40:6158A, 1980.

WUBBOLDING, R., and OSBORNE, L. B., "An Awareness Game for Elementary School Children," *School Counsel.*, 21: 223–227, 1974.

YITZCHAK, B., "An Israeli Experimental Group with Primary School Dropouts Outside the School Setting," *Child Welfare*, 50: 336–340, 1971.

ZIMMERMAN, W. M., "Effects of Short Term Counseling on Gifted Elementary Students," *Dissert. Abst. Intl.*, 40: 6214A, 1980.

Groups in Camps

KURODA, K., "Therapeutic Camp with School Phobic Children," *Japan Jrnl. Child Psychiat.*, 14: 254–257, 1973.

MORSE, W. C., and SMALL, E. R., "Group Life-Space Interviewing in a Therapeutic Camp," *Am. Jrnl. Orthopsychiat.*, 24:1; 27–44, 1954.

YOUNG, R. A., et al., "Treatment Techniques in a Therapeutic Camp, *Am. Jrnl. Orthopsychiat.*, 21:4; 819–826, 1951.

Index